POLITICAL ETHICS

Political Ethics

A HANDBOOK

EDITED BY EDWARD HALL &
ANDREW SABL

PRINCETON UNIVERSITY PRESS
PRINCETON & OXFORD

Published by Princeton University Press
41 William Street, Princeton, New Jersey 08540
99 Banbury Road, Oxford OX2 6JX

press.princeton.edu

ISBN 9780691179681
ISBN (pbk.) 9780691241135
ISBN (e-book) 9780691231310

British Library Cataloging-in-Publication Data is available

Editorial: Matt Roahl
Production Editorial: Sara Lerner
Cover Design: Wanda España
Production: Erin Suydam
Publicity: Kate Hensley and Charlotte Coyne
Copyeditor: Cindy Milstein

This book has been composed in Arno Pro

10 9 8 7 6 5 4 3 2 1

CONTENTS

Contributors vii

Introduction: Dirty Hands and Beyond 1
Edward Hall and Andrew Sabl

1 Lies and Deception 21
Richard Bellamy

2 Compromise 45
Alin Fumurescu

3 Political Integrity 65
Edward Hall

4 The Ethics of Representation 82
Suzanne Dovi and Jesse McCain

5 Leadership and Representation 104
Eric Beerbohm

6 The Ethics of Partisanship 126
Russell Muirhead and Nancy L. Rosenblum

7 The Ethics of Public Administration 147
Joseph Heath

8 Political Corruption 170
Elizabeth David-Barrett and Mark Philp

9 The Public Ethics of Whistleblowing 193
Michele Bocchiola and Emanuela Ceva

10 Political Ethics in the State of Emergency 213
Nomi Claire Lazar

11 The Ethics of Political Lobbying: Power, Influence, and Democratic Decline 236
Phil Parvin

Afterword: Political Ethics and Institutional Renovation 265
Andrew Sabl

Index 281

CONTRIBUTORS

ERIC BEERBOHM is a professor of government and a faculty affiliate in the Department of Philosophy at Harvard University. He is the author of *In Our Name: The Ethics of Democracy* (Princeton University Press, 2012), which considers the responsibilities of citizens for the injustices of their state. His current book projects explore the ethics of electioneering and democratic wrong of gaslighting citizens. He serves as the editor of *NOMOS*, the annual edited volume of the American Society for Political and Legal Philosophy.

RICHARD BELLAMY is a professor of political science at University College London. His publications include *Liberalism and Pluralism: Towards a Politics of Compromise* (Routledge, 1999); *Political Constitutionalism: A Republican Defence of the Constitutionality of Democracy* (Cambridge University Press, 2007), which won the David and Elaine Spitz Prize in 2009; *Croce, Gramsci, Bobbio and the Italian Political Tradition* (Rowman and Littlefield, 2014); and *A Republic of European States: Cosmopolitanism, Intergovernmentalism and Democracy in the EU* (Cambridge University Press, 2019). With Jeff King, he is currently coediting the *Cambridge Handbook of Constitutional Theory*.

MICHELE BOCCHIOLA is a senior researcher and lecturer at the University of Geneva in Switzerland. His main research interests are in public ethics, especially privacy, the ethics of anticorruption, and institutional trustworthiness. He coauthored a book titled *Is Whistleblowing a Duty?* (Polity, 2018), and has published articles in the *Journal of Political Philosophy*, *Journal of Value Inquiry*, and *Philosophy Compass*, among others.

EMANUELA CEVA is a professor of political theory at the University of Geneva in Switzerland. Her main research interests are in the normative theory of institutions. Her most recent coauthored books are *Is Whistleblowing a*

Duty? (Polity, 2018) and *Political Corruption: The Internal Enemy of Public Institutions* (Oxford University Press, 2021).

ELIZABETH DAVID-BARRETT is a professor of governance and integrity at the University of Sussex, and director of the Centre for the Study of Corruption. David-Barrett's key areas of research include corruption at the interface of government and business as well as standards in public life and transnational governance networks to combat corruption.

SUZANNE DOVI is an associate professor at the School of Government and Public Policy at the University of Arizona. She is the author of *The Good Representative* (Wiley-Blackwell, 2006), a book that explores the ethics of democratic representation, and has published extensively on the representation of historically disadvantaged groups. Her current book project is on misogyny and gender oppression.

ALIN FUMURESCU is an associate professor in the Department of Political Science at the University of Houston. He is the author of *Compromise: A Political and Philosophical History* (Cambridge University Press, 2013, 2014) and *Compromise and the American Founding: The Quest for the People's Two Bodies* (Cambridge University Press, 2019, 2021), and coeditor of *Foundations of American Political Thought: Readings and Commentary* (Cambridge University Press, 2021).

EDWARD HALL is a senior lecturer in political theory at the University of Sheffield. He is the author of *Value, Conflict, and Order: Berlin, Hampshire, Williams, and the Realist Revival in Political Theory* (University of Chicago Press, 2020), and has published articles on realist political theory and political ethics. His current book project is on the liberalism of fear in the twenty-first century.

JOSEPH HEATH is a professor in the Department of Philosophy as well as the Munk School of Global Affairs and Public Policy at the University of Toronto. He is the author of several books, both popular and academic. His most recent, *The Machinery of Government* (Oxford, 2020), is a philosophical inquiry into the normative principles that inform the judgment of civil servants.

NOMI CLAIRE LAZAR is a full professor of politics in the Graduate School of Public and International Affairs at the University of Ottawa. She is the author of *States of Emergency in Liberal Democracies* (Cambridge University

Press, 2013) and *Out of Joint: Power, Crisis, and the Rhetoric of Time* (Yale University Press, 2019). She is at work on a new book about apocalyptic politics.

JESSE MCCAIN is a doctoral student in higher education and the sociology of education at the University of Virginia. He is coauthor of the book chapter "Are Lobbyists Lawyers?" (Routledge, 2016). His research uses qualitative methods and social theory to explore issues of inequality and identity in higher education settings, with a particular focus on graduate training. His current project examines professionalization and identity formation in law school.

RUSSELL MUIRHEAD teaches political theory at Dartmouth College as the Robert Clements Professor of Democracy and Politics. He is the author, with Nancy L. Rosenblum, of *A Lot of People Are Saying: The New Conspiracism and the Assault on Democracy* (Princeton, 2019). Muirhead also serves in the New Hampshire House of Representatives.

PHIL PARVIN is a reader in politics at Loughborough University. He is the author of *Political Philosophy: A Complete Introduction* (Hodder, 2012) and *Karl Popper* (Bloomsbury Academic, 2013) as well as numerous articles on lobbying, democratic engagement, and participation.

MARK PHILP is a professor of history and politics at the University of Warwick, and an Emeritus Fellow at Oriel College. His recent publications include *Radical Conduct: Politics, Sociability and Equality in London 1789–1815* (Cambridge University Press, 2020); *Reforming Political Ideas in Britain: Politics and Language in the Shadow of the French Revolution* (Cambridge, 2013); *Re-imagining Democracy in the Age of Revolutions: America, France, Britain, Ireland 1750–1850* (Oxford, 2013), coedited with Joanna Innes; and *Re-imagining Democracy in the Mediterranean* (Oxford, 2018) as well as editions of John Stuart Mill's essays and his own *Autobiography* for Oxford World Classics.

NANCY L. ROSENBLUM is the Harvard University Senator Joseph Clark Professor of Ethics in Politics and Government emeritus. Her books include *A Lot of People Are Saying: The New Conspiracism and the Assault on Democracy* (Princeton University Press, 2019), coauthored with Russell Muirhead; *Good Neighbors: The Democracy of Everyday Life in America* (Princeton University Press, 2016); *On the Side of the Angels: An Appreciation of Parties and Partisanship*

(Princeton University Press, 2010), which received the Walter Channing Cabot Fellow Award from Harvard in 2010 for scholarly eminence; and *Membership and Morals: The Personal Uses of Pluralism in America* (Princeton University Press, 2000), which was awarded the APSA David Easton Prize in 2000. She is also the editor of *Thoreau: Political Writings* (Cambridge University Press, 1996). Rosenblum is a member of the American Academy of Arts and Science, and coeditor of the *Annual Review of Political Science.*

ANDREW SABL is a professor of political science at the University of Toronto. He is the author of *Ruling Passions: Political Offices and Democratic Ethics* (Princeton University Press, 2002) and *Hume's Politics: Coordination and Crisis in the History of England* (Princeton University Press, 2012) as well as numerous scholarly articles. Sabl also coedited, with Rahul Sagar, *Realism in Political Theory* (Routledge, 2018). He is currently completing a project on toleration, and his future work will involve a realist reformulation of liberal political theory.

POLITICAL ETHICS

Introduction

DIRTY HANDS AND BEYOND

Edward Hall & Andrew Sabl

ANYONE WHO HAS TOLD others of having taught or written on "political ethics" is familiar with the rejoinder, "Isn't that a contradiction in terms?" This joke, which may have been fresh a few millennia ago, reflects "a piece of conventional wisdom to the effect that politicians are a good deal worse, morally worse, than the rest of us" (Walzer 1973, 162). An old, long, flattering literature on the nobility of leadership and the dignity of public service runs against a tradition of cynicism also so old that the most ancient school of "democracy," ancient Athens, institutionalized processes whereby its most prominent orators and officeholders were regularly and publicly audited, indicted, or ostracized, lest their disproportionate power go to their head and endanger the polity's welfare.[1] This was so even though politics was overwhelmingly non-institutionalized and far from a professional calling or career (a *politikos* was merely someone who spoke often and influentially in the citizen assembly).

The problem is one of power and interest. In theory, and no doubt in their own heads, politicians claim to further ordinary citizens' interests and channel public power toward common ends. In practice, ordinary citizens often suspect them of furthering their own interests and exerting power in narrow circles of private influence and secret knowledge. As polities grow in size, diversity, and social specialization, and public business becomes ever more technical and

1. Given that Athenian democracy did not include slaves, women, or resident aliens, Athens was in contemporary terms quite far from a democracy. It was arguably a tyranny whose tyrants practiced a form of egalitarianism among themselves in order to muster power against the rest. Yet the influence of its self-perception as a bastion of political equality and rule by "the people" was profound and cannot be ignored.

complex, the participatory methods of Athens—though still objects of nostalgia—become ever less relevant. We rely on politicians more than ever to reach authoritative decisions under conditions of social conflict and disagreement; to produce public goods at a level, and in a variety, that would have dazzled and bewildered the members of all past polities; to administer public business (or rather, select and oversee the specialized administrators who do so); and to regulate enterprises that employ millions and affect billions. Unlike many "professionals," however, whose specialized training is subject to codes of ethics whose violation may be punished by suspending the right of professional practice, those who make politics their calling are often subject to no code. They are certainly responsible to public opinion, as may or may not provide comfort.

Our extreme reliance on political leaders does not, of course, entail extreme trust. On the contrary, we may feel unable, given problems of scale and complexity, to learn about even a small proportion of politicians' incompetent or malevolent acts—let alone to do anything about them given the masses arrayed on all sides of political conflicts. To the extent that we do feel a sense of agency, it may be both small and largely illusory. Under what Max Weber ([1919] 2004, 74) called "spiritual proletarianization"—which he equated to a "loss of soul"—the average citizen may choose among partisan or ideological leaders (as well as, these days, among their ephemeral social media cousins, "influencers"), but cannot hope to have a substantial effect on their own. If, against all odds, an ordinary citizen *does* manage through engagement, activism, or internet notoriety to acquire substantial political influence, this does not solve the problem, but merely transforms that citizen into another politically influential figure whom others simultaneously admire, fear, deride, depend on, and follow (or unfollow). There is no reason to believe that amateurs will respond to such pressure better than professionals.

Political ethics is therefore a complex and paradoxical business. Even those who stress politicians' propensity for evil must acknowledge their role in determining and guaranteeing indispensable public goods. Even those who see politicians as driven by a zeal for public service and the desire to win fame for able stewardship in difficult times must acknowledge that winning office requires compromising with the powerful as well repeating oversimplified messages to sway a mass electorate—and that holding office may produce cluelessness as well as corruption. And the details of politics in both senses, the wielding and the seeking of power, are fiendishly complex and constantly changing. Given all of that, the *second* thing that scholars of political ethics are continually told—"well, you must have a lot to talk about these days"—is predictable without being even slightly wrong.

The Scope of This Book

This handbook is intended to provide a theoretically interesting overview of the central questions of political ethics. The envisioned audience is undergraduate students as well as more advanced scholars seeking concise, though learned, introductions to the ways these topics are addressed in political theory and political philosophy (the difference between the two need not detain us here). Our contributors are not, for the most part, in the business of directly commenting on the specific political controversies that currently exercise political commentators, activists, and engaged citizens. So the chapters that follow do not attempt to definitively outline the ethical misdeeds of the Trump administration (and not just because that would take a frighteningly long time) or pass ethical judgments on other leading politicians of the day. Instead they seek to help readers make sense of the ethical dimensions of political life at some distance from the concrete political controversies of the present, in order to vividly illustrate what is involved in theorizing about politics in an ethically demanding but clear-eyed way. Put another way, though the following chapters do not attempt to straightforwardly instruct readers what they should *do* about many specific issues of contemporary political concern, they demonstrate how we must *think* and what we must think about if we are to make responsible political judgments about such issues.[2]

Each chapter's author or authors offer a unique perspective on the issue they address. All noted scholars, they bring to their contributions their own theses and organizing concepts, and defend their own conclusions. Thus the chapters that follow are not intended to be "objective" or "impartial" summaries of existing work in political ethics. It may be most appropriate to regard them as careful interventions in long-standing debates in the field. The chapters share, then, two primary aims. First, to offer accurate and informative introductions to the topics at hand; second, to spur thought, debate, and discussion by defending a distinct viewpoint on that topic.

This handbook is not a manual for those seeking direct practical strategies for opposing clear political evil. The problems that we address—lies and

2. This explains why we have not included selections by politicians, activists, or civil society leaders in this handbook (though we believe that a good course on political ethics will incorporate such material). We also think that many instructors who assign this handbook will supplement the chapters with topical case studies, as both coeditors themselves do when teaching courses on political ethics.

deception in politics, political compromises, the nature of political integrity, poor representation, leadership in a democracy, excessive partisanship, the ethics of public administration, political corruption, the ethics of public whistleblowing, states of emergency, and lobbying—may be considered relatively minor compared to various "evil" political acts, from directly inciting violence to imprisoning one's political opponents, that unfortunately are not as rare as they should be. But many of these evils are, frankly, obviously wrong, as even autocrats tend to admit in the sense that they deny doing such things rather than defending having done them. For this reason, they are *less theoretically interesting* than the issues tackled in this volume. When one reflects on the topics addressed here, it is genuinely hard to know what to think and do, and it is not clear how we might design institutions, whether in government or civil society, to make them come out right. This makes them gripping topics of normative political inquiry. While there is much to be said about obvious cases of evil political conduct from the perspective of comparative politics or civic activism, there is less of interest to be said from the perspective of scholarly political ethics.

In the remainder of the introduction, we focus on the question of whether or not good political leaders must sometimes violate moral principles and constraints in order to do the right political thing. This is known as the "problem of dirty hands." It is the most apposite entry point into our subject because, in one way or another, it unavoidably affects one's understanding of numerous other topics in political ethics.

The Problem of Dirty Hands

In one of the most famous passages in *The Prince*, Niccolò Machiavelli ([1532] 1998, 61) declares that would-be rulers must "learn to be able not to be good." One tempting reaction, corresponding to the "contradiction in terms" quip just mentioned, is to say that Machiavelli need not have worried: most politicians seem to learn this quickly and well. A more serious and appropriate response, however, is to find disquieting—especially because they can be so seductive—Machiavelli's bold claims about politics' rightful enmity toward morality. Properly understood, Machiavelli does not suggest that politicians must act immorally if they are to successfully pursue their self-interest. If he had said that, those commentators who call *The Prince* simply "a handbook for gangsters" would be right; Machiavelli's work would be simultaneously entertaining and appalling—like a gangster movie—but not worth its reputation and our continued interest.[3] Machiavelli's central point is that a strict adherence to conventional moral standards would leave the prince unable to pursue a set of *worthy political ends* that we all have reason to value highly (see, e.g., Philp 2007, 37–54). It is this idea of Machiavelli's that is genuinely perturbing because it suggests that good politicians cannot be morally good people *and that we should not want them to be.*

The question of whether or not political leaders should sometimes breach significant moral principles and constraints in order to bring about valuable political ends has been known as the problem of dirty hands since Michael Walzer's (1973) article containing that phrase, borrowed from Jean-Paul Sartre's ([1948] 1989) play. According to advocates of the dirty hands thesis, addressing the demands of politics does sometimes require politicians to act "badly," that is, in ways that are *morally* wrong. And if they do, they must accept that they are *guilty*, morally speaking—even if in the end, they chose the correct thing to do, all things considered.

The view that political conduct that is rightly admired often requires moral actions that are rightly condemned generates many troubling questions. How can we be sure that politicians sometimes absolutely *have* to act badly? If these "bad" actions succeed in realizing or promoting genuinely valuable ends, up to and including the physical survival of some of the people for whose welfare the politician is responsible, in what sense does the politician do moral wrong, and why exactly should they feel *guilty*? Most centrally, the dirty hands problem demands that we think hard about the kind of people we want to govern us. How much weight do we want them to give to moral considerations when they are deciding how to act? What character traits and moral dispositions do we need our political leaders to display?

Starting with Walzer's brilliant treatment, the problem of dirty hands has cast a long shadow over the discipline of political ethics. It is not difficult to see why. It not only touches on something of great practical significance for our understanding of political conduct but also raises deep philosophical questions about the relationship between morality and politics that have fundamental implications for understanding the nature and authority of both.

Walzer employs two examples that he claims illustrate why politicians, even if they act rightly, are likely to dirty their hands. The first involves an election candidate who must make a shady deal with a corrupt ward boss who promises

3. Isaiah Berlin (1979, 35) reports Bertrand Russell as endorsing this view. Russell's (2004) *A History of Western Philosophy* reflects a similar sentiment, but lacks this precise formulation.

them votes in exchange for construction contracts. The point of this case is to show why we are right to disparage politicians who want to win elections yet refuse to get their hands dirty. "Assuming that this particular election ought to be won," Walzer (2007, 282) claims, this kind of disparagement is apt: "If the candidate did not want to get his hands dirty, he should have stayed at home. . . . His decision to run was a commitment (to all of us who think the election important) to try to win that is, to do within rational limits whatever is necessary to win." For Walzer, we know that the candidate acts—and crucially, feels and reflects—appropriately if they are reluctant to make the deal, but does so anyway.

Walzer's second example concerns a newly elected politician asked to authorize the torture of a rebel leader who allegedly knows the location of a number of hidden bombs that will shortly detonate, causing great harm and suffering. Just as in the case of the candidate making a deal with a corrupt ward boss, Walzer (2007, 283) insists that in this scenario, the politician should violate the moral prohibition at hand, "convinced that he must do so for the sake of the people who might otherwise die in the explosions—even though he believes that torture is wrong, indeed abominable, not just sometimes, but always." In both instances, Walzer stresses that it is not sufficient to say that the politician should merely feel "very badly" about their decision. Politicians who dirty their hands in these ways, Walzer (2007, 279) asserts, should feel not just badly but also *guilty*: they are "guilty of a moral wrong" and can no longer claim to govern innocently. Indeed, a politician's "willingness to acknowledge and bear [his guilt] . . . is the only evidence he can offer us, both that he is not too good for politics and that he is good enough" (Walzer 2007, 284).

To be sure, there are grounds for holding that the torture example is extremely unhappy given the savage influence of such arguments on everyone from the French in Algeria to the US military in Iraq (Horne 1997; Mayer 2008). In particular, many have maintained that Walzer's stylized illustration is radically untrue to the real-world case in which authorities are prone to resort to torture when they are by no means sure that the victim knows anything or the ticking bomb even exists (Scarry 2004; Shue 2004).[4] Still, the larger

4. In perhaps the closest real-world case to an official's facing a decision to resort to torture to prevent mass destruction—in Algeria, where authorities felt sure that a suspect in custody had an accomplice who had planted a bomb at the gasworks—the official in question decided against torture, and there turned out to be no such bomb (Horne 1997, 203–4). As Jane Mayer (2008) documents, portrayals of torture in popular culture not only severely distorted the

point remains relevant to cases that do not entail defying the absolute prohibition that international law as well as morality has placed on torture: decisions by political, military, and security force actors regarding "the use of force"—a pleasant euphemism—that effectively concern whether maiming or killing people is necessary to achieve higher state purposes.

These two evocative examples, which have now become part of the folklore of political ethics, illustrate Walzer's central point: that good politicians will, when necessary, dirty their hands *and accept that they have done so*. As Walzer (2007, 284) provocatively puts it, "Here is the moral politician. It is by his dirty hands that we know him. If he were a moral man and nothing else, his hands would not be dirty; if he were a politician and nothing else, he would pretend that they were clean." On this view, if necessity demands it, the good politician may have to lie, deceive, break their promises, manipulate others, compromise with morally dishonorable adversaries, even authorize murder and violence, and so on (Williams 1981, 58; Parrish 2007, 2). Outside politics, acting in this way is maligned; in politics, it can be laudable. Indeed, Bernard Williams (1981, 60) claims that "it is a predictable and probable hazard of public life that there will be these situations in which something morally disagreeable is clearly required," and "to refuse on moral grounds ever to do anything of that sort is more than likely to mean that one cannot seriously pursue even the moral ends of politics."

Moving beyond, though building on, Walzer's specific argument, *why* is politics especially likely to generate situations in which political leaders have to dirty their hands? Three reasons seem particularly relevant. First, as Weber famously said, the political state exercises a monopoly on the legitimate use of coercion and violence. Many commentators insist that this matters because it explains why politicians *can* readily dirty their hands:

> Politicians command the resources of the state in pursuit of their ends. They command not only those means of securing the continuing stability of their own regime, but those means—armed forces, intelligence, counter-intelligence and anti-terrorist personnel, diplomatic staff, foreign agents, immigration officers—that are necessary to defend the integrity of its

public's sense of how likely ticking bomb scenarios in fact are, and how certain political actors and security agents can be that such situations are occurring in real time, but also demonstrably influenced the decisions of US policy makers, who ended up approving the torture of suspects who turned out to know nothing.

> borders and its national security. In sum, politicians have the means at their disposal to do considerable wrongs both to their own citizens and to those of other states. (Archard 2013, 780; see also Parrish 2007, 13)

One might add that these considerable means of doing wrong are entrusted to a state monopoly for a reason. If state actors do not deploy them, domestic insurgents, other states, or international groups will be able to do so with impunity, and at the risk of great harm to those whom the squeamish politicians were supposed to protect.

This brings up the second major reason that politics is the distinctive realm of dirty hands: politicians have to act in a climate populated by opponents and adversaries who often act ruthlessly and deviously. In other words, to appreciate the strategic nature of politics, the competitive and resolutely grubby environment in which many politicians have to act, is to change our expectations of political ethics. To some degree, it is futile to expect politicians to adhere to the stringent demands of morality if their adversaries will not. Thus one might say that the nonideal circumstances in which a politician must act "sharply limi[t] the range of effective actions available to the serious politician" (Parrish 2007, 13).

The third reason concerns not the harm politicians can inflict but rather the collective benefits for which they are responsible, ranging from basic security to order, the provision of public goods and other forms of welfare, and retributive and distributive justice. It also matters that in acting to further such goals, politicians act as our representatives, trying—or at least claiming to try—to do well for us (Archard 2013, 779–80).[5] For this reason, it is frequently argued, claims of *necessity* carry a special weight in politics (Parrish 2007, 14). Unlike most of us, politicians have a responsibility to secure specific goods and prevent specific harms. They cannot avoid some blame if they fail in their responsibilities due to constraints—including moral constraints—that they could have overcome.

In focusing on these considerations, theorists of dirty hands insist on the reality of genuine moral dilemmas in public life. That is, they stress that from time to time, politicians—or at least politicians holding sufficiently high office,

5. The fact that politicians act for us has generated a fascinating debate about the extent to which members of the public might be said to have dirty hands if their leaders do—a question sometimes called that of "democratic dirty hands." For discussions, see Archard 2013; Coady 2018; Hollis 1982; Thompson 1998.

especially executive or military—are likely to find themselves beset by situations in which there is "nothing one can do that will not qualify as morally wrong in some relevant respect, where one is literally damned if one does and damned if one doesn't" (Parrish 2007, 4). In other words, there can be situations in which there is no straightforwardly *right* thing to do; in which, regardless of how one chooses to behave, any act will leave a moral *remainder*, an "uncancelled moral disagreeableness" that is not silenced by the fact that the agent may have acted as best as they could in an all-things-considered sense (Williams 1981, 61; on moral remainders, see also Honig 1993). Moreover, theorists of dirty hands often do not merely claim that the dirty hands thesis captures a significant fact about the reality of political life. They contend in addition that politicians' ability to *acknowledge* that politically justified actions can generate moral remainders is likely to have practical benefits. Only those politicians who recognize that the right political decision may have serious moral costs are, on this view, likely to be "reluctant or disinclined to do the morally disagreeable when it is really necessary." Moreover, and at least as important, only those politicians who are attuned to the costs of so acting are said to "have much chance of not doing it when it is not necessary" (Williams 1981, 62).

The dirty hands thesis is puzzling. It seems, to say the least, paradoxical to describe an action—such as authorizing deadly force—as being both the right and wrong thing to do *at the same time*. But this is precisely what the dirty hands thesis asserts. The point is not that overall, making deals with corrupt ward bosses or using threats of deadly force to combat terrorism is morally justified by the good consequences of so doing. These acts remain wrong, and this wrongness is not outweighed by the good consequences of violating moral norms. They are nonetheless taken to be politically necessary (for an admirably clear discussion of this point, see Archard 2013, 778).

This troubles many philosophers because, according to the most dominant approaches in moral philosophy, these kinds of moral dilemmas must in the end be *un*real. In other words (posit these moral theories), politicians might feel as if they are in the grip of a genuine ethical dilemma. If they reason clearly, however, they will recognize that there is not really a conflict between what morality prescribes and how they ought to act in politics—since morality is precisely the inquiry that tells us how we ought to act. Utilitarians, for example, stress that the correctness of a course of action is fully determined by the consequences of the decision at hand. Thus if authorizing the torture of the rebel leader is expected, on the best knowledge available, to produce the best consequences overall, it must therefore be the morally right thing to do, our scruples about torture notwithstanding. Of course, it might be *hard* for the politician asked to authorize the decision to torture the rebel leader to do so, and they may well feel bad about having done so. But when it comes down to it, this is not a genuine dilemma because it is clear that, *from the moral point of view*, the agent must act so as to bring about the best consequences overall. The hands of the agent who does so will hence be clean.

In one of the most engaging defenses of this view, Kai Nielsen (2007, 26) contends that although politicians who find themselves in difficult situations may well feel great psychological anguish and distress about their decisions, it is a philosophical error to suppose that there are *any* acts that we can say should never be done regardless of their consequences. This is because, according to Nielsen, the first responsibility of politics is to do the "lesser" evil. What this involves varies from case to case, and can require politicians to violate standard moral norms. But when it comes down to it, in doing the lesser evil they commit no wrong; they may *feel* guilty, but they are not *actually* guilty (Nielsen 2007, 20–21). Thus when discussing Walzer's second example (torture), Nielsen is adamant that the politician has not departed from the bounds of morality or failed to reason in accordance with the moral point of view. Instead, they have done something difficult that "*everything considered*, was the right thing to do in that circumstance" (Nielsen 2007, 30).

Deontologists—those who believe that certain actions are mandatory, regardless of the consequences, and that certain others are prohibited, regardless of the costs of inaction—disbelieve the reality of dirty hands for rather different reasons. In its most stringent versions, chiefly in the work of Immanuel Kant, deontology presents moral requirements as absolute or "categorical" requirements of reason valid for all rational agents regardless of the circumstances. The moral law set forth by practical reason must always be respected, no matter how the good the consequences of transgressing that law. So if bartering with a corrupt ward boss is immoral, and torture really is wrong "not just sometimes, but always," then no politician may ever do either. On this view, good political ends may not be brought about by doing evil. Though politicians may be *tempted* to disregard morality if they find themselves in the kinds of cases Walzer highlights, deontological approaches to ethics imply that moral politicians will not opt to dirty their hands—or put differently, that actual politicians must not do so.

Utilitarians and deontologists think in these terms because they hold that morality is both *comprehensive* and *dominant*. Morality is supposed to be relevant to all decisions, and if moral considerations conflict with other considerations, the former trump the latter (Coady 2018). Theorists of dirty hands accept that morality is comprehensive; on their view, moral considerations not only are relevant when we assess political action but must, if actors are to retain proper scruples, be *seen* to be relevant too. This is why they hold that a "lingering sense of wrongness should be preserved in our moral judgement of the politician who violates moral principles" (Thompson 1998, 13). Yet they deny that morality is dominant, that it always trumps countervailing considerations, such as those of political necessity and responsibility, or in some cases, political expediency. This is why Walzer claims that the dirty hands thesis tries to make sense of how we can refuse moral absolutism and accept the relevance of consequentialist decision-making in politics "without denying the reality of the moral dilemma" (Walzer 2007, 279).

In this regard, dirty hands theorists argue that political necessity overrides but does not silence morality. Those who think that morality is *irrelevant* to politics, in effect denying its comprehensiveness (such as advocates of crude versions of *Realpolitik*), do not believe that genuine dilemmas of the sort we are concerned with exist. It is important to recognize that though they believe morality cannot claim to straightforwardly legislate for politics, dirty hands theorists *are not* crude realists of that sort.

The philosophical debate between advocates of dirty hands and their utilitarian and deontological opponents is nuanced, and hence too complex to summarize here. As with many other paradoxes, the dirty hands thesis is bewildering and bemusing. Utilitarians are apt to reject it on these grounds, holding that the entire setup of the problem rests on a "conceptual confusion with unfortunate moral residues" (Nielsen 2007, 26). In response, dirty hands theorists raise important questions about whether or not utilitarianism can explain *why* politicians who have violated conventional moral standards should feel anguish and regret for their actions, which seems hard to deny (for this point, see Williams 1981). Many deontologists also maintain that their view is not as stringent and unbending as it may seem, and that exceptions to moral norms can be permitted in situations where this is genuinely required (for a general summary of these moves, see Coady 2018; Parrish 2007, 9). In response, dirty hands theorists reply that although these more flexible versions of deontology reach the right view about how politicians should behave in these cases, they ironically fail to capture the perspective at the beating heart of the dirty hands thesis: that if politicians violate moral norms, they have still committed a moral wrong, even if so acting was on the whole the best thing to do. In other words, flexible deontology, as with all forms of moral reasoning that regard morality as determinate and necessarily dominant, in cases of dirty hands yields the right decision but the wrong view of what is going on—because in such cases the right thing to do is precisely not the *morally* right thing to do.

An alternative way of trying to make sense of the dirty hands thesis in more conventional terms is by invoking the idea of a specific "role morality" for politicians. On such views, alongside a multitude of general moral principles, rules, and obligations, there exist a specific or distinctive set of moral requirements that one inherits when one occupies a particular social role. These two sets of requirements can come into conflict, "as when the lawyer's obligation to provide her client with the best defence and preserve confidentiality can conflict with the demands of impartial justice" (Coady 2018). Thus one might contend that we can explain why political demands sometimes trump moral prescriptions by asserting that when one becomes a politician, one inherits a host of distinctive obligations and duties that override general moral principles and standards.

This route has the advantage of going a long way toward dissolving the paradox at the heart of the dirty hands thesis by explaining why political action may sometimes conflict with conventional morality without, as it were, requiring us to argue that some nonmoral set of considerations trump moral ones. Instead, according to this approach, a distinctive set of moral obligations can supersede a moral general set in some circumstances. The role morality argument also makes clear that there are some political figures who are *not* permitted or required to get their hands dirty, and why. If presidents and prime ministers have special role obligations deriving from their awesome responsibilities, the heads of subway or sanitation authorities probably do not; whatever dilemmas and hard choices they face are no different from those confronting people with substantial private responsibilities.

Yet as C. A. J. Coady perceptively remarks, the central problem with this move is that we ordinarily think that the special obligations and duties associated with different roles are underpinned "by general moral considerations[,] since it is only those roles that can be morally supported by quite general moral considerations that will have a role morality." This explains why, even if the Mafia code may stipulate that snitches must be murdered, it stretches credulity to claim that this is, for a Mafia professional assassin, "a moral imperative of any sort" (Coady 2018). On the other hand, we may accept that lawyers have a genuine obligation to do the best they can for their clients because of the goods that we believe adversarial legal systems promote. (When doing so, we also insist that lawyers must act within certain moral bounds that are consistent with the laudable ends that the legal system promotes; contrary to popular belief, for example, a lawyer is not permitted to tell actual lies in court or written briefs.) In other words, we may believe that there is indeed a role morality for lawyers, but this is because the ends that being a lawyer promotes are compatible with morality properly understood.

If this is the right way to conceive of role morality, then it is hard to see how it can offer a promising route for making sense of the dirty hands thesis. Either the specific obligations of political office are sanctioned in the end by more general moral principles, in which case the purported tension between responsible political decision-making and morality dissolves, or (as in the case of the Mafia assassin) the distinctive obligations associated with the political role lack normative standing altogether. Perhaps the problem of dirty hands is a paradox we cannot do without.

In many respects, these theoretical disagreements about how we should grasp our intuition that politicians should sometimes violate conventional moral standards reflect more fundamental ones about how to philosophize about ethics and politics in the first place. Walzer and Williams, for instance, share a particular view about how we should regard moral feelings and sentiments—as crucial sources for philosophical reflection that we must try to make sense of, rather than trying to reduce to determinate decisions in the name of "reason"—that set them apart from many, if not all, of their moralist opponents, who deny the reality of genuine ethical dilemmas. Walzer and Williams, who may be called "realists" in this antimoralist sense, embrace a certain view of the limits of rationalism in ethics and politics. Some philosophical moralists would argue that if the dirty hands thesis entails this kind of irrationalism, we ought to disregard it. The realists would suggest, on the contrary, that this kind of moralism provides false consolation: it is structurally engineered to obscure troubling truths about the nature of political action, from which we should not avert our eyes.

The problem of dirty hands is unquestionably a vital topic in political ethics, and one that continues to repay study and analysis. Yet the contours of that debate often presuppose various perspectives about the challenges of political ethics, and the structure and nature of political problems, that warrant more fine-grained attention. For example, advocates of the dirty hands thesis frequently observe that we cannot expect politicians to adhere to standards of veracity and truthfulness that we insist on in nonpolitical contexts. But this suggestion regarding truth telling rests on highly involved claims about everything from history to sociology to evolutionary psychology, on what truth is, and why human beings might benefit from gathering and conveying truthful opinions (Williams 2004). Similarly, commentators remark that politicians often have to make morally shady compromises or act in ways that threaten their personal integrity, without examining how we should think about the nature of political compromise, or whether or not there might be such a thing as a distinctively political form of integrity. Likewise, as noted earlier, advocates of the dirty hands thesis repeatedly stress the significance of the idea that politicians are our representatives without delving into the complex debates about the nature and ethics of representation in political theory.

By addressing these topics and many more—including the value of partisanship in politics, the ethics of public administration, whistleblowing, emergency powers, political corruption, and the activity known as lobbying—all the chapters in this book, in one way or another, go *beyond* the problem of dirty hands in order to explore the ethical dimensions of political conduct and practice in the twenty-first century.

Outline of the Book

In chapter 1, Richard Bellamy focuses on lying and deception in politics. After canvassing the work of a number of important thinkers in the history of philosophy—including Plato, Machiavelli, Kant, and Arendt—and showing how their diverse positions are reflected in contemporary theorists' and practitioners' views, he proceeds to scrutinize analytically the concepts of lying and deception, explaining why they are often regarded to be normatively objectionable. Following this, Bellamy discusses the extent to which lying and deception are endemic to liberal democratic politics, and how democracy might be more effective in promoting truthfulness. His analysis avoids both undue optimism and unwarranted pessimism. There are, Bellamy insists, good grounds for holding that in politics, leaders have both pragmatic and principled reasons to be truthful, at least to some degree.

In the next chapter, Alin Fumurescu examines how we should regard political compromises from a moral point of view. Fumurescu's central contention is that appreciating the forgotten history of compromise can help us to correct various inadequacies endemic to work on compromise in contemporary political theory. While the chapter's rich and subtle argument defies easy summary, Fumurescu's analysis suggests on the whole that people are unwilling to compromise when they feel that a particular compromise threatens their group or individual identity. Moreover, he insists that we ought to be deeply suspicious of the search for a neutral or objective standpoint from which we can determine which political compromises are morally acceptable and which are beyond the moral pale.

In chapter 3, Edward Hall asks whether or not we can meaningfully evaluate political conduct by asking if politicians have acted with integrity. To do so, he problematizes common ways that integrity is invoked in popular discourse—roughly, as a synonym for basic moral decency—before arguing that most views of integrity proposed by moral philosophers unfortunately suggest that political integrity may be an oxymoron. Hall, however, offers an account of a distinctively political kind of integrity that he believes can play a useful role in our evaluations of political conduct, drawing out both the negative and positive elements of such an account. On his view, politicians who display a kind of principled commitment to political goals and ends, while avoiding various forms of malfeasance, can claim to act with political integrity even while having to engage in certain kinds of behavior that would seem to threaten one's integrity in nonpolitical contexts.

The next two chapters address issues at the nexus of democratic theory and political ethics. In chapter 4, Suzanne Dovi and Jesse McCain ask what it means to be a good representative. Addressing this question, they contend, requires thinking about what kinds of behavior help the represented to hold politicians to account. In this sense, good representatives facilitate, rather than impede, the political autonomy of the represented. At a minimum, this requires representatives to allow the represented to meaningfully reflect on and influence policy decisions, while also assessing and sanctioning the decisions that politicians make. Drawing on this discussion, Dovi and McCain highlight two nefarious tactics that bad representatives can adopt to promote a worrying kind of "ethical obliviousness"—tactics which they term "self-contradiction" and "disdainful distraction." This is an enlightening methodological move. In accord with what Jonathan Allen (2001) has called "negative morality" (following Shklar 1990), they believe that good representation is best illuminated by examining the vices or misbehaviors that are commonly present instead of positing exalted ideals that will rarely be approached.

Following them, Eric Beerbohm addresses the fraught relationship between leadership and representation. Though many people regard leadership as a counterrepresentational force, Beerbohm shows how leadership can be reconciled with representation by offering a philosophically rich account of how we can say that leaders and followers act together. Beerbohm criticizes agent- and follower-centered models of political leadership before offering his own account, which unifies the attractive features of these models. In making these points, Beerbohm does not shy away from the fact that leadership *can* threaten democracy, but he insists that certain forms of leadership are democratically valuable as they make possible a distinctive form of joint activity.

Nowadays complaints about the partisan nature of politics are legion. In chapter 6, Russell Muirhead and Nancy L. Rosenblum offer a normative defense of parties and political partisanship in the face of detractors who contend that democratic political life would be improved if people refrained from experiencing or engaging in politics as partisans and instead weighed rival claims and political proposals impartially in order to secure the common good for all. They argue that parties play an indispensable role in democratic politics in three distinct ways: by fostering forms of political inclusivity; by offering comprehensive stories about the great economic, social, and moral challenges of the day; and by activating the disposition to compromise that is essential to democratic politics. Muirhead and Rosenblum contend that these three values of parties and partisanship are essential ingredients of a democratic political life, and that those who see them as merely strategic virtues operate with a naive, overly moralistic view of politics.

Most work in political ethics grapples with the conduct of politicians and elected officials. This has meant that political ethicists have had little to say about the duties of civil servants, about how they (and we) should regard the obligations they have toward elected officials and the public they serve. Joseph Heath's chapter is an excellent resource for making sense of the ethics of public administration. Heath charts three different ways in which we can think about the principles and obligations that apply to civil servants. He terms these the hierarchical model (which sees civil servants as mere implementers of policy decisions made by elected officials), the popular model (which sees civil servants as fundamentally accountable to the public), and the vocational model (which sees civil servants as being tasked with securing a set of relatively independent purposes of the state). After highlighting the problems and shortcomings with standard formulations of all three, Heath endorses a qualified account of the vocational model. He argues that although the professional ethics of civil servants must—of course—place great weight on the goals and ends of elected officials, the demands of the role are not wholly subordinate to those goals because the executive branch itself makes a distinctive contribution to the "output legitimacy" of the state—its ability to win popular support not through consent but rather through good performance.

In chapter 8, Elizabeth David-Barrett and Mark Philp address political corruption. They express deep skepticism that the concept of political corruption can provide a clear set of universal standards that we can employ to evaluate the behavior of political agents. They argue, in fact, that seeking universalistic accounts of these matters prevents us from recognizing the diverse range of local factors and expectations that inevitably shape the conduct of political agents. In making these claims, David-Barrett and Philp criticize economic approaches to political corruption, explore the nature of conflicts of interest in neoliberal systems of government, and discuss the shortcomings of moves to build political integrity by introducing codes of conduct for elected officials. They provocatively contend that we must think about political corruption in terms of local circumstances. In so doing, their chapter—like many in this book—illustrates the potential benefits of a realist approach to this contested topic.

Michele Bocchiola and Emanuela Ceva's chapter explores the ethically fraught practice of whistleblowing, asking how whistleblowing can be justified and whether, in certain circumstances, blowing the whistle might be not merely admirable but instead a duty or obligation. They offer an analytically precise definition of whistleblowing, illustrating its relationship to and from other forms of disclosure, and explore the limitations of approaches that attempt to justify whistleblowing in terms of requirements to prevent harm or avoid certain kinds of complicity. They then offer a distinct "relational" account. This view intriguingly justifies whistleblowing as an instance of the duty of "office accountability": actors must blow the whistle if they learn that their organization has been acting in ways that contradict its legitimate mandate. In this sense, the authors derive a stringent duty for institutional organizations to secure safe channels for whistleblowing in order to uphold answerability practices between role occupants. Their challenging and unorthodox argument, while doing justice to more common approaches, promises an entirely new framework.

Nomi Claire Lazar's chapter takes on the ethics of state action in emergencies. She begins by asserting that even the gathering of basic factual information may be practically and ethically difficult in emergencies, before then probing the literature on who gets to decide when and if law applies as usual. After assessing the positions of Carl Schmitt and Giorgio Agamben, Lazar proceeds to explain the problems that both deontological and consequentialist thinkers have in approaching crises, paying particular attention to flexible forms of deontological reasoning. She then inquires into the fraught relationship between emergency decision-making and the rule of law. In conclusion, she contends that ensuring good action in emergency conditions requires the existence, before the emergency begins, of trusting relationships between citizens and their leaders.

In chapter 11, Phil Parvin offers a bracing account of the threat that lobbying currently poses to democratic politics. Drawing on a wealth of empirical work in political science, he maintains that liberal democracies have manifestly failed to ensure that lobby organizations operate in a manner consistent with fundamental liberal democratic principles. This is perhaps not a surprising claim. But Parvin also argues that it is highly likely that states are no longer in a position to implement reforms that can redress these problems. This is because they have failed to ensure that representative institutions are impartial with regard to conflicts of interest, to secure a background distribution of resources that can stop power concentrating in the hands of elites, or to sustain a diverse range of interest groups that can represent a wide array of citizens. In light of this, Parvin contends that lobbying, as currently practiced, not only inhibits states from acting in accordance with fundamental liberal democratic principles but also, much more worryingly, stops states from reforming themselves so that they can live up to their foundational principles. To this end, Parvin suggests that there are grounds for holding that lobbying is the most urgent of all problems faced by liberal states, and one that political theorists continue to ignore at their peril.

In an afterword, Andrew Sabl discusses the lessons for political ethics of quasi-authoritarian populism and the erosion of democracy that it threatens. He links political ethics to constitutional institutions and norms in that both frustrate the immediate, visceral desires of leaders and citizens alike. Populism's appeal thus reminds us that shortsightedness and partiality are natural, whereas political ethics and the constitutional sea in which it swims are artificial, conventional, and opposed to many of our gut instincts. Populism to this extent involves a deliberate rebellion against hard-won, socially learned liberal democratic institutions by those who benefit more, in the short run at least, from grabbing whatever they can. But it also involves real ethical (or antiethical) innovations: redefinitions of desert and justice, the conversion of aristocratic exclusivity into a mass version based on ethnicity, the transformation of despotism into a mass version whereby masses take vicarious joy in the leader's ability to rule by caprice. Against these reversions and innovations, Sabl argues, we can only reprise and reassert political ethics' old and enduring insight: that all of us benefit more, in the long run, from rules and norms that apply to all than by our team's seizing momentary spoils on the expectation that the other team will someday steal them back. To this extent, the proper response to populism is not to question political ethics but instead to double down on its lessons—as the authors of this volume have done.

This book supports a particular approach to thinking about how theoretical insights are related to real-world events—an approach that can be regarded as "realist" in the best sense of that term. The majority of the chapters that follow implicitly explore how the analysis of real politics can improve our understanding of political ethics by helping us to arrive at ethical insights and normative principles that derive from the peculiar circumstances of politics, rather than trying to draw lessons from the small-scale, relatively intimate, and low-stakes circumstances of private life that may not be relevant to politics at all. The theoretical insights gained have real-world relevance not in the sense of telling us exactly what to do but more in the sense of making us wiser and less credulous concerning the threats we face. For instance, realist theory and experience alike, with the former informed by the latter, suggest that ethical standards are neither eternal nor known to all rational beings. They are best regarded as the result of mental habits that derive from past and present political action. And our attachment to those standards may, for better or worse, be weakened or undone given enough experience of their absence, and enough political action dedicated to destroying them.

Thus the prevailing tone of these chapters is one of engaged realism and/or mitigated pessimism. The authors do not shrink from documenting the ethical problems endemic to politics and do not pretend that putting forth glittering normative ideals will make those problems go away. But they also refuse to retreat into a cynicism in which power is politics' only currency and self-interest its only ethical standard. Provided that we recognize politics to be a complex and imperfect business that no theory can render fully comprehensible and no rule can render fully moral, we can reach solid (though always disputable) judgments. Such judgments can hope to distinguish better political conduct from worse, and can guide attempts to reform institutions so that they might address the problems of politics a little better than they otherwise would. It is in that sense, perhaps only in that sense, that political ethics need not be a contradiction in terms.

References

Allen, Jonathan. 2001. "The Place of Negative Morality in Political Theory." *Political Theory* 29 (3): 337–63.

Archard, David. 2013. "Dirty Hands and the Complicity of the Democratic Public." *Ethical Theory and Moral Practice* 16 (4): 777–90.

Berlin, Isaiah. 1979. "The Originality of Machiavelli." In *Against the Current: Essays in the History of Ideas*, 25–79. London: Hogarth.

Coady, C. A. J. 2018. "The Problem of Dirty Hands." In *Stanford Encyclopedia of Philosophy*. https://plato.stanford.edu/entries/dirty-hands/.

Hollis, Martin. 1982. "Dirty Hands." *British Journal of Political Science* 12 (4): 385–98.

Honig, Bonnie. 1993. *Political Theory and the Displacement of Politics*. Ithaca, NY: Cornell University Press.

Horne, Alistair. 1977. *A Savage War of Peace: Algeria 1954–1962*. London: Macmillan.

Levinson, Sanford, ed. (2004). *Torture: A Collection*. Oxford: Oxford University Press.

Machiavelli, Niccolò. (1532) 1998. *The Prince*. Translated by Harvey C. Mansfield. 2nd ed. Chicago: University of Chicago Press.

Mayer, Jane. 2008. *The Dark Side*. New York: Doubleday.

Nielsen, Kai. 2007. "There Is No Dilemma of Dirty Hands." In *Politics and Morality*, edited by Igor Primoratz, 20–37. Basingstoke, UK: Palgrave.

Parrish, John. 2007. *Paradoxes of Political Ethics: From Dirty Hands to the Invisible Hand*. Cambridge: Cambridge University Press.

Philp, Mark. 2007. *Political Conduct*. Cambridge, MA: Harvard University Press.

Russell, Bertrand. 2004. *A History of Western Philosophy*. London: Routledge.

Sartre, Jean-Paul (1948) 1989. *Dirty Hands*. In *No Exit and Three Other Plays*. New York: Vintage.

Scarry, Elaine. 2004. "Five Errors in the Reasoning of Alan Dershowitz." In *Torture: A Collection*, edited by Sanford Levinson, 281–90. Oxford: Oxford University Press.

Shklar, Judith N. 1990. *The Faces of Injustice*. New Haven, CT: Yale University Press.

Shue, Henry. 2004. "Torture." In *Torture: A Collection*, edited by Sanford Levinson, 47–60. Oxford: Oxford University Press.

Thompson, Dennis. 1998. *Political Ethics and Public Office*. Cambridge, MA: Harvard University Press.

Walzer, Michael. 2007. "Political Action: The Problem of Dirty Hands." In *Thinking Politically: Essays in Political Theory*, 278–95. New Haven, CT: Yale University Press.

Weber, Max. (1919) 2004. "Politics as a Vocation." In *The Vocation Lectures, edited by* David Owen and Tracy B. Strong, 32–94. Translated by Rodney Livingstone. Indianapolis, IN: Hackett Publishing Company.

Williams, Bernard. 1981. "Politics and Moral Character." In *Moral Luck: Philosophical Papers 1973–1980*, 54–70. Cambridge: Cambridge University Press.

———. 2004. *Truth and Truthfulness*. Princeton, NJ: Princeton University Press.

1

Lies and Deception

Richard Bellamy

THE BELIEF THAT politicians and the media lie to people and seek to deceive them for self-interested reasons long predates today's accusations of "fake news" (Jay 2010). Although those leveling such accusations invariably contend that the present political class is more mendacious than politicians in the past (Oborne 2005), it is a recurrent complaint going back to antiquity. Yet a distinguished and just as long tradition of political thought treats calls for truth and openness in politics with skepticism (Arendt [1967] 2006).

From Plato through Niccolò Machiavelli to Leo Strauss and Hannah Arendt, numerous political philosophers have seen politics as a realm in which lies and deception necessarily flourish (Jay 2010). Though their reasons for so arguing differ in a number of crucial respects, all agree with Arendt's (1971, 4) claim that "truthfulness has never been counted among the political virtues, and lies have always been regarded as justifiable tools in political dealings." These philosophers consider those who bemoan this state of affairs as either naive fools or devious charlatans, likely to be even greater spreaders of falsehood and deceit themselves. Indeed, as we will see, accusations of lying and deception, on the one hand, and the temptation to lie and deceive, on the other, often prove to be tied up with misplaced expectations, distorted beliefs, and self-deception (Galeotti 2015). Disentangling and distinguishing the one from the other proves harder than one might think.

Lying and deception in politics extend from the outright mendacity of denying or hiding a misdemeanor that might harm a politician's personal reputation, such as adultery or a criminal act unrelated to the exercise or attainment of political office; through seeking to cover up some political offense, such as taking bribes or engaging in electoral fraud; to more accepted forms of being "economical with the truth" that range from protecting state secrets, through dissembling to other politicians or the electorate, as when making them promises one knows one cannot or does not intend to keep; to casting unwarranted aspersions on one's rivals and spinning one's own abilities, achievements, and policies (Mearsheimer 2011, 15–20).[1] Most people would regard some of these lies and forms of deceit as more deserving of condemnation than others. In fact, quite a few people would acknowledge that certain types of dissembling, such as misleading an enemy in war about one's military plans, might be fully justified (Mearsheimer 2011, 40).

This chapter explores these various forms of lying and deception in the context of the norms and practices typically associated with liberal democracy. According to such a system, politicians are considered the authorized and accountable representatives of the electorate, with an obligation to pursue the public interest rather than simply their personal interests or the private interests of a specific group of individuals. To the extent they do further their own interests along with those of their friends or supporters, democratic norms suggest that however hypocritically or implausibly, they must at least claim to be doing so for the common good. To this end, democratic politicians are constrained not only by the democratic process but also by liberal constitutional norms protecting certain individual civil and political rights, such as freedom of speech and association, oriented toward ensuring due process and the equal protection of the law for all.

No democratic system fully meets the standards of the liberal democratic ideal. Moreover, commentators divide over how far it can or should. Some contend democratic politics necessarily involves, and can plausibly require, truth telling, with all lies and deceit consequently damaging democracy to some degree (Bok 1978, 172). If politicians are to rule for the people and be accountable to them, then they believe policy making needs to be transparent, and based on clearly articulated and openly avowed principles and policies. Politicians can only be counted on to rule in the public interest when they are obliged to do so in full view of the public, and under their equal influence and control. By contrast, I have noted already how others regard certain forms of deceit and lying as inherent to politics in general, and democratic politics in particular (Jay 2010, chap. 3). They maintain democracy cannot but rest on a noble lie: pretending

1. While earlier usages exist, the phrase "economical with the truth" gained notoriety when used by the British Cabinet secretary Sir Robert Armstrong in the *Spycatcher* trial of 1986 to distinguish telling an outright lie from giving a misleading impression.

that people can rule themselves through free and fair agreements on those policies that best promote their collective welfare (Canovan 1990). People's values and concerns, however, are too diverse, incompatible, and incommensurable for either public reasons or shared interests to exist. As a result, the democratic ideal proves impossible. Instead, politicians must often employ rhetoric and half-truths to build coalitions between groups of people with conflicting views and interests so as to mobilize sufficient popular support to promote almost any collective enterprise. The falsehood, according to which governments can rule for the common good of citizens, that nevertheless remains so necessary to democratic legitimacy thereby ends up as the source of all the other lies politicians unavoidably tell in politics (Bellamy 2010).

The following analysis of these competing views begins by sketching the classic arguments about the ways lies and deceit are either endemic to politics, or could and should be excluded from it. As we will see, these assertions tend to reappear in later discussions. I then explore what counts as lying and deception, identifying why they might be viewed as normatively objectionable, and distinguishing the different kinds of lies and deceit democratic politicians are apt to commit as well as their motivations for doing so. I conclude with an examination of how truth and truthfulness play out in the circumstances of politics. Although truthfulness in politics will be shown to rest on persuasiveness and opinion as much as logic and facts, it will be maintained that distinctions can be drawn between private interests and public reasons, deception and delusion, and honesty and dishonesty, if not between lies and truth per se. There may be no secure epistemological grounding for the objective truth and morality of most political opinions, but that does not mean politicians can simply say and act as they please so long as the electorate is willing to believe and support them. Rather, we can expect them to offer a minimum of reasoned and evidence-based arguments for their views and actions, which even if not conclusive, can be assessed independently and freely by voters, opponents, and the media with regard to their likely strengths as well as weaknesses.

Noble and Ignoble Lies in Politics: From Plato to Immanuel Kant

The classic historical debates concerning lying and deceit in politics all predate democracy. Yet they prefigure many of the assertions deployed by contemporary politicians and theorists seeking to justify or question political mendacity today. I will briefly explore three arguments about the necessity of lying: Plato's defense of the so-called noble lie, Machiavelli's counsel that a successful prince must be prepared to lie to retain power, and the debate between Benjamin Constant and Kant as to whether lies can ever be morally justified.

Scholars dispute whether Plato's notion of *gennaios pseudos* is correctly rendered as "noble lie" or not (Jay 2010, 3). For our purposes, however, how it has been traditionally understood matters more than what he may or may not actually have intended to say. The argument comes in Plato's ([ca. 380 BC] 1987, 414c) *The Republic*, where he suggests that the rule of an elite group of so-called philosopher kings or guardians might be justified to both themselves and the general citizenry by way of the myth of the metals attributed to the poet Hesiod (Plato [ca. 380 BC] 1987, 414b–c). According to this fable, God had made a golden race to rule, a silver race to be soldiers, and an iron race to be workers (Plato [ca. 380 BC] 1987, 415a–d). Political stability could thereby be secured by reconciling people to their station and its duties as somehow natural. To some commentators, the contention has seemed in tension with Plato's condemnation of the mendacity of the Sophists (Jay 2010, 147–48). Yet Plato ([ca. 380 BC] 1987, 514–21) contended that all but philosophers had access to only the shadows of truth and mere opinion. The rule of philosophers was justified through their having a knowledge of justice that was necessarily inaccessible to the majority of people. Hence in a world of lies and half-truths, the rule of truth had itself to be based on a lie, albeit a justified and "noble" one. Such an argument, though, cannot be easily reconciled with democracy, and for many critics simply offers rulers specious grounds for portraying their self-interest in ruling as being in the interests of those they rule—a line of reasoning all too open to abuse (Bok 1978, 169).

Nevertheless, a number of contemporary writers have defended a parallel argument to Plato's associated with the philosopher and military ruler Xenophon. Although like Plato a student of Socrates and a critic of sophistry, in his dialogue *Hiero*, Xenophon approved the use of guile by an autocrat in order to rule for the benefit of all (Jay 2010, 3–4). This position was later extolled by Strauss (1968) in his influential study *On Tyranny*, a piece that has been credited with inspiring later arguments for mendacity by Cold War strategists in the United States (Jay 2010, 156). Indeed, as we will see, similar reasoning to Plato's and Xenophon's resurface both as justifications of paternalist rule, on the one hand, and a defense of democracy, on the other.

In *The Prince*, Machiavelli ([1513] 1998, chap. 15) also considered politics as being often characterized by lies and deceit. If all people were good, then he conceded it would be wrong to suggest that a prince should not be similarly good. Still, a wise ruler appreciated that unfortunately many people were in fact wicked and would seek to lay traps to supplant them, often lying to gain the prince's trust in order to do so. In such circumstances, it would be wrong for a ruler to keep their word and act honestly when all around them acted dishonestly. As a result, Machiavelli ([1513] 1998, chap. 18) contended that a successful ruler has to be able to act faithlessly, and learn to lie and deceive when it seems prudent. Nevertheless, if the ruler was not to inspire contempt and hatred in the people, it was important to appear to be honest and trustworthy. Indeed, Machiavelli argued that a prince ought only to lie when it was truly necessary, and employ such craftiness against rivals for power rather than against the people, who would generally support them so long as they ruled in the public interest. Lying in the Machiavellian account therefore is not so much self-serving in the narrow sense as it is strategic. That is, he does not suggest that a prince has no duty to be honest, nor that lying for personal advantage is not wrong, but instead that in certain circumstances, lying may be justified if a prince is to hold onto power and that doing so may be generally beneficial.

The final classic account to be discussed is the debate between Constant ([1797] 2003) and Kant ([1797] 1997) as to whether it would be permissible to lie to a murderer who came to your house demanding to know if their intended victim was in. Kant has often been regarded as espousing an extreme position that not only would it be wrong to lie in any situation, including this one, but also that any bad consequences that might arise from the lie would be the fault of the liar. For example, he suggests that if you had lied and denied that the potential victim was in the house, but that unbeknownst to you they had slipped out while you were talking to the murderer, who then encounters them when walking away from the house as a result of your lie, then you would be responsible for the victim's death. Kant's reasoning has been assumed to be that moral principles need to be formulated in a manner that is independent of any calculation of the possible consequences, which are unknowable. Instead, people should only adopt those moral principles that could be adopted universally by all as a consistent principle for action with others, which could not be true of lying. Constant's ([1797] 2003, 36) criticism rested on what he saw as the categorical and formal character of Kantian ethics, and the German philosopher's failure to adopt "intermediate or midrange principles" that apply in less than ideal circumstances.

Although a number of commentators have agreed with Constant's criticism, seeing it as indicating a more general problem with the formalism of

Kantian morality (see, for example, MacIntyre 1998, 125), others, as with Plato, have challenged this standard account. Defenders of the Kantian argument have noted that in his political theory, Kant was accustomed to acknowledge the need to adapt categorical principles to nonideal conditions—as when he proposes articles of just war given that the ideal of perpetual peace remains at present an aspiration. Likewise, while the formula of humanity required that we treat others as ends rather than means, rendering lying immoral as the basis of conduct in taking away the autonomy of the deceived, it is less clear that lying to the murderer was necessarily incompatible with Kant's more formal rule that we only adopt principles that could be espoused universally. After all, a lie would only work in a circumstance where the murderer could be assumed to think you were telling the truth. So to lie in such a circumstance is not to advocate a universal policy of lying because if we all knew that everybody lied, then nobody would ever believe what anyone said—the murderer included. Advocating a universal policy of lying would be pointless, therefore (Korsgaard 1986). Of course, the deceit does not treat the murderer according to the ideal of seeing others as ends in themselves. Yet Kant actually grants Constant's point that such absolute duties only apply in situations where there are reciprocal rights, and he considered that there could not be a right to do wrong.

Even those critics unconvinced by the coherence in Kantian terms of this potential response to Constant grant the general Kantian point that the very possibility of language and other meaningful intersubjective social relations and practices assumes truthfulness among their participants (MacIntyre 2006, 103–5, 137–38). Their claim is merely that it is coherent to argue that in an imperfect world, lies may be legitimate as the least harmful option to uphold the integrity of truthful relationships against those, such as the murderer, who seek to subvert and destroy them (MacIntyre 2006, 138–39). In other words, truth is a universal assumed even by liars; who would believe them otherwise? Nonetheless, exceptionally some lies may be told for the sake of truth, although which lies and when remains controversial.

Philosophy as a whole has been characterized as a series of footnotes to Plato, and thinking on lying and deception proves no exception. If Plato offers one of the earliest and most compelling accounts of the contradictions behind the allure of lies and deception, he also provides one of its most seductive defenses. Meanwhile, Machiavelli indicates why politicians may have no alternative than to deceive and lie if they are to hold onto power in a world where so many others are dishonest and unscrupulous. Finally, Kant's arguments likewise still resonate behind many objections to lying, even if his assertions suggest that we need to draw a distinction between the ethical requirements of ideal and nonideal circumstances. In what follows, we will see how all of these arguments continue to play out in contemporary debates.

Lies and Deception: Definitions and Democratic Objections

This section starts by defining lying and deception before turning to what renders such practices objectionable within a democracy. Neither the first task nor, as a consequence, the second proves entirely straightforward.

Lying and Deception Defined

Both lying and deception can be defined as a deliberate attempt by a person or persons to assert (Fallis 2009, 33)—and possibly mislead another person or persons into believing (Bok 1978, 13–16)—something that the liar(s) knows or thinks is false. Though lying often involves deception, it need not always deceive, however, or at least not straightforwardly so (Fallis 2009, 41–43). Nor need all deception involve lying.

For example, a cancer patient may lie to their family about how they are doing by saying they're fine, knowing full well that their family is aware they are lying and in fact they are doing rather badly. But the lie and the family's acceptance of it may ease some of the emotional stress each feels about the situation. At best, it is a willed self-deception on all sides. Likewise, some forms of deception can comprise telling a misleading truth, such as a half-truth that does not reveal all one knows (Weissberg 2004, 169), or failing to correct another's misperceptions, misunderstandings, or false assumptions, or even lack of knowledge, rather than outright lying. Nevertheless, lying and deception are alike in involving an intention on the part of those who commit them to create or sustain what they consider to be an erroneous opinion in others. To the extent that lying is objectionable, so it might be thought is deception.

Yet perhaps that goes too far. Maybe lying is worse than deception. For instance, in a criminal trial we think it reasonable and even appropriate that the defense lawyers should place the best-possible gloss on their client's behavior, leaving it to the prosecution to expose the flaws in their account. If the prosecution fails to do so, so that a guilty person goes free, the defense team may have succeeded in deceiving the jury, but it has not lied to the jurors.

Many people will feel that in such a case, the defense has simply done its job and will blame the prosecution lawyers for failing to do theirs. The line between deception and lying may be fuzzy therefore, but it is right to distinguish the two. Advocacy ought to stop short of lying, but it may encompass, possibly unavoidably, elements of deception simply in highlighting certain facts and reasons as opposed to others. After all, limited time and knowledge, and an inevitable partiality to certain views deriving from our education and experience, mean that some degree of selectivity proves inescapable when presenting any argument.

All the same, although the selectivity typical of any kind of advocacy may seem like deception, at least superficially, it need not involve any intent to deceive. Someone who *inadvertently* creates a false impression in the mind of another through unwittingly either holding mistaken views themselves or possessing incomplete or flawed information may mislead others, but clearly does not lie to or deceive them. They may be open to criticism and censure for their stupidity, ignorance, or culpability in failing to become better informed, but their fault is different from that of a liar or deceiver who intends to mislead. Likewise, we can distinguish between those defense lawyers who vigorously defend the innocence of their clients while knowing they are guilty and those lawyers who, as is generally the case, give their clients the benefit of the doubt and deliberately avoid raising the issue of their clients' possible guilt so as not to morally compromise their ability to advocate on their behalf. In the first case, the lawyer has willfully deceived others in a way tantamount to lying. By contrast, in the second instance the lawyer has at worst deceived themselves. Yet lawyers in this second category might regard the obligation to uncover the truth as resting as much with the prosecution and jury as themselves. They may feel that upholding truthfulness cannot be achieved simply by trusting everyone to act without deception or lies but also involves being prepared to challenge and question what they say. It is a shared responsibility of the actors within the system.

In politics, likewise, truth and falsehood are not always entirely clear-cut. People may often reasonably interpret the significance of various facts differently when making a political or moral judgment about a particular policy. Of course, that does not mean that all views are equally well supported either by the evidence, or by similarly coherent and relevant arguments. But in many areas of human life, both the known facts and practical reasoning can support a range of reasonable views. Naturally, politicians—no less than political philosophers debating such questions in a seminar—will seek to put the best gloss on their preferred view, choosing which facts and arguments to highlight accordingly. It is debatable whether in so doing, however, they deceive or lie. Perhaps they do so if they fail to mention a fact or argument that provides a particularly strong objection to their own position—one to which they feel they have only a weak response. Yet it might be maintained that their duty is to advocate as well as they can the position that best serves the interests of the people they represent, or cause or position they consider most worthy or valuable. As with the example of the defense lawyer given above, though, there may be limits to how partial in the selection of evidence and arguments such advocacy can go before it involves deception and lying. Here, too, we rely on the effectiveness of opposing politicians and philosophers to reveal the weaknesses of each other's arguments.

In the United Kingdom, the nongovernmental parties are termed Her Majesty's Loyal Opposition in recognition of their legitimate as well as crucial role within the political system as licensed critics and challengers of the government who play a key function in ensuring that ministers are both competent and honest. And of course, such opposition also appeals ultimately to voters and citizens, who perhaps have an obligation to become informed. From this perspective, truthfulness proves an attribute of the political (or in the lawyer's case, judicial) system as a whole—something that not just individual politicians but all citizens have a duty to uphold too. I will develop this argument further below. Before doing so, however, I wish to turn to the claim that lying and deception form an intrinsic aspect of politics, as noted in the previous section.

The Democratic Objection

In a Kantian manner, Glen Newey (2001, 1) has argued that the core consideration behind the normative objection to lies and deceptions rests on their taking away our capacity to consent or not to them as a principle of action. I will suggest below that this reasoning constitutes too high a standard. The importance we attribute to consent, however, rests in its turn on regarding individuals as autonomous agents, entitled to equal concern and respect. The equal political status of all citizens, whether they are the head of state, minister in the government, famous scientist, singer, football player, or unemployed laborer, forms an important democratic norm, and its possible infringement when politicians and public servants lie or deceive their fellow citizens arguably explains the normative concerns underlying such actions (Christiano

2008). From this perspective, to lie to or deceive someone is objectionable when it involves exercising an illegitimate form of power over that person that undercuts their ability to think as well as act autonomously. As Robert Goodin (1980, 62–63) notes, it constitutes a form of manipulation that involves a duplicitous interference designed to lead those subject to it to act contrary to their putative will. Such behavior fails to treat others with equal concern and respect as persons capable of making their own judgments and choices.

For example, suppose a political leader makes a deliberately false claim that the government has credible evidence that a neighboring state not only possesses weapons of mass destruction but also is preparing to use them soon—their intention being to sway public opinion toward supporting a preemptive strike against that state.[2] To put the best gloss on the case, imagine that the politician believes the neighboring regime does indeed possess such weapons and a preemptive strike offers the most appropriate way of addressing the situation, but simply has no firm evidence to back their conviction. Most citizens are as aware as the politician that their neighbor could be prone to such acts; it is, after all, an authoritarian military regime, ruled by an unstable dictatorial ruler. But a majority read the situation differently than the politician. Many doubt that their neighbor has been able to develop or acquire such weapons, and even more believe the questionable morality and likely consequences of starting a war make such a policy less justifiable than one of preparing for the worst while continuing to work toward reducing the capacity or probability of this regime using such weapons. In such a case, the politician's deception—however well-intentioned—denies the right of their fellow citizens to make their own judgment about the situation. After all, their interests are as much at stake in this collective decision as the politician's. By deceiving them, the politician undermines their ability to judge for themselves and manipulates them toward their own preferred view.

Such cases are objectionable because they involve the liar regarding themselves as having superior judgment to the deceived and hence not as their equal. In the process, those who deceive diminish the freedom of the deceived by manipulating their choices in directions favored by the deceiver and that the deceived might not have chosen for themselves had they possessed fuller information.

2. What follows is a stylized account of the Blair government's policy toward Iraq between 1997 and 2002. For an account of the alleged lies and deception involved, see Oborne 2005, chap. 8.

At best, such acts involve a degree of paternalism that the liar or deceiver considers to be warranted. Most people acknowledge that healthy adults can in specific circumstances justifiably claim to be better able to make choices that serve the interests of children or individuals afflicted by certain mentally or emotionally disabling conditions than they could themselves. Even so, how far anyone need or should engage in lies or deceit when doing so is less clear. Where rational argument has failed, or is unlikely to work, and a shift in behavior is genuinely needful, then lying or deception may be preferable to coercion. If telling a small child that they may be eaten by a sea monster proves more effective at inhibiting them from bathing in a hazardous sea than explaining the dangers of tidal currents, then such deception may be a preferable alternative to preventing them physically from entering the water. Much depends on the context and the individuals concerned. Yet a democratic system derives its rationale from assuming that citizens are for the most part better judges of their own interests than others are likely to be, with fairness requiring that what touches all should be decided by all. As such, the paternalist justification surely cannot apply, suggesting honesty to be the only defensible policy.

John Mearsheimer has pointed out that motivation can make a difference. He distinguishes selfish or self-serving from strategic motivations (Mearsheimer 2011, 11). By the former, he has in mind those lies and deceptions designed to preserve a politician's personal reputation or to cover up a criminal act. These motivations, especially the second, provide the clearest case of an objectionable form of lying. Mearsheimer defines strategic lying as lying for reasons of state. In wartime, for example, democratic politicians have occasionally deceived their own citizens, but only in order to gain an advantage against the enemy, as when the British government and its Allies sought to mislead the Germans as to the location as well as timing of the D-Day landings during the Second World War. More problematically, democratic politicians have also denied negotiating with those they have hitherto condemned as "terrorists" or "enemies" in order not to arouse domestic opposition prior to obtaining a peace deal they believed would ultimately serve people's interest. For instance, former British prime minister John Major repeatedly and vehemently denied speaking with the Irish Republican Army when making the initial moves that eventually gave rise to the Good Friday Agreement. Likewise, a prominent politician might feel justified in hiding a terminal illness, say, when their leadership is believed crucial to maintaining domestic morale during an emergency or crisis.

What renders a "strategic" lie justified (or at least acceptable) or not appears to depend on a number of not entirely congruent factors. On the one hand, there are moral considerations of different kinds. If the liar and deceiver is an honorable person, then the good intentions of their lie seem at least more trustworthy as not stemming from mere self-regarding interests (Walzer 1973, 166). These considerations echo earlier theological debates as to whether it was justified for a Christian to escape persecution for their religious beliefs by pretending to conform outwardly to the faith imposed by their potential oppressors while holding to their original beliefs "in their heart" (Oborne 2005, 116–22). The difficulty with this argument is that the conviction that one is "right" in one's "heart" is a self-legitimating reason that could be deployed both honestly and dishonestly, and involve a high degree of self-deception (Oborne 2005, 135–37). Virtue may not always be able to wear its heart on its sleeve, but how can we trust it if it does not? The worry is that politicians who engage in what they regard as justified strategic lying may be simply self-deceived.[3] In these cases, the motivation makes little difference; their acts may have been well-intentioned, but their unfounded and misguided lying will still be objectionable as involving unwarranted manipulation as well as paternalism.

Moral reasoning of a consequentialist character potentially enters at this point. Machiavelli ([1513] 1998, chaps. 15 and 18) can be read as arguing that lying may be a justified means if it can be shown to serve good ends, as most commentators believe was the case with the secret negotiations that ultimately brought peace to Northern Ireland. Some see such cases as instances of Machiavellian political *virtù*, in which a wrong action proves allowable when it is necessary to achieve a valid political goal such as peace and stability, from which all will benefit (Berlin 1971). Yet as Machiavelli remarked, a tension between the good result and wrong action remains even here; the one may partially excuse, but it does not remove the other (Walzer 1973, 175–76).

Note that paternalism is not involved in a scenario where citizens have delegated the making of a decision to the executive in specific circumstances. One can imagine a situation where the politician really does have reliable information regarding an imminent attack and needs to react immediately. Most democracies empower their executives to act without prior consultation in such situations, although they generally put systems in place aimed at verifying that such an emergency truly exists for which such action would be proportionate. For example, the agreement of senior members of the military and possibly

3. Such was the conclusion, for example, of inquiry chair John Chilcot's (2016) *Iraq Inquiry* report with regard to former UK prime minister Tony Blair's belief in the Iraqi regime's possession of weapons of mass destruction.

judiciary, both of whom should ideally have some independence from the government, is typically required for such actions.

Some commentators contend that democracy can be reconciled with deceit and lying by politicians in a parallel manner if it can be argued that voters have consented to the use of deceit and lies by governments, at least in exceptional circumstances such as these, where national security might be at stake (Bok 1978, 172, 181). Such consent obviously cannot be given to any particular lie or deception without being self-defeating. But it could be justified in general terms and consent given through the passing of legislation or a constitutional provision giving the executive certain emergency powers to act deceitfully (Thompson 1987, 22–23, 25–26). Indeed, as Mearsheimer (2011, 72–74) observes, precisely because democracy standardly requires transparency and allows for criticism, the need for deception and lies in democratic states might be greater than in autocratic ones if governments are to act expeditiously.

Granting politicians such powers, however, depends on their being trusted to act according to their mandate. Even with controls, such as those described above, such trust may be open to abuse. Meanwhile, to use executive privilege to lie in these circumstances without the requisite evidence or justification would be deceitful, and subject to the same strictures as apply to the original case.

Does Democracy Rest on a Lie?

So far we have assumed that lying and deception are generally incompatible with democracy. But that assumption perhaps moves too fast. I noted above Newey's contention that key to the democratic critique is the notion of consent, with liars and deceivers by their very nature appearing to undercut the possibility of someone giving their consent to them, albeit with the potential exception of a generalized consent to certain exceptional cases of necessary lies and deception. We accept some such standard in commercial transactions. Buyers are exhorted to beware, but certain forms of deception amount to fraud and invalidate the contract as inconsistent with genuine consensual agreement by the purchaser. Yet this standard seems impossibly high for politics. Most proponents of the social contract tradition have acknowledged difficulties in claiming any existing political community to be based on the actual consent of its founding members, let alone its current ones (Lessnoff 1986). Nor can the presence of a functioning democratic system be plausibly viewed as a mechanism that ensures all acts of government enjoy the tacit, let alone explicit, consent of the people. At best, they may enjoy the support of only a majority or, more likely, plurality of the population. Meanwhile, how far such support can be regarded as involving rational consent to every aspect of a government's program remains dubious. A majority of voters may simply be persuaded that on balance, the policies and personnel of a given party represent the least bad of the available alternatives.

Some political philosophers argue that political legitimacy only requires that the basic principles underlying a liberal democratic constitutional order should be such that one could imagine people hypothetically consenting to it, or at least having no reasonable grounds to dissent. Yet even liberal democratically inclined philosophers disagree as to which constellation of principles ought to command our rational consent, and how they should be ordered and applied. If a freely arrived at rational consensus cannot be assumed even on the fundamentals of a liberal democratic society, does that mean that the very idea of a political community built on the free and equal consent of its members must itself be deemed a big lie, with the policies settled on by liberal democracies themselves the product of numerous smaller lies? After all, if the possibility of all reasoning to the same conclusions is not plausible, how else can agreement be reached among people except through some deceiving others into believing what they know cannot be proved and may well be false?

A number of philosophers have thought this to be so, with some regarding it as a pernicious lie and others as a "noble" one (for a discussion, see Canovan 1990, especially 5–9). Much as parents collude in their children's false belief in the existence of, say, Santa Claus because they regard this fantasy as part of the magic of childhood and as such something of value that they wish their children to enjoy, so citizens and politicians within a liberal democratic society can be regarded as colluding in supporting the myth of a society of free and equal individuals. Indeed, one can plausibly see such a myth as one to which to some degree all parties consent. Like a magical childhood, a liberal democratic society has a genuine value for most citizens. Rights may not be "natural" but rather contingent and vulnerable historical achievements. But regarding them as if they did inhere in human beings as such, and that the legitimacy of any political society rests on it being possible for citizens to claim them, arguably serves as an important political myth, which usefully raises the expectations citizens have of their governments (Canovan 1990, 13–17).

Liberals tend not to employ such fictions, however, while conservatives—who do use them—typically do so to criticize the liberal's reliance on appeals to reason alone, maintaining that it can only result in a disorder of conflicting individual assertions (Burke [1790] 2014, 35, 95). Instead, conservatives appeal to the need to preserve the "mystery" of the historically contingent customs and traditions binding societies together, and supporting existing social entitlements and obligations. On this account, viewing the aristocracy, say, as truly noble and entitled to rule not only encourages deference from the lower orders but also fosters a genuine nobility of spirit among the upper classes (Burke [1790] 2014, 78). By contrast, the standard liberal view holds that it is precisely such a social order that encourages deceit and lies, with the lower classes forced into adopting falsely flattering and fawning behavior to curry favor among those with power over them, and whose position and condescending behavior rests on little more than fraud. Not only will honesty only flourish within an egalitarian society, where no one is owed deference on the basis of birth or position alone, but also, so they claim, such a society will be one that has no need for dishonesty to sustain it (Paine [1791] 2000, 97). Meanwhile, the worry arises that if democracy was thought to be nothing but a "big lie," designed to give a false veneer of legitimacy to the rule of the few over the many, then that would in its turn delegitimize all appeals to truth in democratic politics—suggesting that all truth claims are "fake news" (Hahl, Kim, and Zuckerman Siva 2018).

Is Democratic Rhetoric a Form of Lying, or Worse, Bullshit or Even Post-Truth?

If, as I suggested above and will argue more fully below, no rational consensus on which all reasonable and rational individuals could be expected to converge exists, so that we can always expect people to reasonably disagree, then how can collective agreements be legitimately concluded? In gaining support for any program or proposal, politicians make as much—if not more—use of rhetoric as they do reason. Persuasion can take many forms. Clear, coherent, logical, and evidence-based reasoning undoubtedly can and does play its part, but so do oratory and charisma that appeal to people's passions and emotions. Indeed, in situations where an appeal to reason and fact alone will only get so far as to suggest a range of views as reasonable, then rhetoric is likely to be necessary to garner support behind one of those views.

How far can lying and deception be seen as rhetorical devices? The Socratic condemnation of the rhetoric of the Sophists reported by Plato tends in that direction, and lives on in the standard definition of sophistry as specious and false reasoning, with the intention to deceive. The contemporary adoption of "spin" and advertising techniques by politicians has often been characterized in these terms. Whether a "sexed-up" or "dodgy" dossier, overselling the likelihood that a foreign power possesses weapons of mass destruction, can be distinguished from an outright "lie" may itself seem an example of captious and sophistic reasoning.[4] Even if we envisage spinning and being economical with the truth as resting on a continuum between truthfulness, on the one side, and outright mendacity and duplicity, on the other, most would accept that a valid distinction exists between presenting one's case effectively and in the best possible light versus lying and deception. The difficulty resides in where to draw the line.

Part of this difficulty rests on practical judgments in the realm of human affairs not being capable of justification on the basis of either "rational" or "factual" truth alone. A distinction made by Arendt ([1967] 2006, 226), the first refers to the logical and propositional reasoning typical of mathematics, and the second to the empirical reasoning of the natural sciences. While both have their role, neither fully determines our political judgments.

In the areas of logic and mathematical reasoning, or what Arendt ([1967] 2006) calls "rational" truth, these processes are more or less self-validating a priori as a means for generating correct answers in their respective domains. Two plus two equals four because math as a coherent and consistent system of logical reasoning involves that necessarily being the case. The key features of such reasoning consist of its being public, in the broad senses of being in principle accessible to all with the mental ability and training to follow it, and hence transparent and demonstrable of "proof" in the technical sense.

Reasoning in other areas of human knowledge proves less certain. Within the natural sciences, the experimental method has allowed for the testing of hypotheses and their provisional empirical validation, at least until later refinements in both reasoning and experimental technique lead to their being reconfirmed or falsified. As such, an epistemological basis exists in this domain for grounding what Arendt ([1967] 2006) terms "factual" truth. Once again, both the formulation of hypotheses and their experimental testing involve the characteristics of publicity noted above, with such processes possessing the same key features of being replicable and capable of peer assessment.

4. On September 24, 2002, the Blair administration published a dossier titled *Iraq's Weapons of Mass Destruction: The Assessment of the British Government* (British government 2002). The document included a claim that Iraq could deploy weapons of mass destruction against the United Kingdom within forty-five minutes—an assertion that was widely criticized as at best exaggerated ("sexed-up") and at worst fallacious ("dodgy").

That does not mean that there are no matters even in the domain of natural science that are not subject to controversy through being less than clear-cut. Some hypotheses may remain, provisionally at least, untestable yet necessary to fill gaps in our current understanding of certain phenomena; such was the case in the past for the general theory of relativity. There have also been instances of such theories later being shown to be misguided, as proved the case with theories of phlogiston prior to the discovery of oxygen in the eighteenth century and may well be true of what contemporary physicists term "dark matter." In these sorts of instances, however, a public method for testing such claims exists, even if it may not be always immediately possible for it to be deployed.

Global warming has been seen as pointing to difficulties in objectively grounding "factual truth" even in natural science. The multiple physical and social factors involved in anthropogenic climate change initially made the complex causal dynamics hard to identify and assess in a way that could lay claim to general acceptance. Nevertheless, the steady accumulation of evidence through public methods has now made those who deny the existence of humanly caused global warming akin at best to those who continue to assert that the earth is flat. Their thinking is simply incomplete, be it through ignorance and an inability to follow what is nonetheless open to public reasoning, or willfully and for self-serving motives.

Although both logical and factual truth play an important part in political reasoning, they cannot fully determine it. As John Rawls (1993, 55–56) noted, practical reasoning on political issues has a normative dimension and consequently labors under what he called the "burdens of judgment." The factual information required for deciding what policy we ought to adopt to best address any social and economic problem can be complex, and its exact bearing on the matter at hand is open to varying assessments. This proves especially the case given disagreement over the weight to be given to different normative considerations, and how particular values are in any case to be understood and specified. What people consider the most plausible way of interpreting and balancing the relevant facts and normative considerations will tend to reflect their own experiences and knowledge, which not only are unavoidably limited and liable to be oriented toward their own concerns but also inevitably differ from those of people with different experiences and knowledge. For example, people hold different views on the role of different social and moral factors in crime, and hence of the most appropriate forms of punishment and policy responses. If some emphasize individual responsibility and retributive concerns, others are inclined to adopt more complex assessments that diminish the salience of these factors.

None of this means that logical and empirical reasoning can be ignored, or has no independent weight in political decision-making. Take the example of global warming and climate change denial. Reasonable disagreements of the Rawlsean kind can occur over issues such as who has responsibility for mitigating climate change—for instance, should developed countries accept greater responsibility than developing ones—which of a range of policies such as carbon taxes and carbon offsetting might be regarded as the most effective, or which policies might be fairest, both among current generations and toward future ones, and so on. These disagreements can give rise to a wide range of policy recommendations, some of which will be in conflict with others. None of them, however, need deny either the fact of global warming, or the desirability of providing a coherent as well as evidence-based proposal as to how it might be most successfully and equitably tackled. By contrast, climate change denial seeks to either misrepresent or ignore rational and factual truth in this area. Some types of denial may take the form of lies or misleading half-truths that conceal or distort the import of pertinent arguments or facts. Companies may use such tactics to avoid costly and constraining regulations by seeking to diminish the risks of their activities, or politicians may employ them to curry favor with voters by suggesting that certain burdensome measures are neither urgent nor even necessary. Yet such misrepresentation conceals the truth; it does not deny it, and as such is capable of being revealed as a distortion of the truth.

The more pernicious forms of climate change denial, though, take the form of what has been called bullshit and post-truth. Harry Frankfurt (2005) has famously defined bullshit as a disregard for truth, which takes the form of employing spurious and possibly meaningless arguments, and simply making up the evidence. Post-truth goes further, denying the very existence of truth; all views are simply a matter of opinion. Whereas the liar seeks to conceal the truth and the bullshitter sidelines it as irrelevant, the post-truth advocate disputes its very existence. These rhetorical strategies become possible the more inaccessible the relevant reasoning and facts are to most people. If these can only be fully understood by those with the relevant expertise and training, and cannot be easily or straightforwardly related to peoples' everyday experience—as is the case with some of the evidence for global warming—then people may be open to those who cast doubt on its value and validity. That becomes all the more likely if truth is of an inconvenient nature and has potentially costly consequences for people, especially if they feel that these costs are not being fairly distributed, which is a matter of reasonable disagreement.

As a result, we need a way of distinguishing reasonable from unreasonable disagreements. Neither technocratic government nor rule by philosopher kings is possible, because unlike the purely logical and natural scientific disagreements, no public epistemological processes are available to settle disputes between rival ontological claims about the just or even the most efficient society. Logical reasoning can help clarify what is in dispute, and empirical evidence can offer important background information. A concern with truthfulness in the sense identified by Bernard Williams (2002, 11)—that is, as a regard for the virtues of sincerity and accuracy—can encourage people to engage with each other's arguments and concerns, and argue in less self-interested, narrow, or myopic ways. But there is no guarantee that people will converge through the force of reason and weight of evidence alone on a given position, or that if they did that such a consensus would necessarily be the correct position to take. On many of these issues, though, a collective decision needs to be taken despite these disagreements. If outright coercion is to be avoided, then some process seems necessary for reaching agreements that the vast majority, if not all people, will accept as legitimate.

Democratic politics offers itself up as a legitimate process of this kind. Therefore a key issue is how far the democratic process is capable of weeding out lies, bullshit, and post-truth from legitimate attempts at persuasion. To return to the earlier example of a court of law, and the opposing arguments of the prosecution and defense lawyers—just as these contesting advocates attempt to persuade a jury of their case, in part by uncovering flaws in each other's reasoning and evidence, can we see democratic politicians as engaged in doing something similar with regard to the electorate? If not, what will prevent democratic decisions from being based on lies and bullshit, and as such deeply flawed? The question to which we now turn, then, is how effective is democracy in promoting truthfulness by encouraging a respect for it among politicians and citizens alike?

Truthfulness within the Circumstances of Democratic Politics

Like logical reasoning and the experimental method, democracy is in many respects a public process. It possesses similar epistemic qualities to only a limited degree, however. Democracy is public in supplying a form of collective decision-making that offers each person a single vote, and by conducting elections and the aggregation of votes under certain known and settled rules of the game. As we saw above, ideally such rules should allow all voters to be treated as free and equal, capable of making their own decisions and able to express their views, and operate in a fair manner through not being biased toward any given view and treating all of them equally, with majority rule an impartial means for settling a standoff among different perspectives. Some epistemic gains can be attributed to such a process of collective decision-making. For example, both the Marquis de Condorcet's jury theorem (List and Goodin 2001) and the "wisdom of the crowds" thesis (Surowiecki 2004) suggest that given certain assumptions, the more people involved in making the decision, the more accurate it is likely to be. Democratic systems should also allow a plurality of different views to be aired, and for advocates of each of them to challenge the factual and rational basis of the other views. More generally, democracy offers a mechanism for gathering information about people's needs and concerns. Still, while the goal of an ideal democracy might be to offer an equal say to all involved and a fair mechanism for deciding differences, it cannot be claimed that a democratic process produces "correct" answers in the manner of a logical proof or confirmation of hypotheses in the manner of an experiment. It merely indicates the degree of support that certain propositions can obtain among a relevant group of people, and provides a neutral and equitable way of resolving conflicts. There can even be reasonable disagreement on which electoral systems and rules best realize the democratic ideal, given that notions of fairness and equity are themselves open to a variety of interpretations.

Nevertheless, democracy operates as a public method that incentivizes politicians and citizens to express their views openly as well as engage with the opinions of others. Given the need for democratic politicians to gain the support of a plurality or even majority of the electorate, depending on the voting system, and the acceptance of their right to rule by most of the rest, it becomes necessary for them at least to claim to govern in the public interest. The truth of that claim, however, cannot be demonstrated unequivocally. Various forms of evidence may be recruited to defend it, but citizens can and will evaluate their relevance and bearing by different criteria. As I noted above, rhetoric and persuasiveness are ineliminable aspects of politics, as they are of much argument in the humanities and social sciences. Yet that need not mean that logic and evidence, on the one hand, and the virtues of sincerity and accuracy associated with truthfulness, on the other, count for nothing. Citizens will still have good reasons to want their politicians to be consistent in their principles, and propose policies that are realistic and effective. How will they be able to trust them otherwise, and be able to select those they feel likely to pursue programs that promote their interests and sanction them if they fail?

Some philosophers have worried that truthfulness as well as truth have become ever harder to achieve in contemporary politics. Arendt believed that rational truth in particular had limited application to politics. In her account, the truth of political argumentation was necessarily a matter of public opinion rather than of logic and depended on the debating skills of those involved. But that did not mean politics had no use for truth of any kind. She felt that factual truth did hold an independent validity within political argument. Yet she feared that facts were increasingly distorted in politics. Commenting on former French prime minister Georges Clemenceau's remark that while he did not know how guilt for the start of the First World War would be apportioned by future historians, he did know for certain that "they will not say Belgium invaded Germany," Arendt ([1967] 2006, 234) observed that such a rewriting of the facts was precisely what totalitarian regimes attempted. Although the facts allowed for different historical interpretations, including a lively debate about the causes of the First World War in Germany and elsewhere, they also placed a constraint on allowable interpretations of a kind that totalitarian regimes will frequently seek to deny.

Indeed, Arendt's worry was that for slightly different reasons, a parallel denial of "fact" was occurring in democracies too. Discussing the lessons to be learned from the Pentagon Papers (Arendt 1971), her argument once again was that they revealed a failure to engage with factual truth.[5] On the one hand, she contended that successive presidents misled the US electorate about the conduct of the Vietnam War by believing that elections had more to do with advertising and spin than being honest. Worse, politicians and their advisers came to believe their own hype. As a result, they failed to acknowledge the manifest shortcomings of the military campaign. On the other hand, policy makers based their policies on theories grounded in suppositions regarding human behavior that were unsupported by any evidence, and in particular, any historical evidence about the region, its lack of strategic importance, and its culture.

Nevertheless, in the case of both totalitarian and democratic regimes, Arendt contended that what she calls the contingency of historical fact ultimately

5. The Pentagon Papers, as the *Report of the Office of the Secretary of Defense Vietnam Task Force* came to be known, offers an account of the United States' military involvement in Vietnam from 1945 to 1967. It has been held to suggest that the administration of President Lyndon Johnson systematically lied to the public and Congress about the conduct of the war and its chances of success.

wins out against all attempts to deny factual truth. Ultimately, neither citizens nor governments can consistently live a lie. The dramatic transformation of the public sphere by new media since the 1960s and 1970s, when Arendt wrote her essays on truth and politics, has led some commentators to fear we are now moving into a post-truth era (see, for example, Davis 2017). They worry that facts about the world are no longer accessible to citizens, even with regard to their own lives. Jeremy Bentham famously defended democracy on the grounds that although the electorate might not be able to judge how best to make a shoe, it could judge when the shoe pinched and hence be capable of removing politicians whose policies left it worse off (Harrison 1983, 209). If politicians can always blame others for their failings, asserting that all criticism is simply fake news, then no such control can operate. As Arendt ([1967] 2006) noted, within a democratic society, one needs independent sources of both rational and factual truth about the politicians themselves and their supporters—including independent media and universities. When these come under political attack and get undermined, the possibility for a democratic system to operate as a mechanism capable of promoting truthfulness gets correspondingly diminished.

Democracy and Truthfulness: Lies Will Find You Out, Maybe . . .

In his study of lying in international politics, Mearsheimer (2011, 25–30) contends that leaders rarely lie to each other, at least in peacetime, but frequently do so to their own citizens. He surmises that in the international sphere, trust is paramount because no authority exists with a legitimate monopoly of coercive force capable of enforcing agreements between states. As a result, if agreements are to be long-lasting, then they must be honestly made. In the domestic sphere, by contrast, politicians can afford to be untrustworthy because they can rely on the apparatus of the state to secure their position.

While the point about the international sphere is well taken, the inference he draws with regard to domestic politics appears overdetermined. At least within democratic states, the foregoing analysis suggests that leaders have pragmatic as well as moral reasons to be truthful to some degree. Lies will find you out. Yet politics is the realm of opinion, and truthfulness is a systemic property rather than something any individual citizen or politician can be expected to possess alone.

References

Arendt, Hannah. (1967) 2006. "Truth and Politics." In *Between Past and Future: Eight Exercises in Political Thought*, chap. 7. London: Penguin Books

———. 1971. "Lying in Politics: Reflections on the Pentagon Papers." In *Crises of the Republic*, chap. 1. San Diego, CA: Harcourt Brace and Company.

Bellamy, Richard. 2010. "Dirty Hands and Clean Gloves: Liberal Ideals and Real Politics." *European Journal of Political Theory* 9 (4): 412–30.

Berlin, Isaiah. 1971. "The Question of Machiavelli." *New York Review of Books*, November 4, 1971.

Bok, Sissela. 1978. *Lying: Moral Choice in Public and Private Life*. New York: Vintage Books.

British government. 2002. *Iraq's Weapons of Mass Destruction: The Assessment of the British Government*. London: Stationery Office. https://nuke.fas.org/guide/iraq/iraqdossier.pdf.

Burke, Edmund. (1790) 2014. *Reflections on the Revolution in France*. In *Revolutionary Writings*, edited by Iain Hampshire-Monk, 1–250. Cambridge: Cambridge University Press.

Canovan, Margaret. (1990. "On Being Economical with the Truth: Some Liberal Reflections." *Political Studies* 38 (1): 5–19.

Chilcot, John. 2016. *The Iraq Inquiry*. Her Majesty's Stationery Office. https://webarchive.nationalarchives.gov.uk/20171123122743/http://www.iraqinquiry.org.uk/the-report/.

Christiano, Thomas. 2008. *The Constitution of Equality*. Oxford: Oxford University Press.

Constant, Benjamin. (1797) 2003. *Des reactions politique*. Electronic edition produced by Jean-Marie Tremblay, Chicoutimi, Quebec, March 21.

Davis, Evan. 2017. *Post-Truth: Peak Bullshit—and What We Can Do about It*. London: Little, Brown and Company.

Fallis, Don. (2009. "What Is Lying?" *Journal of Philosophy* 106 (1): 29–56.

Frankfurt, Harry G. 2005. *On Bullshit*. Princeton, NJ: Princeton University Press.

Galeotti, Anna Elisabetta. 2015. "Liars or Self-Deceived? Reflections on Political Deception." *Political Studies* 63 (4): 887–902.

Goodin, Robert E. 1980. *Manipulatory Politics*. New Haven, CT: Yale University Press.

Hahl, Oliver, Minjae Kim, and Ezra W. Zuckerman Sivan. 2018. "The Authentic Appeal of the Lying Demagogue: Proclaiming the Deeper Truth about Political Illegitimacy." *American Sociological Review* 83 (1): 1–33.

Harrison, Ross. 1983. *Bentham*. London: Routledge.

Jay, Martin. 2010. *The Virtues of Mendacity: On Lying in Politics*. Charlottesville: University of Virginia Press.

Kant, Immanuel. (1797) 1997. "On a Supposed Right to Lie from Philanthropy." In *Practical Philosophy*, translated by Mary J. Gregor, 605–16. Cambridge: Cambridge University Press.

Korsgaard, Christine M. (1986. "The Right to Lie: Kant on Dealing with Evil." *Philosophy and Public Affairs* 15 (4): 325–49.

Lessnoff, Michael. 1986. *Social Contract*. London: Macmillan.

List, Christian, and Robert E. Goodin. 2001. "Epistemic Democracy: Generalizing the Condorcet Jury Theorem." *Journal of Political Philosophy* 9 (3): 277–306.

Machiavelli, Niccolò. (1513) 1995. *The Prince*. Edited and translated by David Wootton. Indianapolis: Hackett.

MacIntyre, Alasdair. 1998. *A Short History of Ethics*. 2nd ed. London: Routledge.

———. 2006. *Ethics and Politics: Selected Essays Volume 2*. Cambridge: Cambridge University Press.

Mearsheimer, John. 2011. *Why Leaders Lie*. London: Duckworth.

Newey, Glen. 2001. "Truth and Deception in Democratic Politics." ESRC Grant Reference R000223151, Research Summary. https://researchcatalogue.esrc.ac.uk/grants/R000223151/outputs/read/04637d31-6dc1-4493-bcb7-89df4ca21cfb.

Oborne, Peter. 2005. *The Rise of Political Lying*. London: Free Press.

Paine, Thomas. (1791) 2000. *The Rights of Man, Part 1*. In *Political Writings*, edited by Bruce Kuklick, 57–154. Cambridge: Cambridge University Press.

Plato. (ca. 380 BC) 1987. *The Republic*. Translated by Desmond Lee. Harmondsworth, UK: Penguin Books.

Rawls, John. 1993. *Political Liberalism*. New York: Columbia University Press.

Strauss, Leo. 1968. *On Tyranny*. Ithaca, NY: Cornell University Press.

Surowiecki, James. 2004. *The Wisdom of Crowds: Why the Many Are Smarter Than the Few*. New York: Doubleday.

Thompson, Dennis. 1987. *Political Ethics and Public Office*. Cambridge, MA: Harvard University Press.

Walzer, Micheal. 1973. "Political Action: The Problem of Dirty Hands." *Philosophy and Public Affairs* 2 (2): 160–80.

Weissberg, Robert. 2004. "Mr. Pinocchio Goes to Washington: Lying in Politics." *Social Philosophy and Policy* 21 (1): 167–204.

Williams, Bernard. 2002. *Truth and Truthfulness: An Essay in Genealogy*. Princeton, NJ: Princeton University Press.

2

Compromise

Alin Fumurescu

IN RECENT YEARS, the unwillingness to compromise has become the staple of national and international politics alike, expanding its scope beyond the "classic" controversial issues, such as ethnic or religious conflicts, abortion, euthanasia, and the like, to encompass more mundane ones, from minimum wage to tax reform, and from health care to trade agreements. Amy Gutmann and Dennis Thompson (2012) advanced as an explanation the obvious gap that exists in US politics between the demands of governing and those of campaigning, with each requiring different *mindsets*. Campaigning, especially in the primaries, requires an uncompromising mindset: standing by principles, and mobilizing one's hard-core supporters by emphasizing irreconcilable differences with the other camp, thus increasing polarization. Once in office, however, governing requires a compromising mindset in order to get things done by putting the general interest over partisan ones. The observation is undoubtedly accurate, particularly nowadays, when by all measures, campaigning never stops even between elections. Nevertheless, since the same uncompromising attitude is evident not just in the United States but also various settings from Russia to the European Union, and from Venezuela to the Philippines, this is bound to remain just a partial explanation.

It seems that today, nearly any political disagreement becomes automatically a matter of principle, and as the orthodoxy has it, principles cannot be subject of compromise. Apparently gone are the days when Robert Paul Wolff (1965, 21) could write with little fear of being contradicted that "the genius of American politics is its ability to treat even matters of principles as though they are conflicts of interest." Nowadays it seems that all politics is French, as per Wolff's (1965, 21) description: "It has been remarked that the genius of French politics is its ability to treat even conflicts of interest as matters of principle." All humor aside, the observation captures a truth that begs an explanation: How did we get here? Why is politics no longer considered "the art of compromise" all across the world?

As we will see, the answer is relatively straightforward: people are unwilling to compromise whenever they feel—whether rightfully or not is immaterial—that their identity qua individuals or groups is under threat. It follows that many of today's political stalemates are, directly or indirectly, related to what is loosely called "identity politics" and the frequent appeals to the rights associated with it. The diagnosis comes with bad news and good news. The bad news is that since identities are likely to be increasingly inflated *and* challenged by the digital revolution, political compromises can become more and more difficult. The good news is that *precisely because* all of these inflated identities are constantly challenged, they become increasingly fluid and mutable. Hence what today is perceived as a serious identity threat by one group or another might well lose its menacing edge for a redefined identity.

It goes without saying that under these circumstances, a hefty amount of responsibility falls on the shoulders of politicians in charge of not only protecting or promoting identities but also redefining the terms of the debates in which they are protagonists. To give just one example for now, during the 2017 discussions on the new US budget, the issue of building a wall between the United States and Mexico became contentious when framed in terms of identity politics ("us" versus "them") and thus a moral problem. Unsurprisingly, neither side showed a willingness to compromise and so the possibility of a governmental shutdown became a real threat. Nevertheless, a bipartisan agreement was reached once $1.5 billion were allocated for "increasing border security" spending. The rewording allowed each side to claim victory. "The [budget] deal does not fund President Trump's *immoral and unwise* border wall or create a cruel new deportation force," House minority leader Nancy Pelosi said in the aftermath. On the other side, then White House budget director Mike Mulvaney touted, "You can call it new wall, you can call it replacement, you can call it maintenance, *call it whatever you want to*. The President's priority was to secure the southern border and that's what this does."[1]

Obviously, not every issue can be so easily reworded as to be made suitable for compromise, and not every one should be, for if everything can be subject

1. Quoted in Jeremy Diamond, "White House Says Budget Deal Contains Wall Funding," CNN, May 3, 2017, http://www.cnn.com/2017/05/02/politics/mick-mulvaney-wall/ (emphasis added).

to compromise, there is *nothing left to be compromised*. The fear of entering a "rotten compromise" (Margalit 2009) and thus being compromised (Lepora 2012) is not to be easily dismissed, for this is precisely what makes compromise an ethically charged concept. After all, if no moral dilemma were even remotely involved in a compromise, we would call it a "negotiation," "bargain," or "trade-off"—all concepts related to compromise, yet nonetheless distinct. Hence the major challenges of the debates surrounding the role that compromise is or ought to be playing in politics remain less practical and more ethical: *What* qualifies as a compromise? *How* can one distinguish between the "right" compromise from the compromising one? And *who* is entitled to pass the judgment in relation to the first two questions? The variety of answers provided so far to these questions appear to agree on just one conclusion: we are yet far from—shall we say—a compromise on the proper role of compromise in politics.

I will argue that partially responsible for this lack of agreement is the largely ignored history of the concept and almost exclusive focus on its normative aspects. Though "compromise" had two distinct meanings by the seventeenth century, becoming the "boo-hooray" concept (Margalit 2009) that we have so much trouble managing these days, compromise for centuries had some relatively neutral meanings that are worth remembering. Unlike most scholars today, medieval people did not argue about what qualifies as a compromise, good or bad, nor about its usefulness—and not for lack of conceptual sophistication. As we will see, the reason is to be found in the particular understanding of identity, both at the individual and group level. And while it would be futile to try to resurrect the same understanding today, there are lessons worth recalling. For the same technological and media changes that presently appear to threaten various identities might very well forge a new understanding that in some important respects mirrors the medieval one.

Let us not forget, today's millennials are but the second wave. The first "millennials" faced their own identity crisis, resulting in what is now called the renaissance of the twelfth century.

The Forgotten History

From the beginning, compromise was meant to expediently solve otherwise difficult to overcome disagreements.[2] The word *compromissum* appeared for the first time in Latin and initially meant just what it says: to co-promise—to promise together. Two parties in dispute, unable to reach an agreement,

2. This section is largely informed by Fumurescu 2013.

acquiesced to subject themselves to the arbitration of an independent and unbiased third party—a *compromissarius*—promising to respect their decision. Simply, it was a paralegal, private method of solving disputes while avoiding the hassles of appearing in front of a judge. It was a *promise* accepted as a *verbal contract* to respect the authority of the *arbitrator*, yet a contract acknowledged as such even by the courts, in the public sphere. Furthermore, the arbitrator had much more power than an official judge because in passing judgment, they were not restricted by any existing laws. Their authority, in other words, was absolute.

What can we infer from this information? First, that in order to commit to a compromise, one had to make oneself equal to the other party, at least insofar as the matter in dispute was concerned. In effect, this equality was a cause of the disagreement since it made difficult for one side to accept the other side's opinion as better or more just. The first French dictionaries of the seventeenth century spelled this condition out: "*To compromise is to make oneself equal to the other party*" (Richelet 1680, 205; Furetiere 1690). That is why, warned the same dictionaries, a prince should never compromise with his subjects, for by doing so, he would be making a superior equal to an inferior. One can further infer that there was in the dispute something morally doubtful for both parties. One entered a compromise because one wanted to avoid a formal trial and hence taking public responsibility. Here, once again, the first French dictionaries made it clear: "*One puts on compromise only the doubtful affairs*" (*Dictionnaire de l'Académie Française* 1694, 39; Richelet 1680; Furetiere 1690). Third, it also meant that one was willing to accept the risks involved in the *undisputed* and *unrestricted* authority of an arbitrator.

During the Middle Ages, the original meaning of compromise was enlarged to encompass a method of election as well. After all, what are elections but methods to solve public disagreements? Unanimity in any election was seen as the sure sign of revealing God's will, yet no matter how often sought, this ideal was rarely reached then as now. Given this, compromise became the favorite method of election in a society structured as a corporation of corporations. If there were disagreements on how to count votes, each smaller community—guilds, nobles, peasants, and so forth—from inside the larger whole, such as a parish, designated its own representative as an arbitrator.[3] The only condition was that the number of arbitrators had to be odd in order

3. In medieval times, the principle of majority was qualified by the one of seniority or wisdom—or seniority and wisdom were qualities easily disputable. Also, perhaps surprising for

to avoid further stalemates. These trusted arbitrators were the ones making the final election—that is, the compromise, properly speaking. The assumption of equality between parties remained in all cases unscathed, for formally at least, all corporate communities were equal, regardless of their size or relative importance, and each arbitrator's vote held the same weight. To summarize, various groups of people with conflicting opinions or interests each selected their own representative, aka arbitrator, to make a compromise on their behalf. If it sounds familiar, it should, for there are no major differences from many contemporary elections. So why were people not worried about compromising?

To answer this question, we have to remember that during medieval times, the self was understood as being composed of two forums dependent on each other, constituting each other. *Forum internum*—the internal self—was the forum of uniqueness and complete freedom. No one could regulate or control one's inner self, not even the almighty church. On the other hand, in *forum externum*—the external self—one was an "I" insofar as one was sharing in the membership of various communities and played by the rules of that corporation—the church, to be sure, but also the township, a certain guild, and so forth. It was the forum of sameness and conformity. Only in this capacity—as a member of some community—could the individual have been represented and/or become part of a compromise. Therefore while corporations (or offices) could be represented and/or engage in making compromises, unique individuals could not. The general understanding was that no one could represent someone else in full given that no one could represent someone else's uniqueness or be virtuous in their place. Regardless of the circumstances, for the medieval individual, compromise could only involve the external, public self, never the inner, private one. Thus there was no fear of "being compromised."

This understanding changed drastically at the beginning of early modernity, when the medieval dialectic between the two forums started to be forgotten, and the one-dimensional self came to replace the bidimensional one by reducing the understanding of the self to one forum or the other. Modern individualism was born altogether with a new understanding of compromise. Unsurprisingly, the period also marked the disappearance of a key element of compromise, namely the third party, the arbitrator, for once the distinction between the

---

many, but disadvantaged categories of people, like women, the poor, and so on, enjoyed this right as well.

private and public self was lost, the need for an indifferent third party arbitrating disputes involving exclusively the public self was no longer felt. Yet this simplification came with a cost.

The first negative connotations of the word surfaced in France by the end of the sixteenth century, and were all connected with the unique identity of the person or community. Then as now, people worried about compromising their honor, virtue, conscience, and so on. For example, according to essayist Michel Montaigne and theologian Pierre Charron, no decent person should compromise their integrity, conscience, and the like—that is, their authentic self. In France, from the end of the sixteenth century to the end of the seventeenth, the individual, faced with absolutism and an increased pressure for conformity in the outer self, came to identify the "true self" solely with their inner one. The external, public self became, as Charron put it in 1601, a mere costume. Thus identity came to be threatened by compromise, not just at the individual level, but at the communitarian one. Throughout the seventeenth century, many, including Cardinal Duc de Richelieu, warned kings about the possibility of "submitting the whole France to compromise" (Fumurescu 2013, 77–78).

On the other side of the Channel, in Great Britain, no such concerns were yet voiced. Moreover, unlike their French counterparts, the first British dictionaries of the period failed to mention any negative connotations for "compromise." Here, because of the religious fragmentation increased by the Anglican Church, the inner, private self came to be viewed with suspicion precisely because it was beyond anyone's control. As a result, the emphasis switched to the public self, the only one that could be observed and judged. It is worth remembering that the success of the Elizabethan reign was largely due to its insistence on outward conformity and the acceptance of the Book of Common Prayer, allowing individuals to privately interpret its doctrine as they pleased. As Thomas Hobbes would later theorize, the inner life was to be of no concern to the government. To use Charron's imagery, the costume became the person in Britain.

Under these circumstances, covenants, compacts, and contracts became necessary for maintaining the social and political order, so the instances in which "compromise" was used as "contract" or "promise" increased dramatically over the course of the seventeenth century. There was no fear of compromise because the equality of the parties was assumed, sometimes in the least likely scenarios; even God compromised with humans since by entering into a covenant (of grace) with them, he became their equal (see Fumurescu 2013,

87). In turn, the Church of England was seen as a safe compromise between Catholicism and Protestantism (Adair 1982, 89–90).

But British religious fragmentation made obvious the necessity of creating an arbitrator with an indisputable authority, based on something other than a disputable divine right, controversial tradition, or contested merit. It was this problem that Hobbes hoped to solve once and for all. From this perspective, his social contract theory is nothing but a generalized compromise meant to create an indisputable and unrestricted authority of an overarching arbitrator. The only distinction for Hobbes was that the sovereign authority was not the arbitrator because of its qualities and lack of bias but rather because of the co-promise made by all people willingly entering the contract to delegate their rights. Granted, Hobbes never used the word "compromise" (nor did he use, for that matter, the celebrated formula of a social contract). Instead he preferred covenant, promise, or arbitration. Meanwhile, his contemporary Gilbert Burnet (1688, 2 [emphasis added]) had no problem using "compromise" versus "contract" in a similar context:

> The true and Original Notion of Civil Society *and* Government, is, that it *is a Compromise* made by such a Body of Men, by which they resign up the Right of demanding Reparations, either in the way of Justice against one another, or in the way of War, against their Neighbours; to such a single Person, or to such a Body of Men as they think fit to trust with this.

Modern Interpretations

The famous Hegelian saying that "the owl of Minerva spreads its wings only with the falling of the dusk," applies well to the scholarly awareness of compromise. One pays attention to what is already problematic. The theoretical interest in compromise has had many ups and downs over the past two hundred years, and an attentive observer can notice some correlations between theory and practice. With a few (yet sometimes notable) exceptions in between, the literature that has seriously tackled the concept of compromise from both an ethical and political perspective has clustered around a few important historical periods: the second half of the nineteenth century, the second decade of the twentieth century, the beginning of the Cold War, and the fall of the USSR. For different historical causes, all of these periods are characterized by an increased awareness of the significance of political compromise. The reasons encompassing the second and third periods' scholarly interest in this topic are rather easy to discern. The label "Cold War" is in itself telling, while the fall of Communism in Eastern Europe was marked by bloody interethnic conflicts and sometimes even borders being redrawn, of which the disappearance of Yugoslavia remains probably the most notable consequence of the refusal to compromise. A vast amount of literature is available to document it. The first and last periods, however, are theoretically more challenging and thus potentially more rewarding when it comes to deciphering the rationale behind them. The remainder of this chapter will focus precisely on these two periods.

That the first book fully dedicated to this subject, John Morley's ([1886] 1906) *On Compromise*, appeared in Britain should come by now as no surprise considering the development of representative democracy, the early modern history of the concept, and the British penchant toward it. What is surprising is the accuracy of this early analysis and Morley's ability to identify the major theoretical challenges that the debates that followed faced in the next couple of centuries. Morley was an admirer and disciple of John Stuart Mill ([1840] 1963, 131), who wrote that England "is the native country of compromise" and authored *Considerations on Representative Government* in 1861. From Mill, of whom Morley wrote that he "was less English than French" (quoted in Stansky 1970, 103), Morley inherited a mixed attitude toward compromise.

While agreeing with Edmund Burke (1999, 223) that "all government, indeed every benefit and enjoyment, every virtue, and every prudent act, is founded on compromise and barter," Morley ([1886] 1906, 229) also went to great lengths to ensure "that men will interpret [these words] in all the fullness of their meaning." According to Morley ([1886] 1906, 229 [emphasis added]), in this well-known and widely quoted paragraph, compromise and barter did not "mean the mutilation of both sets of principles. . . . What Burke meant was that we ought never to press our ideas up to the remotest logical issues, without reference to the conditions in which we are applying them. *In politics we have an art.*"

Unlike the French, who tried to impose "a new social order on a number of uncompromising deductions from abstract principles," the English were more "political," looking first and foremost for "practical arrangements," mainly because of their long tradition with representative democracy as embodied in the British Parliament (Morley [1886] 1906, 23). This would be "the English feeling for compromise . . . *on its better side*" (Morley [1886] 1906, 23). There is, however, a dangerous side as well. By overemphasizing the centrality of compromise—Morley ([1886] 1906, 25) warns—his fellow compatriots started "not only . . . [t]o look on its importance as *exclusive* and *final*, but

[had] extended our respect for the *right kind* of compromise to *wrong* and *injurious* kinds." In doing so, the proper limits of an otherwise useful method began to break down. The tool, he claimed, become an end in itself, a principle in its own right, "spilling" beyond the "normal" borders of the political sphere.

Thus as a pioneer in the field of conceptualizing compromise, Morley deserves credit for differentiating "the right kind" of compromise from "the wrong and injurious" ones, connecting the necessity of compromise with representative democracy, warning about the dangers of raising compromise to the rank of a good in itself.

Distinguishing between Compromises

Toward the end of World War II and in the years to follow, the theoretical discussions about compromise—of which the strongest supporter was undoubtedly Thomas Verner Smith (1942, 1956)—centered, perhaps not surprisingly, on the Hobbesian alternative, compromise or violence, with the added corollary, democracy or authoritarianism.[4] For Oliver Martin, however, this either-or alternative was dangerous in its simplicity. By equating democracy with compromise, one automatically precludes the possibility of reaching an agreement via politics not through compromise but instead through rational debates and persuasion. Much as Morley had done almost a century before, Martin (1948, 122) argued that "in making the method of compromise absolute, a doctrine of human nature and a function of reason are implied that restrict the realm of possibilities." "It is impossible," argued Martin, to identify "completely the democratic way with the method of compromise," for that would mean to accept that reason is nonnormative but rather purely instrumental, and "its chief function is to find good reasons for defending what is already willed" (Martin 1948, 120).

In his defense, Smith (1942, 8–9) maintained that there are three limits that allow us to distinguish between "proper" and "improper" compromises: compromise is desirable only when necessary, "and necessary only when somehow desirable"; since compromise is "an alternative to war, it loses its nature if it does not lead to peace," and therefore the Munich Agreement between British prime minister Neville Chamberlain and Nazi leader Adolf Hitler was a "bad compromise" because of the outcome; and finally, if a compromise does not

4. As one may recall, if one accepts that Hobbes's social contract was nothing but a generalized compromise, the alternative remains the war of all against all.

advance the "perfectibility of mankind" but instead breeds further sacrifices, it should be avoided altogether. None of these limits, however, appeared logically persuasive enough for John H. Hallowell. First, he asserted, if compromise is something necessary, it does not follow that it is desirable as well. "The inevitability of the existence of crime will never be an argument for its desirability or for the toleration of criminals." Second, how is one to find "some standards with which to measure the limits of what, in specific situations, can be safely conceded [since] the principle of compromise, as a self-sufficient principle, cannot supply the standard" (Hallowell 1944, 159)? Finally, he asked, "How can individuals possibly know if they are making progress, whether a compromise will hasten or retard this progress?" (Hallowell 1944, 167).

Since differentiating between moral and immoral compromises from some objective perspective appeared an extremely difficult (if not altogether impossible) task, there were two more theoretical possibilities left to tackle this conundrum—and they were both used with mixed results. One was to declare that compromise is essentially a moral political practice, especially in a pluralistic society—a claim that requires a redefinition of morality, compromise, or both—and the other was to argue that compromise is neither moral nor immoral, but amoral.

David Gauthier choose the first path, proposing to save morality from its "foundational crisis" by radically redefining it. In his *Morals by Agreement,* he contended that morality "can be generated as a rational constraint from the non-moral premises of the rational choice" (Gauthier 1986, 4). With the same confidence as his acknowledged inspiration, Hobbes, Gauthier (1986, vi) claimed that *his* definition of morality as the result of contract is nothing less than "the correct moral theory." Like Hobbes (and Glaucon in the Second Book of Plato's *Republic,*) he maintained that prior to the agreement arrived at by bargaining and compromise, there is no such thing as good and evil, no morality and no justice.[5] And once again following in Hobbes's footsteps, Gauthier (1986, 296) was willing to challenge all the traditional conceptions of morality: "If the reader is tempted to object to some part of this view, on the ground that his moral intuitions are violated, then he should ask what weight such an opinion can have, if morality is to fit within the domain of rational choice."

Richard Bellamy's attempt to solve the "morality conundrum" of compromise might be less contentious, but no less ambitious than Gauthier's. Instead of

5. In effect, Gauthier uses "morality" and "justice" indiscriminately, while equating both with the mutual promotion of different parties of their interests.

redefining morality, Bellamy (1999, 94; see also Bellamy 2012) chose to redefine compromise—"the stuff of both democracy, with its concern that everyone has a stake, and liberalism, defending individual and group freedom." As one can see, almost three-quarters of a century after Smith, Bellamy once again equates democracy with compromise. In order to do so, he began by eliminating traders, trimmers, and segregators from the ranks of democratic compromisers.

Traders, such as economist F. A. Hayek (or Gauthier, one may argue), tend to keep politics at bay, and expand the theory of rational choice and "economic" thinking to "mutually beneficial compromises" by trading the resources needed to satisfy subjective preferences. Yet Bellamy (1999, 97) argued that "a theory which makes rational choice a matter of individual self-interest gives no reason to think that a sum of rational choices will be in the collective interest." Not everything in politics can be translated into money and material benefits. "Like Oscar Wilde's cynic, market traders know the price of everything and the value of nothing" (Bellamy 1999, 11).

On the other hand, liberal *trimmers* like Charles Larmore or John Rawls promote a political liberalism that "trims away" all controversial moral positions. Their search for "the lowest common denominator" was a "search for stability, rather than justice *tout court*." But "any attempts to divorce principles of justice from all controversial moral and metaphysical considerations risk vacuity." Accordingly, "trimmers resemble [writer] G.K. Chesterton's man of universal good will, ridiculed for saying, 'Whatever the merits of torturing innocent children to death, and no doubt there is much to be said on both sides, I am sure we all agree that it should be done with sterilized instruments'" (Bellamy 1999, 99–100).

Finally, *segregators,* such as political theorist Michael Walzer, "aim at avoiding compromise by preserving the integrity of each value, culture, or interest within its own domain." This might be easier said than done, though. In practice, "setting the boundaries itself entails compromise and the participant of those affected both within and outside them." But in effect, "segregation to avoid all compromises requires all questioning of existing boundaries be suppressed, and so invariably entrenches the domination of hegemonic elites" (Bellamy 1999, 100–101).

Bellamy's own alternative solution for a "fair compromise" is one that at a closer look, has little to do with today's understanding of compromise, resembling more the Aristotelian arbitrator and their quest for the *juste milieu* or *mesotes*. According to Bellamy (1999, 138), "This model of democracy draws on the pre-liberal notion of political constitution based upon the separation and dispersal of power and the mixing and balancing of social classes," being an approach that "leads to the search for solutions that attempt to integrate the various concerns of the parties involved." This approach resembles Aristotle's constitutional regime (*politeia*) aimed at integrating the concerns of the oligarchs with those of the democrats, without seeking a consensus. In both cases, the underlying accepted assumption is a vision of the common good—a radical departure from today's understanding that generally speaking at least, does not see in compromise a quest for justice or a common good but rather its opposite.

In turn, by embracing an aesthetic theory of representation, Frank R. Ankersmit (2002) claimed to be able to detach political philosophy from ethics, thus transcending the gap between *is* and *ought*. In his reading of modern history, true representative democracy appeared not, as orthodoxy has it, in England but rather in the Romantic climate of post-Napoleonic Europe. Only then was "the very idea of compromise about basic political principles," "*a principled unprincipledness*," really able to flourish (Ankersmit 2002, 27). In England and the United States, he argued, people did not fight against each other over the control of the state. Instead, "they fought together to keep the power of the executive within acceptable limits" (Ankersmit 2002, 29). By doing so, the Anglo-American representative systems ended up reducing politics to mere administration, in sharp contrast to the "creative compromises" typical of the ideological fragmentation of continental democracies.

Yet persuasive as it is, Ankersmit's diagnosis suffers from a major setback: it is not historically accurate, for as we have seen, the French were the ones suspicious of compromise, while English embraced it as a virtue. If Ankersmit can overlook these facts it is because, much like Bellamy, he pays attention to the compromises *institutionally embedded*, especially in the systems based on proportional representation, like France, in counterdistinction to the majoritarian electoral systems in which the winner takes all, such as Great Britain or the United States. Only apparently counterintuitive, the latter are friendlier to *the making* of compromises among political actors, not the former. Yet such a historical myopia brings us to the second major challenge in the process of conceptualizing compromise, namely *who* is entitled to pass judgment?

Politicians as Arbitrators of Compromises?

All puns aside, the question remains a serious one. If initially a compromise began with the *selection* of an impartial arbitrator, it evolved to presuppose the *creation* of an arbitrator via elections in accordance with majority rule and ended up with the modern disappearance of the arbitrator, replaced, supposedly, by the goodwill of the parties involved. But when it comes to analyzing compromises, and separating them into "fair" and "unfair," political theorists nowadays place themselves, often unknowingly, in the position of the impartial arbitrator. From this position, one is tempted to pass "objective judgments" on what qualifies as a compromise, which compromise deserves to be commended or condemned, and even who is a compromiser and who is not, regardless of what the people actually involved have or had to say. Ankersmit, for example, praised French *juste milieu* politicians, and especially François Guizot, as great compromisers, despite the fact that Guizot himself, like all other French people, used the word consistently with negative connotations. In a similar way, Bellamy labeled Rawls (2005, 169 [emphasis added]) a compromiser, even though Rawls distinguished between "compromise" and "consensus," and clearly stated that "a balance of reasons as seen within each citizen's comprehensive doctrine, *and not a compromise compelled by circumstances*, is the basis of citizens' respect for the limits of public reason."

This might be more than a methodological mishap. Avishai Margalit (2005, 194), for example, argued that the Munich Agreement is "a rotten compromise, but it is rotten not because of its content, but because it was Hitler who signed it," and "a compromise with Hitler was a compromise with someone who undermined morality itself." By making this claim, Margalit moved the discussion from the content or consequences of compromise to the morality of the parties involved—in this case, Hitler and Chamberlain. In other words, he switched the emphasis from the morality *of* compromise to the morality *in* compromise (Overeem 2018), or from compromise *as end state* to compromise *as process* (Golding 1979). After all, we sometimes talk about a compromise that "has been reached," and at other times about "a solution being reached *through* compromise."

The distinction between the two is not to be overlooked since "a process approach to the phenomenon of compromise requires that we go beyond mathematical game theory and into the disciplines of psychology, sociology, and moral philosophy" (Golding 1979, 8). Yet it is not an easy distinction to make either. "The degree to which a compromise can be made in a proper way (morality *in* compromise) determines in large part the degree to which it should be made at all (morality *of* compromise). Assessing the former before entering the process may, however, prove an impossible feat" (Overeem 2018).

Let us now return to the Munich Agreement and Margalit's judgment that it was a rotten compromise not because of its terms but instead because Hitler both was and stood for radical evil, and hence one of the parties was, mildly put, morally unfit. Evidently in retrospect, Margalit was right. To what extent in 1938, however, could Chamberlain have been as sure as we are today of Hitler's true intentions? Furthermore, by using the same approach, how can one then excuse the compromises made by British prime minister Winston Churchill with Hitler's equivalent, Soviet leader Joseph Stalin—and unlike Chamberlain, knowing full well with whom he dealing, namely "the devil"?[6] Who is to judge that Stalin was less of a radical evil than Hitler? Churchill or Margalit? Generally speaking, who can judge with infallibility the morality of *the other* party involved in a compromise? It appears rather straightforward that in any type of relationship—from love to friendship to compromise—the only party one can be sure of is *oneself*.[7]

As we have seen, the equality of the parties involved and terms of the exchange are preconditions for any successful compromise. Yet as Christian Thuderoz observes, such equality cannot be assessed objectively by an impartial spectator. For example, on October 2011, the Israeli government reached a compromise with Hamas: after five years of imprisonment, Israel Defense Forces soldier Gilad Shalit was released in exchange for 1,027 Palestinians imprisoned in Israel. Were the terms of the exchange "fair"? Who can objectively say, from the outside, what numbers would be "fair and equal" (Thuderoz 2015, 119, 127)? Thus if compromise is, conceptually speaking, at the intersection of an *intra*- and *inter*actor dimension (Overeem 2018), the defining dimension appears to be the intra- one.

If so, the problem of morality in compromise remains fundamentally one of identity or self-representation. That is the reason why compromises almost always prove impossible in cases of religious or interethnic conflicts, or why any dispute formulated in terms of constitutive rights, like the ones surrounding abortion or, say, gay marriage, is more often than not intractable to compromise. "It is certainly difficult to see how the opponents will come to a compromise if they insist upon standing on their rights" (Golding 1979, 10–11). Most scholars, including Margalit (2005, 203 [emphasis added]), agree wholeheartedly: "What is negotiated in such serious disputes, beyond interests, is sometimes

6. As Churchill (1950, chap. 20) famously said to his personal secretary, John Colville, the evening before Operation Barbarossa, the German invasion of the Soviet Union, "If Hitler invaded Hell, I would make at least a favourable reference to the devil in the House of Commons."

7. Surely one also tends to lie to and be biased toward oneself, but this "prejudice" is part of one's identity as well.

the very identity of the sides to the disputes. *By 'identity' I do not mean reputation in the eyes of others, but self-identification.*" One cannot ask people "to sacrifice all that gives their lives meaning" (Sabl 2002, 26). And yet as Andrew Sabl (2002, 26) was the first to point out, what applies to universalists applies to particularists as well, for one's identity is not "unified and insoluble."

And since political compromises involve by necessity collective, not individual, identities, it appears that the solution is to be found, like in the Middle Ages, in the hands of those trusted to represent various communities. Even an apparently technical question such as a budget allocation for, say, education and defense can be presented as well as argued in terms of either interests or principles. "Politicians, diplomats, mediators, and others on the front of social conflict are . . . often inclined to construe disagreements that may be have been originally formulated in terms of moral values or principles as conflicts of nonmoral interests" (Benjamin 1990, 15). In turn, Sabl (2002, 19–54) maintains that this is no accident, and it is precisely in the field of politics where "principled compromises" ought to be welcomed.

To sum up, it appears that the morality *of* a compromise depends of the morality *in* compromise, which in turn depends on the self-identification of the parties involved—an identity that is not inherently fixed and frequently remains in the hands of professional politicians. Where does this provisional conclusion leave us?

The Gospel of Principled Compromise

Here is the good news for believers in the saying that "*politics* is the art of compromise": their intuition that politics is the domain par excellence of compromise is confirmed by the intellectual history of the concept.[8] Both as a *method* of arbitration and as a *method* of election, compromise was agreed on by *the parties* in dispute, but the *actual* compromise was *settled* by *the representatives,* not by the parties themselves. What otherwise might have been compromising for the individuals was not morally damaging for the representatives acting in their names, not qua individuals, but qua members of a group with a distinct identity and interests. After all, the idea that politics is the domain of a different type of morality has a long tradition, of which Niccolò Machiavelli

8. Etymologically, "gospel" means literally "good spell" or "good message." It is a translation of the Latin *bona adnuntiatio,* itself a translation of the Greek *evangelion,* meaning a "bringing of good news."

and Max Weber are but two of the well-known supporters. It follows that in a representative democracy, politicians are best placed to redefine identities in and of various constituencies, and make compromises beneficial to both sides (Dobel 1990).[9]

These distinctions are easily missed when one looks at compromise from a purely analytic perspective and focuses on the controversy surrounding the possibility of "principled compromises." For example, Simon Căbulea May (2012, 317) has argued that the pragmatic necessity for making moral compromises in politics does not justify the theoretical attempts "to make a virtue of this necessity." The reasons for accepting compromise, he claims, are always of a second order, thus consequential, and never of first order, hence "principled." In reply, other authors have contended that "the negative view of compromise rests on a misconception of the democratic process" (Bellamy 2012, 445) or "if we are to make conceptual space for the notion of compromise, then we have to open the door to the conceptual possibility of there being principled compromises" (Weinstock 2013, 544).

From the perspective advanced here, however, the debate is improperly framed, making its protagonists right and wrong at the same time. May is right, for instance, when claiming that a compromise can be morally damaging for the persons acquiescing to it, yet fails to distinguish between the moral responsibility of the politicians and that of their constituencies. After all, this is behind the crucial distinction that Weber famously made between "the ethics of ultimate ends" and "the ethics of responsibility." "We are placed into various life-spheres, each of which is governed by different laws." Thus "whoever wants to engage in politics at all, and especially in politics as a vocation, has to realize these ethical paradoxes. He must know that he is responsible for what may become of himself under the impact of these paradoxes" (Weber [1919] 2004). Bellamy (2012, 443), on the other hand, understands the distinction between private and public compromises, but concludes that the main problem resides in "the possibility of 'uncompromising' politics provided by the . . . plurality

9. This is not to say that artists are not even more persuasive than politicians, let alone political theorists, when it comes to changing "hearts and minds." After all, Harriet Beecher Stowe's *Uncle's Tom Cabin* did more for the abolitionist movement than any politician or philosopher. In more recent times, popular TV shows such as *Will and Grace* or *Six Feet Under* did more to sway public opinion in favor of gay rights by "normalizing" gay relationships than any activist for gay rights ever did. Nevertheless, it is still up to politicians to channel such transformations or reidentifications into political changes.

voting system." In effect, as we have seen, the unwillingness to compromise is more manifest in systems where compromise is already institutionally embedded, and representation is understood as representations of groups, interests, or ideas, not of individuals, as is typical in majoritarian systems. Finally, while Daniel Weinstock (2013, 553) is right in attacking May's "unspoken equation of 'principle' with 'non-consequentialist' reasons for compromise," he fails to distinguish between "principled compromises" in politics versus the personal lives of the persons engaging in it.

As Burke and Morley had noticed already by the nineteenth century, to govern is to compromise between competing interests, values, or even principles, but being able to do so requires a particular *type of character*. It appears that not everyone is equally endowed with this ability—to change and be changed.[10] Sabl (2002, 15) went a step further, claiming that the "principled plurality of governing institutions implies a principled plurality of office ethics: since the functions of governing offices are diverse, so are the characters and habits that conduce to the good performance of each office." All political offices, he argued, formal or informal, demand some form of political compromise, but the character required for, say, the office of a senator is different from the one of the moral activist or great organizer (for a somewhat similar observation, see Weber [1919] 2004).

Yet if a principled compromise in politics calls for a certain type of character, it may also shape one, thereby bringing compromise into the less explored field of virtue ethics. As Patrick Overeem observes, unlike other ways of engaging the field (consequentialism versus deontology, or universalism versus particularism), virtue ethics does not weigh a single act—in this case, a single compromise—but instead looks at the life of a person as a whole series of choices that help shape a certain type of character. This should not come as a surprise since any ethical decision not only reveals something about the moral character of the person involved but also modifies it ever so little by either strengthening some feats or weakening others. Obviously such an approach might appear less "scientific" for more analytically bent natures. Like most classical virtues—moderation, prudence, decorum, generosity, and so on—it can be only approximated, but never circumscribed with precision. To do so requires *phronesis*—that is, practical wisdom. Furthermore, as many authors from Morley onward have pointed out, knowing when and how to compromise in

10. US president Abraham Lincoln comes to mind, for example, as particularly endowed to redefine identities.

politics is an *art*, and from an art, by definition, one cannot expect the same degree of exactness as from, say, mathematics.

Frustrating as it might be for some political scientists, this return to a more classic understanding of politics, and thus political compromise, might be part of the looked-for solution. We have to recuperate the distinction between private and public, and so between the personal and political. Otherwise the vicious circle of distrust between "us" and "them"—"our" disappointing representatives—will only get worse, together with the enthusiastic and deeply concerning support of any "outsiders" perceived as not part of "the system."

Clearly we cannot and should not change by academic fiat the contemporary understanding of the self so that it matches the medieval distinction between the private and public self, nor can we change overnight the general understanding of representation. The same digital revolution that creates so many of the identity crises that politicians have to deal with, however, also creates new opportunities by questioning the contemporary, one-dimensional understanding of the self, either neoliberal or communitarian. Prudent politicians and theorists alike should learn how to take advantage of these new challenges. As we have seen, the explosion in recent times of identity politics is at least partially responsible for the generalized rejection of political compromises. But not all identities ought to be politicized, and not all would benefit from becoming so. Morley's warning from a century and a half ago is worth remembering: by breaking down the limits of the political sphere, making it encompass all aspects of our lives, we risk being left to choose only between violence and the "wrong and injurious kinds" of compromise.

Considering the alternatives, we could all agree that these are borders whose security is worth defending.

References

Adair, John. 1982. *Founding Fathers: The Puritans in England and America*. London: J. M. Dent and Sons Ltd.

Ankersmit, Frank R. 2002. "Representational Democracy—an Aesthetic Approach to Conflict and Compromise." *Common Knowledge* 8 (1): 24–46.

Bellamy, Richard. 1999. *Liberalism and Pluralism—towards a Politics of Compromise*. London: Routledge.

———. 2012. "Democracy, Compromise, and the Representation Paradox: Coalition Government and Political Integrity." *Government and Opposition* 47 (3): 441–65.

Benjamin, Martin. 1990. *Splitting the Difference: Compromise and Integrity in Ethics and Politics*. Lawrence: University Press of Kansas.

Burke, Edmund. 1999. *Selected Works of Edmund Burke*. Foreword and biographical note by Francis Canavan, Indianapolis: Liberty Fund.

Burnet, Gilbert. 1688. "An Inquiry into the Measures of Submission to the Supreme Authority . . ." In *A Collection of Papers Related to the Present Juncture of Affairs in England*. London.

Churchill, Winston. *The Second World War*. Vol. 3. Boston: Houghton Mifflin, 1950.

Dictionaire de L'Academie Francaise. 1694. 1st ed. Amsterdam: Jean Baptiste Coignard.

Dobel, J. Patrick. 1990. *Compromise and Political Action: Political Morality in Liberal and Democratic Life*. Lanham, MD: Rowman and Little.

Faber, Michael J. 2015. "The Federal Union Paradigm of 1788: Three Anti-Federalists Who Changed Their Minds." *American Political Thought: A Journal of Ideas, Institutions, and Culture* 4 (4): 527–56.

Fumurescu, Alin. 2013. *Compromise—A Political and Philosophical History*. Cambridge: Cambridge University Press.

Furetiere, Antoine. 1690. *Dictionnaire universal*. . . . La Haye: A. et R. Leers.

Gauthier, David. 1986. *Morals by Agreement*. Oxford: Clarendon Press.

Golding, Martin P. 1979. "The Nature of Compromise: A Preliminary Inquiry." In *Compromise in Ethics, Law, and Politics*, edited by Rolland J. Pennock and John W. Chapman, 3–25. New York: NYU Press.

Gutmann, Amy, and Dennis Thompson. 2012. *The Spirit of Compromise—Why Governing Demands It and Campaigning Undermines It*. Princeton, NJ: Princeton University Press.

Hallowell, John H. 1944. "Compromise as Political Ideal." *Ethics* 54 (3): 157–73.

Kuflik, Arthur. 1979. "Morality and Compromise." In *Compromise in Ethics, Law, and Politics*, edited by J. Roland Pennock and John W. Chapman, 38–65. New York: NYU Press.

Lepora, Chiara. 2012. "On Compromise and Being Compromised." *Journal of Political Philosophy* 201 (1): 1–22.

Margalit, Avishai. 2005. "Indecent Compromise, Decent Peace." Tanner Lectures on Human Values, Stanford University, May 4–5.

———. 2009. *On Compromise and Rotten Compromises*. Princeton, NJ: Princeton University Press.

Martin, Oliver. 1948. "Beyond Compromise." *Ethics* 58 (2): 118–22.

May, Simon Căbulea. 2012. "Moral Status and the Direction of Duties." *Ethics* 123 (1): 113–28.

Mill, John Stuart. (1840) 1963. "Coleridge." In *The Collected Works of John Stuart Mill: Autobiography and Literary Essays*, edited by John M. Robson, 131. Toronto: University of Toronto Press.

Morley, John. (1886) 1906. *On Compromise*. London: Macmillan.

Overeem, Patrick. 2018. "Compromise." In *Global Encyclopedia of Public Administration, Public Policy, and Governance*, edited by Ali Farazmand. Cham, Switzerland: Springer Publishing.

Rawls, John. 2005. *Political Liberalism*. Exp. ed. New York: Columbia University Press.

Richie let, Pierre. 1680. *Dictionnaire de la langue francoise ancienne et moderne*. Amsterdam: Chez Jean Elzevir.

Sabl, Andrew. 2002. *Ruling Passions: Political Offices and Democratic Ethics*. Princeton, NJ: Princeton University Press.

Smith, Thomas Verner. 1942. "Compromise: Its Contexts and Limits." *Ethics: An International Journal of Social, Political, and Legal Philosophy* 53 (1): 1–13.

———. 1956. *The Ethics of Compromise and the Art of Containment*. Boston: Starr King Press.

Stansky, Peter, ed. 1970. *John Morley—Nineteenth Century Essays*. Chicago: University of Chicago Press.

Thuderoz, Christian. 2015. "Examining Third Parties, Examining Conflict." *Négociations* 24 (2): 73–86.

Weber, Max. (1919) 2004. "Politics as a Vocation." In *The Vocation Lectures, edited by* David Owen and Tracy B. Strong, 32–94. Translated by Rodney Livingstone. Indianapolis, IN: Hackett Publishing Company.

Weinstock, Daniel. 2013. "On the Possibility of Principled Moral Compromise." *Critical Review of International Social and Political Philosophy* 16 (4): 537–56.

Wolff, Robert Paul. 1965. "Beyond Tolerance." In *A Critique of Pure Tolerance,* edited by Robert Paul Wolff, Barrington Moore Jr., and Herbert Marcuse, 3–52. Boston: Beacon Press.

3

Political Integrity

Edward Hall

MICHAEL WALZER (2007, 279) memorably once remarked that the idea that politicians are "a good deal" morally worse than the rest of us is now simply a piece of "conventional wisdom." But like most pieces of conventional wisdom, this one obscures as much as it illuminates. One does not have to be a hard-headed realist to believe that there is something problematic about judging the conduct of politicians by the standards of personal morality because politics is a distinctive sphere of action that generates unique problems and challenges that need to be resolved by those who exercise power. Indeed, as many theorists who have written on the problem of dirty hands suggest, politicians may have good reasons to violate moral constraints if so doing will avert a serious disaster or bring about important political goods. In a similar way, others have claimed that because politicians are tasked with attempting to realize a set of ends that others have entrusted them to pursue, they have a genuine "responsibility to act effectively, which not infrequently entails the obligation to use the kind of tactics a decent person will regard as intrinsically disagreeable" (Galston 1991, 185). This is one reason why politicians may find themselves in situations in which they have to engage in morally grubby behavior: "lying, or at least concealment and the making of misleading statements; breaking promises; special pleading; temporary coalition with the distasteful; sacrifice of the interests of worthy persons to those of unworthy persons; and (at least if in a sufficiently important position) coercion up to blackmail" (Williams 1981b, 58). The implication is clear: if politicians are to act well *as politicians*, they may have to violate some moral standards that apply to ordinary moral agents.

This indicates that the ethical evaluation of political conduct cannot simply take the form of lamenting the fact that politicians do not act as morality conventionally demands. This point is not inconsequential for it suggests that the conventional wisdom that politicians are morally worse than the rest of us may be misleading at best and irresponsible at worst because it maligns them for falling short of a set of standards that it is futile to expect them to abide by in the first place. Yet recognizing this leaves us in the problematic situation of attempting to work out which standards we should employ to evaluate political conduct.

In this chapter, I focus on one standard of evaluation that I believe can help us to evaluate the conduct of politicians in a more mature and politically responsible manner—that is, by asking whether or not they have acted with integrity. This might cause some consternation. In our current political climate, judgments about politicians' integrity are ubiquitous. But commentators and pundits rarely speak positively about the integrity of elected politicians; it is far more common for them to malign the absence of integrity in public life. Yet beyond a general agreement that calling someone a person of integrity is a way of commending their character, it is surprisingly hard to discern what integrity consists of and why it is supposed to be a value. As a result, it is difficult to determine if integrity is wanting in public life, and, if it is, whether or not this is something that should either surprise or concern us. I hope to make progress on these issues by illustrating that a rendering of integrity that is suitably sensitive to the vagaries of politics can play an important role in the judgments that we make about the conduct of politicians from an ethical perspective, even though integrity is only one of a number of values that ought to play a role in our assessment of political conduct.

In the first section, I address and problematize a common way that claims about integrity are invoked in popular discourse—in which integrity is more or less synonymous with honesty and decency—and explore a number of more sophisticated views about the nature of integrity that have been proposed by moral philosophers, especially those linking integrity to the coherence or integration of a moral self. I argue, however, that all of these views troublingly suggest that political integrity may be something of an oxymoron. Then I probe two alternative ways of thinking about political integrity. In the second section, I examine various "negative" approaches—operative in some of the codes of conduct that seek to regulate political behavior—that claim that in politics, integrity is simply a matter of avoiding various forms of misconduct. I argue that although such considerations are clearly an important element of our judgments of political integrity, as they speak to the idea that admirable politicians must act in light of their sense of the public interest rather than their private interest, we must also ask whether or not politicians have displayed a kind of principled commitment to a set of their political ideals and ends—a set of "positive" considerations that I discuss in the third section. I conclude by developing some of the implications.

Private Integrity: Everyday and Philosophical Views

Around 2010, researchers at the University of Essex's Centre for the Study of Integrity designed an "Integrity Test" that purported to measure the integrity of the British public. The test asked respondents to decide whether or not ten things, such as "Avoiding paying the fare on public transport," "Cheating on your taxes if you have a chance," or "Lying in your own interests," are: "1. Never justified," "2. Rarely justified," "3. Sometimes justified," or "4. Always justified." The lower the score, the greater one's integrity. Thus if you found yourself in the one–fifteen bracket, you were said to be "a very honest person who really wants to do the right thing." Scoring fifteen–twenty supposedly revealed that you had an average level of integrity, but didn't "mind bending the rules occasionally." Things got more problematic from twenty onward. If you fell into the twenty–twenty-five bracket, as about 15 percent of the respondents to a national survey in 2011 did, you were told that you are "relaxed about breaking the rules when it suits you, but you are not fundamentally dishonest." Scoring over twenty-five showed, more worryingly, that you did "not believe in living by the rules and find it easy to break them" when it suits you. Thankfully, only about 5 percent of the respondents admitted to being so feckless (Essex Centre for the Study of Integrity 2012).

Clearly the social scientific significance of this kind of survey is limited. But in its own way, the Essex survey reveals something theoretically interesting: that integrity is a slippery concept to pin down. The survey questions equivocate between seeing integrity as a matter of being "honest" and "living by the rules." The person of integrity is supposedly truthful and complaint, resisting the temptation to lie or break the rules for self-interested reasons. This fits with a reasonably common usage according to which acting with integrity is synonymous with complying with some basic moral obligations. On this understanding, acting with integrity is a matter of showing some kind of basic moral decency by avoiding things like lying, cheating, breaking the law, and so on.

It is hard to deny that when people talk about integrity, they do often mean to refer to something akin to this kind of basic moral decency. Philosophers are, however, generally united in finding this understanding of integrity inadequate. For one thing, it makes it hard to see why commending someone for having integrity is taken to be a distinctive form of ethical appraisal. Certainly most people agree that dishonesty and cheating are vices, and we should abide by the rules and regulations that bind society together. Yet acknowledging one's obligations of this sort is a baseline that we expect people to meet *at a minimum*. Conforming to these standards is therefore not worthy of particularly strong moral admiration. Accordingly, if we think about integrity in these terms, it is hard to see why being called a person of integrity is a mark of high praise, or why an imputation of lacking integrity would differ substantially, or at all, from one of lacking honesty, decency, or a sense of fair dealing.

Most philosophers thus insist that rather than thinking about integrity as a kind of minimal moral decency, we must foreground the idea that "integrity, as its etymology suggests, has to do with integration—*the integration of the self*" (Cottingham 2010, 3). This kind of integration indicates something more laudable than the steadfastness to comply with a set of externally imposed rules or moral obligations. Roughly speaking, the idea is that people of integrity have a clear grasp of their convictions, and in so doing know who they are, while also having the resolve to stick by these convictions even if this ends up being costly or difficult for them. On this view, capitulating on one's convictions when met with various kinds of opposition or temptation, or acting with rank opportunism, is the central mark of a lack of integrity. The person who lacks integrity is a sellout or opportunist, and not merely morally indecent.

The work of Bernard Williams played an especially influential role in putting integrity on the agenda of modern moral philosophy and setting the terms of the debate that followed. Williams famously articulated two thought experiments that were designed to illustrate how utilitarianism was incapable of making sense of the value of integrity. The first example involves George, a recently minted chemistry PhD who is offered a job in a chemical and biological weapons laboratory. George needs a job to support his family, but he has a long-standing opposition to chemical and biological warfare. To complicate things further, it is pointed out that if he rejects the job offer, it will go to someone else who has no scruples about the use of chemical and biological weapons. The second example involves Jim, who, while on a botanical expedition to South America, stumbles on a row of twenty locals awaiting execution in a town square. The local army captain, Pedro, is going to kill the twenty local inhabitants, plucked at random, in order to discourage further protests against the government that have been taking place in the surrounding area. Pedro offers Jim a guest privilege of killing one of the twenty. If he accepts, the other nineteen will be saved (Williams [1973] 2008, 97–99).

According to Williams, utilitarianism holds that George should make some biological weapons, and Jim should do some killing. Williams, though, claims that if we experience a genuine sympathy with the complexity of these situations, and grasp the myriad set of considerations that any careful and thoughtful judgment about how George and Jim should act must take into account, we will come to see that utilitarianism approaches the question of how we should live in an impoverished manner.[1] In particular, he asserts that utilitarianism ignores the role that "ground projects," such as a long-held principled opposition to chemical and biological weapons, play in our lives. Williams (1981a, 12–13) describes these ground projects as a special set of commitments that are closely related to our existence as they give "a significant degree of meaning" to our lives. Because utilitarianism demands that we forgo such commitments when sticking by them will not generate the best overall consequences, Williams contends that it cannot make sense of the value of integrity

Although there is some dispute about the overall adequacy of Williams's position, moral philosophers who have written on the topic generally follow him in holding that an agent possessing integrity shows a particular kind of fidelity to a set of commitments or projects that the agent in some sense deeply identifies with. In light of this, it is generally agreed, to use Cheshire Calhoun's (1995, 250) helpful formulation, that integrity is a matter of "standing for something" insofar as people with integrity resist the temptation to "trade action on their own views too cheaply for gain, status, reward, approval, or for the escape from penalties, loss of status, disapproval [and so on]." As Greg Scherkoske (2013, 29) notes, in this regard, integrity is "most obviously exhibited in a person's resistance to sacrificing or compromising his convictions."

Martin Benjamin (1990, 47–49) usefully outlines five negative character types that elucidate the more positive picture of integrity at work when we

1. This is not because Williams simply disputes the conclusions that utilitarianism delivers about these cases (he rejects the suggestion that George should take the job, but accepts that Jim might have good reasons to dirty his hands). His main point is that utilitarianism simply fails to do justice to the kinds of considerations he draws attention to. As Williams (1995, 211) puts it, "If the stories of George and Jim have a resonance, it is not the sound of a principle being dented by an intuition."

think in these terms. The first, *moral chameleons*, are "quick to modify or abandon previously avowed principles in order to placate others," and given their desire to accommodate others and avoid disagreement, have "little sense of moral identity." The second type, *opportunists*, change their loyalties and aspirations in order to further their short-run interests. Third, *hypocrites* lack integrity to the extent that they endorse a set of principles in public in order to make a false impression that masks a more authentic set of commitments or motivations. Fourth, *weak-willed* people lack integrity to the degree that although they have a coherent set of commitments, they do not have the courage to act in accordance with them when they are faced with external opposition even though this opposition could be resisted. Finally, *self-deceivers* lack integrity because even if they do not recognize this themselves, external observers can see that there is a gap between the values and principles they affirm and their actions.

While work that addresses integrity in moral philosophy has much to be said for it, it generates a puzzle for political ethicists. This is because thinking in such terms strongly implies that it is futile to expect elected politicians to be people of integrity.[2] It is frustratingly hard to see how politicians—at least those who are concerned with improving the political status quo by acting in concert with others—can hold to their convictions in the kind of ways that moral philosophers typically insist that people of integrity do. Politics is, in large part, a matter of creating coalitions, both within and between political groupings, in order to generate a large enough number of supporters to back various political positions. This requires politicians to negotiate, conciliate, compromise, and on occasion, back a set of proposals that fall short of the principles and values they affirm. Thus as Benjamin (1990, 141) aptly notes, "One who cannot abide by the glad-handing and the various 'compromises' . . . often required to get elected or who takes no enjoyment from the rough and tumble of political bargaining and negotiation is probably not cut out for the life of a democratic politician."

2. Calhoun (1995, 260) insists that "acknowledging others as deliberators who must themselves abide by their best judgment seems part of, not exterior to, acting with integrity. . . . This is to say that when what is worth doing is under dispute, concern to act with integrity must pull us both ways. Integrity calls us simultaneously to stand behind our convictions and to take seriously others' doubts about them. Thus, neither ambivalence nor compromise seem inevitably to betoken lack of integrity." Still, she appears to see ambivalence and compromise in epistemic terms. The compromises, negotiation, and bartering that make up a lot of political activity often cannot be understood in these terms, however, for the simple reason that frequently when politicians act in these ways, they are rarely taking seriously others' doubts about their convictions, but acting pragmatically and strategically.

Accordingly, if one insists that the person of integrity simply refuses to *trade action* on their principled political commitments, one appears to end up in the uncomfortable position of having to conclude that the only way for politicians to maintain integrity is to be utterly intransigent as far as their principles and political commitments are concerned. Although some people are drawn to thinking about politics in these terms, most recognize that political actors have special reasons to be concerned with the consequences of their actions (Hampshire 1983; Mendus 2009; Nagel 1978; see the discussion of Max Weber below). This suggests that talk of "political integrity" has something of an oxymoronic status. Even if we may sensibly hope that ordinary citizens display the kind of integrity that moral philosophers focus on, the realities of political life indicate that this kind of integrity is not something we would actually want politicians to strive for. Indeed, if politicians were too concerned with maintaining their moral integrity, one might reasonably worry that they would be unable to think in the strategic and pragmatic ways that they frequently have to if they are to achieve the political ends we want them to secure.

So if claims about the integrity of politicians are going to be relevant to our assessment of political conduct, we need to think in more distinctively political terms. In the remainder of this chapter, I sketch two sets of considerations that can help us reflect on the integrity of politicians in a more appropriately political way. The former are various types of misconduct not commensurable with the behavior of a politician of integrity. The latter set requires us to assess whether or not a politician can meaningfully be said to have *stood for* a settled set of deep political commitments in a principled way while acknowledging that it is futile to expect politicians to display the kind of uncompromising and pure stance that moral philosophers highlight.

Political Integrity: Negative Considerations

The first set of considerations stress that when we complain about a politician lacking integrity, we are not really making any claims about whether or not they have achieved some kind of self-integration but merely observing that they have not fallen short of a set of distinctive standards that we can rightly expect politicians to observe. So far as I am aware, this view has not received much in the way of academic articulation but instead is implicit in some codes of conduct that purport to guide the action of elected public officials. There is a structural similarity between this way of thinking about political integrity and the "minimal moral decency" view that I introduced earlier, but this way of thinking about political integrity does not hold that politicians of integrity must respect the same set of moral standards as ordinary citizens. Rather, the central point is that the politician of integrity acknowledges the obligation to further the public interest over their private interest and that their actions conform to this demand.

A publication written by political theorist Mark Philp for the United Kingdom's Committee on Standards in Public Life succinctly outlines the theoretical ballast that underpins this way of thinking about the central ethical demands of politics.[3] As Philp (2014, 5) sees it,

> Political ethics is not the same as personal morality and the two sets of requirements do not always align. Political ethics broadly covers standards, rules, norms and precepts that relate to the roles and functions that political office serves and the concomitant responsibilities that incumbents of office undertake to fulfil. These responsibilities are not identical to acting "morally" or with personal integrity. Indeed, there is some similarity to other professions in the separation of personal morality and professional ethics. A doctor with a strict personal moral code deriving from religious commitments must distinguish between what her formal responsibilities for the care of a patient requires and what she would herself opt to do in a similar situation as a patient. Similarly, politicians may not always be able to do what their consciences demand because, in accepting the responsibilities of public office, they accept duties that it would be inappropriate (unethical or "dishonourable") to ignore even when these clash with their personal moral convictions. For example, they have duties to represent their constituents' interests even where they regard aspects of those constituents' lives as morally reprehensible or repugnant. In no case are such conflicts easily resolved, but the potential for such clashes highlights the fact that role requirements differ from those of personal morality.

According to Philp, then, the correct standards for evaluating the conduct of politicians are in some sense sui generis; they relate to the distinctive ends that political office aims to secure, and must be sensitive to the ways that the demands of politics are not simply derivable from a more basic or fundamental set of general moral standards.

3. As its website explains, "The Committee on Standards in Public Life (CSPL) advises the Prime Minister on ethical standards across the whole of public life in England. It monitors and reports on issues relating to the standards of conduct of all public office holders." https://www.gov.uk/government/organisations/the-committee-on-standards-in-public-life.

Philp makes this claim in a publication that discusses the rationale behind the seven *Principles of Public Life* that the Committee on Standards in Public Life proposed to guide the political conduct of elected politicians in the United Kingdom. Interestingly, Philp is clear that the seven principles are not meant to be interpreted as guides to morality. Instead, they "set out the standards that those in public office must respect in their *capacity as holders of public office*" (Philp 2014, 5).[4] The principles were originally published in 1995. Integrity was listed alongside selflessness, objectivity, accountability, openness, honesty, and leadership. Having been revised in 2013, political integrity is now described in the following terms:

> Holders of public office must avoid placing themselves under any obligation to people or organisations that might try inappropriately to influence them in their work. They should not act or take decisions in order to gain financial or other material benefits for themselves, their family, or their friends. They must declare and resolve any interests and relationships. (Committee on Standards in Public Life 1995, 24).

Thinking in these terms encourages us to see political integrity as a matter of politicians resisting the temptation to use public office to promote their financial self-interest in inappropriate ways. So long as politicians do not engage in any kind of misconduct of this sort, the *Principles of Public Life* imply that their integrity should not be impugned.

Unsurprisingly, many politicians in Westminster now talk about their integrity in such terms when their conduct is scrutinized by the media or public. For example, when Jack Straw, the former British home secretary (1997–2001) and foreign secretary (2001–6), was recently embroiled in a cash-for-access scandal, he took it on himself to stress that throughout his parliamentary career, he had sought to "observe the highest standards of conduct and integrity." In particular,

4. In this regard, Philp (2014, 12) insists that "when aspects of politicians' private lives are presented as evidence of hypocrisy or as a lack of commitment to the office, this may often be a matter of private morality being inappropriately brought into the public sphere." The majority of the theoretical discussions that examine when politician's private actions may be rightly disclosed by the media broadly agree with Philp on this point (Nagel 1998; Thompson 2004; Dobel 1999, 170–92). The fact that the media so often claim that splashes concerning politician's private lives are in the public interest shows that this distinction between private and political morality is far from uncontroversial. Yet that there are grounds for asserting that members of the public actually think about the relevance of politician's private lives in a much more nuanced manner than the media do is well brought out in Allen and Birch 2015.

Straw talked up his honesty and openness by stressing that he had never misused parliamentary resources (House of Commons Committee on Standards 2015, 40). To this extent, then, Straw was happy to insist on his integrity because he avoided breaking various financial regulations while in office.

Although the definition offered in the *Principles of Public Life* clearly captures one serious kind of failure of political integrity, it is hard to believe that it is exhaustive of the kind of behaviors that would impugn a politician's claim to act with integrity. The underlying rationale at work suggests that if politicians violate the public trust that is placed in them, by prioritizing their private interests over the public interest, then we can impugn their integrity. Politicians, however, can clearly betray the public trust that is placed in them in other ways than those highlighted by the definition offered in the *Principles of Public Life*. For instance, they can engage in electoral fraud, fail to abide by norms that uphold important democratic standards, or purposefully mislead the public on matters of great importance. Thus a more adequate negative approach must operate with a broader understanding of the ways that politicians can betray the public trust placed in them if it is to generate plausible views about the nature of political integrity (Hall 2018, 398).

Still, even if we think in such terms, it is not obvious that conceiving of political integrity as a matter of refraining from misconduct is satisfactory. Just as the minimal moral decency view that was discussed earlier runs into the problem that it describes a baseline of acceptable behavior rather than anything particularly laudable, so does this way of thinking about political integrity. If we adopt this way of conceiving of integrity in politics, it thus becomes hard to see why calling a politician a person of integrity is considered a form of high praise. This has problematic consequences, both practical and theoretical. In practical terms, it encourages the idea that in politics, asserting one's integrity is merely a way of batting away accusations of misconduct. This, in turn, has a theoretical cost; it forecloses the idea that we might be able to meaningfully invoke considerations of integrity to make more positive judgments about a politician's character and behavior.

Political Integrity as a Positive Ideal

Although refraining from promoting one's personal interest over the public interest is clearly a necessary condition of describing a politician as displaying integrity, it is hard to believe that it is a sufficient condition. If we are to preserve the sense that there might be such a thing as a distinctively political kind of integrity, and that the politicians who display it do more than merely refrain from various kinds of misconduct, we need to ask whether any further considerations exist that should influence our assessment of whether or not politicians have grasped the requirements of the distinctive role they occupy.

At this point, I think we do well to return to some of the points that Weber raised in his celebrated lecture on the vocation of politics. Weber (1994, 360) famously rebuked those who held that their main responsibility is to ensure "that the flame of pure conviction . . . is never extinguished" so that "to kindle that flame again and again is the purpose of his actions, actions which, judged from the point of view of their possible success . . . can and are only intended to have exemplary value." Yet he also asserts that there is "no more pernicious distortion of political energy than . . . [the] worship of power for its own sake" (Weber 1994, 354). Weber develops this point with reference to his idea of a *cause*: the "meaning and purpose" that the politician seeks to serve by striving for and using power. Although Weber (1994, 355) claims that the "*nature* of the cause the politician seeks to serve" is ultimately "a question of faith," he is adamant that some kind of belief must motivate their political strivings if their political achievements are to avoid being "cursed with the nullity of all mortal undertakings." In this sense, a commitment to some kind of cause is a necessary requirement of admirable political conduct. This is why Weber (1994, 368) insists that the ethic of conviction and the ethic of responsibility are not "absolute opposites," and the most admirable politicians combine conviction and responsibility.

Weber's idea that politicians who fail to act in the service of some kind of cause do not show the right kind of orientation to politics can help us to make further progress in our thinking about the requirements of political integrity. Although we cannot expect politicians to show the same kinds of unwavering commitment to a set of principles that moral philosophers who have written on integrity highlight, Weber is adamant that some kind of meaningful commitment to a set of political ends is an ineliminable element of admirable political conduct.

Political commitment differs from private commitment in various respects. As Lea Ypi (2016, 604) recently put it,

> Political commitment is public rather than private. It involves a distinctive kind of activity, one where agents seek to shape and design political institutions in accordance with particular principles and aims. Political commitment is driven by a critical scrutiny of the exercise of power, and either the

> endorsement or rejection of the reasons and structures that shape the institutional rules on the basis of which power is exercised or reproduced.

This definition is purposefully broad, but helpfully suggests that political commitment is a matter of acting in light of the beliefs one has about how their political institutions and practices should be ordered if they are to bring about the common good. If we think about political commitment in roughly these terms, we can make sense of the idea that politicians may be able to display a distinctively political kind of integrity if they show a kind of fidelity to principles or ends that are, in some sense, constitutive of their identity as political agents. That is, if a politician holds to some deep political commitments in a principled and resolute way over a long period of time, we might come to see that it makes sense to say that they have achieved some kind of meaningful integration, not necessarily of the self, but at least between their actions *in politics* and their deepest *political* principles and commitments. Such behavior can be presented as a political analogue of the kind of behavior that moral philosophers claim that the person of integrity evinces. In a sense, we might say that such politicians are dedicated to a set of identity-conferring ground projects, and therefore display a particular kind of political integrity if they stick by such projects in the face of external pressure and opposition (Hall 2018).

It is common for us to admire politicians who display such commitment even if we do not happen to endorse their particular political views, and we do often say that such politicians display a kind of integrity. For example, this is a how a slew of commentators regard US senator Bernie Sanders—that is, as a principled advocate of various political and economic positions that would, if implemented, have deleterious consequences. In a British context, it is possible to think the same of some of the more thoughtful, long-standing advocates of exit from the European Union even if one regards Brexit as a serious mistake. On the other hand, those who cannot plausibly be said to act in the service of a set of deep political commitments, either because they shift principled positions so frequently that any supposed commitment to a set of ends is highly dubious, or because their supposed endorsement of various principles or ends is obviously opportunistic and self-serving, simply seem to lack the kind of character that enables them to be classed as politicians of integrity even if they are politically successful in certain other respects. (At the time of this writing, it is impossible to reflect on this point without the bottle-blond vanities on either side of the Atlantic—Donald J. Trump and Boris Johnson—coming to mind.)

What it means to stand for something politically diverges from our understanding of what it means to stand for a set of private moral principles or ground projects in some significant ways. It is futile to claim that politicians who engage in compromises necessarily lack integrity if they support a political compromise that falls short of their avowed principles and ends because doing so is frequently a necessary cost of improving on the status quo. Indeed, there is a sense in which politicians who refuse to engage in principled compromises may actually fail to display *political* integrity because outright intransigence will rarely enable one to promote and further a set of political commitments. In this sense, Weber is surely correct to note that the ethic of pure conviction is often worryingly antipolitical. Moreover, as many commentators who are concerned by the increasing uncompromising mindset evident in much contemporary politics have remarked, there is something foolishly moralistic about views of politics that fail to grasp that such compromises are central to the art of governing (Gutmann and Thompson 2012).

Of course, bargaining on matters of principles can be unprincipled. But there is a sense in which such behavior can also be a requirement of resolving political conflict through democratic discussion and debate. As Andrew Sabl has claimed, reflective observers "realize that opinions will vary among legislators because of diversity in constituencies, party, and ideology, without anyone's [opinion] necessarily being irrational or insincere." The correct response is for politicians to neither "demonize opponents' positions as false, unjust, or stupid, nor expect their opponents ever to be fully persuaded by the argument," but instead to accept that they can sometimes show respect to each other by being prepared to bargain "*even on matters of principle*" (Sabl 2001, 163). This kind of activity does not necessarily undermine a politician's integrity so long as they do not lose sight of their commitments. This requires strength of character; as Susan Mendus (2009, 51) notes, "After years of attention to consequences, the politician might cease to have any deep or serious commitments of his own."

If we think about political integrity as a matter of a politician displaying the right kind of practical commitment to a set of political principles or ends, we must acknowledge that plausible judgments about a particular politician's integrity will often be extremely complex. To be sure, it will sometimes be easy to identify clear failures of integrity; it is hard to regard the decision to recant on one's principles for the promise of a promotion or to escape some negative headlines in the press as being compatible with the behavior of the politician of integrity. Nevertheless, more positive judgments will require us to decide whether or not a politician stood for a set of deep principles or commitments in a politically responsible way while engaging in the kind of compromises and bargaining that politics frequently involves. It almost goes without saying that this is difficult. Some of the time, making a concession on matters of principle is not only politically excusable but also the right thing to do. Thus plausible judgments about political integrity require us to ask whether or not a politician showed the right kind of commitment to their deepest principles given the unique confluence of factors that confronted them. We can only really make such judgments responsibly if we have a sense of a politician's motivations and a clearheaded grasp on what was politically possible for them. Similarly, we will often only be in a position retrospectively to make a considered judgment about whether or not doing so was, all things considered, the right thing to do. Interestingly, this suggests that particular decisions or cases are often the wrong units for judging integrity. Rather than focusing on discrete decisions, realistic judgments of political integrity should consider political agency and dispositions of character over time. The kicker is that because time is scarce, and the relevant information is (to say the least) hard to come by, this is extremely tough to do.

Two outstanding issues that must be attended to by those who are attracted to this way of thinking about the contours of political integrity are worth highlighting. First, a serious question presents itself concerning the *source* of the commitments that politicians must stand for if they are to be said to have acted with integrity. As William Galston (1991, 183; see also Walzer 2007) has observed, Weber's account of the ethic of conviction flirts with the "quasi-Nietzschean image of the politician as a solitary hero." This is arguably undemocratic insofar as we, as democrats, hope that at least for the most part, politicians will act as agents of the public.

With these considerations in mind, one might be tempted to maintain that in a democracy, politicians will display integrity by standing for the principles and ends that voters authorize them to pursue at the ballot box. This certainly will play a large role in our assessments of political integrity in democratic settings. After all, there is a clear sense in which, if a politician claims to be committed to one thing and does the opposite when in office, people will not be able to know whom to vote for. As a result, some form of integrity is a necessary condition for representation working on pretty much whatever view of representation that one adopts. I think we ought to resist the temptation, however, to entirely reduce our understanding of political integrity to these representative obligations. Alongside such concerns, we also recognize that politicians may endorse a set of political commitments that they take seriously, and that may indeed have driven them into politics, but that may not form part of their party's manifesto and on which they may not campaign. Sticking by these commitments politically, by working to get others to endorse and advocate for them, also seems to be commensurate with the behavior of the politician of integrity even if the pursuit of these commitments has not been sanctioned by voters in any plausible sense. It is possible that these two kinds of commitments may conflict as well. If they do, I cannot see how we can conclude, a priori, which ought to be pursued and which relinquished on the grounds of integrity alone.

In addition, there is some dispute about whether or not some political commitments are so morally unacceptable that regardless of how steadfastly one clings to them, they are simply incapable of conferring integrity in any plausible sense. Mendus powerfully brings this point into focus by discussing Nazi politician Heinrich Himmler, the leader of the SS during World War II. In a speech, Himmler (quoted in Mendus 2009, 18) is reported to have said,

> What happens to a Russian, a Czech, does not interest me in the slightest. What the nations can offer in the way of good blood of our type, we will take, if necessary by kidnapping their children and raising them here with us. Whether nations live in prosperity or starve to death like cattle interests me only in so far as we need them as slaves to our *Kultur*; otherwise it is of no interest to me. Whether 10,000 Russian females fall down from exhaustion while digging an antitank ditch interests me only in so far as the antitank ditch for Germany is finished.

As Mendus (2009, 18) notes, most of us would recoil from the idea that Himmler could be classed as a politician of integrity even "though he knew what he stood for and had settled reasons for taking the stand he did." This suggests that *some* moral considerations constrain our sense of which ground projects or deep commitments are potentially integrity conferring. I cannot hope to resolve where this line should be drawn here. (In fact, I am skeptical that we could ever conclusively determine where such a line should be drawn.) Yet even if this is indeed the case, we must avoid falling into the trap of insisting that we can only say a politician has integrity if we happen to endorse the particular political ends or projects they pursue. It is perfectly ordinary to admire someone's resolve and character even if they hold to a set of ends we do not endorse. Plausible understandings of political integrity must accept this.

The Messiness of Political Integrity

As I have illustrated in this chapter, the models of integrity proposed by most moral philosophers cannot be straightforwardly applied to the political realm in order to deliver conclusive judgments about the integrity of politicians. Any viable understanding of political integrity must be cognizant of the fact that politicians have a responsibility to be politically effective even though the conditions of political effectiveness can often be incompatible with the requirements of personal morality. Thus if integrity is to be a meaningful standard of political evaluation, we need to think hard about the distinctive demands of political office, and the ways in which politicians can violate the trust that is placed in them or fail to match up to the demands of the role.

Some egregious failures of political integrity, situations in which politicians clearly promote their personal self-interest over the public good by engaging in various forms of misconduct or malfeasance, are not especially hard to decipher so long as we have a clear view of the facts on the ground. But reaching more positive views about the integrity of politicians requires attention to a host of other considerations that are a great deal more complicated. We need to ask if a politician stood for a set of deep commitments in a politically meaningful way over a long period of time. This requires us to have a good understanding of what kinds of actions were possible for them and what types were not, and a plausible account of their motivations for acting as they did. Needless to say, it is difficult to make particularly conclusive judgments of this sort because political commitment is not best understood in all-or-nothing terms. Much of time, politicians will engage in compromises on matters of principle in the hope that this will have fortuitous long-term consequences. For this reason, plausible assessments of political integrity will inevitably be messy, provisional, and highly controversial.

References

Allen, Nicholas, and Sarah Birch. 2015. *Ethics and Integrity in British Politics: How Citizens Judge Their Politician's Conduct and Why It Matters*. Cambridge: Cambridge University Press.

Benjamin, Martin. 1990. *Splitting the Difference: Compromise and Integrity in Ethics and Politics*. Kansas: University of Kansas Press.

Calhoun, Cheshire. 1995. "Standing for Something." *Journal of Philosophy* 92 (5): 235–60.

Committee on Standards in Public Life. 1995. "Standards in Public Life: First Report of the Committee on Standards in Public Life." http://www.public-standards.gov.uk/.

Cottingham, John. 2010. "Integrity and Fragmentation." *Journal of Applied Philosophy* 27 (1): 2–14.

Dobel, J. Patrick. 1999. *Public Integrity*. Baltimore: Johns Hopkins University Press.

Essex Centre for the Study of Integrity. 2012. "Take the Integrity Test." University of Essex. https://www1.essex.ac.uk/government/documents/integrity-test.pdf.

Galston, William. 1991. "Toughness as a Political Virtue." *Social Theory and Practice* 17 (2): 175–97.

Grant, Ruth. 1997. *Hypocrisy and Integrity: Machiavelli, Rousseau, and the Ethics of Politics*. Chicago: University of Chicago Press.

Gutmann, Amy, and Dennis Thompson. 2012. *The Spirit of Compromise: Why Governing Demands It and Campaigning Undermines It*. Princeton, NJ: Princeton University Press.

Hall, Edward. 2018. "Integrity in Democratic Politics." *British Journal of Politics and International Relations* 20 (2): 395–408.

Hampshire, Stuart. 1983. "Public and Private Morality." In *Morality and Conflict*, 101–25. Oxford: Basil Blackwell.

House of Commons Committee on Standards. 2015. "Sir Malcom Rifkind and Mr Jack Straw: First Report of Session 2016–16." https://publications.parliament.uk/pa/cm201516/cmselect/cmstandards/472/472.pdf.

Mendus, Susan. 2009. *Politics and Morality*. Cambridge, UK: Polity Press.

Nagel, Thomas. 1978. "Ruthlessness in Public Life." In *Public and Private Morality*, edited by Stuart Hampshire, 75–92. Cambridge: Cambridge University Press.

———. 1998. "Concealment and Exposure." *Philosophy and Public Affairs* 27, (1): 3–30.

Philp, Mark. 2014. "Public Ethics and Political Judgement." https://www.gov.uk/government/uploads/system/uploads/attachment_data/file/336977/2902536_CSPL_PublicPolitical Ethics_acc.pdf.

Sabl, Andrew. 2002. *Ruling Passions: Political Offices and Democratic Ethics*. Princeton, NJ: Princeton University Press.

Scherkoske, Greg. 2013. "Whither Integrity I: Recent Faces of Integrity." *Philosophy Compass* 8 (1): 28–39.

Thompson, Dennis F.. 2004. "Private Life and Public Office." In *Restoring Responsibility: Ethics in Government, Business, and Healthcare*, 227–44. Cambridge: Cambridge University Press.

Walzer, Michael. 2007. "Political Action: The Problem of Dirty Hands." In *Thinking Politically: Essays in Political Theory*, 278–95. New Haven, CT: Yale University Press.

Weber, Max. 1994. "Politics as a Vocation." In *Weber: Political Writings*, edited by Peter Lassman and Ronald Speirs, 309–69. Cambridge: Cambridge University Press.

Williams, Bernard. (1973) 2008. "A Critique of Utilitarianism." In *Utilitarianism: For and Against*, by J. J. C. Smart and Bernard Williams, 77–150. Cambridge: Cambridge University Press.

———. 1981a. "Persons, Character and Morality." In *Moral Luck: Philosophical Papers 1973–1980*, 1–19. Cambridge: Cambridge University Press.

———. 1981b. "Politics and the Moral Character." In *Moral Luck: Philosophical Papers 1973–1980*, 54–70. Cambridge: Cambridge University Press.

———. 1981c. "Utilitarianism and Moral Self-Indulgence." In *Moral Luck: Philosophical Papers 1973–1980*, 40–54 Cambridge: Cambridge University Press.

———. 1995. "Replies." In *World, Mind and Ethics: Essays on the Ethical Philosophy of Bernard Williams*, edited by J. E. J. Altham and Ross Harrison, 185–224. Cambridge: Cambridge University Press.

Ypi, Lea. 2016. "Political Commitment and the Value of Partisanship." *American Political Science Review* 110 (3): 601–13.

4

The Ethics of Representation

Suzanne Dovi & Jesse McCain

FOR MANY, democracy is associated with the people participating directly in politics, such as by voting, protesting, and exercising their free speech. Most democratic institutions, however, require the people to have representatives. Elected officials, lawyers, political parties, lobbyists, and the media (to name a few) construct as well as advance claims about policy preferences and political issues on the behalf of others. Representatives do the substantive work of democracies—that is, they govern them. In the process, representatives shape democratic citizens' political identities, dictate the rules and procedures used to resolve political conflicts, and make us feel part of a polity. How good a polity is depends importantly on the ethical actions of representatives.

But what is ethical representation? For many democratic citizens, the answer to that question seems to be "something we don't have." In the United States, public approval ratings for the president, Congress, and political parties generally have fallen abysmally. Since 1937, half of all elected US presidents have never achieved an average approval rating above 50 percent. In 2018, President Donald J. Trump's average approval rating sat at the record low in that recorded history of around 38 percent (Gallup 2018). The distaste for elected representatives is not just a US phenomenon, though.

Such distaste can be found throughout the globe as the rise of populist movements attests. For example, the Mass Observation Archive has documented the shifting language that British citizens use to describe their politicians. In 1945, British citizens predominantly used measured terms to portray their representatives, while they currently depict them as "arrogant, boorish, cheating contemptible, corrupt, creepy, deceitful, devious, disgraceful, fake, feeble, loathsome, lying, money-grabbing, parasitical, patronising, pompous, privileged, shameful, sleazy, slimy, slippery, smarmy, smooth, smug, spineless, timid, traitorous, weak, and wet" (Mass Observation Archive, n.d.). Such visceral descriptions reflect the anger and distaste that democratic citizens can feel toward their elected officials. The intensity of these emotions can partially explain why populist movements like Brexit in Great Britain and the Five Star Movement in Italy have taken hold. Citizens are against current political elites and want the voice of the people better (more directly) expressed in democratic politics. They want something different from what their democratic institutions seem to offer.

This anger toward elected representatives and representative institutions can easily turn to cynicism. According to Jason Stanley (2012), people in the United States "no longer expect or care" whether politicians tell the truth. Some stress how the existing choices of representatives are all the same (read corrupt). For instance, Noam Chomsky (2008) famously stated that "the United States has essentially a one-party system and the ruling party is the business party." Others emphasize the meaninglessness of the existing choices of representatives available to democratic citizens. As Slavoj Žižek (2012) reminds us, "We do not get to vote on who owns what, or on relations in the factory and so on, for all this is deemed beyond the sphere of the political, and it is illusory to expect that one can actually change things by 'extending' democracy to people's control." Existing representative processes are dismissed as ineffective and crooked. Citizens simply vote for "the least bad" among seemingly meaningless choices.

The pessimism regarding good representation is reinforced by much of libertarian thought, supporting the impulse to give up on government initiatives and embrace the free market as the de rigueur solution to any problem. According to this way of thinking, the inefficiency of representative institutions combined with unresponsive accountability mechanisms fosters tyrannical political power. The free market is the proper check to corrupt representative processes.

Although democratic citizens are pessimistic about ethical representation, the theoretical literature on representation celebrates its ethical significance. In fact, Nadia Urbinati (2006) and David Plotke (1997) equate representative institutions with democratic ones. Representation is not an unfortunate "second best" option to direct participation; rather, it possesses independent moral political value. Representation creates *mediated* participation that provides the time and reflection needed for responsible governance as well as checking the fickleness of public opinion.

The question "what is ethical representation?" therefore is a timely one. In this chapter, we survey the relevant literature on ethical representation and uncover some persistent problems that complicate assessments of individual representatives. Instead of identifying what policy positions good representatives should hold, or how they should determine these positions, we maintain that good representatives are accountable ones. More specifically, good representatives protect and foster the capacities of the represented to be politically autonomous (Dovi 2018)—that is, to have and make choices that can approximate to the degree possible their deeply held values and priorities as they sustain democratic legitimacy. (For a more detailed discussion of political autonomy, see Christman 2015). Such capacities require reliable and actionable information.

To be accountable to diverse populations, good representatives will at a minimum do two things. First, they must *structure* and *pluralize* the choices available to the represented, allowing them to reflect on and influence their policy options. By pluralizing the options, good representatives sustain the capacity of the represented to disagree with each other as well as their representatives. Second, good representatives should construct the political identities of the represented with the aim of developing and maintaining their capacities to assess and sanction their representatives.

In order to hold representatives accountable, however, democratic citizens need to recognize when their representatives have importantly violated democratic norms. To that end, we identify two tactics adopted by bad representatives: self-contradiction and disdainful distraction. Both tactics promote an ethical obliviousness (Dovi and McCain 2017). By ethical obliviousness, we mean the inability of democratic citizens to identify and autonomously assess the moral norms that underpin as well as justify the actions and beliefs of their representatives. Ethical obliviousness prohibits the ability of relevant parties to identify the moral norms at stake, and thereby obscures their ability to monitor and regulate norm violations. By facilitating a moral free-for-all, ethical obliviousness undermines the capacities of the represented to hold their representatives accountable.

Focusing on negative morality—that is, the characteristic activities of bad representatives—reveals what is democratically at stake when representatives do not properly attend to democratic governance. Not only can bad representatives undermine the mechanisms of accountability, but they can change political norms so significantly that vices can be seen as virtues. In this way, we identify what a good representative should *not* do.

Literature Review: How to Identify a Good Representative?

Typically, discussions about the ethics of representation orient themselves around the question, What should a good representative do? The answers to this question vary. Some stress that a good representative should do what the represented wants. If the represented wants lower taxes, then the representative should cut taxes. In other words, good representatives are good *delegates* who follow the instructions of the represented. Others contend that good representatives should do what they believe is in the represented's best interests. Good representatives will cut or increase taxes based on their own assessments about the "preferable" tax policy. Here, good representatives are good *trustees*.

The delegate and trustee paradigms, though, can generate different and sometimes mutually exclusive standards. For when the represented's preferences conflict with what the representatives believe is in the represented's best interests, the standards for evaluating representatives' behavior become paradoxical (Pitkin 1967). Under such circumstances, no matter what a good representative does, they will violate the ethical standards of representation, such as the requirements to be a good delegate or good trustee. If they do what they think is best, the representative is not being a good delegate. If they do what the represented wants, they are not a good trustee. Thus political circumstances can prohibit representatives from being good representatives.

Such dilemmas suggest that democratic citizens need to ask additional questions when assessing their representatives. In particular, they should attend to two questions, Who is helped and harmed by a representative's activities? Are the benefits gained from a particular course of action worth the harms obtained? These questions provide an alternative starting point for evaluating representatives. They do not assume that all constituents agree about what should be done or what is in their interests; rather, these two questions highlight the vulnerability of the represented to being manipulated and exploited by their representatives. Focusing on the harm and help provided by representatives draws our attention to what is politically at stake for the relevant actors, and whether certain communities are disproportionately bearing the costs of representatives' decisions. To the extent that the harm seriously impedes the capacity of the represented to evaluate, let alone sanction representatives, such harms violate sacrosanct democratic standards and thereby ethical representation.

Of course, this alternative starting place does not "solve" the controversy about what a good representative should do. For what the represented want and what is in their interest can be identified in different and contradictory ways. Consider how the following questions generate different understandings of preferences and interests:

- What do *most* people being represented want? What is in the interests of most people being represented?
- What do the privileged members of the represented (for example, the educated or well-off) want? What is in the interests of the privileged members of the represented?
- What do the allies and supporters of the representative want? What is in the interests of the allies and supporters of the representative?
- What do the most vulnerable and marginalized members of the represented want? What is in the interests of vulnerable and marginalized members of the represented?

The answers to these questions generate different understandings of what a representative should do. In this way, ethical standards that require representatives to be good delegates (or good trustees) need further clarification regarding who counts as the "represented" and how representatives should handle conflicts of opinions among the represented. In any case, it is important to recognize that representatives have a choice regarding how to be a good delegate/trustee. If, and when, members of the represented disagree about what can and should be done, representatives can appeal to those who agree with them as evidence of being a good representative. But adopting either a trustee or delegate approach to ethical representation does not settle the question of how good representatives should act.

Building on the insights of the literature on intersectionality (see, for example, Crenshaw 1989; Hancock 2016; Collins and Bilge 2016), it is important to attend to how privileges and disadvantages are mutually constructed. Sometimes doing what one's supporters want can be at the expense of what most people want. Sometimes, the actions of representatives can benefit both some of the privileged *and* disadvantaged groups while harming others. Consequently, it is critical to attend to whether representatives only help disadvantaged groups when it is in the interests of privileged groups to do so. The Fourteenth Amendment to the US Constitution, for example, which forbids the states from restricting the basic rights of citizens or other persons, has not only protected the rights of former slaves but also served as the legal foundation for recognizing the personhood of corporations. According to attorney and civil rights activist Derrick Bell (1980), legislation that benefits Black people has often benefited Whites in the United States too. Noticing the contradictory incentives behind certain decisions becomes key to assessing the democratic ethics of a representative—that is, whether a representative is selling out or supporting democratic forms of governance in order to advance a representative's career/policy preferences. Because representatives are not likely to make everyone happy, and politics demands that they take sides, conflict itself is not antithetical to democratic representation or governance. Indeed, those who advance antagonistic notions of democracy maintain that conflict is an essential part of democratic politics (see, for example, Connolly 2002; Wenman, 2013). Yet, it is important to recognize that representatives have the power to structure and regulate conflict in ways that undermine democratic authority, and thereby its legitimacy, such as through gerrymandering.

Suzanne Dovi (2006) offers three criteria for identifying those actors who represent in a democratic fashion. Good democratic representatives are ones who display three virtues: they must be fair-minded, build critical trust, and be good gatekeepers. Importantly, Dovi recognizes these virtues depend on the capacities of democratic citizens. Consequently, in some circumstances, good democratic representation might not be possible or desirable. Good *democratic* representation crucially depends on what democratic citizens want.

To be sure, there is no agreement within democratic theory about how representatives should resolve disagreements among the represented. Representatives can use their discretionary power to construct the identities of those they represent in order to support their particular aims. Representatives can employ symbolic politics to make people feel represented even when their preferences are being ignored. Sometimes, the mere willingness to notice or meet with the represented is sufficient for earning their approval. President Trump's willingness to visit coal mining towns like Pittsburgh and Scranton boosted his popularity in traditionally working-class regions rife with economic depression (Schwarz 2017).

Of course, offering emotional speeches and photo ops to groups is different than fulfilling one's campaign promises. Here it is important to focus on the impact that a representative has on different communities as well as on democratic institutions. For a gap can exist not only between what a representative does and says but also between what a representative does and how that representative makes you feel.

Niccolò Machiavelli famously advised princes that while it is better to be feared than loved, it is crucial to avoid being hated. For Machiavelli ([1513] 1995, 50–51), good rulers should not be afraid to violate moral norms; in fact, good political leaders must "learn how not to be good, and use that knowledge, or refrain from using it, as necessity requires." The need to break moral rules in politics can be unavoidable and sometimes even desirable.

Although a Machiavellian ethics seemingly dictates that "good" representatives will sometimes be required to violate moral prohibitions, such as against lying or violence, based on the contingent demands of politics, Michael Walzer (1973) cautions against giving up on one's political ideals completely. He offers an alternative vision of political ethics—one that recognizes the moral dilemmas facing political actors. Walzer argues that good political actors are ones who possess moral principles, but are willing to violate those principles for the greater good. In other words, they are willing to get their hands dirty.

For instance, Walzer contends that if an elected representative is faced with the decision to order the torture of an alleged terrorist to get information about an impending attack, then they should do it. But ethical political action does not stop there because even if the action produced the desired effect (stopping the attack), the representative must still be accountable to those they represent. Walzer suggests that such a representative should submit themselves to the rule of law, explaining why they violated the prohibition against torture (and the law) and offering some evidence, such as their resignation or guilt, that they recognized what they did was wrong. For this reason, a representative who inauthentically professes certain morals or acts without remorse toward the human costs of their policies is an undesirable public servant. The internal life of a representative is evidence of good representation.

While Walzer stresses how guilt provides internal constraints on the actions of political actors, Dennis Thompson (1980) argues that the problem of dirty hands in democracies requires institutional solutions. For democratic governance can spread responsibility so wide that it becomes impossible to hold anyone accountable for bad decisions. Democratic representatives are obliged to preserve the institutional conditions that allow those who are represented to assess the hands of their representatives. Certain institutional solutions like oversight committees or selective transparency are possible, albeit limited, mechanisms for preserving the conditions needed to evaluate representatives' performance. Because what representatives do is authorized by others, the authorizers must be able to assess the policies, impacts, and reasons behind representatives' actions.

Hanna Pitkin (1967) offers alternative advice regarding how representatives should negotiate competing standards: representatives of liberal democracies should justify their decisions to their constituents when they *consistently* go against the represented's revealed preferences. For Pitkin, representation requires protecting the autonomy of both the representative and represented. Transparency about what one has done and why it is essential for maintaining the political autonomy of the represented (albeit with the aim of trying to get the represented to agree with/condone the actions of the representative) is imperative. Implicitly, Pitkin's accounts assume that the ethical problems with representation fall away when the representative and represented agree. Representation become a moral free-for-all only when the preferences of the representative and represented conflict.

The theoretical literature on representation has responded to the difficulties in identifying agreed-on standards for evaluating representation by shifting away from the language of interests and preferences. This leads to the second kind of ethics found in the literature on representation: the constructivist approach to representation. Instead of thinking of representation as a principal-agent relationship—that is, as a relationship between the represented and representative that is structured by processes of authorization and accountability—some theorists recommend understanding representation as the process of claim making.

Michael Saward's *Representative Claim* is exemplary. For Saward (2006, 302), representation is constituted by a set of relationships: "A maker of representations (M) puts forward a subject (S) which stands for an object (O) which is related to a referent (R) and is offered to an audience (A)." Representation is how agents construct claims on the behalf of others. This abstract understanding of representation allows it to apply to different institutional contexts. Saward's characterization of representation updates our understanding to include its performative and aesthetic dimensions.

For Saward, the representative not only constructs claims but also constructs the political identity of groups. Saward understands representatives as determining who is inside and outside the referent group. The tendency of representatives to justify what they are doing by invoking notions of "the people" or "my supporters" is constitutive of representation. To be sure, representatives can construct those identities in manipulative and hateful ways. Yet Saward himself does not focus on the question, How should we identify problematic instances of identity construction or claim manipulation?

Rather, Saward's contribution holds two important normative insights. First, he stresses that "the appropriate constituency" must retain "the ultimate say" in approving and rejecting claims made by representatives (Saward 2014, 733). The appropriate constituency consists of those parties affected by the claims made. Second, Saward identifies legitimate representation emerging not from the relationship between individual representatives and the represented but instead from the collective conditions in which representative claim making specifically takes place. As a result, good representation refers to the collective conditions that permit contestation and inclusion. Representative claims need to be properly challenged, and the affected parties need to be included in representative processes. The relationship between the representative and represented is only important to the degree to which it encourages the appropriate constituency to accept its representative's claims. The context is therefore considered more morally relevant than any given representative's claims or the effect of particular actions of a representative on the represented.

Instead of focusing on the trustee/delegate tension or claim making, we approach the concept of ethical representation through a different perspective—one that revolves around the capacity of the represented to hold its representatives accountable.[1] As Thompson (1987, 131) wrote, "At a minimum, democracy requires that citizens be able to hold officials accountable, and to do that citizens must know what officials are doing and why." Similarly, ethical representation requires representatives to keep the represented informed about their activities. Instead of understanding ethical representation primarily in terms of how representatives act or deliberate on behalf of the represented, let alone as a process of claim making that allows appropriate audiences to have the ultimate say, we explicate *how bad representatives undermine the capacities of the represented to hold their representatives accountable.*

The need to maintain citizens' capacity to evaluate their representative should be readily apparent. As *Vox* writer Sean Illing (2017) observed (citing Nancy Bermeo), "Democracies don't merely collapse, as that implies a process devoid of will. Democracies die because of deliberate decisions made by human beings. Usually, it's because the people in power take democratic

1. Within political science, there is a rich and extensive literature on accountability. See, for example, Przeworski, Stokes, and Manin 1999; Schedler 1999; Mulgan 2003; Day and Klein 1987. This literature offers various typologies of different kinds of accountability mechanisms. See, for example, Grant and Keohane 2005; O'Donnell 1998, 2003; Goetz and Jenkins 2001.

institutions for granted. . . . They develop interests separate and apart from the voters. They push policies that benefit themselves and harm the broader population." Similarly, Scott Mainwaring and Aníbal Pérez-Liñán (2013, 124) maintain that a democracy's "prospects for survival is affected by whether actors normatively (that is, intrinsically) value democracy as a political regime." They found that democracies start to break down when elected officials do not privilege the fairness and legitimacy of democratic processes over policy gains. For this reason, both representatives and democratic citizens must recognize the value of democratic norms, and the need to preserve the mechanisms of accountability that allow democratic processes to resolve political disagreements fairly and peacefully. Any useful ethical account of representation should address the ways that representatives can go bad.

Problems with the Literature

As can be seen, the literature on ethical representation holds many important normative insights regarding how citizens should identify good representatives. Two developments in this literature, however, significantly complicate attempts to identify both good (and bad) representatives. First, the concept of the representative has been stretched to include a variety of political actors. Representatives are no longer limited to formally elected officials (and therefore the notion that disagreements about good representation can be settled through elections); rather, interest groups, political parties, nongovernmental organizations, social movements, bureaucrats, and even ordinary citizens "represent" themselves and others in democratic politics (Urbinati and Warren 2008). As a result of this conceptual stretching, the roles and responsibilities of representatives as well as the relevant ethical and legal codes have grown significantly. The various institutional locations of the representative seemingly defy ethical generalizations.

Ethical understandings of representation depend on the representative's role. As Andrew Sabl (2002) insightfully pointed out, senators have different ethical obligations and duties than do leaders of social movements. Consequently, the criteria for evaluating representatives have proliferated. Such multiple and often conflicting criteria can lead citizens to turn to "the marketplace" as the primary method for determining whose preferences and voices are voiced as well as heard. The criteria for evaluating representation has in a critical sense become privatized. Citizens are understood as consumers. Politics is merely "transactional." Representatives test market what they can get away with, and citizens perceive the rhetoric of the representative as just another form of "entertainment" (Postman 2006). To be sure, the public performance of representatives can seem scripted, directing representatives to denigrate their political opponents, and celebrate what favors them and theirs, as opposed to enacting and enforcing a public ethos that underlies legitimate democratic authority. Voicing principled moral commitments can be cynically perceived as a public relations strategy or window dressing for selfish interests.

A second, related development in the literature of representation that complicates the moral evaluation of representatives is the tendency to "contextualize" those moral assessments (see Carens 2004). More specifically, the focus becomes how *collective* representative processes construct claims (Saward 2006; Disch 2012). This development shifts the lens from the duties and obligations of individual representatives to the represented, to the cultural and institutional norms in which a representative's activities are embedded. In this way, the symbolic meaning of a representative's actions to the represented and fairness of the decision-making procedures have more moral significance than the impact of the policies on the affected actors. Representation is understood as a collective process that makes you feel represented to different degrees, not as a power-infused relationship between the represented and representative.

While the political context certainly should inform moral evaluations of a representative's actions, we maintain that evaluating the ethics of representation primarily through collective contingencies obscures the dangers to democratic governance. Put bluntly, the emphasis on collective processes masks how individual representatives participate in and perpetuate systemic injustices. They can shape the preferences of the represented so as to manipulate them into accepting their representatives' claims instead of contesting them. They can transform vices into virtues. Focusing on collective processes is a biased ethical approach—one that favors those who currently occupy positions of power.

In any case, we charge that these two developments in the literature of representation have contributed to the perception that specifying ethical standards is not possible (because of disagreements) and not even desirable (because democratic citizens should decide for themselves what ethical representation is). Articulating and defending ethical standards allegedly curtails, as opposed to informs, citizens' political judgments. As a result, general accounts of ethical representation that aim to identify good representation have become too indeterminate and lost their critical purchase.

Instead of articulating ideal standards of ethical representation, we concentrate on identifying some characteristic behaviors of bad representatives. We do so because we believe that one task of political theory is to "analyze evils as evils" and "alert us to their presence in the conduct of everyday affairs" (Allen 2001, 341). By identifying such evils, humans are in a better position to fight against and limit such behavior. On our view, political theory plays an important role in educating citizens about the political stakes of the bad behaviors of representatives and thereby in assisting citizens' judgments. Focusing on vices (negative morality) instead of virtues reveals the limitations of idealized standards that can mask the harms of (and need to prioritize eliminating) particular vices.

Another reason for focusing on negative morality is our understanding of contemporary politics. The extent to which contemporary politics is marked by antipolitical and antiestablishment attitudes—that is, an explicit rejection of and disgust for democratic norms and practices—reflects a frustration with expressed "positive" political moralities. The expression of political ideals is associated with empty rhetoric, clichés, and broken promises. As a result, the transparent expression of political vices have begun to be seen as a political virtue, reflecting authenticity and sincerity. Violating civil behavior—for instance, being obviously racist or misogynist—and rejecting the normal pathways of political elites—for example, gaining political experience and knowledge—can make a representative seem closer to the people (as opposed to part of the corrupt political establishment). Being anti political establishment has become a political ethos that not only undermines the checks and balances of democratic governance but also resonates with those who feel abandoned by economic developments and "liberal" political institutions. Feeling left out generates a politics of resentment that demands vitriolic, nonnormal expression.

The Tactics of Ethical Obliviousness

In the rest of this chapter, we identify two tactics used by bad representatives. By *bad* representatives, we mean those representatives who undermine the publicity and transparency needed for democratic citizens to mobilize against, constrain, and sanction their representatives. Instead of focusing on what representatives need to do in order to be good, we concentrate on two ways that representatives can get things wrong. What is distinctive about these tactics is their ability to hide the moral and political stakes of their actions: they weaken citizens' capacities of judgment. Here our analysis of bad representatives challenges the constructivist assumption that democratic citizens will simply "know" violations of good representation when they see them. Articulating standards has been equated with recommending that those standards should be universally applied in all circumstances and that citizens do not need to evaluate their representatives on their own terms. In contrast, we observe that the tactics of bad representatives can disguise the political and ethical implications of their actions. On our view, such tactics, other things equal, violate the democratic norm of political autonomy. By identifying these tactics, we aim to assist, not impede, citizens' evaluations of their representatives.

Those who recommend understanding good representation as consistent with "whatever arises from representative processes" or "whatever democratic citizens want," downplay the abusive and manipulative power of bad representatives. For representatives can significantly obscure the moral and political costs of their actions. Thus silence about the ways that representatives hinder political judgments empowers the autonomy of representatives, not the represented. In order to make up for the current lacuna regarding bad representation, we illustrate how the ability of representatives to construct their claims can block and deter the judgments of the represented. We argue that bad representatives prohibit accountability by promoting ethical obliviousness. Good representatives should facilitate political judgments, not cloud them.

We assume that at a minimum, good representatives must obey the law and act in ways consistent with democratic norms. Consequently, democratic citizens must be able to identify and sanction their representatives when they engage in ethically questionable behavior, let alone violate laws. When representatives seek solutions outside formal legislative processes and regulations, let alone are removed from public input and scrutiny, it becomes difficult, if not impossible, for democratic citizens to assess the activities of their representatives, and hence act on their own moral and political norms of representation. Such ambiguity creates an environment where moral norms are dubious and allow for the proliferation of ethical obliviousness (Dovi and McCain 2017).

So what are the tactics of bad representatives? To identify the tactics that good representatives should not use, we examine the claims of one particular representative, specifically Trump. Although other representatives can employ similar tactics, we focus on Trump's tactics when president because of their transparency. In particular, we consider how Trump's method of claim making facilitates moral confusion and ambiguity at the expense of democratic autonomy. We highlight two tactics that promote ethical obliviousness: self-contradiction and disdainful distraction. These strategies effectively nullified the capacity of democratic citizens to keep Trump in check. For these tactics allow representatives to circumvent criticism, preserve deniability, and undercut the political mobilization necessary for democratic mechanisms of accountability.

Self-Contradiction

The first tactic promotes moral confusion and ambiguity through flux. By constantly changing and offering unstable as well as inconsistent positions, such as denying previously made public statements and thereby rewriting history, Trump's method of claim making generates a stream of steady confusion regarding what he believes, wants to happen, and stands for. As a result, his self-contradictions make him unaccountable for any particular stance he takes. Consider how when president, Trump flip-flopped not only on his current views but also on what his views were previously, sometimes in mid-sentence. During a CNN interview on June 28, 2015, Trump said that he was pro-choice only to apologize seconds later and reiterate that he is pro-life (Bump 2016). A few months later in Cleveland, Ohio, he restated that he was "very, very proud to say I'm pro-life." On March 30, 2016, in a campaign statement, Trump's views on abortion faced increased scrutiny and the president opted for another strategically altered version of his stance: "My position has not changed—like Ronald Reagan, I am pro-life with exceptions." One day later, on April 1, Trump's views on abortion shifted yet again when he commented on CBS News that "the laws are set now on abortion and that's the way they're going to remain until they're changed."[2] Thus Trump's positional malleability is susceptible to maneuvering within months, days, or even seconds in mid-conversational stream. Such instantaneous shape-shifting is not an attempt to include diverse communities, as Saward claims (2014), but instead a strategy for absorbing the public's attention, thereby increasing the size of his audience.[3] While good representatives can change their minds (especially in light

2. CNN interview, July 28, 2015, http://www.cnn.com/videos/tv/2015/08/11/donald-trump-part-five-interview-newday.cnn; Cleveland speech, August 6, 2015, https://www.washingtonpost.com/news/post-politics/wp/2015/08/06/annotated-transcript-the-aug-6-gop-debate/?utm_term=.aba7faa4dbe9.

3. Saward (2014, 735) stresses that "there is nothing *intrinsically* good or bad about shape-shifting representation." Saward acknowledges that the shape-shifting representative can be difficult to "pin down," yet he still contends that shape-shifting is valuable for increasing the number of claimants/subjects being represented. In contrast, we focus on how Trump's

of new evidence or changing circumstances), what is distinctive about Trump's flip-flopping is two factors. The first is its speed. His self-contradictions occur in such rapid succession that it is difficult to know which position is actually his. His claims are a response to what is "trending" and a political form of moment marketing (Dovi 2017). The second factor is that Trump will explicitly deny his contradictions. In this way, Trump does not seem to care if he lies. He adopts the disposition of a bullshitter. According to Harry Frankfurt (2005, 55), the intention of a bullshitter "is neither to report the truth nor to conceal it. . . . [T]he motive guiding and controlling it is unconcerned with how the things about which he speaks truly are." The essence of bullshit is not that it is false but rather that it is phony. In other words, bullshitters try to get away with speaking about things that they do not know. So while liars must carefully monitor the truthfulness of their statements to make sure their lies are not caught, bullshitters concentrate on the impression that they create with their words. Trump's claims work because they elicit an emotional reaction in the audience that allows him to capture its attention. Such claim making works by resisting clarification attempts. In fact, Trump seemingly relishes all attention, even the attention produced by his contradictions.

Trump's self-contradictions are not just about particular policies but also about his own political identity. For instance, Trump claimed on CNN that he is "not a politician," yet around the same time, on July 28, 2015, argued in the *New York Times* that he is "no different than a politician running for office." Similarly, Trump blurs his partisan commitments. As he asserted on CNN on March 21, 2004, "You'd be shocked if I said in many cases I probably identify more as a Democrat." More recently, during a speech in Burlingame, California, on April 29, 2016, Trump embraced a right-leaning identity while simultaneously delegitimizing the importance of party affiliation altogether: "Folks, I'm a conservative, but at this point, who cares?" Trump's fluctuating political identity prohibits citizens from making judgments about where he is on the political spectrum as well as where his ethical bearings lie. As Trump said in a CBS interview on April 29, 2017, "I don't stand by anything. I just—you can take it the way you want."[4] Trump's willingness to suggest that it doesn't matter

---

self-contradictions are in tension with democratic accountability, not the legitimacy of democratic institutions.

4. *New York Times*, July 28, 2015, https://www.nytimes.com/2015/07/29/us/politics/depositions-show-donald-trump-as-quick-to-exaggerate-and-insult.html?_r=3; CNN, March 21, 2004, http://www.cnn.com/2015/07/21/politics/donald-trump-election-democrat

what he stands for limits democratic citizens' ability to determine whether his actions are consistent with ethical democratic representation.

But such contradictions also foster deniability, and thereby prevent him from being accountable for what he says and does. The tactic of self-contradiction suggests that it doesn't matter what he says or does because his political performance is not based on advancing any specific policy agenda; rather, it simply generates new needs and expectations (Dovi 2017). When he was president, Trump did not represent by articulating and defending substantive policies that become the basis for democratic governance; he constructed inconsistent and contradictory statements that did not have any overt political significance. In this way, Trump's method of claim making changed the aims of political representation. Instead of placing the resolution of political conflicts on the distribution of goods, such as "who gets what and when," as the primary purpose of democratic politics, Trump understood his role primarily in terms of the entertainment industry. His political success while president was defined by the number of followers (regardless of whether they agreed or disagreed with him) and ability to control the agenda by creating an audience that capitalized on current expectations (see Dovi 2017). His demand for "high ratings" and large numbers of followers suggested that being watched or "grabbing the public's attention" was more important than expressing what he really believed, or advancing a particular policy agenda.

Trump's Twitter performance while president was remarkably reminiscent of cultural critic Neil Postman's *Entertaining Ourselves to Death*. Postman (2006, 3–4) warned that "all public discourse [in the United States] increasingly takes the form of entertainment. Our politics, religion, news, athletics, education and commerce have been transformed into congenial adjuncts of show business, largely without protest or even much popular notice." Trump's shifting positions satisfied his followers' demand for new material—something to retweet—but did not enhance the capacities of citizens to hold him accountable.

Zygmunt Bauman and Leonidas Donskis's (2013) analysis of what they called "moral blindness" illuminates what is troubling about this tactic. Trump's self-contradictions allow him to control and monopolize the attention span of democratic citizens. These contradictions distract citizens from

/index.html; Burlingame speech, April 29, 2016, https://www.nytimes.com/2016/04/30/us/politics/trump-campaign.html?smid=fb-nytpolitics&smtyp=cur; CBS, April 29, 2017, https://www.cbsnews.com/news/president-trump-oval-office-interview-cbs-this-morning-full-transcript/.

thinking in a sustained fashion about the suffering of others and duty to respond to that suffering in a sustained fashion. The constant bombardment of different kinds of wrongs and harms shortens our attention regarding others' suffering, and thereby fosters a dangerous insensitivity to the suffering of others.

Self-contradiction also allows the bad representative to shape and erase the past in order to manipulate the present. The contradictions foster a loss of memory. As Bauman and Donskis (2013, 28–29) assert, "By losing their memory, people become incapable of any critical questioning of themselves or the world around them . . . [and] lose their basic moral and political sensibilities." Being unsure about what really happened, such as what one's representative says and endorses, allows individuals to distance themselves from their responsibilities to other human beings. Contradictions therefore weaken democratic citizens' empathy toward others and attenuate the judgments necessary for ethical understanding. Among the greatest threats to democratic processes are not those acts that are deliberately immoral but rather those that circumvent clear right versus wrong accountability by questioning the legitimacy of engaging in the debate at all. In this way, bad representatives are not accountable to either side. They represent nothing, and it is difficult to approve of or disagree with a representative's claims if one cannot detect what they are.

Disdainful Distraction

The second tactic used to promote ethical obliviousness occurs when representatives produce an endless stream of personal attacks that replace substantive policy discussions. For example, after coming to office, Trump targeted his critics—whether they were his opposing party, own party, administrative appointments, or even the media. Trump's tweets created anticipation regarding "who is he going to disparage next?"

Disdainful distractions are often ad hominem attacks, such as against the personal appearance of another person or their character. So in Trump's tweets, US senator Ted Cruz became "Lyin' Ted" and former US secretary of state Hillary Clinton became "#CrookedHillary."[5] Bad representatives attack

5. Twitter, March 22, 2016, http://thehill.com/blogs/ballot-box/presidential-races/271746-trump-digs-at-cruz-calling-him-lying-ted; Twitter, August 25, 2016, http://www.msnbc.com/brian-williams/watch/trump-reignites-feud-with-crooked-hillary-in-late-night-tweets-1046261827987.

individuals instead of solving issues of governance. When a representative responds to an issue by attacking the person and fails to address the argument, the possibility of democratic dialogue and political compromise is diminished. This what-will-they-say-next, media-fueled sensationalism frequently draws attention away from pressing political issues, like climate change, Syrian refugees, or a nuclear war with North Korea, toward hollow, slur-based zingers. Trump's "off-the-cuff" statements during his presidency effectively ended substantive democratic deliberation. Thus this second tactic further dissolves the potential for democratic engagement into a "disavowal of free discussion and its smothering before it has even started" (Bauman and Donskis 2013, 39). As such, disdainful distraction is indicative of a bad representative to the extent that this tactic works against using peaceful and fair legal procedures to adjudicate disagreements. Put bluntly, refocusing attention on name-calling and sensationalist hate speech suffocates the critical analysis and sustained attention needed for effective policy making.

To be sure, these personal attacks can elicit strong emotional reactions and thereby enhance symbolic representation, yet disdainful distractions too often replace specific accounts of the wrongs committed or the actual problems with proposed policies. Playing verbal gladiators is simply more entertaining than articulating the values and an accurate cost-benefit analysis of one's proposed policy platforms. As a result, democratic discussions have been effectively bulldozed by bombastic verbal sparring. Critical engagement with meaningful issues dies before national conversations even have a chance to begin.

Interestingly, Bauman and Donskis (2013, 39) conceptualize such vitriolic rhetoric as intimately intertwined with self-contradiction: "A brutal type of discourse cutting down others and oneself, that is, social and political commentary as a slow process of self-negation and self-destruction, has truly nothing in common with a critical attitude." Disdainful distractions reinforce not only confusion about what should be done but also skepticism about what can be done.

What makes disdainful distraction a tactic of *bad* democratic representatives, though, is when such tactics undermine democratic accountability mechanisms. Trump's willingness when president to dismiss and denigrate democracies' institutions, such as voting, media, courts, and law enforcement, delegitimized democratic checks and balances along with due process. Such denigration might have gained him support from antipolitical followers, but it did so at the expense of the rule of law and democratic governance. So when citizens derived pleasure (and their satisfaction with Trump) from watching his offensive and off-the-cuff tweets, it also made watching the failure of democratic institutions "entertaining."

In particular, by criminalizing his opponents, Trump invoked the authority of the president to silence dissent. To be sure, jailing one's political opponents is a tactic used by many political representatives, both totalitarian and democratic ones. For instance, in 2017, Venezuela's President Nicolás Maduro jailed two of his most vocal opposition members, Leopoldo López and Antonio Ledezma (Casey and Herrero 2017). Disdainful distraction criminalizes one's opponents instead of compromising with them and thereby weakens the political compromise necessary for shared governance. It also prevents citizens from considering issues from their fellow citizens' perspective. Given this, disdainful distraction dehumanizes segments of a political community and fosters divided political identities.

Thus, both self-contradiction and disdainful distraction can prevent citizens from reflecting on their policy preferences, and significantly impair their capacity to hold their representatives accountable. These bad forms of claim making displace democratic norms of deliberation. The refusal to take words seriously goes against democratic politics, which relies on words (as opposed to guns) to settle conflicts.

To be sure, this negative morality is transparent. President Trump was up-front about his self-contradictions and disdain for other citizens. His willingness as president to flaunt conventional democratic ethical norms, such as disclosing and eliminating conflicts of interest, reflected a disrespect for representative institutions. Such disrespect is enjoyable for those who do not perceive themselves as benefiting from the status quo. Representation becomes valuable not as a form of governance but rather as a form of entertainment.

To take seriously the autonomy of democratic citizens, one needs to recognize how representatives can focus citizens' attention on the hateful or fleeting, and how such a focus can weaken citizens' appreciation for democratic authority and governance. The role that representatives can play in shaping democratic citizens' understanding of their political identities as well as policy preferences can reduce citizens' political autonomy and democratic accountability. Identifying the two tactics of ethical obliviousness is an important first step in acknowledging how representatives can change democratic norms in undesirable ways. This acknowledgment, in turn, will allow us to denounce bad representatives for their undemocratic practices.

References

Allen, Jonathan. 2001. "The Place of Negative Morality in Political Theory." *Political Theory* 29:337–63.

American Presidency Project. n.d. University of California at Santa Barbara. http://www.presidency.ucsb.edu/data/popularity.php?pres=45&sort=time&direct=ASC&Submit=DISPLAY.

Arendt, Hannah. 1987. "Collective Responsibility." In *Amor Mundi*, edited by James Bernhauer. Dordrecht: M. Nijhoff.

Bauman, Zygmunt, and Leonidas Donskis. 2013. *Moral Blindness: The Loss of Sensitivity in Liquid Modernity.* Cambridge, UK: Polity Press.

Bell, Derrick A. 1980. "Brown v. Board of Education and the Interest-Convergence Dilemma." *Harvard Law Review* 93 (3): 518–33.

Bump, Philip. 2016. "Donald Trump Took 5 Different Positions on Abortion in 3 Days." *Washington Post*, April 3. https://www.washingtonpost.com/news/the-fix/wp/2016/04/03/donald-trumps-ever-shifting-positions-on-abortion/?noredirect=on&utm_term=.0a34770db062.

Carens, Joseph H. 2004. "A Contextual Approach to Political Theory." *Ethical Theory and Moral Practice* 7 (2): 117–32.

Casey, Nicholas, and Ana Vanessa Herrero. 2017. "Jailings Raise Fears of Dictatorship in Venezuela." *New York Times*, August 1. https://www.nytimes.com/2017/08/01/world/americas/venezuela-opposition-nicolas-maduro.html.

Chomsky, Noam. 2008. "The United States Has Essentially a One-Party System." Interview by Gabor Steingart. *Der Spiegel Online*, October 10. https://chomsky.info/20081010/.

Christman, John. 2015. "Autonomy in Moral and Political Philosophy." *Stanford Encyclopedia of Philosophy*, edited by Edward N. Zalta. Spring ed. https://plato.stanford.edu/archives/spr2015/entries/autonomy-moral/.

Collins, Patricia Hill, and Sirma Bilge. 2016. *Intersectionality.* Cambridge, UK: Polity Press.

Connolly, William E. 2002. *Identity/Difference: Democratic Negotiations of Political Paradox.* Minneapolis: University of Minnesota Press.

Crenshaw, Kimberlé. 1989. "Demarginalizing the Intersection of Race and Sex: A Black Feminist Critique of Anti-Discrimination Doctrine, Feminist Theory, and Anti-Racist Politics." *University of Chicago Legal Forum* 140:139–67.

Day, Patricia, and Rudolf Klein. 1987. *Accountabilities: Five Public Services.* London: Tavistock.

Disch, Lisa. 2012. "Democratic Representation and the Constituency Paradox." *Perspectives on Politics* 10 (3): 599–616.

Dovi, Suzanne. 2002. "Preferable Descriptive Representatives: Or Will Just Any Woman, Black, or Latino Do?" *American Political Science Review* 96:745–54.

———. 2006. *The Good Representative.* Oxford: Blackwell.

———. 2009. "In Praise of Exclusion." *Journal of Politics* 71 (3): 1172–86.

———. 2017. "Name Brand Populism." *Critique, January* 15. http://www.thecritique.com/articles/namebrandpopulism/.

———. 2018. "Good Representatives Foster Autonomy." *PS: Political Science and Politics* 51 (2): 323–26.

Dovi, Suzanne, and McCain, Jesse. 2017. "Are Lobbyists Lawyers?" In *Ethics in Politics: The Rights and Obligations of Individual Political Agents*, edited by Emily M. Crookston, David Killoren, and Jonathan Trerise, 319–38. New York: Routledge.

Frankfurt, Harry G. 2005. *On Bullshit*. Princeton, NJ: Princeton University Press.Gallup. 2018. "Presidential Approval Ratings—Gallup Historical Statistics and Trends." http://news.gallup.com/poll/116677/Presidential-Approval-Ratings-Gallup-Historical-Statistics-Trends.aspx.

Goetz, Anne Marie, and Rob Jenkins. 2001). "Hybrid Forms of Accountability: Citizen Engagement in Institutions of Public-Sector Oversight in India." *Public Management Review* 3:363–83.

Grant, Ruth W., and Robert O. Keohane. 2005. "Accountability and Abuses of Power in World Politics." *American Political Science Review* 99 (1): 29–44.

Hancock, Ange-Marie. 2016. *Intersectionality: An Intellectual History*. New York: Oxford University Press.

Illing, Sean. 2017. "20 of America's Top Political Scientists Gathered to Discuss Our Democracy. They're Scared." *Vox*, October 13. https://www.vox.com/2017/10/13/16431502/america-democracy-decline-liberalism.

Machiavelli, Niccolò (1513) 1995. *The Prince*. Translated by George. Bull. London: Penguin Books.

Mainwaring, Scott, and Aníbal Pérez-Liñán. 2013. "Democratic Breakdown and Survival." *Journal of Democracy* 24 (2): 123–37.

Mass Observation Archive. n.d. "The Mass Observation Archive." http://www.thekeep.info/collections/mass-observation-archive/.

Mulgan, Richard. 2003. *Holding Power to Account: Accountability in Modern Democracies*. New York: Palgrave.

O'Donnell, Guillermo. 1998). "Horizontal Accountability in New Democracies." *Journal of Democracy* 9 (3): 112–26.

———. 2003. "Horizontal Accountability: The Legal Institutionalization of Mistrust." *Democratic Accountability in Latin America* 22:34–55.

Pitkin, Hanna. 1967. *The Concept of Representation*. Berkeley: University of California Press.

Plotke, David. 1997. "Representation Is Democracy." *Constellations* 4 (1): 19–34.

Postman, Neil. 2006. *Amusing Ourselves to Death: Public Discourse in the Age of Show Business*. New York: Penguin Books.

Przeworski, Adam, Susan C. Stokes, and Bernard Manin, eds. 1999. *Democracy, Accountability, and Representation*. Vol. 2. Cambridge: Cambridge University Press.

Sabl, Andrew. 2002. *Ruling Passions: Political Offices and Democratic Ethics*. Princeton, NJ: Princeton University Press.

Saward, Michael. 2006. "The Representative Claim," *Contemporary Political Theory* 5 (3): 297–318.

———. 2010. *The Representative Claim*. Oxford: Oxford University Press.

———. 2014. "Shape-Shifting Representation." *American Political Science Review* 108 (4): 723–36.

Schedler, Andreas. 1999. "Conceptualizing Accountability." In *The Self-Restraining State: Power and Accountability in New Democracies*, edited by Andreas Schedler, Larry Diamond, and Marc F. Plattner, 13–28. Boulder, CO: Lynne Rienner.

Schwarz, Sam. 2017. "Donald Trump Has Only Delivered 1,200 Coal-Mining Jobs, Despite Claiming to Have Created 45,000." *Newsweek*, December 19. http://www.newsweek.com/donald-trump-has-only-delivered-1200-coal-mining-jobs-despite-claiming-have-751885.

Shklar, Judith. 1984. *Ordinary Vices*. Cambridge, MA: Harvard University Press.

Stanley, Jason. 2012. "Speech, Lies, and Apathy." *New York Times*, August 30. http://opinionator.blogs.nytimes.com/2012/08/30/speech-lies-and-apathy/.

Thompson, Dennis. 1980. "Moral Responsibility of Public Officials: The Problem of Many Hands." *American Political Science Review* 74 (4): 905–16.

———. 1987. *Political Ethics and Public Office*. Cambridge, MA: Harvard University Press.

Urbinati, Nadia. 2006. *Representative Democracy: Principles and Genealogy*. Chicago: University of Chicago Press.

Urbinati, Nadia, and Mark E. Warren. 2008. "The Concept of Representation in Contemporary Democratic Theory." *Annual Review of Political Science* 11:387–412.

Walzer, Michael. 1973. "Political Action: The Problem of Dirty Hands." *Philosophy and Public Affairs* 2:160–80.

Wenman, Mark. 2013. *Agonistic Democracy: Constituent Power in the Era of Globalisation*. Cambridge: Cambridge University Press.

Žižek, Slavoj. 2012. *The Year of Dreaming Dangerously*. Brooklyn: Verso.

5

Leadership and Representation

Eric Beerbohm

LEADERS MAKE CAMEO appearances in political ethics. They face dilemmas, and if all goes well, resolve them, sparing us the decisional burden. We pass the buck to them. On the classic depiction of dirty hands, the leader "hustles, lies, and intrigues *for us*," insulated from our say or will (Walzer 1973). Or leaders buck our strongly held opinions, knowing the political consequences full well. When they lose their next election, they become "profiles in courage" (Kennedy 1955). Either way, leadership in electoral politics and democratic governance comes to look like an activity that is, at its core, counterrepresentational. There is no clear sense in which democratic citizens are involved in the exercise of leadership. Indeed, the *independence* of the leader is taken to be constitutive of leadership.

This chapter examines the complex relationship between representation and leadership. No plausible theory of democracy can do without a concept of representation. The thought that elected officials stand for us—in some meaningful way—is too central to democratic politics practiced on a mass scale. This tempts us to construe leadership as a contrastive term so that it becomes a counterrepresentational force. We should push back against this view. Leaders and followers *act together* in a way that forces us to reconsider the usual accounts of coagency. If we come to see leadership as making possible a distinctive form of joint activity, our conceptions of representation and leadership needn't vie for our democratic loyalties. Instances of leadership can be paradigmatic moments of representation.

We precede in five steps. The first section offers two explanations for the low profile that political ethics assigns to leaders. The story isn't a failure of oversight but instead a philosophical consequence of reducing the phenomenon to counterrepresentation. The second section considers two models for identifying the exercise of leadership. On the one hand, the agent-centered model begins with a unifying set of characteristic traits and actions of leaders. On the other, the follower-centered model inverts the relational structure. It asks what happens to followers when leadership is successful; successful leaders do not merely take their followers' goals and preferences as given but rather change them substantially and often permanently. The third section presents a model of leadership that attempts to unify the agent- and follower-oriented models. If we construe leadership as a unique species of joint activity, we can constructively draw on material from both approaches. The next section considers ways that leadership can sustain *and* upend relationships of political equality. Some threats that leadership poses to democracy, while incurable, can be managed. Others are terminal. The chapter closes by imagining how leadership, despite its inherent threat, is an indispensable feature of representative democracy.

An Underrepresented Concept

Leadership has an ambient presence in social life. Leaders manage to get people to do or think things. They show the way, setting patterns of action or thought among their followers. They do this not by issuing coercive threats but instead through speech acts alone. The phenomenon ranges across associative, political, or academic domains. Put in its most general form, leadership is ever present. In democratic politics, things look different. It is ritual to decry the *lack* of the phenomenon. There is an expressed hunger for more instances of authentic leadership. In the musical *Hamilton,* George Washington reports that the people are "asking me to lead" (Miranda 2016, 137). What, exactly, are they asking? Philosophical work in political ethics and democratic theory around the concept is underpopulated. When invoked, the concept has received a reductive treatment. Leadership becomes a service performed for us, but not with us. Let's rehearse two views of this kind.

Dirty Hands

Leaders tend to get typecast as the solution to a problem. Adapting the term "dirty hands" from Jean-Paul Sartre's eponymous play, Michael Walzer (1973) frames the problem as one that arises when we ask what political leaders are for. His answer is that leaders occupy a role that insulates them from the usual ethical constraints on action that you and I face. They perform the dirty work of politics. Think of former President Lyndon Johnson threatening to blackmail a segregationist opponent, shouting on the phone, "I'm going to run over you if you challenge me on this civil rights bill" (quoted in Updegrove 2012, 55). If leaders cannot avoid dirtying their hands, they find themselves in a kind of dead-end. As Walzer (2004, 46) sees it, "Leaders may sometimes find themselves in situations where they cannot avoid acting immorally." An air of inevitability marks this discussion. Part of the job of leadership is to make decisions that are, to use Bernard Williams's (1978, 71) polite phrase, "morally disagreeable or distasteful."

Political ethicists have assumed that "dirty hands" is the answer to the question: What are leaders for? I propose that this conclusion constitutes a case of mistaken identity. Leadership's relationship to power is not monocausal. In some cases, leadership can serve as an all-purpose means to attain, keep, or deploy power. But this doesn't exhaust the concept's meaning. Now we can see how the problem of dirty hands has been a source of misdirection. Leaders, when successful, come to hold and deploy power. And it may well be that individuals in power face dilemmas that raise the philosophical difficulties of dirty hands. So it's tempting to infer that political leadership, at its core, is the business of dirtying of one's hands. But this conclusion fails to distinguish the characteristic *position* of a leader—power bearing—from the conditions that mark out an *activity*: the exercise of leadership.

Dwelling on the dilemmas of dirty hands delivers a highly constricted view of leadership—one that is confined to an agent acting in a profoundly individualistic way. It leaves us with a misleading model, where leaders are portrayed as solitary and brooding—not to mention that their role as leaders is short-lived.

Sacrificial Roles

A second explanation for the underrepresentation of leadership involves representation itself. If representatives stand in an agency relationship with us, this can seem to crowd out the phenomenon of leadership altogether. In her classic analysis of representation, Hanna Pitkin noticed this tension. For what Pitkin calls descriptive accounts of representation, there is no obvious space for instances of leadership. If representation is constituted by acting as a "mirror" of a constituency, then exercising leadership—acting on one's own initiative, independent of one's constituents' wishes—is a distinctively grave way to *fail* at representing others. Seen as a profile in courage, leaders stand in a zero-sum relationship with representatives. On this account, exercises of leadership are necessarily counterrepresentative. What is less noticed is that Pitkin didn't limit this incompatibility to descriptive views.

On any theory of representation where *you* act for or on behalf of another, profound limits on your discretion seem to kick in. You can take risks, improvise solutions, and "wing it" when you are acting only for yourself—as Thomas Hobbes would say, when you are serving merely as your own spokesperson—but not another's. "What is courage or daring on our own behalf," Pitkin (1967, 118) warns, "becomes irresponsibility when committed on behalf of another." The intuitive appeal here is clear. If you serve as a decision surrogate for another, the range of options you may permissibly select is constrained. This holds true even if you see yourself as a benefactor, trying to maximize some metric of flourishing in the person you represent. Even Burkeans don't seem to have room to lead. Rather than moving public opinion, they bracket it. Their solitary judgment is what they owe to constituents.

These two pictures of leaders have more in common than has been appreciated. The first has leaders *violating* moral principles so that the citizens for whom they act for are insulated; the second has leaders *honoring* moral commitments despite their constituents' blinkered wishes. What connects these cases is that the constituencies for whom they act are, in the end, held constant. They don't participate in the activity of leadership in any meaningful way. Either way, we are spared. We neither dirty our hands or undo our own irrational views. We even depose our agents because they have failed to follow our wishes. The thought that the exercise of leadership *changes followers* is crucially missing from both accounts.

Parsing Leadership

In everyday politics, we call occupants of certain official positions "leader" as a functional title. This naming scheme is even hardwired in the rules and procedures of legislatures. Consider the majority or minority leader of the US Senate. Let's not read too much into this linguistic practice. Conflating a functional position with a normative exercise of leadership can be a source of confusion. Is the Senate majority leader a leader? If we are invoking a more thickly normative concept, this is a perfectly sensible question. Still, it doesn't follow that leadership's exercise need be morally laudatory. The concept, as I'm imagining it, is only partially moralized. It's not conceptually possible for me to lead you by directly threatening you with violence to follow me. Let's consider two identification strategies, which begin from opposite ends.

Agent-Centric Approaches

The first method fixes on the properties of leaders themselves. We canvas for character traits that leaders share. In "Politics as Vocation," Max Weber (1994) presents leaders as possessing "personal charisma," which brings followers to "believe" in them (see also Keohane 2012; Galston 2012; Swaine 2013). Accounts of this kind treat character traits as stable dispositions to act in a certain way. This approach invites the objection that it builds the fundamental attribution error into its methodology (Ross and Nisbett 1991). It's a standing temptation to assume that individuals' actions turn on what kind of people they are, neglecting the environmental factors that influence them (Goodwin 1998). Character-theoretic views of leadership typically start with a pool of leaders, which fit our pretheoretical intuitions, and then attempt to explain what is common among this group by looking for shared traits. This makes them prone to neglect the characteristic situations that people exercising leadership find themselves in. If we have inflated beliefs about the significance of personality traits, we may fail to exercise caution in relying on methods that treat such traits as the most essential elements of the theory.

A more targeted approach directs our attention away from character traits in general. *Virtue-theoretic approaches* focus on the virtuous character traits shared by leaders. We treat the relevant virtues, or "habits of governance," in a functional way. We search for the traits "conducive to acting well in office" (Sabl 2002, 7). This method guards against attribution errors in its sensitivity to the environment in which leaders operate. It identifies traits in distinctive political habitats, ranging across the offices of the legislator, organizer, and activist. With this approach, Andrew Sabl identifies "middle virtues" like sympathy and toleration. If there is a master virtue of leaders, it is "democratic constancy," the effective pursuit of interest, broadly construed. What emerges is a view of leaders that allows for a permissible mix of moral and self-regarding considerations.[1] We can usefully contrast this partially moralized approach

1. Whether this virtue-theoretic approach remains vulnerable to attribution errors is an open question. The approach does assume that virtues track reliable behavioral disposition. It is precisely the steadiness of democratic constancy that makes it appealing for leaders of all stripes, whether the activities or senator.

with purely instrumental accounts, popular in leadership studies. Leaders possess whatever traits that allow them to accomplish their preset ends. Their skill lies in handling power, however monstrously it is deployed.[2]

Faced with philosophical concerns about character traits, this approach may limit its purview to the characteristic *actions* that exercises of leadership share. Leaders "take a stand," frequently improvise solutions, and when they err, take responsibility for their actions (Mansfield 1989). This explains why instances of leadership are more salient in less than ideal background conditions. Injustice doesn't *create* leaders, but it may present many more opportunities for would-be agenda setters. This includes ample opportunities to make mistakes, however well-intentioned, and take responsibility for them in a public manner.

Action-centered views can usefully distinguish between leadership action *types* and action *tokens*. We can describe the action type of sticking one's neck out or focus on action tokens, where particular leaders bear risks. The former approach will unfold in a deductive manner, picking out the classes of actions that together make up leadership. The latter will proceed inductively, starting with handpicked cases. Its focus on tokens of leadership makes a theory more flexible but less determinate.[3]

A recent action-theoretic approach views leadership as an essentially risk-bearing activity. James Read and Ian Shapiro conceive of leaders as engaging in a distinctively "risk-embracing" activity. The conditions for this activity are familiar to any collective action theorist. Leaders find themselves in a strategic dilemma, where they must choose between cooperating with opposing parties or defecting: "Individual leaders can initiate new, tentatively co-operative approaches more readily than can whole communities, but in the process they accept a different degree of risk than the community does. In addition to political failure and repudiation, such leaders risk assassination by extremists on both sides" (Read and Shapiro 2014, 42). This account brings to light a distinctive contribution of leaders: they are uniquely placed to launch a new cooperative scheme; they can come to reimagine a zero-sum conflict as a variable-sum opportunity. Their actions are characterized by a kind of "strategic hope": they take calculated risks in the service of cooperative outcomes.[4] When cooperation

2. Sabl draws this contrast with Richard Neustadt's means-ends account.

3. See, for example, Dennis Thompson's (2010) discussion of "constitutional character."

4. In game-theoretic work, leaders are routinely absent. Robert Axelrod's indefinitely iterated prisoner's dilemma has no place for leaders. See Axelrod 1984, 1997.

breaks down, a leader's decision to restore it—offering a "contrite" tit for tat—is always a risky move. Leadership emerges as a unique mix of actions; leaders absorb risk in the service of overcoming our strategic dilemmas.

This argument for leadership turns on a key assumption. It applies in cases where most members of each group will benefit more from cooperation than from any outcome involving separate action. We badly need assurance that others will go along. If we suspect others won't cooperate, we will hedge our bets and opt out. Leaders, in supplying this assurance, will antagonize members with more radical beliefs. These "extremists" will favor noncooperation precisely because they don't share the interests of more moderate members of the group. It follows that leadership is a double-edged sword: in solving one assurance problem, leaders bear the brunt of risk.

Follower-Centric Approaches

The second way of identifying leadership starts with its characteristic effects on followers. Follower-centered views, as I'm calling them, assign conceptual priority to followers. They deliberatively put the cart before the horse, starting with the post-treatment effects of leadership. Something happens to the followers of this activity. Once we pinpoint this cluster of symptoms, we will have identified the phenomenon of leadership. Transformational theories in this vein are organized around leadership's momentous effects on followers.[5]

Joseph Schumpeter offers a paradigm of a follower-centered approach. Leadership makes a productive contribution to followers. In this case, the production is literal. Leaders *manufacture* their follower's will; there is no prefabricated will of the people. If we look at the pedigree of leaders—some chain of authorization in their assent to power—we are looking in the wrong place.[6] We need to look upstream. Schumpeter's theory of leadership is powered by a puzzle: How can a collective, without a will of its own, act? When we act in some collective vein, there is powerful evidence that we have received a leader's treatment. The theory, in effect, has us derive the presence of Neptune from its surrounding moons. We notice an emergent phenomenon, collective

5. Thus as James MacGregor Burns (1978, 52) understands it, "Leadership theories . . . feature profit-maximizing elites who manipulate fixed preferences, or conversely attribute extraordinary transformative powers to individual leaders."

6. Theorists who have allegiance to the Schumpeterian program include Richard Posner (2003) and Ian Shapiro (2003).

activity, so we infer the conditions that made this possible. Schumpeter (2010, 270) concludes that "collectives act almost exclusively by accepting leadership." This view has no patience for theories of representation. It just isn't possible for officials to "carry out the will of the people exactly as a doctor acts to carry out the will of the patient to get well" (Schumpeter 2010, 250). The political activity of leadership altogether displaces representation.

The ensuing theory of democracy is reductive. *Accepting leadership* or *withdrawing acceptance* are the two activities available to democratic citizens. This has led some commentators to distinguish *approval* from mere *acceptance*. "Acceptance is an undemocratic notion," Gerry Mackie (2009, 143) holds, maintaining that "those who only accept leadership, by definition, have no further inclinations to approve or disapprove of it." But this conclusion comes too quickly. When we "go along" with the proposal of another, we are in the role of a follower. Why should we assume, though, that this attitude—lacking full-throated approval—is less of an action? Perhaps the thought is that acceptance, as an attitude, is generally less reflective, or more lukewarm in character.[7] Yet as a pro-attitude, acceptance comes in grades, from wholehearted to begrudging. Nor does acceptance have to be a passive activity. I can see my own agency perfectly clearly when I follow you, even if I haven't initiated the action. So we might conclude that worries about the democratic credential of acceptance turn on some underlying concern. In Schumpeter's theory, if our acceptance is part of the material manufactured by leaders, then we may be suspicious of its normative force.

Follower-centered views needn't result in a democratically hampered view of leadership. Hannah Arendt presents leaders as initiative takers, whose success hinges on the resulting actions of followers. She rejects views of leadership that see rulers as directing or managing our activity. Here is Arendt's (2003, 47) target:

> Every action, accomplished by a plurality of men, can be divided into two stages: the beginning, which is initiated by the "leader," and the accomplishment, in which many join to see through what then becomes a common enterprise. In our context, all that matters is the insight that no man,

7. David Hume's ([1748] 1987, 475) description of the begrudging individual dragged onto a ship conjures the idea of bare *acceptance:* "We may as well assert, that a man, by remaining in a vessel, freely consents to the dominion of the master; though he was carried on board while asleep, and must leap into the ocean, and perish, the moment he leaves her."

> however strong, can accomplish anything, good or bad, without the help of others. What you have here is the notion of an equality which account[s] for a "leader" who is never more *primus inter pares*, the first among his peers.

Arendt refuses to see politics as "rulership"—as what some *do* to others. She uses scare quotes when identifying leaders to separate herself from a more agent-centered view. On her account, initiative taking that marks out leadership is wholly underwritten by the support of followers. Leadership, when successful, is sustained by a pattern of action taken by followers. Arendt directs our attention to the essential role. Precisely how leaders get us to do things is left open. What matters is how their actions thread their followers' actions together, producing "concerted action" (Arendt 2003, 40). An updated version, offered by Mark Philp (2007, 77), sees leadership as producing "patterns of action for others." The activity is constituted not by *how* it creates templates that followers together act on but instead by its effects on followers interested in coordinating their actions. How do we get past our uncertainty and excessive self-interest? Leadership may be understood as the solution to our chronic coordination problems (Calvert 1992).

Follower-centric views can take on an instrumental cast. Economists describe leaders as offering a distinctive service for would-be groups. For Norman Frohlich and Joe Oppenheimer, leaders and followers stand in a bartering relationship. For the price of solving coordination problems, the leader extracts a payment in money or honor. After all, they have provided a specialized service, created by a peculiar kind of market failure. And they deserve something for this service. The leader, a skillful entrepreneur, brings a particular set of skills, "supply[ing] a collective good without providing all of the resources himself" (Frohlich and Oppenheimer 1971, 6).

This concept of leadership isn't cashed out in terms of the motives, aims, or character traits. Nor does it specify the characteristic means by which this service is supplied. The leader changes our strategic environment, not by transforming us, but by channeling our actions. That's the indirect treatment effect that allows us to identify instances of leadership. On this view, it seems, the motives and beliefs of followers are held constant. They remain the underwriting source of power: leaders enable us to act in patterns that wouldn't be possible without their orchestrating role. But in an important sense, the collective aim is *ours*. "The leader's power," given this perspective, is "founded upon his ability to solve derived coordination problems. Here the leader causes followers to act in concert, whereas they would not otherwise have been able to do so" (Calvert 1992, 19). What emerges is the image of the traffic guard, who makes it possible for us to get where we already want to go. The treatment on followers in this case is indirect. Leaders shape our environment, channeling our preexisting ends, but we remain unchanged.

A Shared Agency Approach

We now have two blueprints for constructing a full-fledged theory of leadership. Agent-centric views draw our attention to the traits, habits, and action types that we associate with leaders. If we have strongly held intuitions about tokens of leadership, why not attempt to find traits, virtues, or habits that they exhibit? There was also theoretical force in approaches that took followers as primary. What is most interesting about leadership is what it leaves in its wake. Followers are affected, sometimes profoundly so, by this distinctive treatment. It follows that we should look at the downstream effects on *us*, whether individually or collectively, after being led. It seems that we face a chicken-and-egg problem with a methodological flavor: What is conceptually prior, the leader or follower?

There's a way out of this deadlock. Rather than starting with *one* of these two characters, we can investigate the structure of the relationship itself. What is shared between leaders and followers in an authentically *democratic* politics? In that setting, we might suppose, leadership isn't something done to us but instead *with us*. By posing the problem in this way, we naturally invite our intuitive reactions to cases where we have democratic unease. Demagogues get us to do something by subverting our reasoning. There's no sense in which their actions are compatible with democratic values. By their counterexample, they sketch a way forward.

We can start with the assumption that leadership, at least in its democratic form, must be an activity that followers partake in. If we are looking for the sharing in actions, not mere beliefs, the relevant material is *intentions*. In perfectly ordinary activities, like going on a walk, our intentions need to be interlocking in a characteristic way. Suppose you are a slower walker, and my natural pace is faster. Without a shared intention to coordinate our movements, we'll soon be blocks apart from each other.

The shared material between leaders and followers is analogous to our walkers. Their interlocking intentions allow them to pursue actions in concert. Political activity is notoriously failure prone and so it's natural to search for a hardier species of intention. We generally call this form of intention a "commitment"—whether in a marriage ceremony or movement politics. On this view, leadership involves proposing a commitment that the leader will share with prospective followers. This brings out the creative and even improvisational dimension of the activity. Leadership has a discretionary character; it resists algorithmic reasoning. "Leadership is not wholly rule- and norm-bound," Philp (2007, 83) writes, observing that "it requires innovation, the interpretation of norms, and an ordering of values and commitments that are not covered by some further set of norms."[8] Sometimes this ordering will be audacious. US president Abraham Lincoln attempted to reframe the Civil War as collective effort for human equality (Wills 1992). It was hardly obvious that this proposal—launched at Gettysburg—would receive widespread uptake.

On the shared agency view, leaders get people to share a commitment and mobilize them to honor that commitment. In democratic politics, it can take on these forms:

Commitment setting: leaders propose that *we* (leaders and followers) bring about a political end.

Commitment sustaining: leaders mobilize existing followers to act together in bringing about a political end.[9]

Seen this way, leadership is a relational property in two ways. The ensuing commitment is shared between the leader and followers—vertically—*and* it is shared among followers horizontally. The proposed commitment isn't agent neutral. It doesn't say that *someone* or *anyone* should bring about some political change. It folds leaders and their followers into the commitment itself. That our coagency is recruited is central to the activity. The leader doesn't get followers to form a commitment that *someone else* should act on. Of course, leaders can and do call on others agents to act. You can spearhead a petition, directed to a university governing body, that my university divest from its carbon investments. But your *leadership*—as opposed to the effects that it may bring about—consists in you getting your body of followers to commit to this public speech act. The commitment is irreducibly about what *we* will do, not some third party.

It's dangerous to assume that democratic citizens are commitment types. After all, asking voters or movement members to share a bold commitment

8. This theme is sounded in popular accounts of leadership. Walter Isaacson (2010, 12) notes that leaders "know when to be flexible and pragmatic, on the one hand, and when it is, instead, a moment to stand firm on principle and clarity of vision."

9. For this approach, see Beerbohm 2015.

can seem outlandish. Martin Luther King Jr. (1960) asked his followers to commit to nonviolent resistance, which he claimed served as the "guiding light of our movement." King (2010, 63–64) defended this commitment against severe criticism, insisting on its centrality to the civil rights movement: "Occasionally in life one develops a conviction so precious and meaningful that he will stand on it till the end. This is what I have found in nonviolence." He set down a commitment to a nonviolent means in service of political equality. The shared ingredient of leadership can be about means, ends, or some aim that defies these political categories. For King, an essential feature of the commitment was that his proposed means were constitutive of the end. His refusal to cooperate with unjust structures delivered the appropriate forms of protest as well as the end vision of social and political equality.

If leaders aim to get followers to form a joint commitment, we can see why this activity has been seen as inherently risky. In small-scale actions, this is familiar. We commit to running a marathon together. Or we commit to jumping "on the count of three" on a base jump. Here our decision to engage in these activities together increases our odds of success. Our shared vow functions as a precommitment device. Even if my odds of success at base jumping aren't affected—whether I perform the action alone or with someone else—the odds of my sticking to my commitment may depend crucially on our willingness to bear this risk together. This seems to hold true for "moon shot" proposals in politics. The original proposal of this kind was shot through with risk. On September 12, 1962, then US president John F. Kennedy invited his national audience to share a decade-long commitment—one that he would share with them posthumously:

> We choose to go to the Moon in this decade . . . not because [acts like these] are easy, but because they are hard; because that goal will serve to organize and measure the best of our energies and skills, because that challenge is one that we are willing to accept, one we are unwilling to postpone, and one we intend to win, and the others, too. (Brinkley 2019, 363)

The speech is powered by a first-person plural voice. This isn't presented as a public service announcement: "I'd like you to know what NASA is planning to do over the next decade." Kennedy isn't alerting his audience of a policy undertaking that he is personally committed to. The speech is built around the proposal of an intention—one that must be shared for the political end to have any chance of success. Precisely how much uptake the proposal received is contentious. In response to the speech, then ex-president Dwight Eisenhower (quoted in Brinkley 2019, 384) rejected it wholeheartedly: "Anybody who would spend $40 billion in a race to the Moon for national prestige is nuts."

Let's assume, plausibly, that Kennedy knew that public support for the Apollo space program was relatively low. Was his proposal counterrepresentational? On a simple theory of representation, which takes the public opinion in a narrow time slice, then it surely was: the public's shared commitment grew over time, so that by Apollo 11, a commanding majority supported the program. If Kennedy had some confidence in his power to shape the opinions and commitments of the public over time, need his leadership be at odds with his role as a representative? Anticipatory accounts of representation suggest that there needn't be a tension. They tend to focus on representatives who anticipate changes in public opinion that are out of their control. But on another model, an official can anticipate the views of future constituents who shift in response to their own leadership. This view has a wrinkle. It's plausible to think that leaders tend to be overconfident in their ability to persuade others to join them on behalf of a cause. So we need to ask whether it is reasonable for them to anticipate a recruitable set of followers. Even with this caveat, this view subjects leadership to a kind of moral luck. If Kennedy's moon shot proposal doesn't find early uptake, at some point his attempts to move the public will reflect a disconnect from reality rather than anything resembling leadership.

This brings us to the *mobilizing* dimension of the activity. Leaders don't just create the background conditions for shared agency. They also mobilize that constituency to enact a shared commitment in law and public opinion. And indeed it can take as much effort to sustain a sturdy intention as to bootstrap it into existence. By 1967, King acknowledged that significant numbers of followers were flagging in their commitment to nonviolent resistance. King (2010, 45) diagnosed the fragility of the commitment in this way: "We maintained the hope while transforming the hate of traditional revolutions into positive nonviolent power. As long as the hope was fulfilled there was little questioning of nonviolence. But when the hopes were blasted, when people came to see that in spite of progress their conditions were still insufferable . . . despair began to set in." On his view, the true test of this commitment came when movement members' confidence was weakening.[10]

10. In his analysis of Hume's political morality, Sabl (2012, 36) stresses the sense in which leader's attend to the needs of followers, particularly their assistance in resolving social dilemmas.

If we see leadership as a distinctive form of joint activity, we can draw on insights from the two approaches discussed in the last section. For a proposal to get uptake from prospective followers, we would expect patterns of personality traits to play a central role. The bundle of traits, including charisma, rhetorical savvy, and overconfidence (even against all available evidence), will often serve as necessary psychological ingredients. So, too, do the virtue-theoretical traits of leaders have considerable explanatory power. Leaders don't frame a candidate commitment as wildly at odds with the interests of followers. They propose commitments that defy simple binaries between altruistic and self-interested aims. They may enlarge the appeal to include the moral interests of followers. King insisted on the commitment to refuse cooperating with evil—an appeal that could be put in terms of his follower's *good* or universal values of justice and peace. Indeed, he reframed the choice as between nonviolence or nonexistence.

Follower-centered approaches also supply rich material for making sense of leadership as a joint activity. Leaders *do* provide a kind of coordination service. But to cash this contribution out as a kind of transactional "skimming" is misleading. In small-scale problems of this kind, we tend to imagine decisions that are morally underdetermined. We must pick which side of the road to drive on, and so long as *someone* proposes a solution, we will drive content. In politics, however, our decisions don't typically have this character. We don't see leaders as third-party arbiters who broker coordination deals and take a cut of the transaction. Once we conceive of leadership as an irreducibly shared activity, we can see the mechanisms by which coordination problems are overcome. In *Hamilton*, Washington (and later Alexander Hamilton) report that people are "asking them to lead." We can make sense of this kind of request. Under certain conditions, leadership is a genuine service performed *for* followers. Yet it is also performed *with* followers, at least when placed in the setting of democratic politics. Transactional accounts focus on the former, occluding the joint character of the activity.

To see this, we can turn to an unabashedly undemocratic setting. Jean Hampton (1987) finds a leadership selection problem at the center of Hobbes's political theory. In the state of nature, we recognize that we can't spontaneously realize an optimal outcome. The variety of coordination problems that we face is too great. We need to empower a leader with vast coordinating power. They will then propose a shared framework and threaten punishment if we veer from our commitments (a decidedly Hobbesian form of mobilization). The conditions of the state of nature are sufficiently unpleasant that we are willing to precommit to honoring nearly any plan that the selected leader proposes, if doesn't fly in the face of our interest in avoiding recurring wars. Leaders, on this view, render a specialized coordination service for followers. But they needn't bring any special traits, whether charismatic or epistemic. The Hobbesian leader, in this sense, is unremarkable. We won't find anything extraordinary if we focus on their distinctive traits or even set of virtues. Still, it is no understatement to say that they transform us (Tuck 2004). Hobbesian leadership promises to rescue us from fear—so long as we sustain our shared commitment to invest exclusive authority in the selected leader.

Compatibility Testing

Views on leadership's relationship to representative democracy fit into a binary. On the one hand, we may hold little hope for compatibility. Leadership is an invasive species in democracies. Its place in democracy is incoherent and even paradoxical (Kane 2007; Sartori 1987). Benjamin Barber, for example, viewed the exercise of leadership as probative evidence of a democratic failure. For him, the activity is perpetually "opposed to participatory self-government" (Barber 1984, 237). Leaders can't help but displace action by individual citizens; they shrink the domain of collective choice. Barber's (1984, 237) conclusion leaves little room for moderation: "Complete self-government by an active citizenry would leave no room for leaders or followers." As democracy flourishes, we should expect and hope for a withering away of leadership.

The other pole dissolves the tension entirely. After worrying that descriptive theories of representation would make leadership impossible, Pitkin (1967, 233) offers her official line: that political representation, properly understood as a type of responsiveness, is "perfectly compatible" with leadership. She argues through a process of elimination. We first reflect on the line between leadership and manipulation—one that she acknowledges is difficult to draw. We then borrow from Ludwig Wittgenstein's (1953, 621) strategy for analyzing action: "What is left over if I subtract the fact that my arm goes up from the fact that I raise my arm?" What *remains* is supposed to be my action. Pitkin performs a parallel move. Leadership is what remains when we subtract manipulative acts from those actions that get people to do things. Why is this difference central for Pitkin (1967, 233)?

> Leadership is, in a sense, at the mercy of the led. It succeeds only so long as they are willing to follow. Thus it is not incompatible with our requirement

> that the represented be able to get their way when they have an explicit will. Manipulation by a ruler, on the other hand, is imposed on the ruled, and threatens their capacity to reject a policy or initiate a new one.

This argument recasts the leader as an agent and the followers as principals. Our *willingness* to follow is what preserves our agency in this activity. The coagency that Pitkin underscores is perfectly familiar: we *go along* with your proposal. We may do so begrudgingly, but we won't deny that this is an activity that we play some meaningful role in. Not so when we are victims of manipulation. In paradigm cases, manipulated individuals are not even aware of this treatment. Our subrational faculties are targeted, bypassing our reasoning altogether. On Pitkin's definition, leadership *can't* be manipulative and poses no threat to representative democracy. The tension is dissolved by conceptual fiat.

Neither view registers the complexity and potential compatibility of the relationship between representation and leadership. If we see the two concepts as standing in a zero-sum tension, we will overlook a class of cases where leadership seems to facilitate representation, and vice versa. And if we conceive of the concepts in a way that ushers away any tensions, we won't be able to appreciate the difficulties chronic to this relationship. Even if we aren't clear victims of manipulation, leadership can whittle away at our ability to see ourselves as equals, view ourselves as sharing in authority, and recognize ourselves as authors, not editors, of a democratic polity. To bring out these three potential sites of tension, we can run three kinds of compatibility tests between these models of leadership and representation: equal standing, coauthority, and coauthorship.

Equal Standing

Representatives, former and informal, wield far more power than any one of their constituents. How can we reconcile this inequality with the democratic value of equal standing? If legislators are agents and their constituents are collective principals, there is no necessary social inferiority in this relationship. Lawyers and accountants act on behalf of others. These agent-principal dyads seem consistent with relationships of equality. Once representatives play a more active role in shaping the convictions that they claim to represent, the egalitarian standing of the parties gets murkier. Was Kennedy representing his future constituents, who he believed would come to support an expensive moon shot? At the time of his speech, it's hard to cast his language in ways that are responsive to a broad constituency. Perhaps he saw himself as honoring a more general principle held by his constituents: committing to the United States' own leadership into new frontiers.

This suggests a sense in which his moon shot proposal was simultaneously an act of representation and leadership. He claimed to *represent* normative commitments; his leadership consisted in connecting those principles to a concrete policy goal. If he had failed to connect principles to policy, he could not have sustained the funding for the Apollo mission. In this sense, he was ultimately dependent on public opinion. And it is this veto point that gives the constituency a collective power that no act of leadership can surmount. As Lincoln put it, "With public sentiment, nothing can fail, without it nothing can succeed" (quoted in Basler 1989, 525). But as he recognized, public opinion can be shaped in an egalitarian direction (Young 2000, 26). In 1901, the White House released one of the first press releases of Theodore Roosevelt's presidency. It read simply, "Booker T. Washington of Tuskegee, Alabama, dined with the President last evening" (Morris 2010, 54). Roosevelt didn't explicitly invite his broad audience to join him in undermining white supremacy, but his one-sentence note was a powerfully understated way of proposing a commitment to racial equality as a central part of his presidency (Grantham 1958). This isn't an instance of Roosevelt deploying the "bully pulpit," a term that he famously coined. It's a restrained way of testifying to human equality. As an expressive act, it is far upstream from the civil rights legislation that enshrines equality in institutional forms.

Coauthority

Leaders claim the authority to speak and act in the name of their followers. But this claim can seem unearned. Claiming to speak for others can be a deeply vain and self-serving act. Walzer imagines two different "would-be leaders." The first finds "warrant in his ideology alone"; the other "finds his warrant in the fact that he can give his ideology currency among the oppressed themselves" (Walzer 1970, 55). For Walzer, only the latter can be a genuine leader of the oppressed who can speak on their behalf. Even if the former advances their interest, they lack a crucial element of authority: the uptake of followers, who take the leader's proposal as diagnosing their own subordination. In this kind of case, a leader's legitimate claim to speak for followers can empower them, enabling their voice and raising their consciousness. Precisely *how* uptake by followers occurs isn't obvious. There are clear cases where an unofficial representative seems to earn this authority. King (1987) describes the process by which he came to speak for the Montgomery bus boycott in a community that he had no roots in, and without seeking an official office:

> That afternoon, I returned to Atlanta to make at least an appearance at the meeting of Negro leaders. There I found an enthusiastic group of almost a hundred men from all over the South, committed to the idea of a Southern movement to implement the Supreme Court's decision against bus segregation through nonviolent means. Before adjourning they voted to form a permanent organization, the Southern Christian Leadership Conference, and elected me president, a position I still hold. (King 2010b, 168)

When a constituency provides evidence of uptake, the relationship between representation and leadership can be mutually supportive. King describes a preexisting commitment among movement leaders: the use of nonviolent means to end segregation in public transportation. Of course, King's own prior leadership on nonviolent resistance played a significant role in this commitment. Leadership in this case helped pave the way for King's representative role. He didn't get out ahead of the boycott leaders, claiming to act and bargain on their behalf, until he was officially recognized by the newly founded Southern Christian Leadership Conference.[11]

Coauthorship

If leaders typically generate commitments that followers come to share, how can ordinary citizens view themselves as coauthors, rather than coeditors, of political institutions and policies? Even if agency is shared among these actors, the form of agency that followers contribute may appear less significant. Nelson Mandela worried about this problem in his autobiography, *Long Walk to Freedom*. He imagined the leader who "stays behind the flock, letting the most nimble go out ahead, whereupon the others follow, not realizing that all along they are being directed from behind" (Mandela 1994, 57). The means by which leaders can channel convictions into an achievable route isn't best modeled by audacious proposals. There are subtler, nonmanipulative ways that leaders can

11. W. E. B. Du Bois (1903, 46) welcomed this selection problem: "The way in which groups of human beings are led to choose certain of their number as their spokesmen and leaders is at once the most elementary and the nicest problem of social growth. History is but the record of this group leadership"

set a pattern of action for followers. Leaders can draw on innovations from their broad base. Even if they serve as the principal initiative takers, it doesn't follow that their source material must be drawn from elites.

Political morality underdetermines our collective choices. How we choose to respond to an appalling injustice won't be settled alone by a set of political principles. This opens up considerable authorial space for leaders. They can channel general obligations held by followers—say, to seriously respond to inequality—into specific obligations to participate in redistributive policies. A constituency may feel strongly about a precise political end, but have wide discretion in the means by which to pursue that end. Consider the commitment to bring about a living wage. The Fight for $15 movement set an unambiguous end. But it left open-ended the means by which union organizers pursued that end, state by state. When movement members and elected officials settled on a means, they engaged in a coordinating act of leadership. They formed concrete intentions about how to pursue a preset policy commitment. On a popular view of representation, elected officials have discretion to determine the means to achieve ends that are set by their constituency (Christiano 1996). When legislators enacted a $15 minimum wage in several states, we could characterize their actions as a hybrid: they represented constituents' policy ends and exercised leadership in selecting the political strategy that was most effective in achieving those ends. Here again, a binary view of these two activities lacks explanatory power.

The authorial character of leadership can derive from the public. Think of a mass initiative with a genuinely democratic pedigree. It's no stretch to say that the people are leading, and the elected representatives, perhaps fearing a defeat in the next election, are following. This kind of populism is compatible with and even supportive of democratic ideals. But we are familiar with leadership from the bottom that is menacing to our equal standing. A riotous crowd can get reluctant elites to go along with unjust ends. If leadership is, at its core, about the sharing of commitments, there's no guarantee that its ends will be morally welcome. Even if representation and leadership can be mutually supportive activities, this shouldn't dampen the threat of antidemocratic leadership. Demagogues bring followers to commit to policies and institutions that disempower them. In Plato's phrase, demagogues "lead people into fear."[12] Leadership can get followers to act on what political scientists have called unenlightened self-interest, coming to share a commitment to policies that make them materially worse off (Bartels 2005).

12. Plato, *The Laws*; I thank Jacob Abolafia for this translation.

A Cautious Partnership

In democratic politics, leadership is perpetually perceived as an endangered species of collective action. We hear despair over its alarming infrequency, and references back to a time when it was deployed in the service of momentous causes of justice and peace (Goodwin 2018). The literature in political ethics is also marked by the underrepresentation of this core political concept. I have offered two explanations for this neglect, and canvased ways we can get a greater philosophical grip on the concept. In democratic politics, leadership can be a counterforce to representation, but it can enable unexpected forms of representation that enlarge the possibilities of collective action too.

We might close by taking a leaf from Judith Shklar's (1989, 37) view that democracy and liberalism are in a marriage of convenience. Leadership's relationship to representative democracy is a similarly fraught partnership. Democratic politics needs forms of leadership for it to respond to its deepest failures, even while leadership will always retain its potential to undermine our democratic norms.

References

Arendt, Hannah. 2003. *Responsibility and Judgment*. Edited by Jerome Kohn. New York: Schocken Books.

Axelrod, Robert. 1984. *The Evolution of Cooperation*. New York: Basic Books.

———. 1997. "The Dissemination of Culture: A Model with Local Convergence and Global Polarization." *Journal of Conflict Resolution* 41 (2): 203–26.

Barber, Benjamin. 1984. *Strong Democracy: Participatory Politics for a New Age*. Berkeley: University of California Press.

Bartels, Larry. 2005. "Homer Gets a Tax Cut." *Perspectives on Politics* 3 (1): 15–31.

Beerbohm, Eric. 2015. "Is Democratic Leadership Possible." *American Political Science Review* 109 (4): 639–52.

Brinkley, Douglas. 2019. *American Moonshot: John F. Kennedy and the Great Space Race*. New York: HarperCollins.

Burns, James MacGregor. 1978. *Transforming Leadership: A New Pursuit of Happiness*. New York: Atlantic Monthly Press.

Calvert, Randall. 1992. "Leadership and Its Basis in Problems of Social Coordination." *International Political Science Review* 13 (1): 7–24.

Christiano, Thomas. 1996. *The Rule of the Many: Fundamental Issues in Democratic Theory*. Boulder, CO: Westview Press.

Du Bois, W. E. B. 1903. *The Souls of Black Folk: Essays and Sketches*. Michigan: A. C. McClurg and Company.

Frohlich, Norman, and Joe A. Oppenheimer. 1971. *Political Leadership and Collective Goods*. Princeton, NJ: Princeton University Press.

Galston, William. 2012. "Reforming Institutions: The Next President Should Not Miss This Moment to Make Government Work." Brookings Report, July 24. https://www.brookings.edu/research/reforming-institutionsthe-next-president-should-not-miss-this-moment-to-make-government-work/.

Grantham, Dewey W. 1958. "Dinner at the White House: Theodore Roosevelt, Booker T. Washington, and the South. *Tennessee Historical Quarterly* 17 (2): 112–30.

Goodwin, Doris Kearns. 2018. *Leadership in Turbulent Times*. New York: Simon and Schuster.

Hampton, Jean. 1987. *Hobbes and the Social Contract Tradition*. Cambridge: Cambridge University Press.

Hodgkinson, Christopher. 1983. *The Philosophy of Leadership*. Oxford: Basil Blackwell.

Honig, Bonnie. 1993. *Political Theory and the Displacement of Politics*. Ithaca, NY: Yale University Press.

Hume, David. (1748) 1987. "Of the Original Contract." In *Essays Moral, Political and Literary*, edited by Eugene F. Miller. Rev. ed. Indianapolis: Liberty Fund.

Isaacson, Walter. 2010. *Profiles in Leadership: Historians on the Elusive Quality of Greatness*. New York: W. W. Norton.

Kane, John. 2007. "The Ethical Paradox of Democratic Leadership." *Taiwan Journal of Democracy* 3 (2): 33–52.

Kennedy, John F. 1995. *Profiles in Courage*. New York: Harper.

Keohane, Nannerl. 2012. *Thinking about Leadership*. Princeton, NJ: Princeton University Press.

King, Martin Luther, Jr. 1960. "Pilgrimage to Nonviolence." April 13. https://kinginstitute.stanford.edu/king-papers/documents/pilgrimage-nonviolence.

———. 1987. *Stride toward Freedom: The Montgomery Story*. New York: HarperCollins.

———. 2010. *Where Do We Go from Here: Chaos or Community?* New York: Beacon Press.

———. 2010b. *Stride toward Freedom: The Montgomery Story*. Edited by Clayborne Carson. New York: Beacon Press.

Mackie, Gerry. 2009. "Schumpeter's Leadership Democracy." *Political Theory* 37 (1): 128–53.

Mandela, Nelson. 1994. *Long Walk to Freedom: The Autobiography of Nelson Mandela*. Boston: Little, Brown and Company.

Mansfield, Harvey C. 1989. *Taming the Prince*. New York: Free Press.

Miranda, Lin-Manuel. *Hamilton: The Revolution*. New York: Grand Central Publishing.

Philp, Mark. 2007. *Political Conduct*. Cambridge, MA: Harvard University Press.

Pitkin, Hanna Fenichel. 1967. *The Concept of Representation*. Berkeley: University of California Press.

Posner, Richard A. 2013. *Reflections on Judging*. Cambridge, MA: Harvard University Press.

Read, James H., and Ian Shapiro. 2014. "Transforming Power Relationships: Leadership, Risk, and Hope." *American Political Science Review* 108 (1): 40–53.

Ross, Lee, and Richard E. Nisbett. 1991. *The Person and the Situation: Perspectives of Social Psychology*. New York: McGraw Hill.

Sabl, Andrew. 2002. *Ruling Passions: Political Offices and Democratic Ethics*. Princeton, NJ: Princeton University Press.

———. 2012. *Hume's Politics: Coordination and Crisis in the History of England*. Princeton, NJ: Princeton University Press.

Sartori, Giovanni. 1987. *The Theory of Democracy Revisited*. Chatham, NJ: Chatham House.

Schumpeter, Joseph A. 2010. *Capitalism, Socialism and Democracy*. Abingdon, UK: Routledge.

Shapiro, Ian. 2003. *The State of Democratic Theory*. Princeton, NJ: Princeton University Press.

Shklar, Judith N. 1989. "The Liberalism of Fear." In *Liberalism and the Moral Life*, edited by Nancy L. Rosenblum. Cambridge, MA: Harvard University Press.

Swaine, Lucas. 2013. "Moral Character for Political Leaders: A Normative Account." *Res Publica* 19:317–33.

Thompson, Dennis F. 2010. "Constitutional Character: Virtues and Vices in Presidential Leadership." *Presidential Studies Quarterly* 40 (1): 23–37.

Tuck, Richard. 2004. "The Utopianism of *Leviathan*." In Leviathan *after 350 Years*, edited by Tom Sorell and Luc Foisneau, 125–38. Oxford: Oxford University Press.

Updegrove, Mark. 2012. *Indomitable Will: LBJ in the Presidency*. New York: Crown.

Walzer, Michael. 1970. *Obligations: Essays on Disobedience, War, and Citizenship*. Cambridge, MA: Harvard University Press.

———. 1973. "Political Action: The Problem of Dirty Hands." *Philosophy and Public Affairs* 2 (2):160–80.

———. 2004. "Emergency Ethics." In *Arguing about War*, 33–50. New Haven, CT: Yale University Press.

Weber, Max. 1994. "Politics as a Vocation." In *Weber: Political Writings*, edited by Peter Lassman and Ronald Speirs, 309–69 (Cambridge: Cambridge University Press.

Williams, Bernard. 1978. *Descartes: The Project of Pure Enquiry*. New York: Penguin Books.

Wills, Garry. 1992. *Lincoln at Gettysburg: The Words That Remade America*. New York: Simon and Schuster.

Wittgenstein, Ludwig. 1953. *Philosophical Investigations*. Oxford: Basil Blackwell.

Young, Iris Marion. 2000. *Inclusion and Democracy*. Oxford: Oxford University Press.

6

The Ethics of Partisanship

Russell Muirhead & Nancy L. Rosenblum

OVER THE PAST FIFTEEN YEARS, we have contended that partisanship is central to democratic theory (see Rosenblum 2008; Muirhead 2014; Muirhead and Rosenblum 2006, 2015, 2016). Our argument is a response to the gap between the political science of democracy, which shows parties and partisanship to be essential, and normative democratic theory, which is often silent on parties and partisanship (or when it is not silent, sees them as defective and dispensable). This gap is nothing new. E. E. Schattschneider ([1942] 2004, 4, 16) noticed it in the mid-twentieth century; although parties "created democracy," they "are still the orphans of political philosophy," he wrote. Today the distance that separates the institutional necessity of parties and their normative stature is less stark than it was only ten or fifteen years ago, as a wave of contemporary political theorists have sought to integrate parties into political theory. Yet much work remains to be done to fully bridge the gap.[1]

1. Aside from our own work on the subject, this literature includes the following important books: Bonotti 2017; White and Ypi 2016; Bonotti and Bader 2014. It also includes the following articles: Disch 2009; Ebeling 2016; Goodin 2008; Hendricks, Dryzek, and Hunold 2007; Herman 2017; Johnson 2006; Landis 2017; Leydet 2014; Van Blezen and Saward 2008; Waldron 2016; Wolkenstein 2016. We recognize the editors of the *American Political Science Review, Perspectives on Politics,* and *Journal of Political Philosophy* for the important role those journals have played in advancing and developing the political theory of partisanship.

Legitimacy and Agency

For our part, we argue that democracy needs parties and partisanship—and benefits from them. Our reasoning begins with the observation that parties are an essential ingredient in democratic legitimacy and democratic agency. Popular rule requires coming together. Yet *the people* do not stand together spontaneously; bringing people together is the creative work of partisans—ambitious office seekers and believers in a cause who want their allies to get elected, and need a coalition in order to succeed. Partisans (and the parties they sustain) bring and hold people together. No other force can do this—at least nothing that has been tried since modern democracy was invented in the late eighteenth century. Without parties in legislatures (what political scientists often call the "party in government"), legislatures would be incoherent collections of hundreds of individual political entrepreneurs (Key 1964, 656). Without parties in the broader society (what political scientists often call the "party in the electorate"), the connection between the legislature and people would be attenuated, if not severed (Key 1964, 209–17). Parties are what bring citizens and their representatives together in groups sufficiently large that they can claim to govern with majoritarian legitimately.[2]

This is why partisan commitment is consistent with good citizenship. The strongest version of this claim would say simply that to be a good citizen, one needs to be a partisan. More precisely, good citizenship involves an ability to combine identification with a party, on the one hand, with valuing the institution of regulated party rivalry, on the other. Good citizens are partisans who can see the political opposition as a loyal opposition, not an enemy. They must see parties as a key incarnation of political pluralism and not just a glum concession to the ineradicable "circumstances of politics" (Waldron 1999, 102).

We also maintain that the partisan's stand is in general more admirable than the Independent's. In the Independent's worldview, politics would go better if instead of parties and partisans, there were only freethinking, independent-minded citizens and representatives who weigh rival claims, and then go where the facts and evidence lead them. In our view, this would in fact destroy any prospect of democratic political agency. In the absence of some kind of

2. The institutions of direct democracy—referenda and so on—are outside the scope of this analysis, except to note that it may be theoretically possible to dispense with both representative legislatures and parties.

collective coordination, it is not clear that any majority could form in a legislature of radically independent political entrepreneurs. If one were to spontaneously form, it would not likely hold itself together long enough to defend its own decisions. It would pass something today only to see it defeated tomorrow. And even in the unlikely event that the spontaneous majority of legislators could hold itself together throughout a legislative session, it would be vulnerable to being defeated in the next election unless it also coordinated an electoral campaign that aimed to persuade voters to reelect it. To get anything done in politics, one needs a party—at least where politics takes the form of representative democracy with the elected legislature at its center.

There is no way to accomplish anything in politics—for instance, to pursue a program of action by passing a variety of laws all pursuing the same purpose—without parties and partisanship as well as recognizing the value of regulated party rivalry. This fact underlies what we call "the moral distinctiveness of partisanship" (Rosenblum 2008, 348–52, 362–68). Unlike Independents, partisans acknowledge that democratic legitimacy depends on building a coalition; they acknowledge this by their willingness to belong to, identify with, and help sustain a group that is striving to become large enough to govern constitutionally. Independence may have a kind of moral integrity that cannot be denied insofar as the Independent is never called on to trim or compromise. Independents can think solely about what they are willing and able to *stand for*. Partisans, however, cannot be morally self-indulgent because legitimate democratic politics is not only about *standing for* a set of principles, programs, and policies; it is also about *standing with* others, including those with whom we cannot agree about everything. *Standing for* this or that limits the set of people with whom one can make common cause; *standing with* imposes limits on what one can stand for. Unlike the Independent, the partisan must balance considerations about what it is right to *stand for* against considerations about who it is possible to *stand with* in common cause. This is what it means to be political, to think and act like a democratic citizen.

Inclusivity

To stand with others is to be inclusive, which is one of the principal qualities in our ethics of partisanship. At the individual level, the commitment to inclusivity may be more of a strategic matter than an ethical one: partisans want to win, and in order to win, they need to form an electoral coalition that can deliver them to victory. One might see less inclusivity in proportional electoral systems with low thresholds than one does in first-past-the-post systems or two-stage systems such as California's top-two primary since a party can win legislative seats with a low vote share. In such systems, the moment of inclusivity comes at the stage where the parties in a parliament negotiate to form a majority coalition. So the extent to which partisans are inclusive depends on institutional incentives.

Notwithstanding the way that norms are embedded in institutions, we regard inclusivity as a partisan virtue—a quality that partisans at their best exemplify. It is a virtue that partisans in high-threshold proportional representation or first-past-the-post systems will have more incentive to develop, to be sure. But it is a democratic virtue nonetheless because of the way it acknowledges the moral authority of the demos. Inclusive partisans want to win, yes. They also want the authority, though, that comes from "the great body of the people." As Alexis de Tocqueville (2002, 127) saw, democratic partisans often want the backing of a large and inclusive group for more than strategic reasons: "The parties have a great interest in determining the election in their favor, not so much to make their doctrines triumph with the aid of the president-elect as to show by his election that those doctrines have acquired a majority." Partisan inclusivity comes not only from the strategic need but also the moral desire to stand *with* one's fellows, in a group large enough to legitimately claim the authority of the people.

As things stand today in the democracies of Europe and the United States, the value of partisan inclusivity is imperiled. The great catchall parties of Europe are losing their allure in the face of more sectarian and divisive appeals by extreme parties, especially of the Right (Ignazi 2003). The great Social Democratic and Christian Democratic parties that dominated politics in the postwar era were models of partisan inclusivity; they did not exclusively represent, and did not claim to do so, specific social groups even if in their origins they came from concrete groups like labor unions or churches. They became inclusive and democratic institutions that sought to expand their support without limit, and in the process, unify society.

But in part because of their success, the inclusive parties of European democracy have lost their hold on popular identifications as they have become agents of the state—more like bureaucracies and less like social movements. Perhaps no one documented this development more acutely than the late political scientist Peter Mair (2013), who saw the fragility of even great and affluent democratic states that lacked the connection to the populace that only inclusive and vital parties can provide.

Amid their decay, smaller, more ideologically extreme parties with more forthrightly exclusionary appeals have grown. The traditional inclusive parties of Germany, the Social Democrats and Christian Democrats, lost enormous support in the elections of 2017 (even as they continue to be the major parties). Close on their heels is the Alternative for Germany, a nationalist-populist party that was only founded in 2013. In France, the nationalist party National Front was one of two final contenders for the final round of presidential elections in April 2017 (when its leader, Marine Le Pen, decisively lost). While the combined vote share of the Labor and Conservative Parties in the 2017 parliamentary elections in Europe was the highest since 1970, this came amid the disarray of Brexit, which was adopted by a 2016 referendum that the governing Conservatives felt compelled to offer in order to stem losses to the nationalist right-wing United Kingdom Independence Party. This is not to mention the right-wing New Democrats in Sweden, Finns Party in Finland, or Fidesz, the right-wing party that governs Hungary. The inclusivity that we put at the center of ethical partisanship is imperiled across Europe.

The same can be said of the United States, though the path is different. In the United States, the broad ideological ground, ideologically speaking, collided in the center, just as economist Anthony Downs's (1957, 118) median voter theorem would predict. This changed after the passage of the Civil Rights Act of 1964 and Voting Rights Act of 1965, when the Republican Party aimed its appeal at disaffected whites in the South (the "Southern Strategy"), with the consequence that the Republican Party became more exclusive in its racial appeal and more uniformly conservative. The Democratic Party became more uniformly liberal. As the parties polarized, they became more distinct—and less inclusive (Pildes 2011).

Since Philip Converse's (1964) article "The Nature of Belief Systems in Mass Publics," it has been widely appreciated that ordinary citizens are not all that ideological. They do not know what ideological labels mean, and their positions on issue A do not predict their positions on issues B, C, and D. In other words, ordinary citizens do not align their own views according to an ideological constraint. Everyday citizens are all over the road, ideologically speaking (Converse 1964; Noel 2013, 67–92). Yet increasingly in the US, their parties—and those who run for office—are ideologically narrow and extreme. The consequence is a disconnect between citizens and their representatives (Fiorina and Abrams 2011). Nonideological citizens are represented by a governing class that is ideological. This is one reason why, when they have the chance, some American citizens often identify as Independents rather than as Democrats or Republicans.[3]

More important, it is also a challenge for parties that want to build a durable governing majority and make the government govern. Since then US president Lyndon Johnson signed the Civil Rights Act in 1964, neither party has been able to construct a constitutional majority that can reliably control the House of Representatives, Senate, and presidency. That the US Constitution simultaneously checks the powers that it creates and authorizes (the Senate checking the power of the House, for instance) is a staple of civics education. Yet if the Constitution were solely about checks and balances, it would be a device that impeded popular power as opposed to one that facilitated it; *we the people,* the empowering and democratic aspect of the Constitution, would be overwhelmed by checks and balances that were hostile to any exercise of governmental power. In fact, the Constitution both impedes and facilitates. It is meant to impede what we now call "rent-seeking" behavior, or power exercised by special interests that is contrary to the common interest or rights of individuals. But it is meant to facilitate power exercised by and on behalf of the great body of the people. Indeed, within certain familiar constitutional constraints (such as in the US case, the limitations laid out in the Bill of Rights), it allows the people to rule without limitation, but only if the people stand together in a great and durable coalition that can reliably elect majorities to the House of Representatives, Senate, and presidency. Building such a coalition is the task of parties.

Neither of the great parties in US politics has been able to succeed in recent decades. Each has had its chance. With the election of Ronald Reagan in 1980, the Republican Party succeeded in mounting a direct challenge to the ethos of New Deal liberalism for the first time since 1932—but Republicans were unable to elect a majority to the House of Representatives (Reagan enjoyed a Republican majority in the Senate for only the last two years of his presidency, 1986–88). Democrats took full control of the government in 1992, for the first time since 1968—but they were only able to hold control for two years, as hostility to President Bill Clinton's effort to pass national health insurance reform allowed Republicans to take control of the House of Representatives in 1994, for the first time since 1952. The Republican Party then won full

3. This is in cases where people are given a three-way choice between Democrat, Republican, or Independent (and not taking into account leaners). See Gallup 2018.

control of the government in 2002, with George W. Bush in the White House.[4] Although Karl Rove, Bush's political adviser, deliberately aimed to create a durable Republican majority, Republicans lost control in 2006, as popular frustration with the Iraq War allowed Democrats to take control of the House and Senate in 2006. Democrats in turn won back complete control in 2008 with the election of Barack Obama to the White House—but they were able to hold control for only two years as opposition to Obama's health care reform and the bailout of the banking industry following the 2008 financial sector crash allowed Republicans to win the House in 2010.

In 2016, Republicans again controlled two of the institutions of federal government, but only by virtue of a president—Donald J. Trump—whose fidelity to the Republican Party was questionable. And neither Trump nor Republicans in Congress were inclined to assemble a broad and inclusive coalition that could govern across a number of election cycles. On the contrary, President Trump was more concerned with gratifying his base by feeding its resentments and fears than he was with expanding his base to achieve a broad and durable majority coalition.

Trump is only the most recent and extreme manifestation of the tendency in US politics to play to the base rather than the center. The Downsian logic of politics—where amid a unimodal distribution of public opinion, the parties move to the center—has been overwhelmed by a polarized logic of politics, where the parties play to the extremists who are more likely to contribute money to campaigns and vote, especially in primary and midterm elections.

In short, the principal virtue of partisanship—inclusivity—is endangered. The parties are not symmetrical in this. The Right has gone further in rejecting the virtue of inclusivity, yet the Democratic Party too has been unable to build a durable governing majority. As we write, President Joe Biden enjoys unified party control of the government, but the majority is slim and its durability endangered. Perhaps the parties are victims of their own prior inclusivity: having become so inclusive as to stand for nothing (in the case of the ideologically

4. Note that the Senate during the 107th Congress (2001–3) flipped back and forth between the parties. With Bush's inauguration, the Senate was split fifty-fifty, and Vice President Richard Cheney had the deciding vote. In June 2001, Republican senator James Jeffords of Vermont switched to an Independent and began caucusing with the Democrats, giving the Democratic Party control of the Senate. In October 2002, Senator Paul Wellstone (D) of Minnesota died, and a Republican was elected to replace him, giving control back to the Republican Party. This underscores the fact that neither party has been able to form a durable majority.

indistinct parties of postwar United States) or so inclusive as to become synonymous with the state (as in Europe), they lost their ability to inspire people to identify with them. And perhaps the parties are overwhelmed by the growing fragmentation of the larger society, and find themselves unable to build a diverse coalition and hold it together. And perhaps forces of raw exclusion are at work, such as racial exclusion, or other sources of bias and animus. The formula of *out of many, one*, gives way to *out of many, many. E pluribus plures.*

The decay of inclusivity will mean that parties no longer create the conditions for democratic legitimacy on their own terms. Legitimacy in the real-world sense (what one might call descriptive legitimacy rather than principled or theoretical legitimacy) comes from the actual connection between citizens and their government. The primary function of modern partisanship is to sustain this kind of legitimacy (Landis 2017). It does this by drawing popular interests and passions to a team that at least on occasion, shares in rule and by connecting popular passions toward the contest for office. To the extent that neither party can form a durable coalition, neither side can ever hope to rule. The most that partisanship can accomplish is to defeat the aspirations of the other side. The Constitution comes to appear a broken instrument for facilitating popular rule. In other words, the failure of the parties to perform their fundamental aggregational function—to build a coalition large enough to rule constitutionally—nourished a legitimation crisis where the democratic constitution itself comes to seem unworkable and unworthy.

Comprehensiveness

What is at stake in the capacity of parties to build a governing coalition is the very idea of the common good. We admire not all parties equally, but especially parties that advance a comprehensive conception of the common good. At their best, partisans tell a comprehensive story about the economic, social, and moral changes of the time. Partisanship is a general orientation—one captured by the general ideological spatial metaphor of left-right, or general terms like conservative, socialist, and liberal. As with inclusiveness, the comprehensiveness of partisanship is, on the one hand, a strategic necessity for partisans: insofar as they want to rule and need to win elections, they have an incentive to appeal as broadly as possible. But it is also, we think, an internal commitment for partisans at their best.

Comprehensiveness is what definitionally separates a party from an association dedicated to the interest of one particular group, like a union. What's good for the members of the Correction Officers Benevolent Association (the union that represents prison guards who work at Rikers Island in New York) may or may not be good for the citizens of New York City, the state of New York, or the country. It may or may not be aligned with the cause of human rights and justice. To the dues-paying members of the union, none of that matters. The union is there to represent them and advance their cause, regardless of how that affects the larger interests of the public.

The comprehensiveness of partisans is again most evident in electoral systems that privilege large coalitions, like first-past-the post systems. Proportional representation with low thresholds provides less incentive for parties to be comprehensive. Yet even there, one sees the inner logic of comprehensiveness at work; after all, no party wants to be accused of being indifferent to, much less against, the interest of the whole. Consider, for instance, the Dutch animal rights party, which has been accused of being a single-issue party, more like a lobby or interest group, than a true party. In response, Marianne Thieme, the leader of the "Party for the Animals," turns the tables on its accusers. "Traditional parties are in fact the single issue parties," she says. "Political Parties for the Animals have a broader vision. They do not put the short term interests of people first, but of the whole planet and all her inhabitants instead."[5] Our point is not whether animal rights parties are more or less comprehensive than traditional ones but instead to show that partisans care about comprehensiveness, even in electoral contexts where it is not strategically essential that they care (because they can win seats with only a small share of the vote). What differentiates a party from a pressure group, lobby, single-issue advocacy group, or faction is that parties speak in a comprehensive way. They make lofty notions of the common good real and concrete.

In this sense, parties are what make possible a politics of public reason. Public reason is a philosophical idea advanced in one way by John Rawls and in another by Jürgen Habermas that says the coercive power of the state has to be justified in a particular kind of way if its exercise is to be legitimate.[6] For Rawls (1999), public reason is a stringent philosophical concept; it refers to terms of argumentation that are analytically consistent with the idea of citizens as free and equal. For Habermas (1995, 1996), public reason is the product of an actual political process of argumentation and contestation. For both, public

5. Dutch Party for the Animals (Partij voor de Dieren), https://www.partyfortheanimals.nl/.

6. On Rawls and parties, see Muirhead and Rosenblum 2006; Bonotti 2017.

reason is the reason that the whole public can recognize; it addresses public things in a comprehensive way.

Public reason is an ideal that is fulfilled (in Rawls's account) whenever public officials and candidates give reasons for supporting fundamental political positions in terms that respect other citizens as free and equal. Beyond this, the reasons that officials and others offer should be rooted in a complete conception of political justice rather than reflect a series of disconnected ad hoc arguments. In Rawls's view, judges, especially Supreme Court judges, epitomize the ideal of public reason: they make decisions and offer extensive, written reasons for those decisions, and take pains to ensure that the reasons they offer in any particular case square with those they have offered in other cases. But the ideal applies to all public officials, and even candidates and ordinary citizens as well, insofar as complying with the ideal of public reason is how we succeed at regarding other citizens as our equals (Rawls 1999, 576).

Public reason is a simple ideal in a sense. It is based in the elemental notion that to regard another as our equal is to act from reasons that the other can see and could also accept. It is also a demanding ideal, though. Rawls himself says that it does not apply to the "background culture" of society—that is, to every conversation citizens have with each other in the privacy of their homes, at their churches, or over a beer. Public reason does not police everything we think and say. It instead applies to laws that are enforced by the coercive power of the state. The idea is that the coercive power of the state—the power that can deprive citizens of their lives and liberties—must be justified in terms that respect every citizen's freedom and equality as opposed to the interests of a dominant group.

The question for us, and one that Rawls does not take up, is how to connect the background culture of society, which is full of religious, moral, and philosophical ideas that do not comply with public reason, with the public culture of democracy, where we should expect that arguments about fundamental political justice should exemplify the spirit of public reason. We believe that parties are the single best institutions to build a translation bridge between the background culture and public culture of government. Parties have a foot in each camp. They appeal to and connect with the discrete social groups to which citizens belong (churches, unions, and organized "identity groups" that desire equality, for instance). Partisan candidates for office have to speak in the vernacular; they must express an immediate understanding of the way of life, values, and habits of those they seek to represent. At the same time, once elected, partisans become state officials, and they have a duty to justify the ways they want to use the coercive power of the state in terms that all can expect. Partisans are the only actors who are in both the background of popular culture and the formal state; they are the bridge between these two worlds, and as such, they—more than any other political type—are capable of creating a real culture of public reason.

We do not mean to say that every partisan succeeds at this or even tries to. Many simply want to be elected (and reelected), and will say or do anything to succeed at their strategic purpose. Some see society as composed of elementally warring groups, and amid that contest, pick a side and do not care to offer terms that the other side can accept. They want to use the power of the state to serve their own, and in some cases, oppress others. But many care about justice as the kind of thing that all in principle can agree to, and these types will be drawn to public reason (regardless of whether they are familiar with the philosophical term).

Some might argue that partisanship is only justified insofar as partisans actually succeed at justifying their conceptions of fundamental political justice in terms that align with the strictures of public reason. Or put differently, that ethical partisanship has *justification* at its core—the practice of giving reasons that one can reasonably expect all other citizens to accept. Recent political theorists of parties have offered defenses of partisanship that take this form. On the one hand, some look to a Habermasian conception of public reason to argue that partisans serve democracy by creating the conditions for justification (White and Ypi 2016). On the other hand, other accounts are concerned with how parties might contribute to the process of public reasoning that is central to Rawls's theory (Bonotti 2017).

We agree that parties and partisanship are better able than any other institution or identity to contribute to a culture of public reason. Broadly speaking, party rivalry focuses attention on problems, information and interpretations are brought out, stakes are delineated, points of conflict and commonality are located, the range of possibilities is winnowed, and relative competence on different matters is up for judgment. Without parties, democratic theory's "trial by discussion" cannot be meaningful. It will not be if the inclusion of interests and opinions is exhaustive and chaotic; parties are about selection and exclusion. Nor will it be fruitful if interests and opinions are disorganized and not brought into opposition, their consequences are not anticipated, and argument is evaded. Only then can "public reasons" be offered.

But we want to be precise about what we're saying. We think parties and partisanship are defensible even when they do not accomplish this, and we do not think that the normative stature of parties should depend primarily on their service to creating a culture of public reason. We do not hold that parties are defensible *only* insofar as they conform to public reason—for that is to see parties only as agents of the state, or bureaucratic entities charged with exercising the coercive power of the state, and morally bound to exercise that power in ways that pass the justification test. This diminishes their roots outside the state in civil society. To see parties only as agents of the state in this way is to obliterate their linkage function between the state and civil society, with deleterious consequences for the vitality of partisanship and democratic politics (Mair 2013).

When we say parties should have a foot in each camp, we mean that parties should place a value on the way they speak to nonpolitical identities that flourish in civil society and connect these to the political world. They do this through being attuned to what Rawlsians would call the "comprehensive conceptions," or religious and ethical conceptions of life, that define the free associational life of civil society. Partisans come from the communities that are defined by these conceptions; they appeal to and reflect such conceptions, and honor such comprehensive conceptions by giving them public voice. As candidates and officials, partisans may trespass the boundaries of public reason; indeed, it is only because they trespass such boundaries that they are able to breathe vitality into the impersonal institutions of the state by connecting them with the natural life of civil society. Parties at their best are *bilingual*: they know how to speak the language of public reason. But they know how to speak in the vernacular as well.

So we agree with those who say that parties and partisanship can contribute to the circumstances of justification. We agree that they might contribute to a culture of public reason. Yet we do not think parties are defensible only insofar as they do this, nor that they are only good when they follow the strictures of public reason. On the contrary, it is because parties—unlike courts—can trespass beyond the terrain of public reason that they can do the essential work they are meant to do for democracy.

Our appreciation of parties and partisanship is informed by the ways in which parties, especially those that seek to govern, are inclusive and comprehensive. We hesitate to endorse a maximalist ethics of partisanship, however, where parties and partisanship are only defensible when they satisfy certain demanding standards (such as compliance with public reason). Our ethical ideal of partisanship is minimal in its moral demands and centers on a steadfast resistance to using violence as a mode of getting one's way in politics. The renunciation of violence and acceptance of a regulated rivalry of contending parties are at the core of ethical partisanship. Identifying these elements at the minimal core of ethical partisanship is consistent with praising parties for their inclusivity and comprehensiveness when those qualities are manifest. But we would not want to make those qualities in their most demanding forms the necessary conditions of ethical partisanship.

Compromise

In addition to inclusiveness and comprehensiveness, the third distinctive quality we require of good partisans is a disposition to compromise (Gutmann and Thompson 2012). As an adjective, "compromised" is not a compliment; to compromise is to give up on something good, right, and true. This is why politics itself is a morally compromised activity for there is no peaceful and respectful politics without compromise, which is to say, without relaxing the insistence on winning all of what is good, right, and true for the world right now. Under conditions of equality and freedom, people will not agree on the good, right, and true. So to insist on winning the whole truth for politics is ultimately an invitation to violence. And the rejection of violence is the cardinal virtue of partisans. Partisans at their best are not purists; they are open to compromise.

Some argue that in the United States, partisans have become purists. This dates back to 1964, when the Republican Party nominated Barry Goldwater for the presidency rather than less ideologically conservative and presumably more electable sorts like Nelson Rockefeller (Tulis and Mellow 2018). The trenchant piece "Purists, Politicians, and the Two-Party System" by Aaron Wildavsky sought to explain how an ideologically amorphous catchall party could elect an ideologue like Goldwater. In Wildavsky's (1965) view, the Goldwater nomination represented the triumph of a new kind of person in US politics: a principled purist for whom politics is an ideological quest, over the traditional politico for whom politics is about patronage jobs and material rewards. What was unusual in 1964 is now the norm. Research on the kind of people who run for Congress shows that US politics is dominated by those who care more about devotion to an ideological cause than about building a diverse and durable electoral coalition (Thompsen 2017).

The rise of a more pure and principled orientation to politics might seem to make politics more noble than it was when partisans were more shameless about material rent seeking—such as distributing patronage jobs to supporters. The purist, after all, exemplifies the ideal of morally worthy action, which is motivated solely by a rational apprehension of duty and in no way by a sense of self-interest. But—and this is central to our defense of partisanship—we do not think that the purely principled posture is an admirable one in the context of democratic politics. One might ask, for instance, what the moralist should do when others who profess also to be "on the side of the angels" think that duty points a different way? Does one dig in, from a stubborn sense of self-righteousness? Such a person is often less a saint than a fanatic, blinded by the lethal mix of conviction and pride.

The fact of disagreement should inject a measure of humility even in those who believe they are right. It should nourish a moderating, temporizing, *political* approach to politics. It should open one to the *political* virtue of compromise. For the principled and pure, compromise is derogated and mocked, and used as a rationale to "primary" someone out of office—that is, run a more principled person against an incumbent officeholder in a primary election (Boatright 2013). Consider, for example, the Farm Bill, an omnibus law that packages together agricultural subsidies for farmers and nutrition assistance for the poor. The bill is unified by the theme of "food," but there is no principle that would bring together rural agricultural interests and the mostly urban poor who depend on nutritional assistance. The Farm Bill does not follow a philosophical or moral logic, or even a policy one; it follows a *political logic.* It is, in essence, a way of creating a majority coalition. No interest gets everything it wants, but every party to the deal gets something, and the political logic of the bill says that something is better than nothing. And politics is iterative—an ongoing political process of amendment and change. The Farm Bill goes back to 1938 and is updated every five years. Until recently, it was impossible to beat, but Tea Party purists defeated it in the House of Representatives in 2013. While it was ultimately passed in 2014, its fate is precarious—testimony to the inability of members of Congress to compromise.

The Farm Bill was a way of generating a bipartisan compromise, and whether a party should compromise with other, rival parties will depend on context-specific calculations. Compromise with rivals may or may not be a good thing on balance. Still, the compromise we admire most is the disposition to compromise with fellow partisans. Any party that aspires to *govern* is a compromise of various groups, sometimes competing and conflicting. Partisanship is a kind of solidarity, and during campaigns, partisans are militants—not least because elections are win-or-lose affairs. Yet parties are not enclaves of the like-minded. Intraparty dissension flares up all the time.

Partisans conflict over the direction of their party, the candidates who will receive its nominations, and the policies it prioritizes. Great parties are not only agents of public discussion; they are *arenas* of it. The discussion is so intense, and the disagreements so severe, that without the spirit of compromise, parties would fragment and splinter. Of course, some compromises are intolerable; partisans will refuse to vote for the party nominee, or in an extreme case, bolt from the party entirely. But the great prize of standing together is the prospect of *rule.*

In the United States in recent years, the spirit of compromise *within* the party has decayed, especially in the case of the Republican Party. John Boehner, speaker of the House of Representatives from 2011 to 2015, had great difficulty holding his own party together in large part because of an invitation-only group of Republicans that called itself the Freedom Caucus (Lizza 2015). As Boehner (quoted in Alberta 2017) later said of the caucus members, "They can't tell you what they're for. They can tell you everything they're against. They're anarchists. They want total chaos." In calling the Freedom Caucus "anarchists," Boehner puts his finger on how the spirit of compromise relates to partisanship at its best: partisanship arises from the rejection of violence and peaceful contest for *rule,* and peaceful rule requires *rules.* In a democracy, these rules will be majoritarian or even supermajoritarian. They will privilege large and lasting coalitions. To make and sustain such coalitions is the work of the parties. A party that cannot hold itself together cannot govern, even if its members constitute a nominal majority.

The Trumpist Assault on Parties

Populism has arisen around the world from Turkey to India, from the United Kingdom to the United States. The singular mark of the populist is the insistence that only one person or party represents the true people. It's a denial of not only political pluralism but also the three qualities we've underlined as the hallmarks of ethical partisanship.

The Trump presidency was the incarnation of populist assault on pluralism. What's often overlooked, perhaps because Trump took over the Republican Party, is his assault on partisanship. True, his presidency was characterized by larger immoralism: cruelty, disregard for the consequences of his actions on the nation, and the damage done by incessant, malignant conspiracist thinking. But our focus here is how he led his party in its attack on the three key elements of partisan ethics.

Inclusiveness: After the razor-thin victory of Bush in 2000, the Republican Party exploited the old means of partisan gerrymandering (now perfected with the latest technology) and voter suppression to secure power without a majority coalition. Because of the Senate, Electoral College, and Supreme Court, the party was able to win national office without winning national majorities. It did not try to expand its electorate but instead relied on these methods of self-entrenchment. This policy of the party became explicit with Trump's presidency; he stated outright that only by suppressing the votes of racial minorities in particular could he and his party retain office. He claimed that every election they lost was "rigged!"

Schattschneider's formulation that parties created modern democracy suggests that the logic of self-interest impelled partisans to win over a majority of voters and even to expand the electorate—to make democracy more democratic. He did not imagine that a major political party would have an incentive to shrink the electorate—to gain power by excluding voters. We now see that inclusiveness depends not only on the rules of an electoral system but also on an ethic of inclusiveness built into the democratic ideal of representation.

Comprehensiveness: This element of the ethic of partisanship speaks not only to broad ideology and wide attention to national needs but governance on their behalf too. Before Trump, Republican policy already reflected a truncated set of governing ambitions, such as reducing taxation on the top echelons of the wealthy and making conservative judicial appointments. From the start, Trump was altogether indifferent to governing, and his party in Congress was submissive. Without any concern for policy making in the national interest, agency appointments reflected cronyism and became scenes of kleptocracy. This divergence of government from a comprehensive view of the general welfare to private desires became fatal in the United States when COVID-19 struck, and the administration's public health policy was characterized by mismanagement and misinformation before it finally gave up the pretense of attempting to control the pandemic at all.

Compromise: The ethic of compromise within and between parties was violated by Trump and his followers in the legislature. Within the party, Republican officials and elected representatives at the

> federal and state levels went along with every presidential crime, conspiratorial allegation, and degradation of constitutional norms. Within the party, there was no brokering between the legislature and president; there was no compromise.
>
> Above all, the party in Congress and the states went along with the president's assault on the opposition as illegitimate. Democracy cannot exist without a party system, which cannot exist without acceptance of opposition: winners who refuse to harass, intimidate, humiliate, imprison, or kill their opponents, and losers who are willing to peacefully walk away after an election. Trump identified Democrats and "weak Republicans" as enemies. His 2016 campaign slogan "lock her up" was as frontal a rejection of the ethic of compromise and legitimate opposition as anything in US politics since the 1798 Alien and Sedition Acts. After the 2020 election, Trump propagated the conspiracy claim that the election was rigged and manufactured evidence that his "victory" was stolen. His assault on political opposition culminated with his incitement of followers to attack the US Capitol on January 6, 2021, as a joint session of Congress was certifying the election results of his defeat by Biden.

The ethical limits of political opposition have been addressed in terms of "militant democracy": anticipatory measures taken by states to prohibit the formation or participation in the elections of parties that exploit electoral politics to undermine democracy. Trump's dangerous conspiracist charges, violation of constitutional essentials, and incitement of domestic terrorism are grounds for democratic self-defense. The "paradox of democracy"—restricting the rights of political association if they threaten democracy—is not a paradox at all if we assume that "a Constitution is not a prescription for suicide" (Barak 2002, 44). This was the ultimate path of Trumpist populism, which exploited democracy to install authoritarianism. The US Constitution does not offer textual grounds for democratic self-defense of this kind, so challenges to Trump's violation of foundational democratic norms have taken the form of litigation against voter suppression, and articles of impeachment brought in 2019 (and voted down by a Republican majority in the Senate in 2020) and for a second time in 2021.

Unless candidates and officials are committed to ethical partisanship, the incentive structures set by the institutions of liberal democracy will not be sufficient to give them life.

The Moral Distinctiveness of Partisanship

The three values we isolate—inclusiveness, comprehensiveness, and compromise—are in a sense three angles on the same quality: a willingness to form and maintain a coalition that can rule peacefully and legitimately. It has always been tempting (and wrong) to think *the people* stand together as a natural whole. Indeed, the traditional opprobrium that attaches to parties charges them with destroying the natural wholeness of the people. But holism is a fallacy—or perhaps better, a fantasy. For some, it is a worthy ideal that might be approximated though never achieved; for others, it is a morally objectionable rejection of individuality and pluralism. In any case, parties do not destroy the natural wholeness of the people. On the contrary, they counteract the natural fragmentation of the people. They bring people together and try to hold them together in spite of the natural associability of human beings, in spite of the diversity and difference that flourish under conditions of civil and economic freedom.

Partisans at their best are inclusive. Parties at their best offer comprehensive terms of social cooperation that address the *common* good. Parties and partisans at their best exemplify a spirit of compromise. They are all of this, and they do all of this, because they want to govern, and in order to rule, they have to win elections—and in order to win elections, they need a large group of citizens who back them.

Moralists might be inclined to disdain the virtues we pick out as merely strategic, useful for the sake of winning elections, rather than as qualities chosen for their own sake. Yet it is never right to see the great qualities of partisanship—inclusiveness, comprehensiveness, and compromise—as merely strategic. They are strategic, but they are never only that. Partisans at their best want to win according to the rules of democratic contestation because they believe in those rules and democracy. Democracy cannot work unless the people—some large share of the people—stand together, at least for a while. Partisans want to make democracy work.

Even more disturbing, the strategic incentive to be inclusive, comprehensive, and disposed to compromise are apparently not enough to sustain these qualities into the twenty-first century. The desire to rule, democratically and constitutionally, is not enough to tempt partisans to build a large and lasting coalition. As a result, the great qualities of partisanship are increasingly vulnerable. Partisans today often give up on inclusivity and settle for a bare majority—or worse, winning by disenfranchising marginal voters, gerrymandering districts, or corrupting elections by gutting campaign finance restrictions. Rather than offer a comprehensive account of the common good, they settle for activating their base. Instead of building a legislative coalition through compromise, they impede and obstruct on principle; they prefer chaos to governing.

Political theorists have come to parties and partisanship late in the day. As Schattschneider said, since the dawn of modern democracy, parties have been the orphans of political theory. Perhaps we have come to appreciate parties and partisanship just as the virtues of partisanship are disappearing: the owl of Minerva flies at dusk.

Is society so fragmented that the partisan quest to build a lasting majority is doomed to fail, thus depriving qualities like inclusiveness, comprehensiveness, and accommodation of their strategic force? Or is it rather that the *political virtues* have been derogated in comparison to those of integrity and independence or ideological purism, giving rise to an orientation that is more disposed to self-righteous principled postures and to delegitimating the opposition than to the gritty, compromising task of making democracy work? We hope that it is generational, and that this will pass when a generation of citizens comes to appreciate parties and partisanship anew. More urgently, we hope that the danger to the constitutional fundamentals of representative democracy posed in the recent past by elected leaders in a number of democracies around the world will motivate candidates and voters who understand that inclusivity, comprehensiveness, and compromise are vital not only to build a durable electoral coalition and govern but also to defeat political forces antagonistic to democracy.

References

Alberta, Tim. 2017. "John Boehner Unchained." *Politico, December.* https://www.politico.com/magazine/story/2017/10/29/john-boehner-trump-house-republican-party-retirement-profile-feature-215741.

Barak, Aharon. 2002. "A Judge on Judging: The Role of a Supreme Court in Democracy." *Harvard Law Review* 116 (1): 16–166.

Boatright, Robert. 2013. *Getting Primaried: The Changing Politics of Congressional Primary Elections*. Ann Arbor: University of Michigan Press.

Bonotti, Matteo. 2017. *Partisanship and Political Liberalism in Diverse Societies*. Oxford: Oxford University Press.

Bonotti, Matteo, and Veit Bader, eds. 2014. *Parties, Partisanship, and Political Theory*. London: Routledge.

Converse, Philip. 1964. "The Nature of Belief Systems in Mass Publics." In *Ideology and Discontent, edited by David E. Apter.* New York: Free Press of Glencoe.

Disch, Lisa. 2009. "Parties, Partisanship, and Democratic Politics." *Perspectives on Politics* 7 (3): 621–24.

Downs, Anthony. 1957. *An Economic Theory of Democracy*. Boston: Addison-Wesley.

Ebeling, Martin. 2016. "Epistemic Political Egalitarianism, Political Parties, and Conciliatory Democracy." *Political Theory* 44 (5): 629–56.

Fiorina, Morris, and Samuel J. Abrams. 2011. *Disconnect: The Breakdown of Representation in American Politics*. Norman: University of Oklahoma Press.

Gallup. 2018. "Party Affiliation." http://news.gallup.com/poll/15370/party-affiliation.aspx.

Goodin, Robert. 2008. "The Place of Parties." In *Innovating Democracy: Democratic Theory and Practice after the Deliberative Turn*, edited by Robert Goodin, 204–23. Oxford: Oxford University Press.

Gutmann, Amy, and Dennis Thompson. 2012. *The Spirit of Compromise: Why Governing Demands It and Campaigning Undermines It*. Princeton, NJ: Princeton University Press.

Habermas, Jürgen. 1995. "Reconciliation through the Public Use of Reason: Remarks on John Rawls's Political Liberalism." *Journal of Philosophy* 92 (3): 109–31.

———. 1996. *Between Facts and Norms: Contributions to a Discourse Theory of Law and Democracy*. Cambridge, MA: MIT Press.

Hendricks, Carolyn M., John S. Dryzek, and Christian Hunold. 2007. "Turning Up the Heat: Partisanship in Deliberative Innovation." *Political Studies* 55 (2): 362–83.

Herman, Lise Esther. 2017. "Democratic Partisanship: From Theoretical Ideal to Empirical Standard." *American Political Science Review* 111 (4): 738–54.

Ignazi, Piero. 2003. *Extreme Right Parties in Western Europe*. Oxford: Oxford University Press.

Johnson, James. 2006. "Political Parties and Deliberative Democracy." In *Handbook of Party Politics*, edited by Richard S. Katz and William J. Crotty, 47–50. London: Sage.

Key, V. O., Jr. 1964. *Politics, Parties, and Pressure Groups*. 5th ed. New York: Crowell.

Landis, Joel. 2017. "Whither Parties? Hume on Partisanship and Political Legitimacy." *American Political Science Review* 112 (2): 219–30.

Leydet, Dominique. 2014. "Partisan Legislatures and Democratic Deliberation." *Journal of Political Philosophy* 23 (3): 235–60.

Lizza, Ryan. 2015. "A House Divided: How a Radical Group of Republicans Pushed Congress to the Right." *New Yorker, December 6*. https://www.newyorker.com/magazine/2015/12/14/a-house-divided.

Mair, Peter. 2013. *Ruling the Void: The Hollowing of Western Democracy*. New York: Verso.

Muirhead, Russell. 2014. *The Promise of Party in a Polarized Age*. Cambridge, MA: Harvard University Press.

Muirhead, Russell, and Nancy L. Rosenblum. 2006. "Political Liberalism vs. 'the Great Game of Politics': The Politics of Political Liberalism." *Perspectives on Politics* 4 (1): 99–108.

———. 2012. "The Partisan Connection." *California Law Review Circuit* 3:99–112.

———. 2015. "The Uneasy Place of Parties in the Constitutional Order." In *The Oxford Handbook on the U. S. Constitution*, edited by Mark Graber, Sanford Levinson, and Mark Tushnet, 217–40. Oxford: Oxford University Press.

———. 2016. "Speaking Truth to Conspiracy: Partisanship and Trust." *Critical Review* 28 (1): 23–88.

Noel, Hans. 2013. *Political Ideologies and Political Parties*. New York: Cambridge University Press.

Pildes, Richard. 2011. "Why the Center Does Not Hold: The Causes of Hyperpolarized Democracy in America." *California Law Review* 99 (2): 273–334.

Rawls, John. 1999. "The Idea of Public Reason Revisited." In *John Rawls: Collected Papers, edited by* Samuel Freeman, 573–615. Cambridge, MA: Harvard University Press.

Rosenblum, Nancy. 2008. *On the Side of the Angels: An Appreciation of Parties and Partisanship*. Princeton, NJ: Princeton University Press.

Schattschneider, E. E. (1942) 2004. *Party Government*. New Brunswick, NJ: Transaction Publishers.

Thompsen, Danielle. 2017. *Opting Out of Congress: Partisan Polarization and the Decline of Moderate Candidates*. New York: Cambridge University Press.

Tocqueville, Alexis de. 2002. *Democracy in America*. Edited by Harvey C. Mansfield and Delba Winthrop. Chicago: University of Chicago Press.

Tulis, Jeffrey, and Nicole Mellow. 2018. *Legacies of Losing in American Politics*. Chicago: University of Chicago Press.

Van Blezen, Ingrid and Michael Saward. 2008. "Democratic Theorists and Party Scholars: Why They Don't Talk to Each Other and Why They Should." *Perspectives on Politics* 6 (1): 21–35.

Waldron, Jeremy. 1999. *Law and Disagreement*. Oxford: Oxford University Press.

———. 2016. "The Principle of Loyal Opposition." In *Political Political Theory: Essays on Institutions*, chapter 5. Cambridge, MA: Harvard University Press.

White, Jonathan, and Lea Ypi. 2016. *The Meaning of Partisanship*. Oxford: Oxford University Press.

Wildavsky, Aaron. 1965. "Purists, Politicians, and the Two-Party System." *Review of Politics* 27 (3): 386–413.

Wolkenstein, Fabio. 2016. "A Deliberative Model of Intra-Party Democracy." *Journal of Political Philosophy* 24 (3): 297–320.

7

The Ethics of Public Administration

Joseph Heath

COMPARED TO THE FIELD of business ethics, the field of "public administration ethics," or "ethics for civil servants," is relatively underdeveloped. While there have been some noteworthy contributions, there are no distinguishable schools of thought, nor is there much sustained engagement between thinkers with different points of view.[1] While there is some literature on "public integrity," the discussion tends to focus disproportionately on the behavior of politicians and elected officials at the expense of any concern over the behavior of civil servants. Some attempts have been made to develop a general framework for the "ethics of management" or "ethics of bureaucratic organizations" that would encompass both private and public sectors, and yet these tend to founder when confronted with the extreme heterogeneity that one finds within the public sector in terms of the kinds of organizations, the tasks they must discharge, and the complex relations they have in regard to both citizens and elected officials. The resulting intractability is reflected as well in many of the codes of ethics developed for civil servants, which often wind up being just

This chapter presents, in abridged form, material previously published in Joseph Heath, *The Machinery of Government: Public Administration and the Liberal State* (New York: Oxford University Press, 2020).

1. Noteworthy contributions include Rohr 1989; Cooper 2006; Lewis 1991; Thompson 1985, 2005; Applbaum 1993.

a laundry list of "values," with no particular guidance about how they are to be implemented, much less reconciled in cases of conflict.[2]

And yet it is not difficult to see that the basic question of which principles or values should guide the deliberations of civil servants as they go about their duties, and how they should conceive of their obligations toward elected officials, state institutions, and the public more generally, is of the utmost significance. Indeed, considering the fact that almost all state employees work for the executive branch, it is extraordinary how much attention is lavished on the legislature and judiciary to the exclusion of the executive.[3] There are three levels on which the ethics of civil servants "matter." First, because a great deal of compliance with the law is morally motivated, ethical conduct on the part of state employees tends to be prophylactic against various failures of the "rule of law," ranging from petty bribery at one extreme to military coups at the other. Public sector "ethics" in this sense tends to be the preoccupation in low and middle-income countries, particularly where systemic corruption is a major problem. The second major issue is executive discretion. Laws are usually written at a high level of generality—in many cases, intentionally so—leaving civil servants with considerable latitude when determining how they are to be implemented (Zacka 2017). Civil servants therefore require some set of principles in order to guide their decision-making and conduct within these interstices—or in some cases, lacunae—of the law. This issue is particularly important in the United States, where "delegated" rule making has become a major feature of congressional legislation. Finally, there is the fact that civil servants, especially in the upper echelons or within powerful agencies, have the capacity to exercise significant influence over the legislative process. In liberal democracies, most serious or complex policy initiatives originate within the civil service, and in many instances, legislation serves merely to ratify policies that have long been established in practice (Carpenter 2010, 192; see also Carpenter 2001). This issue is particularly important in Westminster-style systems, in which the tradition of civil service neutrality creates a "permanent"

2. For the Canadian federal government code, see Treasury Board of Canada 2011. The UK Civil Service Code can be found at https://www.gov.uk/government/publications/civil-service-code. The United States is more complicated. A useful compendium of codes can be found in the Illinois Institute of Technology's Ethics Codes Collection (http://ethicscodescollection.org/), which provides links to all important federal government executive orders, supplementary agency codes, and state codes.

3. The US literature represents a partial exception to this generalization because of the enormous attention lavished on the president.

class of officials with considerable expertise, while the structure of parliamentary elections generates significant turnover among elected officials, resulting in sometimes serious information asymmetries between members of the executive and their supposed political masters.

Seen from this perspective, public administration ethics does not deal with small or inconsequential questions of personal morality but rather with major issues concerning the disposition of state power. John Rohr (1989, 3) articulated the stakes quite well in an early and influential contribution to the literature, observing that "the bureaucrat's position is sharply distinguished from that of the elected official, even though . . . he or she shares governing power with the elected official. The combination of these two ingredients—governing power and independence from the electorate—presents a significant problem for a democratic society. It is a problem that cannot be answered without a serious look at the ethical norms bureaucrats bring to their governing role."

In the discussion that follows, I will defend my own framework for organizing the various strategies that have been proposed to address this problem. Abstractly, there is little disagreement that the civil servant should be committed to serving the "public interest" or "general good." Things get difficult when it comes to the institutional specification of this ideal, both *how* it gets defined and *who* has the authority to define it. Typically, civil servants have available three distinct "poles of allegiance." The first is to elected officials, the second is to the public directly, and the third is to some independently determined interests of the state. Under happy circumstances, the three will be aligned: politicians will be tolerably responsive to the wishes of the public, while the public will prefer outcomes that can reasonably be construed as serving the general good, and professional norms will therefore recommend allegiance to all three. Difficult circumstances arise when the three become misaligned so that the civil servant is forced to choose one over another or perhaps even over the other two. It is when confronting these sorts of "hard cases" that questions about the fundamental obligations of the civil servant arise.

Preliminary Clarification

I would like to begin with a clarification that may seem rather subtle, but that is actually quite important for understanding some of the constraints that structure the discussion that follows. My intention is to explore the *professional* morality of civil servants—that is, the moral obligations that arise specifically from their institutional role. The philosophical way of expressing this qualification would be to say that the inquiry is into the moral obligations of the civil servant qua civil servant (as opposed to qua individual or qua citizen). Crucial here is the thought that the institutionally defined role of the civil servant imposes not just legal obligations on the individual occupant of that role but moral obligations as well. Furthermore, these moral obligations are sometimes distinctive to the role; they are not obligations that fall on members of the public generally or even occupants of other professional roles. Thus I would like to distinguish between the demands of professional morality (that the individual is subject to qua civil servant) and those of everyday morality (that the individual is subject to qua individual).

This way of looking at things is somewhat at variance with a commonsense view, which regards the "moral problems" that civil servants typically encounter as involving a conflict between, on the one hand, some set of institutional demands (for example, an order from a superior to destroy a document), and on the other hand, some private moral conviction (for instance, the belief that the public has a "right to know" the contents of that document). Faced with such a conflict, the dominant impulse—at least among those who are outside observers to the conflict—is to recommend that the individual "do the right thing," which is to say, act in accordance with the private moral conviction. Yet this response, far from constituting a solution to the problem, is actually a reductio of the conceptual framework that generates it. If the answer to the question "When should I do what I'm told?" is simply "When what you're told to do is right," and the answer to the question "When shouldn't I do what I'm told?" is "When what you're told to do is wrong," then whatever view generates these answers is simply failing to take institutional roles seriously. Most obviously, if people actually acted this way, then organizational hierarchy would be impossible. (If people obey orders only when they happen to agree with them, then there is no point giving orders.) Thus the view is antiauthoritarian in the strict sense of the term. Now there may be something to be said for antiauthoritarianism as a social philosophy, but it stands to reason that antiauthoritarianism cannot be a governing philosophy *for employees of the state.*[4]

4. One can find a similar argument in Carol Lewis (1991, 11), criticizing what she refers to as the "integrity" approach: "When reduced to simplistic do-good exhortation, it overlooks the competing claims that perplex an ethical manager. By neglecting the decision-making environment and focusing exclusively on autonomous moral individuals, the integrity approach sweeps aside organizational and other influences that affect behavior." What she proposes, however, is a

The major problem with the antiauthoritarian stance is that it fails to acknowledge the division of moral labor that exists within our institutions. Instead of making everyone responsible for every bad thing that can happen (which frequently results in nobody doing anything), we generally find it advantageous to parcel out the tasks so that *some* people are assigned special responsibility for preventing *some* of the bad things that can happen (which more often results in somebody doing something, even if it is not the ideal intervention). The tough problems that arise all involve this institutional differentiation of role. And yet the conventional understanding of moral problems clearly fails to articulate the institutional aspect because it treats institutions as a source of demands that are entirely external to morality, and so locates morality only in the private convictions of the individual (qua individual). It never really grapples with the hard problem, which is to understand the *moral* obligations that individuals are subject to as occupants of institutional roles (Hardimon 1994).

Furthermore, it is a structural feature of this analysis that if institutional morality differs from personal or everyday morality, then it is possible for a conflict to arise between the two. This has a number of philosophical implications, the most obvious of which is that it makes the standard theories developed in the field of "normative ethics"—Kantianism, utilitarianism, and virtue theory—of limited use in thinking about professional morality. This is because these theories were all developed in an attempt to provide a rational reconstruction of everyday morality (focusing primarily on our basic norms prohibiting harm, dishonesty, and indifference to suffering). But if professional morality can conflict with everyday morality, practitioners are unlikely to regard a particular question as settled just because some course of action would conventionally be regarded as unethical. (For example, the *mere* fact that a press release is likely to mislead the public does not mean that one may not be obliged to issue it. Or the *mere* fact that a person is in desperate need does not mean that one can enroll them in a program for which they fail to meet the eligibility requirements.)[5] To the extent that normative-ethical theories are just systematizations of everyday morality, they are not likely to be regarded as any

"fusion" between a "compliance" framework and the integrity one. Fusion is an unfortunate term because it suggests that moral conduct involves meeting institutional demands halfway. This obscures the fact that the institutions themselves may be the source of the moral demands.

5. For some further examples of the sort of dilemmas that public servants may face, see Lewis 1991, 1.

more decisive by practitioners. In order to provide some useful clarification, what moral theorists need to offer is a rational reconstruction *of professional morality*.

Fundamental Approaches

As mentioned above, many of the ethics exercises undertaken in the civil service wind up producing a laundry list—that is, an unsystematic collection—of abstract values. It is therefore a common strategy in the theoretical literature, among those who adopt a "bottom-up" approach, to start with these values and then try to impose some type of systematic order on them. One influential approach involves grouping these values in accordance with the branch of government from which they originate or with whose operation they seem most strongly associated (Rosenbloom 1983). Thus it is common to distinguish juridical values (such as rights, liberty, and equality) from political values (for example, responsiveness, representativeness, and accountability), and from "bureaucratic" or "administrative" values (for instance, efficiency, economy, and effectiveness) (Christensen, Goerdel, and Nicholson-Crotty 2011; Rosenbloom and Naff 1997). Unfortunately, this taxonomic approach tends to create more problems than it solves. By associating certain values with other branches of government, it treats them as exogenous to the practice of public administration, which suggests that they should function more as external constraints than as internal features of the "ethic" of the executive branch. Moreover, by associating "bureaucratic" values like efficiency so strongly with the executive branch, it raises perplexing questions about the legitimacy of those values. Particularly when a conflict arises between democratic and bureaucratic values, it becomes difficult to see where the executive gets the authority to impose "its" values or even what could justify a balancing of the two (Denhardt 1989, 188–89). Of course this can only be answered by addressing more basic questions of political philosophy. This speaks in favor of a more "top-down" approach, starting with certain first principles, such as fundamental structures of liberal democracy, and then deriving guidance from them for the practice of public administration.

This is the approach adopted by Rohr and Terry Cooper, and in a particularly explicit form in the work of Dennis Thompson. Starting from the idea that civil servants should be committed to promoting the "public interest," the fundamental question becomes how this commitment is institutionalized. Thompson (2005) argues that different answers to this question generate three distinct models of "administrative responsibility," which he calls the hierarchical, participatory, and professional (each of which has, at one time or another as well as to varying degrees, informed the practice of public administration). In the familiar hierarchical model, accountability flows up the chain of command, ending ultimately with the elected official who presides over a particular branch of government. In parliamentary systems, this sort of model corresponds to the well-known doctrine of "ministerial accountability." The participatory model—or as I prefer to call it, the "popular" model—reverses the lines of accountability and tries to make the civil service accountable to the public directly, without the mediation of elected officials. And finally, the professional model requires that civil servants be held accountable to an independent set of professional norms, which in some form express "the universal interest of the state" (Thompson 2005, 57). (I will refer to this, for clarity, as the "vocational" model, since all three models generate a conception of professional ethics.)

These models provide a useful template for organizing the different conceptions of public administration ethics. Unlike the taxonomic approach, which is interested merely in classifying different values, these models all purport to be comprehensive, which is to say, they each purport to offer a *complete* account of the obligations of the civil servant and a framework within which conflicts of obligation can be resolved. This naturally raises the question of which one is right, or more modestly, which one offers the most persuasive reconstruction of "best practices" in the civil service. My objective in the discussion that follows will be to evaluate each of Thompson's models in these terms. The hierarchical model, I would like to suggest, is the least attractive in theory, but it remains influential as the "official ideology" of the civil service. Meanwhile, the popular model is the most attractive in theory, but the least important in practice. Thompson and Cooper are both proponents of the popular model, while Arthur Applbaum (1993) and Rohr defend what amounts to a vocational model. My own sympathies lie with the latter. The major impediment to its more widespread acceptance is that it does not tie the obligations of the civil servant directly to an explicitly democratic source of legitimacy. Thus the major burden of proof lies in showing that this should not undermine its normative authority.

The Hierarchical Model

The hierarchical model is without a doubt the most straightforward way of thinking about the obligations of the civil servant. According to this view, where the public interest lies is determined through the democratic process.

Parties and politicians compete for votes, and those who attract the most are entitled to form the government. Having formed the government, they appoint leaders to each branch of the civil service—in the parliamentary tradition, ministers. The civil servant serves the public by serving either the minister or those who exercise authority delegated by the minister. Thus allegiance and loyalty flow up the chain of command. Furthermore, there is no independent conception of the "general good" or "public interest"; these are fully exhausted by the minister's specification. The civil servant may have *private* views on the matter, but the professional ethic of the civil servant has no notion of it other than the minister's. Loyalty to the minister is not only an institutional expectation but also the *moral obligation* of the civil servant.

This model is obviously a natural fit with a Weberian model of bureaucracy (where the job of civil servants is to deliberate about "means," but not to set "ends") as well as the classic distinction between "policy" and "administration" (in which civil servants are tasked with implementing policy, but not setting it). On the latter view, expressed canonically by Woodrow Wilson (1887; see also Appleby 1947), public administration involves a neutral set of technical skills that can be applied to any goal. This is, of course, a nineteenth-century argument, which is not entirely accidental since many regard the basic view as hopelessly outdated. During the 1940s in particular, influential critiques by Carl Friedrich (1940) and Paul Appleby (1949) were taken to have demonstrated the impossibility of drawing any clear distinction between policy and administration. The perspective has, however, received some recent affirmations, such as the Armstrong Memorandum, circulated to an insubordinate civil service in the United Kingdom in 1985, which declared that "the Civil Service as such has no constitutional personality or responsibility separate from the duly constituted Government of the day" (Armstrong [1985] 1996).

Because the policy/administration distinction is considered so thoroughly discredited, the hierarchical model has received little serious consideration as an explicit conception of professional ethics.[6] This is exacerbated by the ease with which it can be dismissed, in a peremptory fashion, by "playing the Nazi card."[7] Many people have difficulty seeing how there could be any *moral*

6. Perhaps the last explicit academic defense of the model is Appleby 1952.

7. Applbaum (1995) moves from a discussion of Charles-Henri Sanson, the executioner of Paris during the French Revolution, to a fairly lengthy discussion of Nazi SS officer Adolf Eichmann and Nazi war crimes. Interestingly, the revised version of his paper, which appeared as a chapter in Applbaum's (1999) *Ethics for Adversaries*, contains no reference to the Nazis. This is,

obligation to follow orders. On the contrary, "just following orders" is more often regarded as an excuse for immorality. After all, weren't the German concentration camp guards just following orders when they made their contribution to the plan to exterminate European Jewry? Moreover, didn't the Milgram experiments show that people are far too easily influenced by authority and need to learn to exercise independent moral judgment?

The problem with this argument is that it seeks to prove too much, too quickly. From the fact that some individuals have on some occasions been given orders that are outrageous and unconscionable, it moves immediately to the conclusion that whenever anyone receives an order, they should evaluate it from the standpoint of their own moral code and obey it only if the action is considered permissible. This conclusion, as we have seen, fails to take hierarchy seriously. If part of the institutional division of the labor in the state involves giving some people special responsibility for determining what the right thing to do is, all things considered, then it necessarily follows that other people are going to have to follow orders without themselves deciding what the right thing to do is, all things considered. The alternative simply makes the division of labor impossible.

Thus the more forceful objection to the hierarchical model is not based on any principled objection to the idea of obedience to authority but rather the sense that it is no longer *realistic* given the complexity of the modern welfare state. There has always been skepticism about the idea that "policy," in any meaningful sense of the term, is set by politicians, while civil servants limit themselves to "administration" or "implementation" (Cubbon 1993, 9). There was a time when ministers could actually develop a clear understanding of how any department of government functioned, and were even in a position to personally supervise all but the lowest-level employees. The growth of the state, both in terms of scale and complexity, has made this arrangement practically impossible. This suggests that ministers are not just failing to provide guidance for civil servants that is sufficiently concrete for them to be genuinely bound by these directives but also that in principle, they cannot because they simply do not have enough information at their disposal to make expert decisions. Government departments and agencies exhibit an extreme form of what economist Oliver Williamson (1983, 31) referred to as "information impactedness" and so cannot be managed in a top-down fashion. Indeed, there is a large

I would hope, in recognition of the fact that the "Nazi card" has been played one too many times in moral philosophy and seldom helps to advance any discussion.

empirical literature focused on the question of whether and to what degree politicians exercise meaningful control over the public sector bureaucracy (Meier and O'Toole 2006).

The twentieth-century "rights revolution" also significantly increased the extent to which administrative activities were overseen by the judiciary (Sunstein 1990). As a result, civil servants are forced to think of themselves as having, at very least, two masters: elected officials and the courts. This is reflected in the fact that in practice, the civil service has found itself an important custodian of constitutional norms, frequently having to tell politicians what they can and cannot do.

Finally, there is the fact that large segments of the so-called public sector are effectively exempt from direct political control. In many areas, decision-making has been intentionally insulated from political "interference," often to counteract populist tendencies that are judged to be inimical to the formulation and implementation of good policy. One particularly striking example of this is central banking, where the governor of the central bank typically enjoys almost as much independence from democratic control as supreme court justices. The standard approach to the management of state-owned enterprises has also been to "corporatize" them, making managers accountable to an independent board of directors. In all of these different areas, the hierarchical model simply fails to correspond to the institutional reality and therefore is unable to provide useful guidance on questions of professional ethics that may arise.

The Popular Model

The idea that there has been a breakdown in the traditional relationship between elected officials and civil servants is not confined to academic observers. Since the early 1980s, wave after wave of reform movements in the civil service have been initiated, all of them loosely based on the idea that the traditional "ministerial accountability" (or "congressional oversight") model had become unrealistic and unworkable, given the realities—particularly the scale—of the modern administrative state. Furthermore, as the civil service began to provide more and more services directly to the public (health, education, transportation, pensions, and so on), it seemed increasingly strained to suggest that the lines of accountability in frontline service organizations should run up the organizational hierarchy, through the minister and parliament, and then back to the public through periodic elections. It seemed to many that the lines of accountability should be reversed so that they ran down instead of up. Why not have direct accountability to the public for the delivery of government services? This would appear to promote, at the very least, a government that was more responsive to the needs of its citizens. (This line of thinking received additional support from the influence of the "customer service revolution" in private sector management, which was also concerned with the tendency of large organizations to become unresponsive to the public that they served (Jos and Tompkins 2009).

Thompson (2005, 61) refers to this as the "participatory" model of accountability, although I prefer the term "popular" in order to emphasize that it came in both right- and left-wing versions. Both shared a desire to reverse the direction of accountability in the civil service so that it would run down to the public instead of up to elected officials. The left-wing version tried to do this by increasing citizen participation in executive decision-making through exercises in direct and deliberative democracy. The right-wing version tried to do the same by focusing on economic incentives, giving the public the ability to "vote with its pocketbook" and tying the compensation of public sector managers to their ability to satisfy these demands. (Forming a parent's council at a local public school in order to advise on curriculum choice would be an example of the former; the introduction of charter schools with competing curricula and tying funding to the number of students enrolled would be an illustration of the latter.)

New Public Management

The most sustained attempt to implement right-wing populist reforms occurred under Margaret Thatcher in the United Kingdom when as prime minister, she created the template for a set of "new public management" arrangements that were subsequently imitated in many other parliamentary democracies (and in somewhat delayed form, as the "reinventing government" movement in the United States [Osborne and Gaebler 1993]). The traditional public sector employment model is characterized—from the middle management level up—by dull pecuniary incentives combined with a "professional ethic" that is supposed to motivate high levels of dedication and work effort. What many critics of this model were inclined to see instead were simply dull incentives generating a low level of work effort. Their goal was therefore to craft a sharper set of incentives, keyed in to the specific performances that the public would want to elicit. The most important reform initiative involved breaking up traditional departments and transforming portions of them into independent agencies, which would no longer be under direct ministerial control. The goal was to shift the public service away from a more process-oriented model toward an outcome-oriented one of administration. Under the slogan "let managers manage," the heads of these agencies were to be given significantly more discretion and control over most aspects of the operations. In return, they were expected to engage in explicit contracting with the government and implement a set of performance measures that would allow for more precise evaluation of their activities. This was typically accompanied by compensation arrangements tied to these performance measures.

Had this initiative been more successful, we might now be thinking of some kind of "responsiveness to the public" as the most appropriate way to understand the moral obligations of civil servants. The general consensus, however, is that the new public management succeeded in changing little in the way that the civil service operates. In some cases this was explicitly acknowledged; many of the independent agencies that were created were folded back into the departments from which they emerged. Some of this was due to the realization on the part of ministers that they were still being blamed when things went wrong in these nominally independent agencies. As a result, elected officials began to reassert managerial control. In other instances the separation never really occurred; civil servants simply worked around the new organizational structures in order to preserve traditional lines of accountability (Graham and Roberts 2004; Savoie 1995).

The most significant problem with the new public management model involved, again, the information impactedness of modern state bureaucracies. Incentives are easy to create. The tricky part is to create the *correct* incentives in order to encourage the behavior that one wants to encourage and discourage the behavior that one wants to discourage. In order to do this, one needs to have *information* about what one's nominal subordinates are doing. The theoretical literature on principal-agent theory establishes this result in an economical fashion: sharp incentives based on bad information are generally worse than dull incentives. While dull incentives may fail to motivate people to do the right thing, sharp incentives based on bad information will encourage them to do the wrong thing (and furthermore, may "crowd out" whatever moral incentives they have to do the right thing) (Harris-McLeod 2013). This suggests that before implementing a performance pay scheme in order to "incentivize" employees, one must be extraordinarily confident about one's own information state.

It is difficult to see how there could be any basis for such confidence throughout most of the public sector except when it comes to the management of the lowest-level service employees. The problems that the state gets called on to fix are typically the most intractable, frequently because the costs and benefits are the hardest to identify, measure, and control. It is no wonder, then, that it is so difficult to develop a set of "performance measures" to assess the civil service. If the "outputs" could be measured so easily, then there would seldom be any reason for the work to be done in the public sector. This was, in some ways, what wound up being discovered. One of the major institutional legacies of new public management was extensive contracting out and the development of purchaser/provider splits, which were in many cases a salutary development. And yet as a model of public sector management, new public management turned out to be hugely deficient. Not only did it fail to take seriously the information problems faced in any large-scale bureaucracy, it failed almost completely to consider the specific information challenges faced by the public sector.

Participatory Government

The participatory version of the popular model was based on a healthy skepticism about the power of incentives (combined, in many cases, with a somewhat hypertrophied aversion to anything that resembled a "market" pattern of organization). Thus a variety of initiatives were undertaken aimed at involving the public more directly in decision-making. There was, of course, the long-standing tradition of holding public hearings in order to solicit *input* from the public, particularly before a controversial decision was made. These were early on expanded to include tools developed in the field of market research, such as public surveys and focus groups. Many of the deliberative initiatives, however, were designed to go beyond mere consultation in order to give the public some degree of control over decision-making. As such, traditional measures like citizen ballot initiatives were supplemented with negotiated rule-making exercises, citizen review panels, citizen advisory committees, and citizen juries or panels (Fiorino 1990).[8]

There is widespread acknowledgment that this increase in direct participation by citizens can have valuable effects. First and foremost, it helps to

8. For an overview of the relative merits of different procedures, see Rowe and Frewer 2000.

provide better information to policy makers so that goods and services being provided by the state more closely match the actual needs and desires of the public. It can also prove quite valuable in persuading communities to accept the results of decision-making exercises. Hence in both respects, public involvement serves to facilitate the provision of more "responsive" government. At the same time, it is difficult to find anyone willing to claim that this type of citizen participation allows the public to exercise any sort of effective *control* over state bureaucracies or that participatory institutions are able to function as a governance mechanism.[9] (Even Thompson [2005, 66], who is quite sympathetic to these initiatives, admits that "the model bristles with problems.")

Most troublesome is the fact that anything less than the most controlled deliberative initiatives are unlikely to attract a representative sample of the population. The standard public choice model of regulatory capture is based on the observation that concentrated interests will tend to win out over diffuse interests in the quest for political favors simply because they are subject to less serious collective action problems when mobilizing to advance their interests. As a result, the tendency of the political system as a whole will be to generate the exploitation of the unorganized by the organized. One of the major functions of traditional democratic institutions is to diminish the advantage going to the organized—to counteract the fact that "the public," in the most general sense of the term, is at a structural disadvantage when it comes to defending its interests. Thus any participatory model is going to have to explain how groups that are diffuse and unorganized are supposed to assert themselves. Especially given that participation in public consultation is both costly and time-consuming, the deliberative model seems more likely to exacerbate the collective action problems faced by these large groups than to help resolve them. Unless it functions with handpicked representatives (the way that some citizens' assemblies do), participatory forms of decision-making would seem to suffer, at the very least, from a squeaky wheel bias. Generally speaking, the individuals who show up to participate will be those whose time has a low opportunity cost (such as retirees) or else those with a significant economic stake in the decision (like industry representatives). This has long been observed as a defect of public hearings, namely that the "public" one would like to hear from is typically not the "public" that shows up (Checkoway 1981, 568–69; Fiorino 1990, 231).

9. An exception would be Fung 2004.

There is also the fact that public participation seems to be incapable of serving as a genuine governance mechanism. It is one thing for the public to be called on to provide *input* and quite another to expect that same public to exercise *control* over the behavior of public servants. The problem is that effective governance is time-consuming and resource intensive, and so "the public" faces a serious collective action problem when it comes to exercising governance, or even acquiring the information and expertise that are its prerequisite. In many cases, if the public could spontaneously organize to exercise effective governance over the officials charged with resolving a particular collective action problem, then it could probably also resolve the collective action problem directly, without the need for state officials. This is one of the issues that motivated the movement toward "representative bureaucracy" (Dolan and Rosenbloom 2003). The thought was that if the bureaucracy could be reconstituted in such a way that it more closely resembled the public, then its own internal deliberative processes might substitute for the more problematic ones involving the actual public. This is, of course, not an unreasonable ambition, but it constitutes a tacit acknowledgment of the limits of the participatory approach.

Implications

All of this institutional detail should not be allowed to obscure the basic point. With the growing complexity of government and declining trust in democratic institutions, there has been a natural tendency to turn away from hierarchical organizational forms and imagine that a more responsible, more responsive civil service could be created by promoting an organizational culture in which public employees are held directly accountable to the public that they serve. While the associated institutional reforms have no doubt led to a number of improvements in the operations of government (for instance, the "flattening" of organizational structures, increased public consultation, greater focus on quality service delivery, and so on), attempts to change the structures of *accountability*, to make the civil service literally accountable or answerable to the public, have not been met with great success, and in some cases have been an abject failure. In the end, both left- and right-wing populist models had the tendency to free public managers from control by elected officials without substituting any sort of effective control by the public. Because direct accountability to the public has been so difficult to institutionalize and is in direct tension with accountability to elected officials, a civil service *ethic* that encourages public sector employees to think of their moral obligations in terms of service to "citizens" or "the people" threatens to create a situation of enormous indeterminacy. One must put into place at least some effective procedures for determining what "the public" wants or needs, otherwise this kind of an ethic winds up being equivalent to saying to the civil servant "do what you think is right."

The Vocational Model

This brings us finally to the third model of public sector morality—that is, the vocational one.[10] The need for "professional" ethics arises when there is a class of workers engaged in tasks where a division of labor is advantageous, but information asymmetries make it impossible (or exceedingly costly) for a principal to effectively supervise an agent or assess the quality of their work. In such cases, the external control system must be supplemented with an internal one, which motivates the agent to a good faith performance of the task. In some instances, this can take the form of a set of principles that enjoin no more than loyalty to the principal's expressed goals. In other situations, however, the information asymmetries are so significant that the principal may not know what goals they should be seeking or may not know how to translate a more abstract set of interests into an actionable set of goals. Hence the professional group must come up with its own, relatively autonomous description of what counts as doing the job well and what counts as doing it poorly. Physicians, for example, do not merely carry out the desires of their patients but instead define a "standard of care," which is used to guide many aspects of clinical decision-making and resource allocation. Of course, the goals of the principal (that is, the patient) figure prominently within this system of professional norms, but the point is that the norms are not merely subordinate or instrumental to the realization of those goals.

In the case of civil servants, professional morality is also just as clearly organized around an *independent* conception of what it means to do the job well. One must, as Applbaum (1993, 550) maintains, start by asking, "What values and purposes does the institution of the role of public servant aim to realize?"

10. Friedrich (1940) probably made the first attempt to articulate such a model. His model differs from my own in that it does not attempt to articulate a professional ethics specific to the public service but rather in keeping with the "scientific management" fashion of the day, tries to assimilate public sector professionalism to that of science.

The answer, generally speaking, will be that the civil servant's role is to serve the state, not just in any way, but in such a way as to help the state achieve *its* purposes. These purposes, in turn, cannot be defined as simply "whatever the minister says" or "whatever the government of the day happens to want" because our system of governance is not one of unlimited popular sovereignty. Thus as Applbaum (1993, 550) goes on to observe, answering the question about the role of the civil servant requires "at least a rough notion of legitimacy, justice, and goodness in government." Furthermore, this notion must necessarily be *prior* to whatever specific political ideologies acquire influence through the democratic process, precisely because it is these background notions that will specify the particular role that democracy is to be assigned in the overall state structure (most important, it determines which decisions will be made democratically and which will not).[11] So while the professional ethic of civil servants must accord a crucial place to the goals of elected officials, it is not entirely subordinate to those aims.

The obvious objection to this analysis is that modern liberal societies are characterized by pluralism with respect to fundamental values and therefore the liberal state has no single "purpose," or at least none that can be specified uncontroversially (Overeem and Verhoef 2014; see also Spicer 2010; Wagenaar 1999). The dominant response among proponents of the state-centric model has not been to deny this but rather to observe that a liberal state is nevertheless committed to certain principles, which are thin enough to be neutral with respect to the most contested values and yet thick enough to serve as the basis for a robust conception of civil service morality. Rohr refers to these as "regime values" and claims (in a US context) that they are articulated most clearly in the Constitution. He therefore advocates a form civil service morality organized around a commitment to the constitutional values of "equality," "freedom," and "property," further specified through careful attention to US Supreme Court jurisprudence.

There are various problems with this formulation, but it is perhaps sufficient to observe that it does not generalize well beyond the US context, particularly not to countries that have no written constitution or supreme court

11. This is a somewhat elaborate way of saying that the correct answer to the question "What is the purpose of the state?" cannot be "Whatever the current government says it is." This is because the set of procedures that generated "the government" were put in place in order to achieve certain purposes—and may be changed if they fail to do so. They are, as a result, necessarily prior to the will of any particular government.

review of legislation. Thus the more common approach has been to identify a "political morality" for civil servants based on abstract liberal principles, as both Kathryn Denhardt (1989) and in a somewhat different way Applbaum have suggested. The obvious candidate would be something like John Rawls's theory of justice, which is intended to be neutral with respect to the various private moral views (or "comprehensive doctrines") held by citizens.[12] If this approach has a weakness, it is that it relies too heavily on an abstract philosophical reconstruction of the sort of expectations we have about the state—one that in many cases, the state fails to satisfy. A more reconstructive approach would focus instead on practices in an attempt to articulate the understandings that inform existing professional morality as well as the more general normative commitments of the executive branch. For instance, the development of cost-benefit analysis for projects in the public sector (and related techniques, such as cost-effectiveness in health care) was in almost all cases something that arose from and was mandated by the executive branch. (Legislatures have often been cool to the practice, and in many instances, specifically exempt legislation from it.[13] Courts frequently exhibit even more dramatic disregard, particularly when dealing with issues that touch on "rights," which they take to preclude consideration of costs and benefits.) So one might begin by attempting to articulate the normative commitments underlying these practices, which appear to be endogenous to the executive branch.

Another way of approaching the question would be to concentrate on the *legitimacy* of the state, because this taps into broader public perceptions and expectations about the role of the state in society. In other words, the focus on legitimacy provides a different angle of approach for answering the questions of what the purposes of the state are and what "goodness" in government consists in. One can then ask the more specific question of what role the executive plays in securing state legitimacy. Recent philosophical literature on the state has been marked by an overwhelming emphasis on democracy and democratic practices

12. Ideally, it should also be neutral with respect to the partisan ideological positions taken by various political parties, although Rawls's specific conception of justice obviously fails this test (the difference principle articulates a controversial egalitarian commitment). The principles that I articulate below are intended to be "more neutral" in this regard.

13. Prominent US examples include the original Clean Air Act, Americans with Disabilities Act, and Affordable Care and Patient Protection Act (that is, "Obamacare"), all of which rule out cost-benefit analysis for certain decisions.

as the source of legitimacy. This often translates, crudely, into an inability to conceive of ways that the exercise of state power could be legitimate except through the democratic election of the person exercising the power or delegation of authority from a person so elected. From this perspective, the legitimacy of the executive branch is entirely dependent on the legitimacy generated by the legislature through its periodic election. This naturally lends support to the hierarchical model. This is, however, not the only way to think about legitimacy (Sharman 2008). Indeed, it is widely held that the judiciary makes its own, distinctive contribution to the overall legitimacy of the state (one that is not reducible to the fact that judges are appointed by democratically elected politicians) by ensuring that the rule of law is respected, treatment of citizens is fair and transparent, individual rights are respected, and powers exercised by the legislature are appropriately circumscribed in accordance with constitutional norms.

My own view is that the executive branch also makes a distinctive contribution to the legitimacy of the state, and one that is not reducible to its role in facilitating democratic governance. As Ian Shapiro (2016, 46) has argued, an important aspect of the legitimacy of any political order "depends on the problems it solves, and promises to solve, for people who are subject to it."[14] A state that holds democratic elections, but is unable to guarantee security, electricity, or basic sanitation to the population, is likely to suffer a deficit of legitimacy. This is because the state is the central agent of *collective action* in the society, and citizens naturally look to it to solve a certain set of collective action problems—solutions that are not only preconditions for the emergence of stable democratic institutions but create the social conditions required for the development of nonstate solutions to many other problems too. This aspect of legitimacy has been discussed rather extensively in the case of the European Union, which exercises regulatory powers that in many ways outstrip its democratic legitimacy.[15] Fritz Scharpf, for instance, has distinguished between "input" and "output" legitimacy, where the former is established through procedures that give citizens input or "voice" in the political process, while the latter is established through the actual problems confronted by citizens in their

14. The passage continues with "far more than on when, how and by whom it was created" (Shapiro 2016, 46).

15. There has also been some discussion of the issue with respect to transnational institutions. For example, Ruth Grant and Robert Keohane (2005) articulate seven different ways that organizations can be accountable *other* than classic democratic accountability.

day-to-day lives that the state is able to solve. In Scharpf's (2000) view, the central requirement of output legitimacy is "that government should be capable of achieving effective solutions to collective-action problems."

From this concept of output legitimacy, one can develop the notion of the civil service having a job to do—one that can be specified independently of the particular wishes of the government of the day. If the central role of the state in modern societies is to solve the most intractable collective action problems—where individual contracting and informal community action fail—then there will also be substantive normative principles governing administrative action, which arise from the purposes that the state is committed to pursuing. When it comes to resolving collective action problems, the central principle (or perhaps better yet, the guiding idea) is that of Pareto efficiency.[16] This is the rule that says that if it is possible to make some people better off (by their own lights) without making anyone else worse off (again, by their own lights), then one should do so. Collective action problems are simply cases where due to the structure of the interaction, individuals fail to bring about a Pareto efficient outcome through self-interested action. This gives individuals each a reason to accept some form of constraint on their actions on the grounds that when everyone does so, it results in an outcome that is better for all, including themselves.

Thus one can think of the three branches of government as each making its own contribution to the overall legitimacy of the state, animated by its own central principles. The important point is that the executive branch is not just a neutral bystander or servant of the legislature. The executive brings something distinctive to the table in the same way that the judiciary does, and that must be weighed against the contributions and demands made by the other branches. As such, when civil servants exercise discretion or are in a position to influence the policy-making process, their professional morality impels them to act in a way that is guided by these fundamental commitments of the executive branch.

Articulating Best Practices

It is important to keep in mind when talking about the ethics of public administration that the issue is not one of private moral conviction but rather professional norms. In other words, the *ethic* of public administration is already institutionalized in the *practice* of public administration. Civil servants are often in a position where they can abuse their power. In some countries they take

16. For a more extensive discussion, see Heath 2001.

advantage of these opportunities, giving rise to the problem of official corruption. In countries that have achieved relatively noncorrupt governing systems, it is seldom because they have put in place more effective incentive systems; rather, it is because they have developed a professional morality among civil servants that limits these abuses. Thus one of the characteristics of successful or well-governed societies is that they have already institutionalized a strong "ethic" of public administration. The problem is that we lack a cogent theoretical articulation of these commitments. This does not prevent the reproduction of those norms, which continues to occur, somewhat inchoately, through informal socialization in the workplace. It does, however, create difficulties when conflicts occur, institutional reforms are proposed that run "against the grain," or the civil service is called on to explain its practices to the public. The present review, while attempting to advance our understanding, no doubt reveals that we are in a preliminary stage of our efforts to articulate the general ethos that pervades the civil service.

Acknowledgments

Research assistance provided by Hamish Russell. Thanks as well for discussion and comments from Mel Cappe, Alex Himelfarb, Wayne Norman, Andrew Stark, and Sareh Pouryousefi as well as audiences at Carlton University, the Princeton Center for Human Values, and the School of Public Policy and Governance at the University of Toronto.

References

Applbaum, Arthur. 1993. "The Remains of the Role." *Governance* 6 (4): 545–57.

———. 1995. "Professional Detachment: The Executioner of Paris." *Harvard Law Review* 109 (2): 458–86.

———. 1999. *Ethics for Adversaries*. Princeton, NJ: Princeton University Press.

Appleby, Paul. 1947. "Toward Better Public Administration." *Public Administration Review* 7 (2): 93–99.

———. 1949. *Policy and Administration*. Tuscaloosa: University of Alabama Press.

———. 1952. *Morality and Administration in Democratic Government*. Baton Rouge: Louisiana State University Press.

Armstrong, Robert. (1985) 1996. "The Armstrong Memorandum." https://www.civilservant.org.uk/library/1996_Armstrong_Memorandum.pdf.

Carpenter, Daniel. 2001. *The Forging of Bureaucratic Autonomy*. Princeton, NJ: Princeton University Press.

———. 2010. *Reputation and Power*. Princeton, NJ: Princeton University Press.

Checkoway, Barry. 1981. "The Politics of Public Hearings." *Journal of Applied Behavioral Science* 17 (4): 566–82.

Christensen, Robert, Holly Goerdel, and Shaun Nicholson-Crotty. 2011. "Management, Law, and the Pursuit of the Public Good in Public Administration." *Journal of Public Administration Research and Theory* 21 (1): i125–40.

Cooper, Terry. 2006. *The Responsible Administrator*. 5th ed. San Francisco: Jossey-Bass.

Cubbon, Brian. 1993. "The Duty of the Professional." In *Ethics in Public Service*, edited by Richard A. Chapman, 7–14. Edinburgh: Edinburgh University Press.

Denhardt, Kathryn G. 1989. "The Management of Ideals: A Political Perspective on Ethics." *Public Administration Review* 42 (2): 187–93.

Dolan, Julie, and David Rosenbloom. 2003. *Representative Bureaucracy: Classic Readings and Continuing Controversies*. Armonk, NY: M. E. Sharpe.

Fiorino, Daniel J. 1990. "Citizen Participation and Environmental Risk: A Survey of Institutional Mechanisms." *Science, Technology, and Human Values* 15 (2): 226–43.

Friedrich, Carl J. 1940. "Public Policy and the Nature of Administrative Responsibility." In *Public Policy*, edited by Carl J. Friedrich and Edward S. Mason, 3–24. Cambridge, MA: Harvard University Press.

Fung, Archon. 2004. *Empowered Participation*. Princeton, NJ: Princeton University Press.

Graham, Andrew, and Alasdair Roberts. 2004. "The Agency Concept in North America." In *Unbundled Government*, edited by Christopher Pollitt and Colin Talbot, 157–63. New York: Routledge.

Grant, Ruth, and Robert Keohane. 2005. "Accountability and Abuses of Power in World Politics." *American Political Science Review* 99 (1): 29–43.

Hardimon, Michael O. 1994. "Role Obligations." *Journal of Philosophy* 91 (7): 333–63.

Harris-McLeod, Emily. 2013. "Incentives for Public Service Workers and the Implications of Crowding Out Theory." *Public Policy and Governance Review* 4 (2): 5–21.

Heath, Joseph. 2001. *The Efficient Society*. Toronto: Penguin Books.

Jos, Philip H., and Mark E. Tompkins. 2009. "Keeping It Public: Defending Public Service Values in a Customer Service Age." *Public Administration Review* 69 (6): 1077–86.

Lewis, Carol W. 1991. *The Ethics Challenge in Public Service*. San Francisco: Jossey-Bass.

Meier, Kenneth, and Laurence O'Toole. 2006. "Political Control versus Bureaucratic Values: Reframing the Debate." *Public Administration Review* 66 (2): 177–92.

Osborne, David, and Ted Gaebler. 1993. *Reinventing Government*. New York: Penguin Books.

Overeem, Patrick, and Jelle Verhoef. 2014. "Moral Dilemmas, Theoretical Confusion: Value Pluralism and Its Supposed Implications for Public Administration." *Administration and Society* 46 (8): 986–1009.

Rohr, James A. 1989. *Ethics for Bureaucrats*. 2nd ed. New York: Marcel Dekker.

Rosenbloom, David H. 1983. "Public Administration Theory and the Separation of Powers." *Public Administration Review* 43 (3): 219–27.

Rosenbloom, David H., and Katherine Naff. 1997. *Public Administration and Law*. 2nd ed. New York: Marcel Dekker.

Rowe, Gene, and Lynn J. Frewer. 2000. "Public Participation Methods: A Framework for Evaluation." *Science, Technology, and Human Values* 25 (1): 3–29.

Savoie, Donald J. 1995. "What Is Wrong with the New Public Management?" *Canadian Public Administration* 38 (1): 112–21.

Scharpf, Fritz W. 2000. "Interdependence and Democratic Legitimation." In *Disaffected Democracies*, edited by Susan J. Pharr and Robert D. Putnam, 101–20. Princeton, NJ: Princeton University Press.

Shapiro, Ian. 2016. *Politics against Domination*. Cambridge, MA: Harvard University Press.

Sharman, Campbell. 2008. "Political Legitimacy for an Appointed Senate." Institute for Research on Public Policy, September 23. https://irpp.org/research-studies/choices-vol14-no11/.

Spicer, Michael W. 2010. *In Defense of Politics in Public Administration*. Tuscaloosa: University of Alabama Press.

Sunstein, Cass. 1990. *After the Rights Revolution*. Cambridge, MA: Harvard University Press.

Thompson, Dennis. 1985. "The Possibility of Administrative Ethics." *Public Administration Review* 45 (5): 555–61.

———. 2005. *Restoring Responsibility: Ethics in Business, Government and Healthcare*. Cambridge: Cambridge University Press.

Treasury Board of Canada. 2011. *Value and Ethics Code for the Public Sector*. https://www.tbs-sct.gc.ca/pubs_pol/hrpubs/tb_851/vec-cve-eng.pdf.

Wagenaar, Hendrik. 1999. "Value Pluralism in Public Administration." *Administrative Theory and Praxis* 21 (4): 441–49.

Williamson, Oliver E. 1983. *Markets and Hierarchies*. New York: Free Press.

Wilson, Woodrow. 1887. "The Study of Administration." *Political Science Quarterly* 2 (2): 197–222.

Zacka, Bernardo. 2017. *When the State Meets the Street*. Cambridge, MA: Harvard University Press.

8

Political Corruption

Elizabeth David-Barrett & Mark Philp

CASES OF CORRUPTION are among the most public of failures of political ethics. Their condemnation invokes powerful ethical judgments and can provoke wide public protests, forcing resignations and ruining political careers. Yet the discourse around political corruption belies the contested nature of the concept, and the extent to which the standards for conduct vary according to time and place. Some political cultures seem to tolerate what others condemn, while some traditions of thinking about politics, such as classical republican theory, invoke ideals of disinterested civic virtue in the pursuit of the common good that so categorically reject self-seeking behavior, it hardly seems a plausible account of agent motivation except under extremely rare conditions. Certainly in most modern states, people in public service need payment, want careers, and are influenced by status considerations as well as a range of forms of recognition and reward. They are not literally "selfless." Nor are their political masters. It is less clear, however, how much "self" is permissible.

As distinctions between politics, government, and administration have evolved, and the public realm has been differentiated from the private, concerns about the bribery and corruption of those in public office and positions of authority have grown. This is unsurprising; anxieties about the decay of the nature of the political domain have become more precise and articulate as the nature of that domain has been more fully elaborated (Philp 1997, 2015). Most publics become concerned when their systems fail to deliver on their promises, subvert the rule of law, or violate expectations and principles that are central to the popular legitimacy of their system of government, and where they do so because those in power pursue their own interests rather than the public good. Nor is the anxiety wholly a popular one; politicians, too, become concerned when the systems they govern fail to implement their commands, where their opponents misuse state resources to hold onto political power, and when votes and voters are bought and sold. And those in administration may also develop concerns about their office being used for inappropriate ends by their political bosses or subject to inappropriate pressures from those outside the formal political system.

Administrative office is often heavily regulated, but in most modern political systems, political office has also become increasingly subject to certain types of regulation—concerning how politicians finance their campaigns, the kind of gifts they may receive, the degree of favoritism they can show in their appointments, the way they make policy and implement decisions, and so on. Where the mass media is relatively free, it is common to find accusations of corruption whenever politicians are seen to violate or bend the rules for personal or political gain, or abuse their position to cover up earlier misdemeanors or errors. These developments mean that the language of political corruption has become part of an internal policing system for political and administrative conduct that while formally often technical in respect to the precise rules and expectations of office, also operates both much more loosely and more critically in wider public discourse, where it may be linked to strong partisan commitments and even used as a political weapon. In different states, different practices are identified as inappropriate, but there is general agreement that corruption involves violations of existing political and administrative rules and norms, serves interests that should not be served by that office, and fails to serve others that should, and that this consequently distorts the legitimate political process.

Popular claims about corruption frequently draw on wider evaluative languages, such as concerns about deviations from the pursuit of the common good (which derive from early modern republicanism), suspicions about the purity of the motives of those who govern us (which derive in part from reformation critiques of church and scriptural corruption), discourses that emphasize officeholding as a position of trust and on the necessity of selfless public service, and libertarian concerns about government interference in areas of free exchange. These traditions fuel a wide but multistranded, often contradictory public discourse in which a great deal of politics can look distinctly sordid and in need of cleaning up.

The exact standards for probity in political conduct vary from one political system to another, reflecting the distinctive historical paths that states take and the political settlements that have been reached to resolve conflicts. Scholars are often concerned that this local variation requires us to endorse relativism and abandon a critical perspective on local practices, and this has encouraged the academic literature to try to identify more general standards that are posited as implicit in claims about corruption and against which we can judge acts corrupt (even when not locally condemned). One of the most recent arguments is Bo Rothstein's claim that departures from impartiality lie at the core of corruption. When public servants act with bias or partiality, they corrupt the impartiality of the legitimate process for the allocation of services and contracts (Rothstein 2011; Rothstein and Varraich 2017). While deeply plausible as a standard for public administration in mature liberal democratic states, the proposal fails to recognize the inevitably partisan character of politics (as against administration), and has little or nothing to say about corruption in politics where individuals have legitimate partisan commitments.

Other proposals have linked corruption with the absence of transparency (Warren 2004), associated it with the suborning of the democratic process (Thompson 1993), identified it with acts that (however motivated) damage the purposes of an organization (Lessig 2013), or treated it as tracking the more fundamental concept of evil (Underkuffler 2013), and so on. These approaches try to identify a single standard of evaluation by which to assess conduct in office despite the fact that standards in public—and especially political office—vary considerably across countries and over time. They also assume that it is possible to find consensus among the well motivated about such a standard, thereby ignoring the political and contested character of standards in politics, and fail to recognize that any consensus on principle must itself be *politically* forged in what is an intrinsically contestable process.

In this chapter, we argue that the concept of political corruption cannot provide a set of clear and universal standards of conduct to guide those in government and administration. Our collective tendency to deny this and behave as if standards are uncontentious can itself be an obstacle to recognizing the complex factors that shape conduct in political life. We develop our contention in five major steps. First, we identify the failures of economic approaches to corruption that have dominated the literature over the last thirty years, and second, the two central dimensions of politics (drawing on political realism) that demonstrate the core contestability of standards in politics. Next we explore the character of conflicts of interest, and suggest the increasing problems we face in identifying and regulating such interests in neoliberal systems of governance. Fourth, we discuss the tensions involved in the move to focus more on building integrity, manifested in many countries by the introduction of codes of conduct. And fifth, we examine the question of motives in the exercise of office and how to elicit changes in political culture. We conclude by making the case for a more realist, more "local," and less ambitious approach to the understanding of probity and corruption in political conduct.

Economic Approaches and Their Limits

Prior to the late 1980s, the literature on corruption was largely to be found in political science, and it revolved, especially in the United States, around questions of local and city administrations and party funding. There was a debate about the extent to which corrupt transactions could be functional in certain conditions for countries in the developing world, but otherwise there was little interest in the topic on the part of economists. This changed dramatically when the World Bank, which had previously seen corruption as a political issue and therefore not within its remit, announced that corruption was proving a major obstacle to economic growth, and as such, something that the bank (which is apolitical by its charter) could and would be concerned about understanding and combating. This shift in policy followed the formation in 1993 of Transparency International, a new international nongovernmental organization set up by a former member of the bank's team, Peter Eigen, together with other development economists who had been disillusioned by the bank's unwillingness to tackle the issue. These developments, and the taking up of the issue by the Organization for Economic Cooperation and Development, led to an explosion in the economics literature on corruption, relying heavily on public choice concepts and methods in its study; it also fueled the rapid growth of an international anticorruption industry (Michael and Bowser 2010). At the same time, and connected to a "democratization" agenda that emerged after the end of the Cold War, Western governments both adopted and advocated a range of regulatory mechanisms based on this approach, aimed at increasing the accountability of government officials and politicians, coupled with the removal of government interference in the operation of free markets.

Economic accounts began by defining corruption in terms of individual uses of public office to maximize personal income (Leff 1964; van Klaveren 1989). That definition confuses the explanation of corruption with its definition. For an act to be corrupt, it cannot simply be income maximizing; it must be income maximizing in a context in which prior conceptions of public office and principles for its conduct define income maximizing as corrupt. That means that we must look elsewhere for a definition of probity and its corruption—a challenge that economists have largely ignored.

Economic approaches also see individual behavior in cost-benefit terms, and it is assumed that the agent follows or breaks norms and rules according to a calculation of rational self-interest (with the corollary that we can reduce corruption by altering incentives and disincentives). This conception denies an essential aspect of the character of norms and rules. Norms and rules have salience for the individual independent of whether they maximize self-interest, and our behavior in following norms and rules is better explained by an alternative approach that sees our actions as taking place within "logics of appropriateness" (March and Olsen 2004). (Imagine someone playing chess whose only motive is to win and who has a wholly prudential attitude to obeying the rules. Such a player could have no conception of cheating; indeed, it is unclear that they could have a conception of what it is to play chess!) For a norm/rule to exist is for it to be recognized as a prima facie guide to conduct. Rules may be violated for self-interested reasons, but to understand compliance and noncompliance wholly in terms of self-interest maximizing behavior is to deny that something has the status of a rule or norm.

In both of these cases, questions about the weight of norms and rules, and probity and misconduct, raise deeper questions about the character of institutional culture as well as individual intentions and motives for compliance. Yet much of the work in economics has ignored these issues, tended to assume that corruption could be equated with bribery or the abuse of entrusted power for private gain, and relied heavily on Transparency International's Corruption Perceptions Index along with a range of quantitative measures of social phenomena to build explanations and models. Only relatively recently have more behavioral approaches (which we discuss below) come to the fore with experimental economics, for example, seeking to examine how people actually behave and how their behavior can be shaped by different institutional setups (Serra and Wantchekon 2012). There nevertheless remains rather little in the way of field research to shed light on how the conduct of serving officeholders is influenced by formal norms and the requirements of office, and still less evidence on how social expectations and group norms interact with more formal requirements.

Fundamental to the economic approach is the use of principal-agent theory to model corruption and underpin the design of anticorruption tools. Principal-agent theory explores relationships in which one actor (the principal, P) employs an agent (A) to act on their behalf where information about A's behavior is asymmetrical since P cannot observe everything that A does (and A has knowledge and skills that P lacks). The model is typically used in a way that the public is seen as the principal, which seeks to control agents—public officials and politicians. Economic theory generally argues that A will act optimally for P only when doing so coincides with A's own interests. This model has encouraged the development of a range of anticorruption tools that seek to reduce the scope of agent discretion and monopoly power by increasing A's accountability to P (Klitgaard 1991). That proposal, however, ignores the extent to which increasing accountability also risks eliminating the institutions of trust that are an essential component of forms of public authority (Philp 2001). It therefore carries the risk that modes of regulating politics on this basis will undermine rather than further the aim of creating conditions in which public integrity can flourish.

More damagingly, these accounts tend to focus on one principal-agent problem while unintentionally creating others—such as, if you don't trust rulers, you police them, but if you don't trust the police (among whom some of the most entrenched forms of corruption have been found), you have to police *them*, and so on (Anechiarico and Jacobs 1996). Scholars have also pointed out that in contexts of systemic corruption, there might not be any "principled principals" (Persson, Rothstein, and Teorell 2013), and that even citizens may not necessarily be interested in trying to hold leaders to the rules of office but may instead be open to informality so long as it benefits them and their group (Bauhr 2017; Peiffer and Alvarez 2016). In addition, the model assumes that the principal has a single set of ordered preferences or interests, which is not exactly the situation of most mass publics in the world. And where members of the principal (the public) see their interests and objectives in different ways, an agent will face conflicting imperatives and is often able to exploit that situation to their advantage—for example, by casting doubt on the motives of those who seek to hold them to account. The model tends to assume that people agree on the importance of good governance, but in practice, few people are committed to such abstract ideas; rather, they are concerned with getting institutions to work in their interests as far as possible.

A More Realist Approach

Economic approaches tend to assume clarity about interests and objectives as well as incentives and rewards. And they assume that the principal writes the rules that its agents must follow. But for political theorists concerned with standards of conduct in politics (especially in politics as opposed to public administration, although the former has a major impact on the latter), there are two basic problems in discussions of political corruption that must be acknowledged. The first is that corruption involves the violation of standards (rules or norms) deemed natural or essential to a domain of activity, and *political* corruption involves the violation of those rules and norms that are central to the domain of politics. Yet those standards, rules, and norms, particularly those that secure sovereignty in the state, are politically forged and imposed. To a significant extent, those in politics have the power to make and interpret the rules that they abide by, and are engaged in an ongoing contest to determine the essential character and ends of the "game" that they are playing. Various states have sought ways to establish rule-making and enforcement bodies that are "above" politics, such as supreme courts, but where these are enabled to control the formal political order, they too become politicized and contested. The "bending" or reinterpretation of the formal processes of politics in the name of populism has, for example, been a feature of the Donald J. Trump presidency and his bid for reelection in the United States, Viktor Orbán's rule in Hungary, and Recep Tayyip Erdoğan's rule in Turkey. They demonstrate clearly how defining the rules of the political system is a politicized process—and the difficulties that institutions established to be above politics have in restraining concerted attempts to claim a greater legitimacy. At the core of all politics is a struggle over securing and setting the terms of the sovereignty of the political order over the society it rules, which means that politics decides what is to be considered corrupt or legitimate. The catch is that public officeholders may be able to use their political power to redefine what is considered corrupt in self-serving ways—a phenomenon known as state capture.

A second compounding challenge for political ethics is that whereas ethics is generally associated with widely legitimated norms and practices that frame agents' conceptions of how they should act, in politics people have to make decisions and determine how rule should be exercised in areas of fundamental disagreement. If we were wholly in agreement on ethical principles, we would barely need politics. As Henri de Saint-Simon and Karl Marx recognized, the government of humans could be replaced by the administration of things; we might need coordination, but there would be no irreconcilable conflict requiring decision. We have politics precisely because we do not agree, and yet to avoid outright conflict, order must be imposed and maintained through the exercise of power. This means that norms and expectations are forged in what is an essentially political struggle over values and interests, and we should not expect consensus on what those rules and norms should be, or over how power should be exercised.

At the same time, those who engage in such struggles do so for various reasons. Our problem is that we do not have strong grounds for trusting them to act, as far as possible, in disinterested and public serving ways. Those in political office face wide opportunities for furthering their interests, both to preserve and enhance their political power, and for more direct private gain. Experience shows that many politicians have feet of clay, that power breeds hubris, and that personal interests and partisan demands compete with obligations to serve the public interest. This is why corruption is a concern and we demand that those in power be accountable to those they rule. Yet there remains a moment of decision and sovereignty in politics that stands above the order that it rules. If we make some institution more powerful than those in politics, that institution will have to exercise power in situations of conflict and be subject to the very dangers that we have created it to avoid. Regulation can become politicized, as when anticorruption tools are used to smear political opponents or enforcement agencies act in the government's interest. But we also need to acknowledge that in relation to politics, the issue of what the rules are and what the ends of politics should be is always deeply politicized; it involves a struggle to settle the parameters of a game that is evolving, contested, and multidimensional (Philp 2018).

This does not mean that those in power are necessarily venal and self-serving. They have to respond to problems and crises in which different sets of interests, motives, and ends jostle for attention; in weighing responses to a problem, politicians will inevitably reflect on how certain paths might affect the support they rely on from their allies and future electoral prospects. At crisis points in politics, short-term concerns often overshadow medium and longer-term objectives, and that can make it difficult to distinguish between conduct that is responding to the problem at hand, that which is directed toward consolidating and retaining power, and that which pursues more personal political ends or private interests. Politicians have to consider how (and how far) to protect and further their interests and concerns—in the widest sense of these terms, which may incorporate the interests of those they rule (although it is rarely exclusively concerned with these). Those judgements will be affected by institutional location, formal role, public expectations, and the imperatives of holding and retaining power and office. This means that the decisions of officeholders are likely to be systematically more consequentialist than those of ordinary citizens, and their relationship to moral principles will be similarly more conditional. Public office is not a license to act on one's own moral principles but instead imposes sets of duties and responsibilities, and creates incentives that are specific to the role and political system.

In liberal democratic constitutional regimes, *public office* has come to be distinguished from *political office*, and states have drawn lines between administrative and political (usually elected) dimensions of rule, albeit differently in different systems. Typically, public office relates to areas of government and administration that are relatively routine, with prescribed functions that allow for a clear definition of responsibilities for people occupying those offices. Political office relates to the making of decisions and establishing laws in areas of conflict, and thus is directed more to the exercise of power and *determination* of policy than its *implementation*. And while these states have rolled back individual rule, and sought to make government more systematically linked to election and accountability, the proper limits of authority, degree of self-regulation, and appropriate principles for accountability all remain ongoing areas of contestation. These debates are also areas that political theorists ought to be contributing to, albeit doing so requires sensitivity to the precise institutions and practices in play, path dependencies of those institutions, and exigencies of particular political moments.

Conflicts of Interest in Public Office

To illustrate some of the difficulties in arriving at convergence on standards for those in office, even in administrative office, and elaborate on the challenges posed by different contexts and developments in public office, it is useful to consider the concept of "conflict of interest." Much public office ethics relies heavily on this concept in distinguishing legitimate and illegitimate interests for those in office, and much of the apparatus for regulating public office (codes of conduct, registers of interests, and asset declarations) is concerned with managing such conflicts.

A conflict of interest is a set of circumstances that creates a *risk* that professional judgment or actions regarding a primary interest will be unduly influenced by a secondary interest (Thompson 1993). A conflict of interest might occur, for example, if a member of Parliament owns a company in the construction sector and in their role as a legislator is required to vote on a new law regulating safety in construction. If they put their desire to earn income from the company (for instance, by favoring regulation that requires their company to spend less on compliance) above their duties as a legislator to serve the public interest (requiring them to decide on the basis of how best to protect the safety of employees and citizens), they would be regarded as having altered their behavior in office to pursue an illicit interest. A conflict of interest, however, might be deemed to exist even if it did not alter their behavior. Some theorists argue that public officeholders should meet the "appearance standard"—that is, so that there is not even the appearance of any conflict since failing to meet this standard risks jeopardizing public confidence (Stark 2003). According to the Code of Conduct (paragraph 74) guidelines for members of Parliament in the United Kingdom, parliamentarians should declare a financial interest if it "might reasonably be thought by others to influence the speech, representation or communication in question."[1]

The concept relies on three assumptions: first, that there is a clear and agreed-on conception of public office and its associated duties; second, that there is a viable and commonly shared distinction between public and private roles or interests; and third, that people are capable of exercising public roles in ways that avoid their being influenced improperly. All of these assumptions are problematic, and their problematic nature is intrinsic to politics. The first assumption is hard to establish even in mature democracies, and meets serious problems in situations where the political system is young or undergoing transition; moreover, the consensus on what the duties of office are tends to change over time. The second assumption is challenged particularly in societies undergoing a major privatization of public services or on a transition path from communism to a market economy—either of which can occur in both wealthy and poorer economies. The third assumption is challenged by the embedded nature of social norms, which often conflict with our aspirations for how those in public office should behave.

Contention over the duties of public office is especially pronounced in the case of political office. A member of Parliament in the United Kingdom must balance duties as a national legislator, constituency representative, and politician with their own interests who must face reelection against their loyalty to their political party. Suppose the government, of which they are a member, proposes a piece of legislation that is in the national interest, but would lead to job losses in their constituency. How do they balance these competing considerations? These concerns are not necessarily private interests, but they

1. For a fascinating debate on this issue, see "Appendix: Memorandum from the Parliamentary Commissioner for Standards—Complaints against Rt Hon Peter Lilley MP," https://publications.parliament.uk/pa/cm201415/cmselect/cmstandards/951/95105.htm.

nonetheless pull in different directions, and the way that the member of Parliament perceives and makes the trade-offs may be affected by private considerations. If they support the government bill, they might be ousted at the next election. If they oppose it, they might forgo an opportunity for promotion. Their options might be influenced by whether they sit in a marginal or safe seat. Even in a mature democracy such as the United Kingdom, where there is broad consensus about the duties of office, there is no consensus about which considerations should carry the most weight.

In many countries, traditions of self-regulation for the legislative branch mean that parliamentarians have been trusted to make judgments about how far their various interests might influence the exercise of their duties. Individuals may be expected to declare personal interests, in line with the principle of transparency, so that the public can decide whether a conflict exists. Alternatively, individuals may be urged or required to recuse themselves from certain meetings or decisions if they have a conflict. In other cases, regulation seeks to remove the conflict entirely, such as by banning officeholders from owning companies, holding second jobs, or employing relatives as staff members. In all of these cases, the potential conflict is seen as one between personal interests and political decisions; there is no similar attention to the interests associated with reelection, keeping office, partisan loyalties, or political career. In relation to personal interests Andrew Stark's (2003) study of US public life argues that there is an increased tendency to ban a variety of activities without regard for whether individuals facing those circumstances are in fact likely to be influenced in culpable ways. This means that our conception of what an interest is along with its potential to influence judgment has become both narrower in its focus on private interests and much broader in scope.

In younger democracies and less stable states, norms about what is required of individuals in public office are often even more volatile. The practices of the former regime—whether communist, colonial, or relating to a state from which the country has seceded—leave a legacy, and new leaders may wish to make their mark by writing a new constitution and building novel institutions. Yet where these lack local legitimacy or even run counter to ingrained informal rules, such efforts may fail. In Tanzania, for example, Julius Nyerere, the country's first leader after independence from colonial rule, set out clear standards for public officeholders in 1967 in the Arusha Declaration, part five of which states that no politician or public official should hold shares or directorships in a company, or receive income from second jobs or renting property. As such, Nyerere drew a sharp line between public and private interests. Since

Nyerere left office in 1985, however, these standards have been largely abandoned. In today's Tanzania, politicians and civil servants frequently own companies as well as (ab)use their office to benefit those enterprises. Research on public opinion, conducted as part of the work of the Constitutional Commission in 2012, found widespread nostalgia for the code among the population and a sense that its abandonment had left the country without clear ethical direction. Still, clearly the code had not exerted a sufficiently strong grip on the minds of officeholders to endure once Nyerere left office, particularly in the face of a major economic liberalization program.

Indeed, the distinction between public and private has been eroded in much of the Western world since the 1980s as many countries—especially the United States, United Kingdom, and Australia, but also a number of other Organization for Economic Cooperation and Development countries—have adopted "new public management," introducing market forces into public service provisions so as to bring efficiency gains. Although the state retains oversight of services that are provided by the private sector, its management role is often weakened as the internal expertise and capacity necessary for it to be performed effectively is itself eroded by the outsourcing.

These practices, including public-private partnerships, blur previously established distinctions between public and private, and create new types of relationships between public officials and elected officeholders, on the one hand, and private sector organizations, on the other, thereby further complicating the identification of conflicts of interest as individuals move from state-owned utilities into regulatory roles and or roles in the companies delivering the services (David-Barrett 2020). This so-called revolving door movement between public and private sector roles has been encouraged by the new public management; often individuals who have accumulated expertise on a particular topic in the public sector are presented with opportunities in the private sector that are better paid yet require similar skills and knowledge. In addition, the increased complexity of a great deal of public policy has challenged the old model of a professional bureaucracy where individuals have transferable skills and can be moved around among government departments. More commonly now, civil servants lack relevant policy-making expertise, making them more reliant on consulting external actors (whose independence is difficult to guarantee).

Scholars have made considerable efforts to find empirical evidence as to the extent of the first problem: Does the revolving door lead to corruption? What are private sector companies "buying" when they hire people from sectoral relevant positions in the public sector? Is it their expertise or their contacts? The evidence suggests that companies are more interested in connections than expertise (Vidal, Draca, and Fons-Rosen 2012; LaPira and Thomas 2014) and that companies that hire such employees gain more government contracts (Canayaz, Martinez, and Ozsoylev 2014; Lazarus, McKay, and Herbel 2016). Most of this research relates to the United States, but Rory Truex (2012) finds that companies with a deputy on their board perform 4 percent better than their peers, even in China, where the parliament lacks autonomy and is seen as a rubber stamp.

All of these practices pose challenges to traditional forms of accountability that rely on a clear separation between the state and private sector. They raise major concerns about the degree to which the private sector may come to have improper influence over government decisions, and given the appearance standard, may erode public confidence in government even if public duties are not in fact influenced. It is also important to bear in mind that the public/private distinction is not set in stone but instead constitutes a multidimensional set of issues where distinctions serve various purposes. As Raymond Geuss (2001, 109) reminds us, "There is no single distinction between public and private; the various senses of 'public' do not cohere very closely with one another, nor do the senses of 'private'; the various forms of opposition between 'public' and 'private' are neither absolute, nor are they all, in the final instance, insubstantial and illusory." Particular distinctions serve particular purposes, and in our reflection and assessment of practices, it is those purposes that are properly the focus of our attention, more than the conceptual distinctions themselves. That is, we have to ask what drawing distinctions in particular ways does (or fails to do) for us.

Even in wealthy Western countries, the introduction of market forces into the provision of public services is controversial and the evidence on whether it delivers the purported benefits is at best ambiguous (Hood and Dixon 2013). In transitional and low-income countries, with weak budgets and limited capacity to borrow, fiscal pressures are yet greater, and such techniques are often especially attractive. For example, infrastructure is key to economic development, but it requires major up-front investment, which low-income countries with a weak tax base and capital markets that demand punitively high rates of return for state borrowing cannot finance. The private financing of transport infrastructure can enable states to launch major projects that would not otherwise be feasible (and in so doing, promote job creation and economic growth). Such partnerships, however, also bring opportunities for politicians and bureaucrats to exploit their power for private gain (or party finance), and may give companies unwarranted leverage in areas of public policy.

In transitional and low-income countries, government and business are frequently intertwined. In eastern Europe, this is partly a legacy of the way in which the post-Communist transition occurred. Many holders of political power at the point of transition were able to convert this resource into economic power as countries shifted from planned to market economies (Wedel 2003). So-called flex organizations were sometimes supported by international donors as a way of circumventing cumbersome bureaucracies to achieve specific tasks that they saw as being in the public interest. Yet they inadvertently empowered informal networks that undercut the formal political process.

Blurred relationships between the state and private sector are present in low-income countries in African and Asian too. The developmental state model in Asia involves intense collaboration among the public and private sectors, while many African countries are characterized by complex clientelist social patterns where public office is routinely used to extract private benefits from companies as well as reward companies that support political campaigns. Adrian Leftwich (2009, 9), for instance, emphasizes that the way in which state-business relations formed at a particular point in Malawi's history created enduring patterns in which the private sector is alive and well, and owned by the government. Peter Ekeh (1975) meanwhile argued that the occupation of African states by colonialist powers created a sense of there being "two publics," a civic one that is amoral and externally imposed, and a local one that is primordial and moral, although others have questioned the binary and suggested that many situations may involve a range of competing logics (see, for example, Anders 2010, 138). The shift from an authoritarian regime to a democratic one can lead to the formation of competitive clientelist regimes in which political parties and their cronies take turns to "feed" on the state; Gerhard Anders (2010, 124) refers to the "democratisation of appropriation." In Ghana, public officeholders use their power to reward those who have helped them get elected, either by appointing them to prestigious roles in state agencies (from which they may then have access to rent-seeking opportunities) or awarding them state contracts (Abdulai and Hickey 2016; Luna 2019). This system is deeply entangled with party financing, but also with strong local expectations that those who gain public office should use their power to benefit their kin. This, too, makes it difficult to operationalize a concept of conflict of interest.

In such complex relationships, what counts as a conflict of interest? If the duties associated with public office are not clearly defined and have little wider cultural support, we are expecting those in public office to show heroic levels of self-awareness, an ability to resist pressures that may be deeply socially and institutionally embedded, and a willingness to sacrifice their political interests. That few exhibit such capacities may well be a function of the fact that individuals are often unaware of their own biases. Research suggests that being part of a group of cheaters makes one more likely to cheat as well as more likely to accept cheating by other members of one's group (Gino, Ayal, and Ariely 2009; Gino and Galinsky 2012). Even if it is cognitively possible to resist some forms of improper influence and internalize professional ethics, members of Parliament with relationships with lobbying firms or those who accept campaign financing from local businesses will still fail the appearance standard in the eyes of many.

Addressing Public Integrity and Public Conduct

The ascendancy of economics in the study of corruption in the last thirty years has meant that accounts that place weight on norms and rules, recognize a range of potentially conflicting motivations for those in public office, acknowledge the importance of personal conduct and integrity, and see institutional and public culture as important components of the integrity of a political system have had a much less prominent role in the literature on corruption. Proponents of good governance agendas in international organizations have also drawn heavily on principal-agent theory and tended to advocate governance standards that are taken to be generally applicable. Doing so both underestimates the potential diversity of forms of institutional design capable of commanding legitimacy, and operates with a covert thesis of convergence on a single economic and political model for states—an assumption that appears naive, and is increasingly challenged by the rise of populist and authoritarian leaders in many parts of the world. In these approaches, there is an assumption that standards for conducting government and administration will be agent neutral and universal in character.

In practice, it seems much more plausible to believe that we need to address the local and particular demands as well as expectations of public office in order to have an adequate agent-relative account of what it is plausible to expect those in public office to aim for and to do. We need to allow for more localized understandings of what can and should be expected of those in public office, yet we also need to recognize that in many societies, these expectations are in flux and some elements in a society may legitimately aspire to standards that have yet to take hold in the wider society. Seeking to build consensus around new norms and standards is an essential part of politics.

One way of clarifying society's expectations about how officeholders should behave is to introduce codes of conduct for public office, and indeed such efforts have been made in a number of countries in recent years. These codes have been proposed in the spirit of articulating and elaborating the responsibilities of those in public office, and identifying the principles underlying the relationship of trust between them and those whose interests they ostensibly serve. The precise effect of such codes is contested; it is unclear whether they help generate commitment to principles versus merely producing box ticking and lip service. In systems where there are high levels of probity, such codes may well make some contribution to serious reflections on the responsibilities of those in senior political office; in systems with low probity, it is not apparent whether they make much difference (David-Barrett 2015).

In the United Kingdom, the code that forms the basis for more institution-specific codes throughout the public services there is the Committee on Standards in Public Life's seven principles: selflessness, integrity, objectivity, accountability, openness, honesty, and leadership. These are principles that the public seems to recognize as desirable in those exercising public office and that officeholders also recognize as important, although there remain tensions over how far what is expected of public officials can apply to those holding political office.

These principles have been widely copied. For example, chapter six of the 2010 Kenyan Constitution contains references to all of these principles; it renders them legally enforceable too, while leaving considerable room for doubt as to how they are to be understood—and whether they are in fact complied with. In the UK case, as in other countries now regarded as having built fairly robust systems of public integrity (Mungiu-Pippidi 2013; Rothstein and Teorell 2015), there has been a long historical process of evolution of public office in which norms, expectations, and codes have developed that support a particular conception that has wide public salience. But that cultural and historical legacy, which frames the expectations of those seeking appointment and pervades the public service culture, cannot be created overnight; it depends heavily on being able to dominate cultural norms and expectations that are at variance with it, while also needing to be largely internally policed as well as relatively independent from political interference and control. Moreover, it is never entirely secure, with its durability dependent on the willingness of many individuals to protect and defend the norms even if doing so invites the wrath of those in power, plus incurs personal costs.

This focus on the culture of public office is crucial because it connects general issues of the operation of norms and rules of conduct, questions about the particular norms and rules that are constitutive of particular public offices, and issues of what practical and institutional frameworks might help motivate conduct that serves the interests of the population at large, rather than personal, sectional, or bureaucratic interests. There is a distinction in the literature between compliance- and integrity-based approaches to public office (Heywood 2012). The weakness of compliance/incentive-based accounts has been discussed above, but integrity-based approaches are also not without difficulties. One problem is that individual integrity does not necessarily lead to organizational integrity. The latter seems to demand integrity plus—not just doing your job, but doing it with a wider awareness of the importance of promoting ethical standards within the organization. Indeed, the growing literature on "institutional corruption" tends strongly to emphasize that individual probity can in itself corrupt the organization of which it is a part (Lessig 2011, 2013; Miller 2011; Thompson 1995, 2018; for critiques of this literature, see Philp and David-Barrett 2015). There is a genuine problem here about the relationship between individual-level action and judgment, organizational culture, and organizational integrity (essentially, whether it is performing the functions it purports to perform). But exponents of an expanded integrity model themselves tend to understate the extent to which there is contestation within organizations about their goals and how best to achieve them, and thereby overstate the possibility of ethical convergence within complex organizations. Demanding more from integrity than mere compliance requires the exercise of judgment by those in office, and that will not always produce convergence.

The difficulties in creating and sustaining behavior that seeks to promote the public interest are manifold. There are *collective action problems*, where each prefers to act with probity if, but only if, everyone else does because we incur unacceptable costs when we act well and others do not. In societies where facilitation payments are ubiquitous, for example, people often resent paying and yet have no way of generating collective nonpayment while ensuring their own access to the service. Where procurement processes are corrupted, companies that do not play the games of campaign donations or kickbacks will simply lose out to others that do. Equally, in some states, public officials who do not favor party cronies, relatives, or their ethnic group in contract allocations see their status as well as prospects sink.

Some commentators see the collective action problem in relation to probity as the central problem in many developing states (Booth and Cammack 2013). That view, however, tends to overstate the extent to which there is a single collective action problem that has a single coordination point rather than there being multiple potential stable Nash equilibria (in each of which it is in no one's interests to change behavior, but where in response to exogenous shocks, new equilibria might emerge that will be in some respects more, but in some respects less, optimal). If the latter is the case, then the idea that there is a single end state, or single transformative moment or push, becomes dramatically less plausible, and the objectives for change become more complex to specify and more difficult to achieve. Moreover, it is vital to remember that systems that today have low levels of corruption have had lengthy processes of evolution and institutional reform that have been able over time to mobilize elite and wider public support for the state as an impartial system of administration as well as policy making (Knights 2017).

Following developments in behavioral economics, the "philosophy of nudge" has attracted a good deal of attention in public services (Thaler and Sunstein 2009). If you want people to do the right thing, then you make it easier for them to do it; if you want them to eat healthier foods, you put fruit within easy reach, and make sweet and savory snacks less visible. Of course, making it easier for someone to do the right thing does not mean that they do the right thing for the right reason, and the hope must be that new and better habits develop as a result of nudges. There remains a trade-off between upping compliance and embedding commitments to public service norms, and the propensity to do the right thing seems to need a firmer basis than it simply being the easier option—not least because it provides no resilient security in more testing cases where judgment is required. One feature of much public office, both senior administrative and political office, is that judgment is an integral component, and the vast majority of work on nudging is concerned with cases where people operate with low levels of judgment. It is clear that making it easier for people to do the right thing is good, but we should not think that there is a design that avoids the necessity of people having some virtue—and "there is neither continence nor virtue unless there is an urge to the contrary" (Frame 2003, 800).

Most behavioral approaches are uninterested in judgment, or how people construct or construe their situation along with their relationship to those in public office, or for officeholders, in relation to what public office signifies in their context. And rather little attention is paid to the forms of reward and recognition that accompany public office. For both public servants and politicians, we have to consider the form and level of reward they should be given. If the only thing that matters to someone is how much money they get, that is not a good basis for a treasury devoted to the public service or politicians devoted to the common good. Nonmonetary incentives, however, are heavily dependent on perceptions of status within a certain reference group; if your public service medal means nothing in your own community, which values more tangible signs of success and competence, it is unlikely to be an incentive to probity. Moreover, such questions are often going to be local in character, including up to the point at which people begin comparing themselves to groups outside their political system. These issues have not generally played much part in thinking about corruption, yet they seem fundamental to questions of sustaining probity and motivating compliance.

The root ethical difficulty is that universalist standards of ethical conduct for public office are overambitious, while local standards of conduct are frequently underdemanding, conflicting, or unclear. Under these circumstances, it becomes more appropriate to ask questions about how to work from within existing institutions and with existing practices to influence behavior as well as create a more positive organizational culture, and shape the ethical climate of conduct to facilitate the emergence of stable and sustainable practices that can carry legitimacy within the wider community that these offices are intended to serve. This demands a political ethics that is less than heroic, acknowledges the limits of the possible, and works to identify means and ends that are attainable from where people currently are. Although less inspiring as a project, it has the virtue of a realism about the difficulties of getting political power to serve those over whom it is exercised rather than merely those who exercise it.

Politics Ethics in a Minor Key

In the rapidly expanding literature on corruption, the tendency has been to develop agent-neutral or universalist claims about political responsibilities that in practice are deeply embedded in local and particular circumstances, path dependencies, and individual relationships and exchanges. Once we see this, we can also see that the language of evaluation in relation to politics and its corruption will lack complete neutrality and objectivity. At the same time, we need to develop some degree of consensus on how to make these judgments.

This takes us back to the realm of the political and the problem of how to arrive at any kind of general guidance.

The discourse of fighting corruption has become an important theme in twenty-first-century politics, in high- and low-income countries alike. One result is that corruption has entered prominently in the discourse of party politics and become an integral part of partisan struggles in many states. Moreover, the blurring of the public-private distinction has created challenges for our ability to hold officeholders to account and perhaps made it more difficult for them personally to regulate their own conduct.

Corruption discourse may itself be partly to blame—seeing politics itself as inevitably corrupt, looking to reduce the scope for political agency and the state, or by giving the impression that corruption is everywhere, allowing individuals to feel less constrained in indulging in it (Krastev 2004; Cheeseman and Peiffer 2021). Certainly the tendency for Western states to turn up their noses at the practices of low-income states shows a lamentable ignorance of their own histories, vulnerabilities, and inconsistencies. In development discourse, we could do a lot more to try to work out how things work, with what levels of legitimacy, and with what strains and potentials for change rather than assuming that a modern capitalist free market economy with a regulatory state will solve all problems. Furthermore, it is clear that the discourse of corruption can prove dysfunctional for change. Why would those in power admit to doing "that," and why would those denouncing it not exploit what they know for their own ends?

Smaller, more local, and applied questions—about how to get things to work more efficiently, how to motivate compliance with standards, what deals can be brokered as to the interpretations of responsibilities, and so on—may be the basis for a more practical political ethics that is context sensitive as well as committed to realism in its aspirations, methods, and language and conceptual apparatus. That would give us a political ethics in a minor, realist key, but that might do more than a lexicon freighted with the ideals of selflessness and purity of intention, or assumptions about markets, rather than politics being the obvious means to achieve a better world.

References

Abdulai, Abdul-Gafaru, and Sam Hickey. 2016. "The Politics of Development under Competitive Clientelism: Insights from Ghana's Education Sector." *African Affairs* 115 (458): 44–72.

Anders, Gerhard. 2010. *In the Shadow of Good Governance: An Ethnography of Civil Service Reform in West Africa*. Leiden: Brill.

Anechiarico, Frank, and James B. Jacobs. 1996. *The Pursuit of Absolute Integrity: How Corruption Control Makes Government Ineffective*. Chicago: University of Chicago Press.

Bauhr, Monika. 2017. "Need or Greed? Conditions for Collective Action against Corruption." *Governance* 30 (4): 561–81.

Booth, David, and Diana Cammack. 2013. *Governance for Development in Africa: Solving Collective Action Problems*. London: Zed Books.

Canayaz, Mehmet I., Jose Vicente Martinez, and Han N. Ozsoylev. 2014. "Is the Revolving Door of Washington a Back Door to Excess Corporate Returns?" Koç University–TUSIAD Economic Research Forum Working Papers 1507.

Cheeseman, Nic, and Caryn Peiffer. 2021. "The Curse of Good Intentions: Why Anticorruption Messaging Can Encourage Bribery." *American Political Science Review*, 1–15. doi:10.1017/S0003055421001398.

David-Barrett, Elizabeth. 2015. "Nolan's Legacy: Regulating Parliamentary Conduct in Democratising Europe." *Parliamentary Affairs* 68 (3): 514–32.

———. 2020. "Regulating Conflicts of Interest in Public Office." In *Handbook on Corruption, Ethics and Integrity in Public Administration*, edited by Adam Graycar, 406–20. Cheltenham, UK: Edward Elgar.

Ekeh, Peter P. 1975. "Colonialism and the Two Publics in Africa: A Theoretical Statement." *Comparative Studies in Society and History* 17 (1): 91–112.

Frame, Donald M., ed. 2003. *The Complete Essays of Montaigne*. London: Everyman Library.

Geuss, Raymond. 2001. *Public Goods, Private Goods*. Princeton, NJ: Princeton University Press.

Gino, Francesca, Shahar Ayal, and Dan Ariely. 2009. "Contagion and Differentiation in Unethical Behavior: The Effect of One Bad Apple on the Barrel." *Psychological Science* 20 (3) : 393–98.

Gino, Francesca, and Adam D. Galinsky. 2012. "Vicarious Dishonesty: When Psychological Closeness Creates Distance from One's Moral Compass." *Organizational Behavior and Human Decision Processes* 119 (1): 15–26.

Heywood, Paul M. 2012. "Integrity Management and the Public Service Ethos in the UK: Patchwork Quilt or Threadbare Blanket?" *International Review of Administrative Sciences* 78 (3): 474–93.

Hood, Christopher, and Ruth Dixon. 2013. "A Model of Cost-Cutting in Government? The Great Management Revolution in UK Central Government Reconsidered." *Public Administration* 91 (1): 114–34.

Klitgaard, Robert. 1991. *Controlling Corruption*. Berkeley: University of California Press.

Knights, Mark. 2017. "Old Corruption: What British History Can Tell Us about Corruption Today." London: Transparency International.

Krastev, Ivan. 2004. *Shifting Obsessions: Three Essays on the Politics of Anticorruption*. Budapest: Central European University Press.

Krueger, Anne O. (1974. "The Political Economy of the Rent-Seeking Society." *American Economic Review* 64 (3): 291–303.

LaPira, Timothy M., ad Herschel F. Thomas. 2014. "Revolving Door Lobbyists and Interest Representation." *Interest Groups and Advocacy* 3 (1): 4–29.

Lazarus, Jeffrey, Amy McKay, and Lindsey Herbel. 2016. "Who Walks through the Revolving Door? Examining the Lobbying Activity of Former Members of Congress." *Interest Groups and Advocacy* 5 (1): 82–100.

Leff, Nathaniel H. 1964. "Economic Development through Bureaucratic Corruption." *American Behavioral Scientist* 8 (3): 8–14.

Leftwich, Adrian. 2009. "Analysing the Politics of State Business Relations: A Methodological Concept Note on the Historical Institutionalist Approach." Discussion Paper Series No. 23, 1–16. Manchester, UK: IPPG Programme Office,

Lessig, Lawrence. 2011. *Republic, Lost: How Money Corrupts Congress—and a Plan to Stop It.* New York: Twelve.

———. 2013. "'Institutional Corruption' Defined." *Journal of Law, Medicine and Ethics* 41 (3): 553–55.

Luna, Joseph. 2019. *Political Financing in Developing Countries: A Case from Ghana.* Abingdon, UK: Routledge.

March, James G., and Johan P. Olsen. 2004. "The Logic of Appropriateness." In *The Oxford Handbook of Political Science,* edited by Robert E. Goodin, Michael Moran, and Martin Rein. Oxford: Oxford University Press.

Michael, Bryane, and Donald W. Bowser. 2010.0 "The Evolution of the Anti-Corruption Industry in the Third Wave of Anti-Corruption Work." In *International Anti-Corruption Regimes in Europe: Between Corruption, Integration, and Culture,* edited by Sebastian Wolf and Diana Schmidt-Pfister, 159–79. Baden-Baden: Nomos Publishers.

Miller, Seumas. 2011). "Corruption." In *Stanford Encyclopedia of Philosophy,* edited by Edward N. Zalta. https://plato.stanford.edu/entries/corruption/.

Mungiu-Pippidi, Alina. 2013. "Becoming Denmark: Historical Designs of Corruption Control.: *Social Research* 80 (4): 1259–86.

Peiffer, Caryn, and Linda Alvarez. 2016. "Who Will Be the 'Principled-Principals'? Perceptions of Corruption and Willingness to Engage in Anticorruption Activism." *Governance* 29 (3): 351–69.

Persson, Anna, Bo Rothstein, and Jan Teorell. 2013. "Why Anticorruption Reforms Fail—Systemic Corruption as a Collective Action Problem." *Governance* 26 (3): 449–71.

Philp, Mark. 1997. "Defining Political Corruption." *Political Studies* 45 (3): 436–62.

———. 2001. "Access, Accountability and Authority: Corruption and the Democratic Process." *Crime, Law and Social Change* 36 (4): 357–77.

———. 2015. "The Definition of Political Corruption." In *Routledge Handbook of Political Corruption,* edited by Paul M. Heywood, 17–29. Abingdon, UK: Routledge.

———. 2018. "Politics and the 'Pure of Heart': Realism and Corruption." In *Politics Recovered: Realist Thought in Theory and Practice, edited by Matt Sleat, 194–217. New York: Columbia University Press.*

Philp, Mark, and Elizabeth David-Barrett. 2015. "Realism about Political Corruption." *Annual Review of Political Science* 18:387–402.

Rothstein, Bo. 2011. *The Quality of Government: Corruption, Social Trust, and Inequality in Institutional Perspective.* Chicago: University of Chicago Press.

Rothstein, Bo, and Jan Teorell. 2015. "Getting to Sweden, Part II: Breaking with Corruption in the Nineteenth Century." *Scandinavian Political Studies* 38 (3): 238–54.

Rothstein, Bo, and Aiysha Varraich. 2017. *Making Sense of Corruption.* Cambridge: Cambridge University Press.

Serra, Danila, and Leonard Wantchekon. 2012. *New Advances in Experimental Research on Corruption.* Bingley, UK: Emerald Group Publishing Limited.

Stark, Andrew. 2003. *Conflict of Interest in American Public Life*. Cambridge, MA: Harvard University Press.

Thaler, Richard H., and Cass Sunstein. 2009. *Nudge:Improving Decisions about Health, Wealth, and Happiness*. New Haven, CT: Yale University Press.

Thompson, Dennis. F. 1993. "Mediated Corruption: The Case of the Keating Five." *American Political Science Review* 87 (2): 369–81.

———. 1995. *Ethics in Congress*. Washington, DC: Brookings Institution.

———. 2018. "Theories of Institutional Corruption." *Annual Review of Political Science* 21:26.1–19.

Truex, Rory. 2012 "The Returns to Office in a 'Rubber Stamp' Parliament." *American Political Science Review* 108 (2): 235–51.

Underkuffler, Laura S. 2013. *Captured by Evil: The Idea of Corruption in Law*. New Haven, CT: Yale University Press.

van Klaveren, Jacob. 1989. "Corruption: The Special Case of the United States." In *Political Corruption: A Handbook*, edited by Arnold J. Heidenheimer, Michael Johnston, and Victor T. LeVine, 557–66. New Brunswick, NJ: Transaction Publishers.

Vidal, Jordi Blanes I., Mirko Draca, and Christian Fons-Rosen. 2012. "Revolving Door Lobbyists." *American Economic Review* 102 (7): 3731–48.

Warren, Mark E. 2004. "What Does Corruption Mean in a Democracy?" *American Journal of Political Science* 48 (2): 328–43.

Wedel, James R. 2003. "Clans, Cliques and Captured States: Rethinking 'Transition' in Central and Eastern Europe and the Former Soviet Union." *Journal of International Development* 15 (4): 427–40.

9

The Public Ethics of Whistleblowing

Michele Bocchiola & Emanuela Ceva

AN EMPLOYEE REPORTS on a colleague who uses the company's car to drive her husband back and forth from work every day. Edward Snowden, a computer specialist working for the Central Intelligence Agency and National Security Agency, shares his qualms regarding the secret mass surveillance programs of the US and British governments with some of his coworkers, and when not listened to, he reveals these programs to journalists at the *Guardian* and *Washington Post.* A US Marine, Chelsea Manning, leaks classified documents concerning crimes committed by US troops in Iraq and Afghanistan to WikiLeaks, the famous international nonprofit organization created by Julian Assange.

The cases in this seemingly heterogeneous set share an important qualifying feature: they are all instances where the member of an organization reports some wrongdoing, allegedly occurring within their organization, by revealing some piece of information to which they have privileged access. To wit, these cases are all instances of whistleblowing. The study of whistleblowing has been central for quite some time in legal theory (for example, in labor and corporate law), economics (such as in business management and administration), and business ethics. The study of this practice from the perspective of public ethics is still underdeveloped. But this is a perspective from which important insights may derive, especially as concerns the contribution of this practice to the promotion of justice and accountability. In particular, a central yet underexplored question concerns whether and how whistleblowing is morally justifiable, and if so, if it is required as a duty.

The journalists who introduced "whistleblowing" into public debate used the term to characterize the action of professionals reporting such hazards as weaknesses or errors in an artifact's design, with the intent of preventing a threat to customers' safety (see Vandekerkeove 2006, 1–27). Nowadays, whistleblowing has entered common parlance as a way of describing the public exposure of episodes of corruption, fraud, or general abuses of power. Across all of these usages, the term has been characteristically laden with an ambivalent connotation, swinging between the appreciation for a heroic act of denunciation and the suspicion—if not the condemnation—of a revelation, which seemingly entails a breach of confidentiality akin to espionage (see Grant 2002).

To offer a balanced assessment of the specificity of whistleblowing and its normative status, we start by articulating a working definition and illustration of this practice (with special reference to the vicissitudes of Manning) that singles out its essential features, and thus distinguishes it from other forms of disclosures. Then we introduce the problem of justifying whistleblowing as a duty, and discuss current consequentialist and deontological attempts at addressing this problem. We show the limitations of the current received views (which draw, respectively, on harm- and complicity-based arguments), and outline a further deontological and relational account of whistleblowing as an instance of the duty of "office accountability" that applies to any legitimate rule-based organization.[1]

Whistleblowing: A Working Definition

Let us start from this general and minimal definition:

> WHISTLEBLOWING: the practice through which the member of a legitimate organization voluntarily reports some wrongdoing, allegedly occurring within that organization, with the intention that corrective action should be taken to address it. (Ceva and Bocchiola 2018, 21)[2]

This definition of whistleblowing contains six main elements: i) the action of blowing the whistle (a report), ii) the agent of the report (the whistleblower),

1. For an extensive presentation and discussion of the material in this chapter, see Ceva and Bocchiola 2018.

2. This definition encompasses the shared aspects included in many standard accounts of whistleblowing. See, for example, Lewis, Brown, and Moberly 2014, 4; Near and Miceli 1985, 4.

iii) the locus where the relevant facts occur (an organization), iv) the object of the report (the wrongdoing), v) the addressee of the report (either internal or external to the organization), and vi) the motivation of the report (the intention to initiate a corrective action).

Whistleblowing consists in an action of *voluntary reporting*. The report could take the form of either an open or anonymous disclosure, depending on the specific environmental circumstances in which it occurs. *Open* reports are usually considered an act of indictment—that is, a form of public accusation (see Jubb 1999). *Anonymous* reports include "tips"—confidentially disclosed pieces of information—or "leaks"—classified information intentionally revealed to the media. Depending on a country's specific legislation, moreover, reports may be either authorized or unauthorized (see Delmas 2015; Sagar 2013, 153–80).

Besides the form that the action of reporting takes, for a disclosure to count as an act of whistleblowing, it must be the case that its *agent* is a member of the organization where the reported facts occur (Miceli and Near 1992; Miceli, Dreyfus, and Near 2014). To be a *member* of an organization means to occupy a role within it; it means to perform a formal and regulated function coordinated with the functions assigned to other members. A whistleblower is a member of an organization who finds themselves in the circumstances to gain access to relevant pieces of information about some questionable facts. This is the sense in which we can say that a whistleblower is someone who has privileged access to information within an organization. Possible whistleblowers include a company's employees, the officers of a public institution, volunteers in a charity organization, and so on. Membership status can be either *permanent* or *temporary* (e.g., subcontractors). Focus on membership enables us to distinguish whistleblowers from the authors of other kinds of disclosures, such as spies (who secretively reveal information on the activities of an enemy or competitor) and bell ringers (conscientious citizens who report general crimes and misdemeanors) (see Miceli, Dreyfus, and Near 2014).

The analysis so far also points out what the *locus* of whistleblowing is: an organization. Standardly, organizations are embodied structures of interdependent roles (see Miller 2014). They may be *private* (corporations) or *public* (hospitals), or *governmental* (state offices) or *-nongovernmental* (civil society associations). In any of these instances, organizations are defined by their performing certain functions that qualify what their members do collectively. An organization is regulated by and modeled on a statute, or an internal code of conduct, which establish members with a set of rights and duties, in accordance with the role of each and in keeping with a specific set of rules that assigns powers to any one role with a specific mandate. These rules are "public" in the sense that all members, at all levels of the organization, have access to them (for a discussion, see Bovens 1998, 9–21). An organization is legitimate when, from a legal or moral point of view, it is entitled to the power it exercises through the actions of its members. It is necessary to qualify organizations as "legitimate" in this broad sense in order to distinguish whistleblowers from informants, who report, for example, on such criminal (hence illegitimate) organizations as the Mafia. In our discussion, we assume the legitimacy of the organizations where the relevant reporting practices occur without any further argument (see Davis 1996).

What is the *object* of a whistleblower's report? Essentially, it is a wrongful fact that allegedly occurs *within* an organization and is related to the uses of power associated with the roles its members perform. Relevant facts may regard either a more or less systematic organizational practice (such as nepotism) or an individual, more or less occasional behavior (like embezzlement). The common qualifying feature is that there is an arbitrary deviation from the mandate with which either certain rule-based practices should occur or certain members should perform their role within the organization. In this sense, the object of whistleblowing is an *organizational* wrongdoing.

At this descriptive level, we refer to the *alleged* occurrence of organizational wrongdoings, thus excluding any normative restriction regarding either the "seriousness" of the wrongdoing or epistemic status of the reported information (Davis 1996; De George 2010). Moreover, relevant organizational wrongdoing may consist in either an *illegal* or *immoral* organizational practice or individual behavior. The former may stem from either unlawful (such as embezzlement) or illicit activities (say, the violation of some organizational standards). In either case, the wrongness of such activities can be established with reference to the law or an organization's internal norms. The latter kind of wrongdoing concerns actions that although not necessarily either unlawful or in contradiction with the letter of a rule, are nevertheless either contrary to the spirit of the rule or morally impermissible. For example, an organization might not have a written policy about sexual harassment, and the current legislation may be vague about what counts as a criminal offense in this case. Still, to receive unwelcome sexual advances by a colleague is morally problematic and may be the object of a whistleblower's report.

A further element to specify concerns the *addressee* of the report. The relevant distinction is between addressees that are either internal or external to the organization where the wrongdoing allegedly occurs (see Davis 2003; De George 2010). Whistleblowing is *internal* when the report is addressed to the whistleblower's direct superior, higher levels of management, or a dedicated office (like an ethical committee). Whistleblowing is *external* when it is addressed to such entities as the police or media.

Regardless of the internal or external channels that the whistleblowers follow, their disclosure is generally carried out with the *motivation* of urging that corrective action be taken either to prevent an organizational wrongdoing from occurring or stop it. In this light, it is easy to see why whistleblowing has often been presented as a prosocial practice, whose aim is the promotion of justice and moral rectitude within an organization (see Miceli and Near 1992, 28–30). Of course, this is a general characterization; the question of the "real" motivation—the set of individual psychological states and attitudes—behind a whistleblower's decision to report is quite complex. A casuistic phenomenology of whistleblowing suggests that this practice is typically motivated by ethical considerations. But this recurrent factual feature does not automatically exclude that a whistleblower may act with malice (for example, to take revenge over a mean boss), or that their actions are totally independent from the expectations of future rewards.[3] Whether selfish or altruistic, the whistleblowers' actual *psychological* motivations do not seem particularly significant from the perspective of a public ethics of whistleblowing, whose main aim is to offer a characterization (and subsequently, a justification) of the public function of this practice. From this point of view, we think it is sufficient to characterize the whistleblowers' motivations in terms of a commitment to bringing about a positive change in the status quo by urging that corrective action be taken to address the alleged occurrence of an organizational wrongdoing.

Who Is a Whistleblower?

Our working definition of whistleblowing can be usefully employed to analyze such generally discussed cases as that of Chelsea Manning, a US Marine who reported crimes committed by some US soldiers in Iraq and Afghanistan by

3. In some countries, state laws incentivize private individuals to report crimes such as corruption or fraud, which are hard to detect, with a share of the recovered sum. For example, in the United States, with the 2010 Dodd-Frank Wall Street Reform and Consumer Protection Act, those who provide information to the Securities and Exchange Commission about a company's violation of some securities law are entitled to a reward.

disclosing classified information to which she gained access while she was an intelligence analyst stationed in Iraq.[4]

In view of the six elements of our definition, Manning's *action* qualifies as a *voluntary, open,* and *unauthorized* report of classified information, which she was under a legal obligation not to disclose. What is more, when Manning took this action, she was a permanent *member* of the US Marine Corps, a part of the public and legitimate *organization* (the US Army) within which the contested facts had occurred. It was by virtue of her membership status, in the role of an intelligence analyst, that Manning came to know about those facts and that she could have *privileged access* to the classified documents, which constituted the nonpublic evidence on which her report was subsequently based. Manning's case thus provides an up-front illustration of the *agent* and *locus* of whistleblowing.

Manning's report was meant to urge that action be taken to *change* a status quo threatening the life of many innocent individuals. Manning's disclosure related to gross violations of human rights on the part of the US Army; these included the murder of unarmed civilians (such as the Granai air strike in Afghanistan) as well as the brutal treatment of detainees and the arbitrary detention of civilians (which was revealed, for instance, in the Guantánamo Bay files [Leigh et al. 2011]). There is little uncertainty, therefore, that its *object* concerned the allegation of *wrongful practices* and *behaviors* that were both *systemic* (like the prisoners' treatment) and *occasional* (such as the air strikes). While the legality of some of the reported military operations has been a matter of debate (for example, the July 12, 2007, Baghdad air strike), all the relevant facts raise serious *moral* concerns insofar as they violate such individual fundamental moral rights as those to life, security, and bodily integrity (see WikiLeaks 2010b; for a commentary, see Meyers 2010). Finally, notice that Manning leaked the various files to WikiLeaks that she managed to collect without first trying to address her concerns to either other fellow members of the Marines Corps or her direct superiors. The *addressee* of Manning's report is entirely *external.*

While the ethical assessment of Manning's action is a matter of controversy, as we discuss below, the case satisfies the six essential elements that analytically define whistleblowing and thus reference to it provides an apt illustration of this practice. But our definition can also be helpful to unmask false positives.

4. Among the many classified documents that Manning leaked, the most influential have been the "Afghan War Diary" (WikiLeaks 2010a) and "Iraq War Logs" (WikiLeaks 2010c).

Think, for instance, of the position of Assange, the founder of WikiLeaks (the addressee of Manning's report). WikiLeaks is a "multi-national media organization and associated library," whose aim is the publication of "large datasets of censored or otherwise restricted official materials involving war, spying and corruption," having as its goal "to bring important news and information to the public" (WikiLeaks 2011). Assange has been frequently presented as a whistleblower. Now his name is quite rightly associated with cases of whistleblowing, such as that of Manning, as we have seen. Yet our analysis suggests that he cannot be rightly considered a whistleblower. While WikiLeaks has played an important role in exposing major cases of organizational wrongdoing, Assange has always acted from outside the organizations where the reported wrongs had occurred. His role has invariably been that of collecting pieces of information from the members of some defective organization that he then exposed. Rather than being a whistleblower, Assange has been the addressee of whistleblowing (as was the case with Manning). Assange's role is thus closer to that of an investigative journalist. Indeed, sometimes journalists report the same kinds of organizational wrongdoing that whistleblowers report. It seems inappropriate, however, to characterize journalists as whistleblowers: although a journalist may help a whistleblower to report wrongdoings (as Assange did with Manning), a journalist is not a whistleblower themselves because they are not the source of the relevant information (see Ceva and Mokrosińska 2021).

These conceptual clarifications can pin down the specificity of whistleblowing with respect to other kinds of reports. This enhanced understanding allows identifying the object of a public ethics of whistleblowing and hence attending with increased precision to the question of its normative justification.

Whistleblowing as a Duty of Public Ethics

As seen, Manning's case presents all the necessary elements of whistleblowing (concerning the relevant kind of actions, agents, locus, object, addressee, and motivation). But was her decision to report morally good or perhaps even a duty?

Reading the details of her story, many would probably think that what Manning did goes well beyond what most people ought to do in similar circumstances. The risks Manning undertook and tragic personal consequences she suffered provide good reasons to conclude that although some may view Manning's actions as morally praiseworthy, what she did goes beyond her—or any other moral agent's—call of duty. This is true for many other whistleblowers, who might have experienced less tragic personal costs than Manning, but had to put up with the negative consequences of their actions—from retaliation and demotion at work, to discrimination and marginalization in society. These costs seem to render whistleblowing a rather burdensome practice, which exceeds the domain of ordinary morality. On the other hand, although there is no doubt about the gravity of the wrongdoings perpetrated by the US Army, one could argue that Manning's disclosure was morally wrong, all things considered, because having leaked unedited materials, she unnecessarily disclosed names and locations of several US officials, exposing them to serious threats to their safety. On this reading, not only was Manning not morally required to report; her disclosures were not even morally permissible. Either way, no normative consideration seems available that could support the idea that whistleblowing refers to a set of actions that are morally *required* of an agent as a question of *public* ethics.

From the perspective of public ethics, the central questions about the normative status of whistleblowing do not concern whether any *particular case* of whistleblowing, such as Manning's, is morally permissible as an individual conscientious response to an emergency. Rather, they concern the justification of whistleblowing as an organizational *practice*—and in particular, the question of whether or not the practice of whistleblowing is morally required. This perspective allows us to focus on the duties that ought to guide someone's action by virtue of the role they occupy within an organization (and not because of the specific individual they are or the personal qualities they have).

Therefore the relevant question for public ethics is not what Manning—or any other potential whistleblower—ought to do because of the specific person she is; nor is it whether Manning's disclosure was permissible qua a morally good action by virtue of the particular professional tasks she had within her organization. The main question is what practices are generally required of a legitimate organization to counter the wrongful practices or behaviors that may occur within it. A derivative question concerns what is required of the members of that organization who have privileged access to some information concerning those wrongful practices or behaviors. This is the distinct sense in which we ask the question of whether whistleblowing is a duty of public ethics.

Surprisingly, contemporary scholars have been quite uninterested in the question of whether or not whistleblowing is a duty of public ethics. Many commentators have engaged with the justification of whistleblowing as something that a member of a legitimate organization *may* yet ought not necessarily to do in standard conditions. For example, the default position is to think that only legal norms or an otherwise enforceable organizational code of professional conduct could make whistleblowing a duty (Leys and Vandekerckhove 2014; Vandekerckhove and Tsahuridu 2010; Tsahuridu and Vandekerckhove 2008). Physicians, lawyers, and engineers, for example, must report episodes of malpractice as a part of their professional obligations. But if we focus exclusively on these cases, the question of whether whistleblowing is a duty does not seem to require much in terms of moral reasoning because the normative strength and cogency of such a duty would derive from a general obligation to obey the law (Raz 1979, 3–36), and the coercive imposition and threats of sanctions.

In the current normative debate, even those who have tackled the question of whether the members of a legitimate organization have a moral duty to report wrongdoings have made it a limited conditional duty binding on particular individuals (see, for example, Delmas 2015). In particular, two views have been prominent: harm- and complicity-based views. On the former view, whistleblowing is required insofar as it is necessary to stop or prevent some measurable serious harm; on the latter view, the moral status of this practice derives from the necessity of avoiding someone's complicity in wrongdoing. Let us take a closer look at each of these views in turn.

The Harm-Based Justification for Whistleblowing

On the harm-based view of whistleblowing, a member of an organization ought to blow the whistle when doing so may prevent or stop a serious harm stemming from some behavior or practices of that organization, about which they have substantive evidence, at a reasonable cost to themselves (see Bowie 1982; De George 2010). So the occurrence of a "serious harm" triggers the duty to blow the whistle. Harms include those wrongdoings that cause some measurable damage to people's health and welfare (from psychological discomfort to physical impairment) as well as possible environmental hazards, but also such behaviors contrary to the public interest such as fraud and corruption (Kumar and Santoro 2017). The qualification of this kind of harm as "serious" establishes a threshold condition, which discriminates between reports that identify real and sizable damages to individuals and society, and mere complaints (such as those deriving from trivial quarrels between coworkers).

Two factors influence the normative stringency of this duty: on the one hand, the available evidence of the (actual or potential) occurrence of a relevant kind of harm, and on the other, the costs associated with reporting it. If a whistleblower is not able to corroborate their accusation with some substantive evidence, their report might be morally permissible but not required. Richard De George (2010, 302), for example, sets this standard of evidence as having proofs that could convince an impartial observer. But substantive evidence might not justify whistleblowing as a matter of duty if discharging this duty comes at an unreasonable cost for the whistleblower. This cost is determined by the kind of personal consequences that may result from the whistleblower's disclosure (like risks of retaliation), and it should not outweigh the expectation concerning the efficacy of such a disclosure to bring about some significantly positive change to the status quo.

Among the criticisms that have been pressed against the harm-based view (see, for example, Davis 1996, 8–10; Hoffman and Schwartz 2015), the following are particularly important. First, the harm-based view endorses too narrow a characterization of the possible *agents* of whistleblowing. How many members of an organization can be plausibly thought to have the capacity of producing a proof that is solid enough to convince an impartial observer about the occurrence of any wrongdoing? Access to robust evidence of this kind might be available only to a limited number of persons, occupying either managerial or technical positions. While this might have been the case with Manning, lower-level employees may form a suspicion to the best of their possible knowledge, which might be worth pursuing, but this approach risks deflecting. To be internally consistent, this view should assign the relevant normative work for the justification of whistleblowing to the harm to be avoided or prevented rather than drawing on the role that someone occupies within an organization.

Second, and setting this epistemic problem aside, on this view the *object* of whistleblowing is too narrow. Quite clearly, there are actions that may be morally problematic even though they do not produce any measurable harmful consequence. Imagine that Lara, the manager of a state-owned company, owes a debt of gratitude to an accountant, Paul, who has helped her husband to overcome some serious fiscal problems he had a few years ago. When a vacancy opens up at Lara's company, Paul calls her, mentioning that his nephew, Steven, is currently unemployed and it would be great if she could help him out by hiring him as a junior member of her staff. Suppose that Steven is quite lucky and no one else applies for the position. Suppose further that he turns out to be a good employee. Because no apparent sizable harm seems to derive from Lisa's hiring Steven to pay back her debt of gratitude to Paul, this case of favoritism is likely to go unnoticed. But what if someone knew Lara's actual agenda, perhaps because he overheard the phone call between Lara and Paul? On the harm-based view, this person (a potential whistleblower) would not be duty bound to report. Yet this conclusion is questionable, to say the least. There is a sense in which allocating jobs in the public sector by virtue of someone's personal debts of gratitude is morally objectionable in itself even if the circumstances are such that no measurable harm is caused.

While it is clear that there is a duty to react to harmful organizational practices or behaviors, there are some forms of harmless wrongdoing that a legitimate organization must be capable of identifying and redressing. The harm-based view therefore cannot offer on its own an exhaustive account of the duties constitutive of a public ethics of whistleblowing.

The Complicity-Based Justification for Whistleblowing

To avoid these limitations of the harm-based view, proponents of the complicity-based view try to offer a more inclusive justification in deontological terms of the duty to blow the whistle. On this second view, a member of an organization ought to blow the whistle when they believe that doing so could avoid their complicity with the occurrence of some wrongful behavior or practice within their organization, and their beliefs are justified and true (see Brenkert 2010; Davis 1996, 2003).

For proponents of the complicity-based view, independently of the kind of wrong that has occurred, insofar as the member of an organization is somehow related to its occurrence (if only because they are justifiably and truthfully aware of it), whistleblowing is justified. Therefore the employee who is aware of Lara's hiring her new assistant to pay back her debt of gratitude to the appointee's uncle, Paul, has good reasons to blow the whistle even if this appointment has not caused any serious measurable harm for any individual or the public interest. The whistleblower's reasons are grounded in a fundamental commitment to respecting their own integrity, which complicity with the manager's wrongdoing would jeopardize (Brenkert 2010). For some proponents of this view, whistleblowing is required granted that the belief that someone's integrity is at risk because of an organizational wrongdoing is justified and true (Davis 1996).

While the complicity-based view avoids the narrowness of its harm-based sibling, it has its own limitations too. First, the idea of complicity is no less controversial and hard to determine than that of harm (see Lepora and Goodin

2013). Basically, any complicity-based justification should specify what being an accomplice in a wrongdoing means and entails—whether it involves, for instance, somebody's active participation in wrongdoing, or their encouragement or assistance in bringing something wrong about, or both. The employee in our example could find themselves mixed up in, or just become aware of, the manager's hiring process, even though they did not contribute to either setting it up or sustaining its course. Thus they would not be playing any active or willful role in the occurrence of the wrongdoing. Their omission to report might nevertheless condone the occurrence of a morally questionable practice. Does this make them a potential accomplice who, given this, has a duty to blow the whistle on the manager? Depending on the normative view of complicity that we adopt, the stringency of the duty of whistleblowing could significantly vary, but proponents of the complicity-based view have not been forthcoming on this point.

This difficulty granted, an epistemic problem remains concerning the standard of evidence that substantiates the whistleblower's beliefs. For example, Michael Davis (1996, 11) adopts a twofold standard: the whistleblower's beliefs must be justified *and* true. Brought to bear on our example, this standard requires—in the first place—that the company's employee acquire substantive evidence about the manager's personal ties with the appointee's uncle, the nature of their relation of dependence, and the manager's commitment to using her public power to pay back a personal debt. This acquisition involves access to a set of information, and presumes a kind of knowledge and understanding capacity that it seems hardly reasonable to expect of an ordinary agent. As seen also with reference to the impartial observer's test at work in De George's harm-based position, this requirement is epistemically demanding and might be met by only a limited number of people within an ordinary organization (if any).

But even if the whistleblower's beliefs were so grounded, this condition would be insufficient to justify their blowing the whistle as a matter of duty. Their beliefs would also have to be *true*. A true belief is one whose propositional content is a fact—that is, something that is indisputably the case. This requirement raises the bar of epistemic demandingness even higher as it entails that one ought to blow the whistle only when one has a rock-solid conviction that their moral integrity is at risk because they're an accomplice of a wrong that is actually occurring. Yet is this standard of belief ever achieved? And in fact, is it a standard of belief that can be justifiably demanded of anyone? The most common cases of whistleblowing see people who act on reasonable suspicions—a belief formed on specific and articulable facts, along with the rationally entailed inferences. Even in the case of Manning, whose allegations were based on some telling documents (for instance, videos of unnamed people stricken by US drones), the degree of certainty of her implication with an actual wrongdoing is a matter of controversy (and was indeed disputed).

This discussion of the complicity-based view can thus reach a similar conclusion to that articulated with reference to the harm-based one. While it manages to capture an important basis for the justification of whistleblowing as a duty, this basis is too narrow to make sense on its own of the many and various instances where the member of an organization may find themselves in the position of deciding what to do facing a wrongful organizational practice or behavior. But providing such a general justification seems nevertheless worthwhile, and in fact, it is necessary to ground a solid public ethics of whistleblowing as one of the best practices to counter organizational wrongdoing. We set out to propose such a justification in the remainder of this chapter.

The Accountability-Based Justification for Whistleblowing

In this section, we purport to overcome the limitations of the harm- and complicity-based views by offering a more robust and encompassing normative account of a public ethics of whistleblowing.[5] To wit, we aim to offer a general justification of whistleblowing capable of encompassing the instances and conditions of organizational wrongdoing that the other views discuss as well as those they fail to capture. Our view is therefore more general than, rather than an alternative to, the other two. If our argument works, whistleblowing is justified a fortiori also in the other cases (that is, when some measurable serious harm is involved and/or the moral integrity of the whistleblower is at stake).

In order to get our argument off the ground, consider the following thought experiment:

> As a bank clerk, you come to develop the reasonable belief (based on some rumors) that one of your colleagues is using customers' money to trade

5. For an extensive treatment of the arguments in this section, see Ceva and Bocchiola 2018, 69–82.

> online. One day, while you stand next to his desk, by peeking at his computer monitor, you realize that if you call your supervisor in that very moment, you can expose your colleague, thus enabling his arrest in the act by the bank's guard. (Ceva and Bocchiola 2018, 66–67)

To isolate the basic conditions of relevant instances of organizational wrongdoing, assume that no apparent measurable serious harm is caused by your colleague's behavior; they take only small amounts of money from several accounts, which they always return to their owners. We can add that your level of involvement in and contribution to your colleague's misbehavior is totally tangential; your job description does not involve any supervisory function of your colleagues' work, and you are not personally related to your colleague or any of their customers in any way. We can thus exclude that your casual position on that day makes you an accomplice to your colleague's misbehavior. You are just at the right time and place to take action against an objectionable behavior. Ought you to act?

Our suggestion is that an answer to this question cannot be found by considering your own personal position in this specific case in isolation. The source of the duty to blow the whistle must be found in the distinctive set of role-based moral obligations that a person acquires by virtue of their entertaining certain relations of membership within a legitimate organizational setting.

To see why, recall that an organization is an institution constituted by a system of interdependent embodied roles governed by public rules to which powers are attached with a specific mandate (Ceva and Ferretti 2021; Miller 2014; Bovens 1998, 9–20). The rules are "public" in the sense that they are generally known and accessible to the members; the set of powers specifies the appropriate range of actions for each role, whose performance structurally depends on that of the other roles within the organization (by virtue of their being interrelated); and the mandate establishes the appropriate ways in and matters over which such actions should be taken. So conceived, organizations generate a system of rights and correlative duties that people hold only by virtue of their occupying specific interrelated roles within an organization. People have these rights and duties *because* they are the members of a legitimate organization, and therefore the normative structural relations between them are constituted by and not prior to the existence of that organization.

The terms of the mandate with which power is entrusted to each organizational role allow for some discretion. Nevertheless, there is a general expectation that those who occupy those roles do so in a way that they can explain with reference to the rationale (either the letter or spirit) of the rule that governs their role (Ceva and Ferretti 2021, 19–42). Thus when people interact as members of an organization, their primary and essential mode of interaction is through relations of *mutual accountability*. By virtue of the interrelatedness of organizational roles, role occupants are directly accountable to the other members of the same organization for the uses that they make of the powers that come with their role. The exact composition of the community of mutually accountable members varies in consideration of the uses of power at stake and kind of organization under scrutiny. For example, it may include the shareholders of a private corporation or extend to cover the citizenry at large were we to consider a democratic governmental organization. These are important details to assess on a case-by-case basis. The general point we would like to emphasize is that these variations granted, the fellow members of a legitimate rule-based system are the *primary* authorities to whom each of them is accountable for the uses they make of their power of office.[6]

The account that the members of an organization owe to one another for their conduct is of a specific sort. To be true to the source of their role-based power, this account must be capable of showing that any given use of a power of office follows a rationale that is coherent with the terms of the mandate that governs those roles. This is the idea of "a duty of office accountability" (Ceva 2018). The duty of office accountability has more precise a referent than one grounded in the idea of harm or complicity that we reviewed in the previous section. But to see how exactly this duty justifies whistleblowing, we need to revisit our thought experiment.

When your colleague uses customers' money to trade online, they make use of the power they have in their capacity as a clerk of the bank for which you both work. But they are also pursuing an agenda (self-enrichment) that is alien to the terms of the mandate that governs the role that gives them the power to act in that very instance. Now as seen, because of their organizational membership and the capacity in which they are acting, your colleague has a duty of office accountability, which requires that they are capable of showing how the rationale of the agenda guiding their conduct is coherent with the terms of their power mandate. Yet this kind of justification is not available for

6. A possible way to state the point is to say that the structural relations between officeholders are a second-person perspective: "the perspective you and I take up when we make and acknowledge claims on one another's conduct and will" (Darwall 2009, 3; see also Feinberg 1970).

their behavior because the rationale of the agenda they pursue when they trade online is quite obviously extraneous to the terms of the mandate with which the power to handle customers' money was attributed to the role they occupy and therefore ought to be exercised. In this sense, the bank clerk's behavior is objectionable in itself because in executing it, they fail to act on the duty of office accountability that is, however, binding on them by virtue of their organizational membership. The bank clerk's behavior is objectionable independent of whether it generates some measurable harm. We want to show also that their behavior is your concern even if you do not stand in any obvious complicit relation to it.

When you come to know about what your colleague is doing—the moment in which you acquire this particular piece of information by virtue of the privileged position you happen to occupy there and then—the duty of office accountability, which your colleague has forfeited, falls onto you. This is because of the interrelatedness of organizational roles and relations of accountability thereby established between role occupants. Therefore you ought to blow the whistle in order to restore the logic of office accountability that your colleague has altered with their misbehavior. Your action is justified as a matter of duty as an instance of the duty of office accountability both of you owe to all the other members of your organization, when you act in your capacity as role occupants, by virtue of the role-based structural relations you all entertain within the rule-based system set in place with the establishment of that organization.

So to summarize, we submit that whistleblowing is justified as a duty when the member of an organization has privileged access to information concerning uses of powers of office within their organization, which contradict that power's mandate, in order to restore the logic of office accountability that the alleged occurrence of that wrongful practice or behavior has altered. As thus conceived, whistleblowing stands in a twofold relation to the realization of office accountability. First, whistleblowing is an *instrument* to enhance the office accountability of an organization because it is a source of otherwise inaccessible information on organizational wrongdoing, whose disclosure is essential to reestablish disrupted relations of accountability between role occupants. Second, by disclosing information in the first person, the whistleblowers' action *realizes in itself* the logic of office accountability that ought to govern the interactions between the members of a legitimate organization.

To understand whistleblowing as a duty within the coordinates of the relations between organizational role occupants means to justify it as an organizational practice to counter organizational wrongdoing from the inside rather than as an individual act of morally motivated disobedience (see Bocchiola and Ceva 2021). It means, in other words, to justify whistleblowing within a public ethics of office not just as a conscientious act of a single officeholder. From the perspective of a public ethics of office, whistleblowing is thus primarily an organizational duty. This duty is binding on any rule-based legitimate organization, and requires, always and necessarily, the establishment of internal (for instance, a secure website for filing a report) and external (for example, some dedicated authority responsible for providing legal advice to whistleblowers' initiatives) reporting mechanisms through which relevant organizational wrongdoings can be brought to light, and consequently, corrective action may be taken.[7] In this sense, whistleblowing is primarily a corrective organizational answerability practice, which fulfills the general organizational duty of accountability when organizational wrongdoing occurs.

When dutiful corrective organizational actions have been taken and the required reporting mechanisms are in place, any member who had privileged access to information concerning a relevant kind of organizational wrongdoing ought to blow the whistle by resorting to one of the established reporting channels, either internal or external (as the circumstances have it). The specific duty to blow the whistle on any given instance of organizational wrongdoing is imperfect and conditional for any one member of the organization. This means that should the organizational duty not be discharged, no individual action is necessarily required as a moral ought, while it may still be permissible. This twofold line of reasoning, organizational and individual, makes sense and corroborates our initial reaction to the evaluation of Manning's disclosures of US troops' crimes to WikiLeaks. Did Manning have the duty to blow the whistle? Or should we view her report as supererogatory? Manning's disclosures seem permissible, but could not be required as a matter of duty because her organization had not established the necessary answerability practices that the general duty of office accountability in fact required (as the ordeals Manning had to endure illustrate). This reasoning makes unauthorized whistleblowing, such as to the media, an *extrema ratio*, which applies when internal and external authorized reporting mechanisms are missing, or arguably, have been exhausted and proved ineffective.[8]

7. An example of this kind of authority can be found in *Wet Huis voor klokkenluiders (House for Whistleblowers Act)*, which came into effect in the Netherlands on July 1, 2016.

8. For an extended discussion of this point, see Ceva and Bocchiola 2018, 83–115.

When whistleblowing *is* a duty, notice also that it could conflict with other duties that people generally have or that derive from the many roles they may occupy by virtue of their different memberships. For example, Manning had the general duty to avoid unnecessary harm (like killing unarmed people); as a soldier, she had a duty of loyalty to the US Marine Corps as well as a duty of secrecy concerning the US government's operations in which she was involved. Such multiple duties could generate a set of conflicting claims such that the duty to blow the whistle is but *one* duty among other moral and legal duties. Hence there could be situations where an agent needs to balance the normative force of such different possibly conflicting duties. Whistleblowing is certainly not an absolute duty, nor is the exercise of this duty unconditional in any particular instance of organizational wrongdoing. In specific circumstances, which require a case-by-case discussion, countervailing reasons might offer an all-things-considered argument for a particular individual not to act on the duty to blow the whistle (for example, for reasons of national security). These circumstantial occurrences, however, do not undermine our general accountability-based justification of whistleblowing as an organizational duty within a public ethics of office. This duty *is there*, and adequate organizational answerability practices to discharge it ought to be in place.

References

Bocchiola, Michele, and Emanuela Ceva. 2021. "Whistleblowing, or the Resistance to Institutional Wrongdoing from Within." *Harvard Review of Philosophy* 28:53–70.

Bovens, Mark. 1998. *The Quest for Responsibility: Accountability and Citizenship in Complex Organizations*. Cambridge: Cambridge University Press.

Bowie, Norman E. 1982. *Business Ethics*. Englewood Cliffs, NJ: Prentice Hall.

Brenkert, George G. 2010. "Whistle-Blowing, Moral Integrity, and Organizational Ethics." In *Oxford Handbook of Business Ethics*, edited by George G. Brenner and Tom L. Beauchamp, 565–601. New York: Oxford University Press.

Ceva, Emanuela. 2018. "Political Corruption as a Relational Injustice." *Social Philosophy and Policy* 35 (2): 118–37.

Ceva, Emanuela, and Michele Bocchiola. 2018. *Is Whistleblowing a Duty?* Cambridge, UK: Polity Press.

Ceva, Emanuela, and Maria Paola Ferretti. 2021. *Political Corruption: The Internal Enemy of Public Institutions*. Oxford: Oxford University Press.

Ceva, Emanuela, and Dorota Mokrosińska. 2021. "Failing Institutions, Whistle-Blowing, and the Role of the News Media." *Journal of Applied Philosophy*. doi:10.1111/happy.12476.

Darwall, Stephen. 2009. *The Second-Person Standpoint: Morality, Respect, and Accountability*. Cambridge, MA: Harvard University Press.

Davis, Michael. 1996. "Some Paradoxes of Whistleblowing." *Business and Professional Ethics Journal* 15 (1): 3–19.

———. 2003. "Whistleblowing." In *Oxford Handbook of Practical Ethics*, edited by Hugh LaFollette, 539–63. New York: Oxford University Press.

———. 2010. "Whistle Blowing." In *Business Ethics*, 298–318. 7th ed. New York: Macmillan.

Delmas, Candice. 2015. "The Ethics of Government Whistleblowing." *Social Theory and Practice* 41 (1): 77–105.

Feinberg, Joel. 1970. "The Nature and Value of Rights." *Journal of Value Inquiry* 4 (4): 243–60.

Grant, Colin. 2002. "Whistle Blowers: Saints of Secular Culture." *Journal of Business Ethics* 39 (4): 391–99.

Hoffman, W. Michael, and Mark S. Schwartz. 2015. "The Morality of Whistleblowing: A Commentary on Richard T. De George." *Journal of Business Ethics* 127 (4): 771–81.

Jubb, Peter B. 1999. "Whistleblowing: A Restrictive Definition and Interpretation." *Journal of Business Ethics* 21 (1): 77–94.

Kumar, Manohar, and Daniele Santoro. 2017. "A Justification of Whistleblowing. *Philosophy and Social Criticism* 43 (7): 669–84.

Leigh, David, James Ball, Ian Cobain, and Jason Burke. 2011. "Guantánamo Leaks Lift Lid on World's Most Controversial Prison." *Guardian*, April 24. https://www.theguardian.com/world/2011/apr/25/guantanamo-files-lift-lid-prison.

Lepora, Chiara, and Robert E. Goodin. 2013. *On Complicity and Compromise*. Oxford: Oxford University Press.

Lewis, David, A. J. Brown, and Richard Moberly. 2014). "Whistleblowing, Its Importance and the State of the Research." In *International Handbook on Whistleblowing Research*, edited by A. J. Brown, David Lewis, Richard Moberly, and Wim Vandekerckhove, 1–36. Cheltenham, UK: Edward Elgar.

Leys, Jos, and Wim Vandekerckhove. 2014. "Whistleblowing Duties." In *International Handbook on Whistleblowing Research*, edited by A. J. Brown, David Lewis, Richard Moberly, and Wim Vandekerckhove, 115–32. Cheltenham, UK: Edward Elgar.

Meyers, Steven Lee. 2010. "Charges for Soldier Accused of Leak." *New York Times*, July 6. http://www.nytimes.com/2010/07/07/world/middleeast/07wikileaks.html.

Miceli, Marcia P., Suelette Dreyfus, and Janet P. Near. 2014. "Outsider 'Whistleblowers': Conceptualizing and Distinguishing 'Bell-Ringing' Behavior." In *International Handbook on Whistleblowing Research*, edited by A. J. Brown, David Lewis, Richard Moberly, and Wim Vandekerckhove, 71–94. Cheltenham, UK: Edward Elgar.

Miceli, Marcia P., and Janet P. Near. 1992. *Blowing the Whistle: The Organizational and Legal Implications for Companies and Employees*. New York: Lexington Books.

Miller, Seumas. 2014. "Social Institutions." In *Stanford Encyclopedia of Philosophy*, edited by Edward N. Zalta. https://plato.stanford.edu/archives/win2014/entries/social-institutions/.

Near, Janet P., and Marcia P. Miceli. 1985. "Organizational Dissidence: The Case of Whistle-Blowing." *Journal of Business Ethics* 4 (1): 1–16.

Raz, Joseph. 1979. *The Authority of Law*. Oxford: Oxford University Press.

Sagar, Rahul. 2013. *Secrets and Leaks: The Dilemma of State Secrecy*. Princeton, NJ: Princeton University Press.

Tsahuridu, Eva E., and Wim Vandekerckhove. 2008. "Organizational Whistleblowing Policies: Making Employees Responsible or Liable?" *Journal of Business Ethics* 82 (1): 107–18.

Vandekerckhove, Wim. 2006. *Whistleblowing and Organizational Social Responsibility*. Aldershot, UK: Ashgate.Vandekerckhove, Wim, and Eva E. Tsahuridu. 2010. "Risky Rescues and the Duty to Blow the Whistle." *Journal of Business Ethics* 97 (3): 365–80.

WikiLeaks. 2010a. "Afghan War Diary." https://wikileaks.org/afg/.

———. 2010b. "Cablegate." https://wikileaks.org/plusd/?qproject[]=cg&q=#result.

———. 2010c. "Iraq War Logs." https://wikileaks.org/irq.

———. 2011. "About." https://wikileaks.org/About.html.

10

Political Ethics in the State of Emergency

Nomi Claire Lazar

AN EMERGENCY is an urgent situation that threatens life, limb, or property. The threat may result from natural or human causes, intentional or inadvertent. Nature may bring an emergency: a hurricane or tsunami, wildfire, ice storm, or flood. And humans cause many more: economic collapse, the imminent threat of or fallout from war, terror attack, or other form of civil violence. Often human activity combines with nature to heighten the threat, and one type of emergency may lead to another. A natural disaster may lead to disease or economic collapse, which in turn may lead to violence. In a public emergency, the state's capacity to safeguard citizens from such threats is threatened too. The ambulance may lack a passable road to reach you, the banks may lack the liquid funds to give you, and firefighters may lack the personnel, equipment, or information to keep you secure. A public emergency may destroy infrastructure, outstripping the capacity of a government's usual safety responses. In extreme cases, a public emergency may obstruct, disrupt, or entirely halt the normal functions of government itself. It is thus a moral duty incumbent on political leaders in a constitutional democracy to prevent or else effectively confront emergencies, and rapidly restore the state's capacity to secure, respond to, and serve its citizens.

Yet dealing effectively with a public emergency may trample other moral imperatives. Rights may need to be derogated—property commandeered, assembly prohibited, speech limited, or due process constricted. All of these are standard elements of emergency power. Furthermore, power may concentrate in fewer or else different hands. This supposedly increases the coordination of state response. A legislature may grant an executive greater sway, the military may assume civilian powers, and lower-level functionaries may acquire tremendous discretion over lives and property, with no time for appeal.

Because the supreme duty to preserve the *salus populi*, the public welfare, may require the violation of these other fundamental duties, it is sometimes said that there is a separate political ethics of emergency, perhaps governed by an emergency utilitarianism, which is sometimes called a "threshold deontology." This is the view that there is a point at which the consequences of behaving in accordance with duty are so horrific that any reasonable person would, in that instance only, temporarily "switch" from a deontological to a utilitarian ethics. Others argue that on the contrary, exceptional, emergency government simply illuminates the normal case: political power and the actions it enables are always *beyond norms*. On this view, we are always subject to raw sovereign power and the rule of law is nothing more than a thin veneer. Hence there is no separate ethics of emergency. The emergency simply reveals the permanently amoral character of politics: it is in the nature of law to suspend itself, political ethics to mute itself, and checks on power to uncheck themselves at the sovereign's discretion. The rule of law is just a facade.

There is a third perspective, which I will support below: emergencies are *urgent*, but they are not *exceptional*. That is, the urgency of emergencies may require unusual *actions*, yet it does not follow from this that the moral principles involved in the decision to act are distinct. A plurality of moral norms animates all political ethics, in normal times and a crisis. It is not the norms themselves that vary depending on the times but rather what would constitute a defensible judgment on the right course of action. For all political ethics relies not only on the identification of pertinent norms and principles but in the first instance, also on the identification of pertinent *facts*, and in the final instance, on a situation-specific *judgment*—a decision on a course of action in light of those facts and principles. It is the judgment, and not the principles themselves, that may vary in the face of urgency. After the fact, the moral reasons a leader gives for their choice—if they are good reasons—are recognizable as consistent with everyday ethical-political norms and values. On this normative pluralist view, there is moral continuity between times of normalcy and times of crisis, even as judgments can vary with context.

Below I review a variety of moral debates around emergency ethics. I begin by showing how the outlines of a crisis can change rapidly, making it difficult to gather sufficient, stable information to inform a right course of action. That paucity of facts may make consequences difficult to predict, meaning it may not be evident what counts as an emergency in the first place. Does this mean someone needs to decide, beyond the application of a decision rule, when there is an emergency? And if that decision leads to restrictions of rights, is the decider in fact above the law? While this position, first articulated by Weimar (and later, Nazi) legal theorist Carl Schmitt, commands wide assent among theorists, I argue that it is plagued by conceptual and empirical difficulties, and should be rejected. Nonetheless, a paucity of facts makes emergency decision-making a morally fraught activity.

Conflicting norms impact decision in an emergency too, and so I turn next to how deontological and utilitarian perspectives perform in this light. Some scholars maintain that at some threshold, a deontologist must convert to emergency utilitarianism, while others assert this is incoherent. I contend that leaders may sometimes be morally required to do wrong, but when such moral tragedies take place, the acts that brought them about must be *called* wrong and their perpetrators called wrongdoers. With Michael Walzer, I hold that such leaders are culpable for their actions, even when the act was necessary. I go on from there to consider the values underlying the rule of law, which are especially vulnerable in emergencies. The debate between Oren Gross and David Dyzenhaus illustrates what's at stake in designing legal institutions that embrace or exile emergency action, privileging or bracketing the rule of law. I then conclude by arguing that beyond principles and facts, judgment—both on the part of the decision maker(s) and the people after the fact—will always be essential. This is true not only in crisis but in normal times as well. Thus while emergency powers present a variety of acute moral complexities, these are different in timbre, but not in type, from political ethics generally.

Facts

Good Moral Decisions Require Good Information

All moral decision-making begins with ascertaining the facts. These may be straightforward. When faced with the injunction to *not* lie, *not* steal, or *not* cheat, it is normally evident what would count as an instance of lying, stealing, or cheating. But when ethics requires action rather than refraining from action, we need to investigate its character: the context into which the action intervenes and its probable effects. For example, in meeting the duty to behave charitably, it is incumbent to ensure that our actions are actually charitable. Volunteer stints in orphanages, say, lead to instability and the recurrent experience of loss for resident children, and foreign donations to "orphanages" have led to an industry that convinces parents to give over their children, who are then trafficked or paraded in front of tourists to secure donations (Lecoufle 2018; UNICEF, n.d.). What seems like charity is, in fact, not. To meet a duty, we must know the real character of our action. The character of actions, like the meaning of words, depends on their context. For this reason, a good moral choice always requires good information.

Because of the truly vast empirical complexity of the social and political realm, the problem of facts may be the greatest (and least acknowledged) source of challenge and uncertainty in political ethics. How well can a decision maker really understand what they are doing, and anticipate the consequences of a social policy decision, political negotiation, or foreign policy move? Even so-called evidence-based policy making confronts a range of fact difficulties; policy research may suffer from design flaws, and even the best evidence-based policy may not translate from one community to another (Parkhurt 2017; Becker, Bryman, and Sempik 2006; Mendez 2012). The complexities of human social interactions mean negative externalities, initially unrecognized, may emerge over the course of time. And as Horst Rittel and Melvin Webber (1973, 155) argued "in a pluralistic society . . . policies that respond to social problems cannot be meaningfully correct or false; and it makes no sense to talk about 'optimal solutions' to social problems unless severe qualifications are imposed first. Even worse, there are no 'solutions' in the sense of definitive and objective answers." In the social and political realms, moral decisions are always made in conditions of relative uncertainty and the face of possible intractability, and social scientific investigation can only get us some way toward reducing this. I am calling this the problem of facts in political ethics. It is the problem of gathering sufficiently complete and accurate information about what a problem is, and what the likely effects of different means of addressing it might be. Without this information, from a moral perspective, we may quite literally not know what we are doing.

Emergency dramatically compounds these difficulties. Decision makers may have little warning, and the nature and scope of the crisis may change rapidly, as an earthquake becomes a tsunami, and a tsunami becomes a nuclear power plant breakdown. And a compressed time line limits opportunities for gathering information in the first place. Emergencies may come on suddenly and need to be dealt with urgently, and often before the full scope of the situation, which may anyway change from moment to moment, is understood. How can a leader know what is morally required when the shape of the situation remains unclear? At best, they make a best guess.

In one sense, it would be easy to overstate this difficulty, particularly in light of empirical research over the last two decades and the rapidly expanding field of disaster management studies. The fact is that while most *token instances* of emergency arise with limited warning, the more common *types* of emergency with which humans are confronted are of predictable kinds and allow for advance preparation. With the knowledge that token instances of volcanic eruption or epidemic, hurricane or terrorism will, location depending, probably occur over time, impacted jurisdictions now normally have contingency plans in place. In Indonesia, geological early warning systems and innovative public education mean people and livestock can be safely evacuated before a volcanic eruption. Building codes and public education in Japan and along the West Coast of North America aim to do the same for earthquakes. This is to say, while we do not know when an emergency will occur, we know with something approaching statistical certainty that common types of emergencies will take place; there will be novel epidemic diseases, volcanic eruptions, and earthquakes in active seismic zones. Empirical research can inform a state's or the international community's response. For example, an inquiry after the evacuation of Houston prior to Hurricane Rita (2005) found that the evacuation itself had doubled the mortality rate of the hurricane. So with the benefit of this analysis, the mayor of Houston knew *not* to order an evacuation with the approach of Hurricane Harvey in 2017 (King 2017). And Singapore, in the wake of the 2002–3 SARS pandemic, put in place protocols that have worked effectively to minimize the harm of COVID-19. In other words, contemporary leaders can be more prepared in a crisis than they once were, and certainly more prepared than the literature on emergencies sometimes suggests.

Nonetheless, the timing, scope, and effects of any token emergency are uncertain, and novel threats appear and evolve. As the climate shifts, and as humans create novel weapons and novel chemical impacts on the environment, novel forms of crisis are sure to unfold too. Even known, potentially catastrophic events may have poorly understood or rarely experienced effects; we have, thankfully, little experience of nuclear warfare, and our experience with novel pathogens begins afresh with each outbreak. It takes time to determine the mechanism of transmission and effects of a novel disease, as we have seen in the recent cases of SARS, Zika, and COVID-19 and a tailored and morally sensitive response requires this information. Even expected forms of crisis have elements of unpredictability and take unexpected turns. So preparation reduces, but does not eliminate, the problem of facts. Political leaders are thus confronted with the permanent challenge of neither over- nor underreacting, despite limited information. Where leaders have underreacted, as in the 2009 L'Aquila earthquake and flooding following Hurricane Katrina in 2005, this has resulted in mass suffering, and in the case of a city official who downplayed the risk in L'Aquila, a prison sentence for manslaughter (Abbott and Nosengo 2014). Where they have overreacted, as in the cases of Ebola and SARS quarantines, this has had human and political costs too (Schabas 2004; Ohlheiser and Kang 2014).

Without good information, sound moral decision-making is especially challenging, and on the basis of any consequentialist calculation, probably impossible. Because of the moral risks associated with insufficient information, it is incumbent on public officials to prepare in advance to the extent possible for statistically likely emergencies so that situations can be assessed and decisions made on the basis of the best information, most rapidly available. This is a practical moral problem: without a nuanced understanding of both the sciences of disaster in general and an immediate disaster in particular, good decisions will rely partly on luck. The problem of facts thus is the first and fundamental one of moral action in a crisis.

UNCERTAINTY ABOUT FACTS CREATES A MORAL PROBLEM OF DECISION

Amid this constellation of moral problems characterized by a paucity of facts lurks a deeper and much darker moral-epistemic puzzle, which begins from the problem of what counts as an emergency in the first place. How does one know that a situation has moved from the realm of "problem" to that of "emergency"? How many people must be affected, and how proximate must the devastation be? And what if the scenario involved is entirely novel and part of the crisis is precisely the lack of information? If there is no "fact of the matter," then someone needs to decide. That decision will inevitably involve the derogation or limitation of rights, so what does it mean for liberal democracy if there is a "someone" who, at any given moment, has the power to decide when law applies in the usual way and when it does not? This problem was famously identified by Schmitt, who started to write about emergencies in 1921, amid the political and economic chaos in the wake of the Treaty of Versailles. In his book *Die Diktatur*, Schmitt ([1921] 1994) initially identified two historical types of consolidated power for governing in times of crisis. The "commissarial" dictator is granted concentrated but temporary power to bring about the resolution of a crisis and restore the constitutional order. An example here is the Roman institution of the dictatorship. The senate and consuls would, with responsibilities for the decision divided between them, appoint as "dictator" a person of known moral standing to resolve a crisis. The dictator was required to immediately lay down their power on completion of their task, or if after six months they had failed, lay it down then. This form of dictatorship is constitutional and aims to make itself redundant.[1] Its use rests on the assumption that there are distinct periods of crisis and normalcy that are recognizable as well as knowable. Schmitt called the other form of dictatorship "sovereign." The sovereign dictator has power that does not find its source in constitutional law, nor can it be constrained by it. Neither, though, does the sovereign dictator eschew law. Rather, the sovereign dictator is the guarantor of law and person responsible for maintaining the conditions necessary for the law to apply. Norms, Schmitt ([1921] 2015, 19) once said, are applicable only in the normal situation. And for the normal situation to exist, someone must guarantee order from above. The power that someone wields cannot have its source in law because it is through this power that law exists at all. This is sovereign power.

For Schmitt, the guarantor is necessary because emergency is not an ontological category. That is to say, there is no set of criteria against which clear information could be compared to make an empirical, binary determination: yes, this is an emergency, or no, this is not. What will count as an emergency cannot be established by rules in advance, nor can it be discussed and debated in the context of deliberative democracy. Rather, the determination that an emergency, which Schmitt called a state of exception or *Ausnahmezustand*, exists rests on a decision. In deciding when the law applies, is the decider not above the law? Is he not, as Schmitt asserts in his famous opening statement in *Political Theology*, sovereign because it is he who decides on the exception? It follows that there is no such thing as a commissarial dictator who makes himself redundant, and Schmitt moves to reject this category in *Political Theology* (McCormick 1999, 121–56). All dictatorship is sovereign dictatorship. Because a state of emergency cannot be a determination of "fact," because there is no fact of the matter but rather a decision on the matter, all dictatorship

1. For further discussion of the Roman dictatorship, see Kalyvas 2007; Lazar 2006, 2013; Nicolet 1982; de Wilde 2012, 2013.

is sovereign, and all action that pertains to the application of the law is dictatorship. Hence liberal democracy is either doomed or a sham.

The influential thinker Giorgio Agamben, drawing on Walter Benjamin's *Theses on the Philosophy of History*, has gone further. If there is no "fact of the matter" with respect to when an emergency exists, and if, when an emergency is declared into existence, the law is silent, then we are but an arbitrary decision away from losing law's protection. This constant potentiality is as good as a constant actuality; we are always already, to use the term that Agamben (1998, 115) borrows from the Romans, *homo sacer*, ejected from the normal sphere of law, abandoned, free to be killed. The substance of law is ephemeral, continuing to exist only at the pleasure of the sovereign. It is the force of law, a force iconically manifest in the executive decree, that remains (Agamben 2005, 32ff.). For Agamben and his followers, then, that emergency power exists is proof that political power more generally is normatively bereft. It follows that normative questions about law and emergency are moot; sovereignty, after all, "is the point of indistinction between violence and law, the threshold on which violence passes over into law, and law passes over into violence" (Agamben 1998, 32). Thus the indeterminacy of the emergency, the lack of "facts" of the matter, ultimately undermines the moral claims of constitutional democracy entirely.

Decision Does Not Entail Sovereign Power

Were Schmitt, and then Agamben, correct in this analysis, the problem of facts in the study of the ethics of emergency powers would be revealed as oxymoronic. It would no longer make sense to inquire into how emergencies might be handled ethically because, first, emergencies would be revealed to be a normal, not special, case, and second, no ethical political action is conceivable under Agamben's description. There is on this view no issue of emergency ethics because there is only a continuity of possible exposure to sovereign violence. Since sovereign power cannot be governed by norms, since it is, on this view, the source of norms, the realm of the political in a democracy is above ethics as a norm-structured activity.

The Schmitt-Agamben conception of a state of exception is, however, undermined by both logical and empirical difficulties. It is certainly true that particularly because of the problems inherent in determining when an emergency situation in fact exists, law cannot rule on its own. This is an important insight, and one that reveals some of the empirically attested dangers with emergency power. But it is fallacious to jump from this recognition to the assumption that the person who decides is *sovereign*, exempt from norms. For one thing, the problem of facts is not unique to the determination of whether a particular situation is an emergency. Administrative law is full of parallel calls for judgments that necessarily exceed rule-bound determinations based on clear sets of facts. For example, while abstract legal criteria describe who is a refugee, the application of those criteria depend on judgment, case by case, and in the face of sometimes cloudy facts. There *are* in fact guiding legal criteria for what will count as an emergency too, and the tension comes in judging their application. There will be clear and less clear cases, and while a decision (whether about refugee status or emergency) must be made, and while that decision brings a fact into existence, this assertion of fact must be supported by *reasons* in a rule of law society and will often be reviewable. It must bear scrutiny. The Schmitt-Agamben perspective makes sense only in temporal isolation. Any decision to suspend rights in an emergency appears sovereign only in a moment, in temporal abstraction from all the politics and jurisprudence that came before, and everything that comes after. It is in this long view that reason giving takes place.

It is an absurd leap from underdetermination to sovereignty. Flexibility and discretion have always formed part of liberal democratic and republican forms of government. And law and the rule of law are made up of not just "the black letter of the law" but also collective habits of government, unwritten principles, and constitutional conventions and precedents, established, interpreted, and applied by officeholders. Nor must power be sovereign to mute the law. Several other kinds of pre- or coconstitutional powers are available to confront emergencies without resort to sovereignty. These include police (Novak 2000; Freund 1904) and prerogative power (Fatovic and Kleinerman 2013; Goldsmith 2013), ringed around with jurisprudence (Loevy 2016), with informal constraints and political consequences for ill use. Simply put, we don't need sovereign power to make crisis decisions because we have these and other kinds of power in our tradition, beyond explicitly, legally granted forms of power. While ultimately a single person may make decisions in a crisis, such decisions are influenced, structured, and in some cases, constrained by a mass of experience, informal as well as formal legal and moral norms, advice, protocol, preordained bureaucratic procedure, and notably, the decision maker's banked legitimacy. And after the fact, decisions may be subject to judicial or popular review. Importantly, even were there a sovereign power above the law, what would justify exempting this decider from the government of moral norms? A moral order is not dependent on a political order and thus requires no sovereign guarantor.

All emergency action is therefore ringed around with normative constraint both informal and informal, making clear the fictitious quality of Agamben's image of a sinister sovereign who strips us to bare life. Of course, it would be both naive and historically ignorant to assume that leaders will never abuse the power to mute rights in a crisis, or that they will never see a crisis as an opportunity to pursue unrelated aims with more efficiency than justice.[2] Such abuses certainly occur, but they are *abuses*, which rationally can be (and sometimes are) pursued and punished (Roach 2013).[3]

Yet even for those leaders who have the public interest at heart, navigating inadequate information is a persistent and unresolvable problem of emergency ethics. From the perspective of citizens, the occasional necessity of secrecy exacerbates this problem, limiting our capacity to evaluate and judge the legality as well as morality of our leaders' critical decisions. It is in the nature of secrecy that we cannot always judge its warrant for ourselves. Hence even if one rejects the claim of sovereign power, problems of fact are profoundly morally consequential in a crisis. It will sometimes be a matter of judgment whether a situation is an emergency or not, and it will always be a matter of judgment—the leader's and thereafter the people's—how it ought to be addressed. The problem of facts as a driver of moral uncertainty is certainly not unique to emergency, but it is particularly acute there.

2. Notable examples of abuse include the near-continuous state of emergency in Egypt since independence, under which many journalists and opposition politicians have suffered torture and imprisonment; the campaign of forced sterilization done under the cover of then prime minister Indira Gandhi's 1975–77 emergency in India; and the case of the Morant Bay rebellion in Jamaica in 1865, when British governor Edward John Eyre allowed a range of violent reprisals including public floggings and executions without proper trials. Eyre's case became a cause célèbre. Many prominent people called for his indictment for murder while others offered to pay his legal expenses. Ultimately neither Eyre nor his subordinates were held accountable. On the place of emergency powers in colonial rule generally, see Hussain 2003. On the emergency in India, see Dhar 2003. On Jamaica, see Heuman 1994.

3. The case of Kaci Hickox provides a fine example. Hickox is a Doctors Without Borders nurse who traveled to West Africa to serve those suffering in the 2014–16 Ebola epidemic there. On her return, against scientific advice, she was isolated in a tent in New Jersey and initially denied contact with anyone, including a lawyer. The quarantine resumed after she was escorted back to her home state of Maine. Hickox had a judge overturn the order and then later sued New Jersey for the breach of her civil liberties. See Santora 2017.

Norms

Conflicting Norms Are Omnipresent, but Difficult to Resolve in Emergencies

Not just facts but norms are tricky in an emergency. Indeed, emergencies seem to demand the violation of our most treasured moral principles. If the *salus populi*, the well-being of the people, is the highest law, and order is its necessary precondition, then emergencies that threaten order may require both that rights and due process are respected, and in the service of restoring order, that they are derogated. If the fundamental moral purpose of liberal democracy is the prevention of domination, then it seems emergency action may require dirty hands.

What kinds of rights are derogated in an emergency? Because it would be wasteful to stockpile resources that could, in the meantime, be productively deployed elsewhere, a crisis often necessitates the derogation of property rights. Materials, vehicles, equipment, and even whole factories may be commandeered in order to move sandbags, facilitate rescue, treat the wounded, or manufacture munitions. Speech rights may be derogated to facilitate a war effort or cover the movements of security forces attempting to neutralize a terror attack. Due process rights, including in some jurisdictions habeas corpus, may be challenged or curtailed. Both international rights documents and domestic constitutions recognize this need to derogate in a crisis explicitly. Article 4 of the International Covenant on Civil and Political Rights, for instance, states that with the exception of certain nonderogable rights,

> in time of public emergency which threatens the life of the nation and the existence of which is officially proclaimed, the States Parties to the present Covenant may take measures derogating from their obligations under the present Covenant to the extent strictly required by the exigencies of the situation, provided that such measures are not inconsistent with their other obligations under international law and do not involve discrimination solely on the ground of race, colour, sex, language, religion or social origin. (United Nations, n.d., Article 4[1])[4]

4. The nonderogable rights (as enumerated in the United Nations International Covenant on Civil and Political Rights Article 4[2]), include the right not to be arbitrarily deprived of life (Article 6); not to be tortured or subjected to cruel and unusual punishment (Article 7); not to be enslaved or held in servitude (Article 8[1, 2]), although protection from compulsory labor (Article 8[3]) is derogable; not to be imprisoned for inability to meet a contractual obligation

Just about every jurisdiction has domestic emergency provisions that enable derogations, limits, and caveats to rights, both in constitutions and regular statutes. How ought we to understand this challenge to these most fundamental norms and principles in a liberal democratic, constitutional regime?

Moral thinkers of both a deontological and consequentialist persuasion have worked to maintain a consistent, principled approach to the moral complexity of crisis. Because deontology, a duties- and rights-based approach to ethics, does not allow for exceptions, on the face of it, it provides no means of reconciling conflicting duties. Hence some scholars have advocated for the idea that there is a threshold of catastrophe beyond which something that may look like utilitarianism must guide public action. Michael Moore (2010, 719) uses the term "threshold deontology" to describe this view, arguing that "it just is not true that one should allow a nuclear war rather than killing or torturing an innocent person. It is not even true that one should allow the destruction of a sizable city by a terrorist nuclear device rather than kill or torture an innocent person. To prevent such extraordinary harms extreme actions seem to me to be justified."

But this view—that an ethics of rights and duties can be overridden in the most extreme situations—raises many difficulties, some of which have been detailed in the work of Larry Alexander (2000). First, are there limits to what can be done when the threshold is reached? Can you torture the bomb planter to find out its location? Can you torture their parent to make them tell? Is there a limit to the *number* of people you could torture? Then, as Anthony Ellis (1992) has argued, there is the absurdity of attempting to determine the threshold in the first place. For example, either there is some *specific* number of lives, N, which constitutes a breach of the threshold warranting public officials to violate sacred duties (not to torture, say, or not to kill the innocent), or the rightness or wrongness of an action is sometimes arbitrary. If it cannot be the case that ethics is arbitrary, then there must be some number N that constitutes a threshold. But how could we know what that number is? What if it were one less? What if, in the course of whatever action one undertakes, the number of persons in danger changes slightly, dropping below N; must one immediately cease (for instance) torturing the terrorist's parent? Could one be permitted—could one even be morally required—to intentionally endanger another person in order to reach the threshold? (Alexander 2000, 900–910).

(Article 11); and not to be found guilty of an offense that was not, at the time of its commission, an offense (Article 15). They also include the right to recognition as a person before the law (Article 16), and freedom of thought, conscience, and religion (Article 18).

In *Just and Unjust Wars*, Walzer proposes a form of threshold deontology that seems to escape these objections. The concept he proposes there, that of a "supreme emergency," eschews the numerical threshold in favor of a functional/conceptual one. It is not strictly the number of lives at stake but rather a threat to the life of the *state itself*, the collective way of life, that constitutes the threshold. Where an aggressor threatens mass enslavement or extermination, the rules of war, *jus in bello*, are held in abeyance, and it becomes not just permissible but also incumbent on political leaders to kill the innocent, and as many of them as is strictly necessary. "For the survival and freedom of political communities—whose members share a way of life, developed by their ancestors, to be passed on to their children—are the highest values in international society" (Walzer 1977, 254). Walzer's position is distinct from that of Schmitt, who contended that norms are silenced precisely so that the enemy—defined as those who threaten one's way of life—may be identified and neutralized because, as Walzer (1977, 255) observes, danger "makes only half the argument; imminence makes the other half." Furthermore, the party against whom we are arrayed must have been the aggressor; they must have actively sought our destruction. Whereas a Schmittian could justify almost anything as existential somewhere down the road, for Walzer, annihilation must be proximate and the result of the actions of a morally culpable aggressor state. For Walzer, in such times of genuine, justified, and imminent existential terror, a leader cannot put their own moral purity ahead of their peoples' well-being. They must dirty their hands and sacrifice their moral integrity for the peoples' sake.

Even this formulation faces difficulties. Immanuel Kant, the thinker most closely associated with deontology, had argued that each should be treated as an end in themselves and never only as a means, as a resource for others. But as Alexander (2000, 912) asserts,

> The threshold deontologist would have us believe that we switch from not being resources for others to being resources for others when *N* is reached. When *N* is looked at like that, however, it seems downright implausible that the moral universe is so constituted. There may be thresholds at which new phenomena emerge, but it is quite another thing to have thresholds at which things become their opposites.

In light of this objection, could Walzer simply be a consequentialist who moves from a rule- to a case-based version in catastrophic circumstances? Then things would not simply become their opposite at the threshold. That is, one could contend that everyone is better off when persons are treated as ends in themselves and that rights serve as the handy heuristic of this view. But since it is on account of people being better off that rights exist in the first place, it could make sense to say that catastrophe trumps these apparent trumps, and that the criteria of culpability and imminence keep the rules forceful. The rule utilitarian may seem, then, to have a ready-made answer to the tragic norms that seem to govern emergency action.

Yet Walzer is adamant that the supreme emergency cannot negate the ultimate value of those persons whose rights are overruled. For Walzer, and contra Schmitt, norms are for always, not only for the normal situation. They never cease to be in force, even in the supreme emergency, and govern everyone's actions, including those of the political leader or decider. Killing the innocent is never right in itself, it is never praiseworthy, even when it is the *right thing to do all-things-considered*. It is possible, for Walzer, to be morally compelled to do things that are morally repellent. But those people who are used as resources for us, in such cases, are always also understood to be ends in themselves, and their use or loss is tragic. From a utilitarian perspective where everyone counts for one and no one for more than one, a person whose rights are trampled in a crisis may legitimately ask whether their worth as a human being was just a negligible fraction to begin with, a value of one over tens of millions. We must recognize that those whose rights are sacrificed, particularly when they are themselves innocent of wrongdoing, are of the same infinite value as everyone else.

It is thus important that this person who dirties her hands for us is not to be celebrated as a hero but instead shamed or even shunned. Walzer cites the example of Arthur Harris, the Royal Air Force commander responsible for the area bombing campaign that destroyed Dresden and 130,000 of its citizens, among other cities. The Bomber Command crews were refused honors after the Second World War. And while Harris himself was unrepentant, he has remained a figure of great controversy. A statue of him erected in 1992 by Queen Elizabeth met with enormous protest (Walzer 1977, 324; Kinzer 1992). Walzer (1977, 247) says that "in an emergency, neutral rights can be overridden, and when we override them we make no claim that they have been diminished, weakened, or lost. They have to be overridden . . . precisely because they are still there, in full force, obstacles to some great (necessary) triumph for [hu]mankind." If threshold deontology is simply a form of utilitarianism, then the element of shame or solemn regret is negated. The idea is not that one has done the right thing because of the circumstances but rather that one has been forced by the circumstances to do a wrong thing because the alternative was unthinkable. So utilitarianism does not provide the straightforward framework of principles for addressing an emergency that one might hope. Indeed, consequentialists face especially grave difficulties in emergencies because good consequentialist decisions require good information, and a handle on complexity and probability. But as we saw in the section above, urgency and unpredictability may make data hard to come by. It is then exceedingly difficult to calculate the course of action with the best outcome.

A firm command of what duty requires at such times can aid in navigating through the morass. While a clear sense of duty will only get one so far, it will at a minimum make evident that those people whose property is commandeered or labor is conscripted must, at the same time, be treated with respect, their contribution acknowledged, appreciated, and perhaps compensated. It will necessitate the acknowledgment that when the innocent are lost or even murdered for the greater existential good, the loss is infinite, not infinitesimal. The same considerations, principles, and rights will continue in moral force regardless of an emergency.

A clear sense of duty helps, but complexity means that knowledge of duty cannot, on its own, dictate action. Good moral decision-making calls for good judgment to both weigh the facts and balance conflicting principles. And this is not unique to crisis but rather a characteristic of most social and political decision-making—that is, wherever complexity is present. But before turning to the question of judgment specifically, there is one moral principle worthy of separate attention, and this is the rule of law.

Conflicts with the Rule of Law Create Special, Additional Challenges

Respect for legal norms is essential to the rule of law, which in turn is a foundational element of political ethics. Thus extralegal action in a crisis, whatever its broader substantive moral quality, is always a moral problem in itself. Ought action in a crisis, then, to be consistently legal in order to respect the fundamental principle of the rule of law? In contemporary scholarship, the legal modalities of emergency action along with their moral character and consequences have been carefully set out by Oren Gross and Fionnuala Ní Aoláin (2006). They describe three approaches. First, one may insist on the consistent necessity of legality and the rule of law, and employ a business as usual model. Such a model would exclude mention of emergency powers from constitutional documents and reject special legislation. For example, terrorism could be addressed through the normal mechanisms of the criminal law, and quarantine could be voluntary or absorbed under everyday police powers. Here rights are rights, the rule of law is the rule of law, and the limits and derogations imposed by police power are just the normal business of government. Arguably, this is the very meaning of the rule of law in the first place. Such models may seem naive or hypocritical: Is it really the case that in the face of an invasion, government could manage with the usual rights and their everyday limitations? Would it be *moral* to do so given the potential consequences? Might it not be better for states to acknowledge, bring into the open, and then regulate extraordinary measures they may need to take? An expansion of police power in such a situation could have negative consequences for rights in everyday life.

The second approach provides legal sanction for exceptional measures. Gross and Ní Aoláin (2006) call these "models of accommodation." Here flexibility is written right into laws and constitutions so that in times of crisis, leaders may take necessary measures within legal bounds. These legal bounds, however, expand and contract when necessary so that extreme action is confined to crises, and rights (with the usual police limitations) remain firm in times of normalcy. For instance, Canada's Emergencies Act (1985) sets the criteria for an emergency declaration, outlines which rights may be derogated in specific situations, and what will bring the emergency to a close. In this way, exceptions are accommodated within the realm of legality. This is probably the most common, contemporary system for managing emergencies.[5]

But there are problems here as well. First, systems of accommodation have a way of infiltrating regimes of normal law, as several scholars have demonstrated.[6] People become "used" to emergency law, and provisions often remain active long after any immediate danger has evaporated, thereby eroding rights regimes. This happens because, as Dyzenhaus has elegantly argued, the rule of law becomes conflated with and ultimately undermined by rule *by* law. When we demand that all power be legal power, and all action be legally sanctioned action, then the use of legislation to rubber stamp executive action that would normally be extralegal facilitates the creation of insidious "legal gray holes." These are legal black holes into which one could fall, but viewed through a

5. It may be noteworthy, though, that this legislation was used only once in its first thirty-four years in force, despite many regional and provincial emergency declarations.

6. See Donohue 2001; Rossiter 2002; Gross and Ní Aoláin 2006. In the United States, the 1976 National Emergencies Act had as a key aim to resolve the problem of standing emergencies then in effect, which included emergency powers from 1933 (limiting gold hoarding), 1950 (the Korean War), and 1971 (inflation). Since then, however, emergency powers, mostly connected with international trade, have begun to accumulate again.

frosted lens of ad hoc legality (Dyzenhaus 2006, 3). In this way, the appearance of legality in an accommodation model can mask the abuse of state power.

Gross, for his part, advocates a third option. Recalling Walzer's account of exception from moral norms, Gross argues for a similar approach with legal norms. Maintain the integrity of the law and the rule of law, he suggests, and in those really exceptional cases, expect leaders to break the law. After the fact, the leader must admit this, throw themselves on the mercy of the people, and hope for, but not expect, indemnification. Where they are not indemnified, leaders must accept the consequences. This "extralegal measures" model has several advantages, according to Gross. First, it secures respect for the law: law must not be stretched or distorted, even in exceptional circumstances. Second, it prevents the "creep" of emergency measures into the regime of normal law. And third, because it is so extreme and so costly to political leaders, we have some reassurance that such measures will be used only when really necessary. If the rule of law is of fundamental moral value, then this approach, Gross contends, shows it the greatest respect.

Some might question whether it is realistic to expect political leaders to throw themselves on the peoples' mercy as the extralegal measures model requires. There are historical examples, such as US president Thomas Jefferson in the wake of the Louisiana Purchase in 1803, but their rarity is not reassuring.[7] Furthermore, Gross here is focused on the most extreme and dramatic cases of emergency—situations in which terrorist nuclear plots must be foiled or manifest destiny secured. But emergencies are dramatically more common. Extreme weather events like blizzards, ice storms, hurricanes, and floods are increasingly regular features in the shadow of climate change. So are terror attacks and other forms of mass murder. COVID-19 saw most of the world under a state of emergency for years. Dozens of major violent attacks, political and otherwise, are thwarted by police and intelligence services annually, while dozens more succeed.[8] Because crises are so common, the extralegal measures

7. In 1802, France, in desperation, offered the United States the opportunity to acquire a vast territory at the strategic expense of Spain. The treaty was signed in 1803, but Jefferson was profoundly troubled by whether he had the constitutional power to acquire territory through treaty in this way. Ultimately, funds would need to be appropriated by Congress, which was done after the treaty was concluded. And all the officeholders concerned begged the forgiveness of the people after the fact. This is arguably an exercise of prerogative. See Fatovic 2004.

8. In the United Kingdom alone, there were five successful terror attacks in 2017. London mayor Sadiq Khan reported that during the period from March to September of that year, an additional seven terror plots were foiled by police ("Seven Terror Plots" 2017).

model could become normalized as an accommodation model. Moreover, there are practical—and in such scenarios, thus also moral—advantages to having procedures laid out in advance. In those cases where protocols make sense, police and other responders can be trained, thereby minimizing both casualties and unnecessary rights derogations. From this perspective, some model of accommodation seems worthwhile.

How then could the problem of legal gray holes be addressed? Dyzenhaus (2006, 139), in the tradition of Lon Fuller, has argued that legality as such makes sense only when understood to rest on the foundational morality of the rule of law. In a state of emergency, every branch of government must exhibit a collective commitment not just to a rule *by* law but rather a "rule of law project." In this respect, the branches of government ought to be understood not as checks on one another that have been suspended but instead as partners in a collective moral enterprise. Emergencies thus present an opportunity to demonstrate a collective commitment to the rule of law (Dyzenhaus 2006, 62). While this approach to emergency power is, as Dyzenhaus recognizes, somewhat aspirational, we can see concrete examples emerging in the debate and jurisprudence surrounding innovations in a variety of jurisdictions working to mitigate the moral costs associated with emergency detention, for instance. These include procedural protections outlined in the United Kingdom's Terrorism Act (2006) and in Canada after the Supreme Court's decision in *Charkaoui v. Canada* (2007), such as increased judicial oversight and review of evidence. As Kent Roach (2013) has argued, when agents of the state violate the spirit of the law and the rule of law project is robust, they can expect to be harassed and shamed.[9] The moral force of the law matters in guiding emergency action, and how political leaders behave in turn impacts the moral authority of the law. It is one task of the political leader faced with a crisis to treat this special moral character of the law with due concern. It is not just any order that must be restored, but an order worth having as well.

Judgment and Legitimacy

Emergency ethics is fraught with complexity and indeterminacy; facts may be hard to come by, and principles may command contradictory or counterintuitive courses of action. Even the temporal boundaries of an emergency may be

9. It is noteworthy that as of this writing, the Canadian government is in the process of paying out compensation in the range of C$100,000,000 to those whose rights were violated in the wake of the 9/11 attacks.

in doubt. While types of emergency may have some predictability, specific ones may bring novel moral challenges too. There is no way to fully codify the ethics of emergency powers. While one can delineate principles, and pass laws that lay out criteria for the declaration and administration of emergencies, fundamentally these contribute to and do not determine ethical action in an emergency. In this morass of uncertainty and contradiction, action is basically a matter of *judgment*.

Of course, judgment is a necessary element of all moral decision-making, and in particular, political decision-making. At a minimum, judgment is necessary to assess and classify a situation, pick the appropriate norm or exemplar, and mediate between conflicting norms. One must judge what *kind* of moral situation one faces, even if it is then clear what action is necessary to address it. But as in so many other respects, emergency brings this characteristic of political ethics into starkest relief. Legal and political thinkers may debate the right norms to govern states of emergency, but it will always be through judgment that a leader settles on the right course of action. And subsequently, it will be through the peoples' collective judgment that this action is affirmed or rejected in the emergency's aftermath (Lazar 2009).

Does this mean that Schmitt is correct in claiming that some sovereign decision maker decides on the exception? That norms cannot determine that decision? That is, if judgment, not legal and moral norms, determines the course of action, are we truly ruled by sovereign power? This is a fallacy of false alternatives. To say that emergency ethics depends substantively on judgment is not to say that it is arbitrary or subject to individual will. Norms must still *govern*, even when they do not *determine* that decision. In the absence of compelling and determinant rules, one can give reasons and submit these to the judgment of others, both in the moment and after the fact. Furthermore, as Karin Loevy and I have both argued from different angles, it is a fundamental misunderstanding of the temporality of emergency to see the moment of decision in isolation from the laws, decisions, judgments, reflections, and debates that preceded it, and the consequences one can anticipate will follow. A decision need not be Schmittian *decisionism* (Loevy 2016; Lazar 2018).

In the study of emergencies, judgment has received less direct attention than issues surrounding facts and norms. But there are exceptions. Clement Fatovic, for example, has studied how the US founders centralized republican virtue in part because of the importance of judgment to emergency decision-making. Selecting a morally upright and experienced leader is in itself a mode of emergency preparation. As Fatovic (2009, 208–32) concludes, though, republican virtue cannot remain secure unless it is also, at the same time, anchored in widespread civic virtue. For before a political leader can choose well in a crisis, the people must choose their leader well. Leaders, in turn, must make decisions in the knowledge that the people will judge the ethical character of their action after the fact. A leader's anticipation of that judgment, whether in the media, at the polls, or by means of a royal or congressional commission, or in the history books, can play an important constraining role. Dyzenhaus is right to claim that a moral approach to crisis requires that all of those who hold office, regardless of the branch of government, are committed to the rule of law as a moral project. Yet because of this crucial role of the broader public, the public too must be committed to this ethical-political enterprise if emergency government has any hope of being an *ethical* government. Where the public has become cynical or distrustful of government as an enterprise, there we have especial cause to fear emergency powers precisely because if the public does not expect virtue, they will not bother to demand it.

Hence what begins as a recognition of the significance of individual moral judgment underlines the broader moral importance of civic culture along with public trust in times of emergency. Beyond norms, laws, beyond administrative competence and advance preparation, and even beyond the individual leader's experience, virtue, and capacity to judge well, the nature and quality of the relationship between the leader and people makes a critical contribution to the moral character of emergency action.

It follows that if it is incumbent on states to take reasonable measures to prevent and prepare to mitigate the effects of emergencies, then this may extend to the cultivation of civic virtue and to the banking of performance legitimacy. Where a political community is prepared, and its leadership trusted and admired, and where this trust and admiration is grounded in a relationship characterized by civic and republican virtue, there action in an emergency has the best chance of being morally optimal.[10] Of course this is aspirational, but nuance and clarity with respect to aspirations means a better-lit path.

10. This relationship is not uncomplicated, however. For example, Leslie Jacobs points out that during the SARS crisis, the use of quarantine was dramatically higher in Canada than in China or Hong Kong. And while the sense of injustice at being quarantined was similar across these jurisdictions, legal complaints were far more common in China and Hong Kong than in Canada, where there has historically been a higher degree of trust in government. Widespread noncompliance with quarantine orders in Toronto, though, suggests an even more nuanced relationship between the government and people (Jacobs 2007).

References

Abbott, Alison, and Nicola Nosengo. 2014. "Italian Seismologists Cleared of Manslaughter." *Nature* 515 (7526): 171

Agamben, Giorgio. 1998. *Homo Sacer*. Translated by Daniel Heller-Roazen. Stanford, CA: Stanford University Press.

———. 2005. *State of Exception*. Translated by Kevin Attell. Chicago: University of Chicago Press.

Alexander, Larry. 2000. "Deontology at the Threshold." *University of San Diego Law Review* 37 (4): 893–912.

Becker, Saul, Alan Bryman, and Joe Sempik. 2006. "Defining 'Quality' in Social Policy Research: Views, Perceptions and a Framework for Discussion." Social Policy Association and Joint University Council Social Policy Committee, Suffolk, UK. http://www.social-policy.org.uk/wordpress/wp-content/uploads/2014/05/defining-quality-in-social-policy-research.pdf.

Dhar, P. N. 2003. *Indira Gandhi, the "Emergency," and Indian Democracy*. Oxford: Oxford University Press.

Donohue, Laura. 2001. *Counter-Terrorist Law and Emergency Power in the United Kingdom 1922–2000*. Dublin: Irish Academic Press.

Dyzenhaus, David. 2006. *The Constitution of Law: Legality in a Time of Emergency*. Cambridge: Cambridge University Press.

Ellis, Anthony. 1992. "Deontology, Incommensurability and the Arbitrary." *Philosophy and Phenomenological Research* 52 (4): 855–75.

Fatovic, Clement. 2004. "Constitutionalism and Presidential Prerogative: Jeffersonian and Hamiltonian Perspectives." *American Journal of Political Science* 48 (3): 429–44.

———. 2009. *Outside the Law*. Baltimore: Johns Hopkins University Press.

Fatovic, Clement, and Benjamin A. Kleinerman, eds. 2013. *Extra-Legal Power and Legitimacy*. Oxford: Oxford University Press.

Freund, Ernst. 1904. *Police Power, Public Policy, and Constitutional Rights*. Chicago: Callaghan and Co.

Goldsmith, Jack. 2013. "The Irrelevance of Prerogative Power, and the Evils of Secret Legal Interpretation." In *Extra-Legal Power and Legitimacy*, edited by Clement Fatovic and Benjamin A. Kleinerman, 214–232. Oxford: Oxford University Press.

Gross, Oren, and Ní Aoláin, Fionnuala. 2006. *Law in Times of Crisis: Emergency Powers in Theory and Practice*. Cambridge: Cambridge University Press.

Heuman, Gad. 1994. *The Killing Time: The Morant Bay Rebellion in Jamaica*. Knoxville: University of Tennessee Press.

Hussain, Nasser. 2003. *The Jurisprudence of Emergency: Colonialism and the Rule of Law*. Ann Arbor: University of Michigan Press.

Jacobs, Leslie. 2007. "Rights and Quarantine during the SARS Global Health Crisis: Differentiated Legal Consciousness in Hong Kong, Shanghai, and Toronto." *Asia Pacific Dispute Resolution Research Notes* 41 (3): 511–52.

Kalyvas, Andreas. 2007. "The Tyranny of Dictatorship." *Political Theory* 35 (4): 412–42.

King, Bill. 2017. "Houston's Mayor Was Right to Not Evacuate." *New York Times*, August 28. https://www.nytimes.com/2017/08/28/opinion/harvey-flooding-mayor-evacuation.html.

Kinzer, Stephen. 1992. "Honor to R.A.F. Leader Wakes Dresden's Ghosts." *New York Times*, January 6. https://www.nytimes.com/1992/01/06/world/honor-to-raf-leader-wakes-dresden-s-ghosts.html.

Lazar, Nomi Claire. 2006. "Making Emergencies Safe for Democracy." *Constellations* 13 (4): 506–21.

———. 2009. *States of Emergency in Liberal Democracies*. Cambridge: Cambridge University Press.

———. 2013. "Why Rome Didn't Bark in the Night." *Polity* 45 (3): 422–44.

———. 2018. "Decision and Decisionism." In *The Decisionist Imagination: Sovereignty, Social Science, and Democracy in the 20th Century*, edited by Daniel Bessner and Nicolas Guilhot, 109–34. New York: Berghahn.

Lecoufle, Olivia. 2018."Say No to Orphanage Volunteering." Save the Children. https://www.savethechildren.ca/say-no-to-orphanage-volunteering/.

Loevy, Karin. 2016. *Emergencies in Public Law*. Cambridge: Cambridge University Press.

McCormick, John. 1999. *Carl Schmitt's Critique of Liberalism*. Cambridge: Cambridge University Press.

Mendez, Ethel. 2012. "What's in 'Good'?" Ottawa: International Development Research Centre. https://www.idrc.ca/sites/default/files/sp/Documents%20EN/Lit-review-Final-English.pdf.

Moore, Michael. 2010. *Placing Blame: A General Theory of the Criminal Law*. Oxford: Oxford University Press.

Nicolet, Claude. 1982. "La dictature à Rome." In *Dictatures et légitimité*, edited by Maurice Duverger. 69–110. Paris: Presses universitaires de France.

Novak, Williams. 2000. *The People's Welfare*. Chapel Hill: University of North Carolina Press.

Ohlheiser, Abby, and Cecilia Kang. 2014. "Nurse Quarantined in New Jersey after Returning from Ebola Mission Is Released." *Washington Post*, October 27.

Parkhurt, Justin, ed. 2017. *The Politics of Evidence: From Evidence-Based Policy to the Good Governance of Evidence*. London: Routledge.

Rittel, Horst, and Melvin Webber. 1973. "Dilemmas in a General Theory of Planning." *Policy Sciences* 4 (2): 155–69.

Roach, Kent. 2013. "The Law Working Itself Pure?" In *Guantanamo and Beyond*, edited by Fionnuala Ní Aolain and Oren Gross, 201–24. Cambridge: Cambridge University Press.

Rossiter, Clinton. 2002. *Constitutional Dictatorship*. New Brunswick, NJ: Transaction Press.

Santora, Marc. 2017. "New Jersey Accepts Rights for People in Quarantine to End Ebola Suit." *New York Times*, July 27. https://www.nytimes.com/2017/07/27/nyregion/new-jersey-accepts-rights-for-people-in-quarantine-to-end-ebola-suit.html.

Schabas, Richard. 2004. "Severe Acute Respiratory Syndrome: Did Quarantine Help?" *Canadian Journal of Infectious Diseases and Medical Microbiology* 15 (4): 204.

Schmitt, Carl. [1921] 1994. *Die Diktatur*. Berlin: Duncker und Humblot.

———. [1921] 2015. *Politische Theologie*. Berlin: Duncker und Humblot.

"Seven Terror Plots Foiled in Six Months, Sadiq Khan Reveals." 2017. *Telegraph*, September 25. https://www.telegraph.co.uk/news/2017/09/25/seven-terror-plots-foiled-six-months-sadiq-khan-reveals/.

UNICEF. n.d. "Residential Care in Cambodia Fact Sheet." https://www.unicef.org/cambodia/Fact_sheet_-_residential_care_Cambodia.pdf.

United Nations. n.d. "International Covenant on Civil and Political Rights." https://www.ohchr.org/en/professionalinterest/pages/ccpr.aspx.

Walzer, Michael. 1977. *Just and Unjust Wars: A Moral Argument with Historical Illustrations*. New York: Basic Books.

de Wilde, Marc. 2012. "The Dictator's Trust: Regulating and Constraining Emergency Powers in the Roman Republic." *History of Political Thought* 33 (4): 555–77.

———. 2013. "The Dictatorship and the Fall of the Roman Republic." *Zeitschrift der Savigny-Stiftung fur Rechtsgeschichte: Romanistische Abteilung* 130:1–39.

11

The Ethics of Political Lobbying

POWER, INFLUENCE, AND DEMOCRATIC DECLINE

Phil Parvin

LOBBYING POSES an urgent threat to democracy. The problem is not principally one of a lack of transparency, or that lobbyists comprise a secret cabal of antidemocrats at the heart of the democratic system, or even that lobbying is a form of corruption (Parvin 2016). The problem goes deeper and wider, and its solution requires nothing less than a fundamental reordering of the modern state and a winding back of nearly a century of democratic decline. Moreover, it requires action on the part of political regimes that are now dominated by powerful lobbies that have proven themselves unwilling to permit necessary reform.

The story I tell in this chapter is controversial, and I have been told, depressing. But it is a story borne out by nearly a century of empirical work produced by social and political scientists. It is also a largely untold story, at least among Anglo-American political and democratic theorists, many of whom who are largely preoccupied with questions concerning citizen participation and deliberation (Sabl 2015). My story is *controversial* because it suggests that the dominant debates in contemporary democratic theory are not in fact as central or pressing as many democratic theorists believe, and that the growth in interest in deliberation, for example, has squeezed out other, bigger structural issues that pose a far more significant threat to democracy in the contemporary era than deficits in certain forms of deliberation or widespread participation. It is *depressing* because it describes the emergence of a problem that contemporary democracies do not have the resources to resolve, or so it seems. So deep is the problem, and so tightly ingrained is it in the practice of contemporary democracy, that it may be irresolvable. It is currently irresolvable. Whether it remains so depends on whether political theorists, social and political scientists, and politicians grasp the issues, and then work together to seek real change. For reasons I outline later, this is unlikely.

Lobbying poses a complex, macrolevel threat comprising three parts. Furthermore, it poses not a single threat but a dual one—a first- and second-order threat to democratic theory and practice that all political philosophers should consider a priority. Let me unpack these two sentences before presenting my case in more detail. There are two levels at which we might examine the ethics of lobbying in democratic states: the *macro-* and *micro*level. Macrolevel analysis would discuss the appropriate role of lobbying in democratic politics broadly conceived, and seek to determine whether and to what extent *unelected* organizations should be able to exert pressure on *elected* decision makers. Microlevel analysis would explore in detail the behavior of lobbyists themselves along with the techniques that they use to influence decision makers and evaluate them against some independently determined ethical standard. Microlevel analysis is only useful if there are found to be no systemic threats to democracy posed by lobbying at the macrolevel. If lobbying is just contrary to democratic theory and practice, then *any* techniques that unelected organizations might use to exert pressure on elected representatives would also be contrary to democracy. Lobbying *is* a problem at the macrolevel. Hence my discussion herein only tangentially addresses the techniques employed by lobbyists and focuses instead on macrolevel questions about the general role that lobby organizations play, and should play, in liberal democratic states.

For many, the answer is obvious: lobbyists have little or no role to play in liberal democracies. In a representative liberal democracy, power is legitimized through the transfer of sovereignty from citizens to political bodies through elections, they say. In such a system, it is not clear how or why *unelected* groups and organizations should be able to influence the development of public policy, or what the status of such entities should be vis-à-vis states, governments, legislatures, and citizens (Lessig 2011; Dinan and Miller 2007).

But lobbying is an important component of democratic life. The commitment to liberal freedoms of assembly and speech that are supported by democrats of all stripes combine to permit citizens to join with like-minded others and collectively seek to influence decision makers (Levy 2014). Furthermore, democratic citizens are broadly assumed to be able to contribute financially to support these groups' ability to influence politicians on their behalf. Citizens are free to join with one another in an attempt to pressure governments to advance their interests, just as they are free to pay a pressure group, trade association, or trade union to do so on their behalf. Many democrats have emphasized the central need for individuals to be able to affect change through collective action and pressure politics (Cohen and Sabel 1997; Dryzek 2012; Habermas 1996; Young 2000). Even lobbying's harshest critics acknowledge that the ability of groups and individuals to lobby their elected representatives as well as other organs of the state is "central to a healthy democratic system" (Cave and Rowell 2014, 9).

Developing a coherent position on lobbying thus requires us to balance these opposing concerns. But how might we do so? The answer is not obvious. Philosophers and political scientists have long disagreed over the appropriate role of private interest groups or "factions" in political life as well as in democracy more specifically. Some have emphasized their benefits (Benhabib 1996; Dahl 1989; Fraser 2004; Hirst 1994; Putnam 2001; Tocqueville [1835–40] 2003), and lobbyists themselves have often defended their role in providing important information to overworked politicians (Chari et al. 2012; Lessig 2011; Zetter 2014).

More frequently, however, factional interests have been seen as a potential threat. Neopluralists, neo-Marxists, and others have criticized the pluralists' optimistic vision of a self-policing polyarchy, arguing that the capitalist economy will cause certain interests (like those of businesses) to become dominant (Lindblom 1977; Lowy 1979; Miliband 1969). Many libertarians and classical liberals have also criticized lobbying on the grounds that it undermines free markets (Munger and Villareal-Diaz 2019). Still others have questioned the positive role of civil society groups and their compatibility with democracy (see, for example, Boyd 2004). Further back, Plato and Aristotle both believed that private interests jeopardized political stability, and hence the just state. Thomas Hobbes ([1651] 2008) saw factions as the enemy of the state and the cause of potentially ruinous conflict, and Jean-Jacques Rousseau ([1752] 2012) believed that they undermined the general will. Plato, Aristotle, Hobbes, and Rousseau shared the view that it was necessary to impose quite considerable constraints on individual liberty in order to diminish the role as well as influence of factions, or eradicate them.

For the framers of the US Constitution, and James Madison (1792) in particular, however, factions posed a different problem. In the "Federalist No. 10," Madison argued that factionalism posed a fundamental challenge to freedom, equality, and the common good. He also recognized, however, that factions were a *consequence* of freedom and equality, and hence rejected *both* the claim that constraints on individual liberty were a justifiable cost to dealing with them *and* that states should seek to eradicate them. Factions, he believed, were an inevitable product of liberty and human diversity: free citizens will develop divergent interests, which they will seek to advance over those of others either individually or collectively. As we cannot destroy factions without first destroying the conditions of liberty that give rise to them, we instead need to structure social and political institutions in such a way that the emergence and activities of factions can be managed in accordance with liberty, equality, and justice. Madison held that this required three things. First, it necessitated impartial representative institutions capable of adjudicating conflicts among competing factional interests. Second, it required reducing social and economic inequalities in order to ensure political equality for all citizens (Madison 1792). And third, it meant encouraging citizens to form factions in the hope that this would produce a proliferation of many small groupings that would protect against the rise of large, dominant groups.

I draw on Madison's theory of factions and apply it to contemporary democratic states in order to reveal the problem with lobbying, and what, if anything, might be done to tackle it. The lived reality of democratic politics in the contemporary era should lead us to be much more pessimistic than Madison was about the general role of vested interests in political life and the prospects of finding political solutions to the problems they pose. The problem for democracy posed by lobbying is precisely that states have not implemented, and now arguably *cannot* implement, Madison's three-point plan to make factions compatible with democracy. Liberal democratic states should be committed to protecting the individual liberties that give rise to lobby organizations, and they should ensure that any such emergent groups are able to influence the political agenda. Yet these fundamental commitments impose duties on states to also ensure that lobby organizations emerge and operate in ways that are consistent with wider democratic principles. They have not done so, and Madison's theory helps us understand how: they have failed to ensure that representative institutions remain impartial with regard to conflicts of private interest, failed to ensure that resources necessary to preventing the disproportionate concentration of political power in the hands of economic elites are evenly distributed, and failed to encourage the proliferation of interest groups capable of representing the interests of a wide range of citizens.

This is what I meant when I said that the problem posed to democracy by lobbying has three aspects. I outline each of these aspects in turn in the next two sections in order that by the end, we are in a better position to understand both the nature and scope of the problem, and its implications for democratic theory and practice. My overarching claim is that liberal democratic states have experienced profound changes over the past three-quarters of a century that have resulted in a concentration of vast and disproportionate powers in the hands of corporations and lobby organizations that represent the wealthy. They have also fueled widespread citizen disengagement, and declines in trust and the social bases of grassroots politics, thereby marginalizing citizens in general and poorer citizens in particular.

Furthermore, I argue, these changes have entrenched lobbying as a *first-* and *second-order* threat to democracy—lobbying is not a single threat, but a dual one—that renders it uniquely problematic and intractable. Lobbying poses a first-order threat to democracy for the negative effects that it has had, and continues to have, on the ability of states to operate in accordance with democratic principles. But it also poses a second-order threat to the capacity of liberal democratic states to reform themselves in ways that rectify the problem. While it is possible to identify possible first-order strategies that would help bring the lived reality of democracy into line with democratic principles (as I do below), the nature and scope of these changes suggests that there is now almost no possibility of these reforms being implemented.

Two definitions before we begin. For the purposes of this chapter, I use Raj Chari and Sylvia Kritzinger's definition of a *lobbying* organization, whether motivated by economic, professional, or public concerns, as "any group, or set of actors, that has common interests and seeks to influence the policy making process in such a way as their interests are reflected in public policy outcomes" (Chari et al. 2012, 3). Many different organizations lobby decision makers, so our definition needs to be broad enough to encompass them all. Also, it needs to capture all the many different activities in which these organizations engage (Parvin 2007).

I define "democracy" in broad terms as a system of government in which all citizens are understood to be politically equal in two connected senses: all citizens should enjoy the ability to influence the course of political decision-making through their participation in the democratic system, and no individual or group should be excluded from the process of decision-making, or their concerns ignored, on account of the fact that they are a minority. This basic commitment to political equality connects with and facilitates the democratic state's ability to ensure the liberty of its citizens via self-government. Citizens excluded from the democratic system, or whose views are systematically marginalized, are not self-governing, and hence are not free. Democracies are thus charged with protecting the liberty and equality of all individual citizens against the tyranny of dominant factions and majorities, and ensuring that political decisions track the will of the people, while also holding this will subject to constitutional and legislative checks. I henceforth refer to these two principles—of freedom and equality thus understood—as "democratic principles."[1]

1. This definition is not uncontroversial. The history of political thought is replete with alternative and rival conceptions of democracy, and for obvious reasons I cannot engage with them all here. Instead, I present a broad definition that tries to capture what is important in many of these conceptions, and especially in those that are currently most influential

From Government to Governance: The Rise and Scope of Lobbying

Lobbying is not merely the preserve of big business or corporations; it is practiced by a wide range of organizations in the public, private, and third sector, including nongovernmental organizations, think tanks, trade unions, campaign organizations, charities, and trade associations (Parvin 2016). It is also not a niche activity; it is a central aspect of democratic decision-making in Britain, Europe, and the United States, and the conduct of politics at a global and international level. This is the first aspect of the problem. Lobbying is now so ingrained in the political system and so central to the core activities of the modern state that it has forced many political scientists to rethink their understanding of democracy from the ground up (Baumgartner et al. 2009; Berry 1997; Bevir 2010; Rhodes 2017). Political philosophers must do so too.

For as noted above, liberal democratic states have experienced profound change in the past three-quarters of a century—change that exerts pressure

---

in contemporary Anglo-American democratic theory—a definition that states in broad terms ideas of self-government and equality that transcend disciplinary and ideological boundaries. That is, I try to present a conception that is grounded in basic ideas that many theorists from many different political backgrounds have either defended or criticized as necessary components of a democratic regime. My reason for doing so is twofold. First, I have drawn on democratic ideas shared at the general level by contemporary democratic theorists on the Right and Left in order that I might convince them that lobbying is a bigger problem than they seem to think *given their own views about democracy*. Second, I have tried to ensure that the conception of democracy I have adopted is nonpartisan, and genuinely shared by thinkers on the political Right and Left. For instance, something like the idea that democracy is grounded in and should ensure the basic liberty of all citizens to contribute to the process by which decisions are made, and also that the equal capacity to participate is strongly associated with the idea of freedom as self-government, can arguably be found in the work of egalitarian and social democratic democrats (see, for example, Chambers 2009; Mansbridge et al. 2012) *as well as* democrats on the political Right like John Tomasi (2012, 88), who has stated that a society is democratic "to the extent that all members have an equal share of fundamental political power." F. A. Hayek (1978) was a harsh critic of democracy precisely because he shared with many egalitarians and social democrats a vision of what a democratic society would look like. And disagreements among many contemporary deliberative, participatory, epistemic, and other democrats do not turn on whether democracy should be committed to ensuring political equality and liberty as self-government but rather how this project might be best understood and operationalized. In identifying grounding ideas that are widely shared among contemporary thinkers on the political Right and Left, I hope to offer a general view of democracy that will pass the "commonsense test" among nonspecialists, while not being considered reasonable by specialists.

on widespread assumptions about democratic theory and practice as well as conventional understandings of the state and its relationship with citizens. These changes are associated with two interconnected developments: widespread declines in citizen engagement and a rise in elite governance (Parvin 2009, 2011, 2018a). Mainstream democratic theory has long presumed and required the presence of a flourishing civil society that acts as a bridge between citizens and their representative institutions, and builds democratic capacity (Knight and Johnson 1998; Parvin 2015; Putnam 2001) as well as a generally politically active citizenry. Civil associations are a prerequisite for grassroots political activism; they mobilize citizens, educate them about political issues of common concern, and provide a conduit through which the dispersed concerns of members can be brought together and communicated to decision makers (Cohen and Sabel 1997; Habermas 1996; Whiteley 2012). Grassroots associations and broad-based membership organizations facilitate effective representation. They have also long provided an important source of expertise and useful experience on which states have drawn in the process of identifying as well as resolving political problems (Dryzek 2001; Fung 2015; Goodin 2012; Hirst 1994; Landemore 2017; Young 2000). Democracy, many theorists suggest, might best be understood as a "system," or a linked collection of "multiple publics," in which citizens pool their on-the-ground experiences and concerns, and communicate them up to government via "representative" organizations and groupings (Mansbridge et al. 2012; Benhabib 1996; Fraser 2004).

Civil society has declined and changed in ways that undermine democratic theory and practice, however. Numerous factors have combined to weaken traditional associational bonds, and reduce the number and influence of grassroots associations. As a consequence, representative organizations have slowly *replaced* citizens in the democratic system (Putnam 2001; Parvin 2016). This has in turn led to a decline in traditional civic life in many states, but also declines in citizen engagement and trust (Parvin 2015; Putnam 2015; Skocpol 2004; Jacobs and Skocpol 2005). A recent survey found that only 17 percent of UK citizens now "trust the government to put the needs of the nation first" compared to 38 percent two decades ago. Meanwhile, at this writing, trust in the credibility of politicians is now at 9 percent, with disproportionately low levels of trust, participation, and political knowledge reported among citizens at the lower end of the wealth and income distribution (Apostolova, Uberoi, and Johnston 2017; Hansard Society and Electoral Commission 2017). And while there was never a golden age of associational membership, empirical data collected over the past half century nevertheless show a marked decline in citizens' willingness to join a range of associational groups over that period. Membership in political parties in the Organization for Economic Cooperation and Development countries has fallen precipitously since the mid-1950s, for example. In the United Kingdom, the combined membership of the two largest parties—Conservative and Labour—as of this writing is around 676,000, a drop of nearly 2.5 million since the 1950s. Despite recent rises in the membership of smaller parties as well as the Labour Party, party membership remained unpopular among British citizens in 2018, with only 1.4 percent of the United Kingdom's eligible voters a member of any party (Audickus, Dempsey, and Loft 2019). Trade union membership has also fallen from around 13 million in 1979 to around 6.2 million in 2017. These declines are perhaps even more surprising than they seem given that the UK population is actually growing by 6 percent a decade. Many millions of citizens eligible to vote in general elections fail to do so, and even fewer vote in local and European elections, or the newly established elections for local authority mayors as well as police and crime commissioners (all of which see average turnouts of around 30 percent). The number of people *registered* to vote fell by 1.5 million in the five years between 2011 and 2016. In the United States, turnout in midterm and presidential elections remains low, with only 55 percent of voters casting a ballot in the 2016 presidential election, and 36 percent doing so in the 2014 midterms. Declines in turnout over this period are most notable among eighteen- to twenty-four-year-olds (around 10 percent), and the number of eighteen- to twenty-four-year-olds registering to vote has fallen by 14 percent. And like in Britain, membership in political parties and trade unions as well as other markers of civic activism, group membership, and grassroots political action are all in decline (Berry 1997; Macedo et al. 2005; Putnam, with Leonardi and Nanetti 2005; Jacobs and Skocpol 2005).

The business of politics, once connected to citizens by mechanisms that made sense to them, and by bridging organizations and associations that they identified with, now is adrift from them. States and citizens have reacted in their own ways. *States* have retreated further from citizens and looked elsewhere for the epistemic insights that were once provided by citizens through grassroots organizations, driving citizens to the margins of political life (Parvin 2016; Baumgartner et al. 2009). *Citizens*, internalizing their marginalization, have disengaged from politics, and become resentful toward their representatives and the democratic system in general. They have become marginal and cutoff from the business of democratic life, and importantly, have come to *understand themselves* as marginal and cutoff from the business of democratic life (Hansard Society and Electoral Commission 2017; Macedo et al. 2005; Mair 2013).

Grassroots and traditional associations still exist, but the citizens who compose their memberships are not the active ones for whom these organizations were created (Mair 2013; Parvin 2015). They are citizens who have seen their role in the democratic system and the value of their political participation eroded by the liberal state's retreat into elitism. Grassroots organizations have tended to rely on a wide and often dispersed, but active and enthusiastic, membership. Such groups have found it increasingly difficult to rely on the continued support of members who are realizing that the traditional mechanisms of representation offered by these organizations are increasingly ineffective, and are increasingly viewing the requirements that they tend to make of members in terms of participation and time as too onerous (Skocpol 2003; Stoker 2006). Just as representative democratic systems have become increasingly unable to rely on their citizens to engage in the forms of political behavior that they require in order to function as intended, so the groups charged with representing citizens' concerns in the democratic process have become increasingly unable to rely on those citizens who constitute their memberships to engage in forms of behavior that these groups need in order to represent their interests effectively (Achen and Bartels 2016; Hay 2007; Schlozman, Verba, and Brady 2012; Skocpol 2003). Across many liberal democratic states, including the United Kingdom and United States, grassroots organizations have declined in size and strength as the communities that historically provided their core constituencies have all but disappeared (Putnam 2001; Skocpol 2003, 2004; Jacobs and Skocpol 2005; Whiteley 2012).

As civil and associational life has declined and political engagement among citizens has diminished, representative citizen associations and organizations have had to adapt to the rise of new forms of governance in which decision-making and policy formation are the product of deliberations among elite actors, rather than between states and their citizens, and in which expertise, not strength in numbers, is the new currency (Fischer 2009). As liberal democratic states have transitioned away from a model of *government,* in which elected representatives make policy decisions in consultation with citizens, to one of *governance,* in which policy decisions are made by a community of state and nonstate actors at the elite level, decision-making and policy development have been driven ever further from citizens, and ever higher into an elite hierarchy populated by experts and insider groups (Bevir 2010). Consequently, the effective representation of citizens' interests in these processes by representative organizations and groups has required an ability on the part of these groups to engage with this expert community in terms that the members of *this community* understand, rather than in terms understood and expressed by their *own* members.

Hence many organizations that had traditionally relied on direct action and grassroots activism to affect change shifted in the late twentieth century toward a more centralized approach focused more on legal advocacy and professional lobbying (Parvin 2016). In the United States, for example, "where it once made sense to try to get things done by first gauging the opinions of grassroots association members, and influencing officials and representatives in the localities and states, it now made much more sense for civic activists to aim their efforts at national media and engage with staffs or agencies in Washington" (Skocpol 2003, 201–2). Similarly in Britain, Greenpeace concentrates less now on direct action, and more on broader public affairs, media, and lobbying campaigns than it once did, as does Friends of the Earth, Amnesty International, and many other nongovernmental organizations (Berry 1997; Jordan and Maloney 2007).

The dramatic rise in the number and influence of professional lobby organizations in the United States is most obvious from the 1960s on, and was driven in part by the success of the civil rights and women's movements in achieving social and political reform through an emphasis on equal *rights* (Skocpol 2003). As political conflicts increasingly became framed in terms of rights, political organizations reframed their campaign activities within a rights discourse. Consequently, they diverted resources away from the management of relations with members, and toward the employment of policy experts, specialist legal teams, political communications operatives, and so on, in order that they might engage more effectively with those majoritarian and nonmajoritarian institutions charged with the development of public policies and the protection of civil rights, and the various other nonstate organizations that feed into this process (Holyoke 2014). The locus of political campaigning expanded as groups increasingly sought change through the courts as much as they did the government or legislature. And as the tendency to frame political conflicts in terms of rights spread, so did the professionalization of interest groups and marginalization of members from these groups' core activities. While organizations like Greenpeace and Amnesty International continue to enjoy relatively large memberships, they are largely inactive and peripheral. The real business of influence and representation is not conducted through the mobilization of members to engage in campaigning activities but rather via specialist lobbying techniques and strategies as well as professional legal advocacy that the vast majority of members do not understand and do not contribute to, except financially.

The scale of the decline in the power and influence of traditional grassroots movements and citizens more generally, and the concurrent rise of lobby organizations in the contemporary mechanisms of decision-making and policy formation in liberal states, including but not limited to the United States and the UK, should not be underestimated (Knoke 1986). Liberal states have, since the 1960s, witnessed an explosion in the number and diversity of organizations establishing permanent offices in Washington, DC, Brussels, and other centers of policy making in order to more easily monitor as well as contribute to debates among policy makers, lobby key representatives, and raise their agendas with journalists, at the same time as they have witnessed declines in citizen engagement, participation, and trust (Baumgartner et al. 2009; Rauch 1994). There are currently over twenty-two thousand registered interest groups and advocacy organizations based in and beyond Washington, DC, and over forty thousand individuals and groups across the United States lobbying at the state legislature level. According to the EU Transparency Register, around thirteen thousand groups and organizations from the private, public, and third sectors are currently "engaged in activities seeking to influence the EU policy and decision making process" in Brussels (European Commission 2022).

Considerable lobbying activity is also visible at the local and national levels in EU member states, particularly in the major financial and political centers like Berlin, Geneva, and Madrid. Finding out exactly how many lobbyists work in different states is incredibly difficult, however, given the number and diversity of organizations involved. In Britain, the political consultancy sector alone employs around fourteen thousand people and has been valued at over £1.9 billion (Parvin 2007). The true size and extent of private sector lobbying in Britain remains largely unknown, though, as it includes the activities of a wide range of professionals working in a diverse range of overlapping areas including public affairs, government relations, policy research, media relations, strategic communications, crisis management, finance, and law. Add to this those lobbyists who work *outside* the private sector in trade associations, think tanks, and so on, and we can begin to appreciate the full scale and complexity of the British "lobbying industry," and also the many ways in which the British democratic system has afforded these groups greater and greater formal access. Members of Parliament in the United Kingdom may be approached upward of a hundred times a week by lobbyists from a range of organizations and sectors in Britain and beyond, and the government regularly consults outside groups when developing policy (Parvin 2007). Other states, too, have made moves to more fully incorporate unelected representative organizations into the formal system of decision-making and scrutiny. In the United States, think tanks and "special interest groups" occupy an influential place in the legislative process through the various contributions they can make to politicians' election campaigns, their networks, and their lobbyists at the national, state, and local levels. States increasingly draw on the expertise of international nongovernmental organizations, charities, and voluntary bodies in the formation and implementation of policies concerning aid, trade, human rights, and development, and regularly work with professional bodies, intragovernmental organizations, and research institutes on constitutional questions arising out of relations with other nation-states and European institutions.

Furthermore, states increasingly rely on nonstate actors to *deliver* policy. In Britain, for example, third-sector organizations such as Christian Aid and Oxfam exert powerful influence over government policy in areas such as overseas aid and development. But they also receive considerable public funding in order to help them deliver these policies on the ground. Moreover, many services that were once directly managed by the state have, since the 1980s, been contracted out to private businesses at considerable public cost. The National Audit Office (2013) has concluded that around 50 percent of the total money that the United Kingdom spends on public services every year is paid to private companies, which in turn devote a vast amount of time and resources lobbying governments in relevant policy areas.

Recent estimates suggest that the total amount spent by organizations across all sectors on lobbying in the United States alone exceeds $3 billion a year. Taken together, hundreds of millions of dollars a year are spent by organizations of various kinds across the world on influencing policy, gaining access to decision makers, and raising awareness of issues among legislators, the media, and "stakeholder groups," all while the citizen populations of these same states are more disengaged, inactive, and resentful toward politics and democracy than ever.

Lobbying, Inequality, and Access

Lobbying, then, is now central to the business of governance in liberal democratic states. Yet this alone is not what makes it a problem. There is nothing intrinsically undemocratic about a form of politics in which unelected organizations are empowered to represent "special interests" among decision makers at the elite level. The problem is also not that lobbyists comprise a secret and malicious presence at the heart of democracy, or that they are collectively motivated by some pernicious desire to destroy democracy, despite the fact that it is common for critics to portray them as such (see, for example, Cave and Rowell 2014). Lobbyists are not all motivated to do any such thing, and they are not all corrupt. In fact, the vast majority of lobbying is practiced by "decent people, people we should respect, people working extremely hard to do what they believe is right" (Lessig 2011). The problem, as I said in the introduction, is not at the microlevel of individuals' behavior but rather at the macrolevel; it is that all lobbyists are working in a system that no longer ensures the appropriate political conditions for fair access and influence.

It would be possible to explain the changes outlined earlier in terms of a neoliberal power grab, in which corporate interests used their economic advantage to circumvent the democratic system and forced other organizations to participate in a system in which they were less equipped to participate, resulting in the decline of these organizations and the marginalization of citizens (Skocpol 2003). Alternatively, it would be possible to understand it as a pragmatic response by institutions to citizen disengagement and the increasing complexity of public policy dilemmas (Parvin 2015, 2016, 2018a).

The real challenge posed by lobbying does not in fact rely on either of these explanations being true. Whatever the reasons behind the changes outlined above, their occurrence has resulted in a profound disconnect between citizens and states—the effects of which are not distributed equally among citizens. Recall Madison's concerns about factionalism and his three-pronged solution to resolving them: the establishment of impartial representative institutions, alleviation of extreme inequalities in wealth, and encouragement of citizens to create factional groups in order to ensure against domination by large groups. The reason why we should be concerned about the role that lobbying plays in contemporary democracies, I suggest, is because contemporary liberal democratic states have failed to do any of these three things. States have failed to establish the political conditions necessary for lobbying to remain consistent with democratic principles.

Because the problem with the story that I have told thus far is the part that I left out: while it is true that states have retreated from citizens, they have not retreated from all citizens to the same degree. This is the second aspect of the problem, and the one that renders the first especially challenging. The trajectories of democratic reform that I have outlined so far have had a disproportionately negative impact on the poor. While many citizens feel disillusioned with politics and powerless to get their voices heard, the poor feel it most acutely, and with good reason: citizens of low socioeconomic status not only *feel* more cutoff from politics but also *are* more cutoff (Achen and Bartels 2016; Birch, Gottfried, and Lodge 2013; Skocpol 2004; Macedo et al. 2005; Schlozman, Verba, and Brady 2012). Not only are such citizens less likely to engage in political activities, but they are less likely to have their concerns represented by lobby organizations. As Theda Skocpol (2003, 54) put it, in the United States, "the economically disadvantaged continue to be under-represented in pressure politics. Organisations of the poor themselves are extremely rare, if non-existent, and organisations which advocate on behalf of the poor are relatively scarce." The situation has gotten worse since then. Cause-oriented lobby groups "and professionally managed institutions offer wealthy and well-educated Americans a rich menu of opportunities to in effect hire experts to represent their values and interests in public life" (Skocpol 2003, 219). Poorer and less well-educated citizens have not been offered, or have not been able to take up, such opportunities. Grassroots associations have typically been more effective at mobilizing poorer citizens, representing them, and building their democratic capacity. Their decline, and then replacement with hierarchical lobby organizations more suited to advancing the interests of wealthier citizens, has left poorer citizens more marginalized than better-off citizens (Gilens 2014; Putnam 2015; Solt 2008).

The reconfiguration of associational life and rise of elite governance have unarguably benefited well-off citizens more than poorer ones, and the richest citizens most of all. Many states, especially those in which citizen disengagement and the rise of elite governance are most pronounced, are characterized by vast and growing inequalities in wealth. Income and capital have been distributed upward from working- and middle-class citizens to the richest 1 and even 0.01 percent of people, who have seen their share of global wealth quadruple over the past four decades (Parvin 2017; Piketty 2014; Thomas 2017). At the same time as the personal wealth of the richest *citizens* has grown, the wealth held by *corporations* has similarly grown at an extraordinary rate. The world's 10-richest corporations now own more wealth than the poorest 180 *states* combined (Global Justice Now 2016). Walmart's annual revenue is larger than the GDP of Spain, and in 2022, Apple's market value exceeded UK GDP. At the same time, the money that corporations spend on lobbying has risen dramatically. In 2002, for example, Google spent less than $50,000 on lobbying. Ten years later, in 2012, it spent more than $18 million, and in 2018, it spent almost $22 million. Google also spent more than any other corporation in the United States on political donations in the 2016 presidential election. Significant increases in lobbying and campaign spending can be seen across many other sectors too, including health, financial services, and energy.

Noncorporates have not been able to keep pace. For "every dollar [in the United States] spent on lobbying by labor unions and public interest groups together, large corporations and their associations now spend $34. Of the 100 organisations that spent the most on lobbying, 95 consistently represent business" (Drutman 2015). In the years between 2010 and 2020, the US Chamber of Commerce alone spent over $1 billion lobbying for business interests in Washington, DC, and in 2020, the 10-biggest spenders on lobbying in the United States—all of which represent private sector interests—spent $94 million in a single *three-month period* (July–September). Furthermore, in line with the narrative of deep structural change outlined earlier, inequalities in access and influence have tracked wider inequalities in civic and economic life. As wealth has become increasingly concentrated among a smaller and smaller group of high net worth individuals as well as in large corporations, so corporations and the organizations that represent the interests of the wealthy have become more central to the business of governance. Meanwhile, poorer citizens have become peripheral and cutoff from decision-making, and the organizations that represent them have become disproportionately weak or disappeared altogether. As a result, the wealthy have been able to consolidate their own dominance and insulate their wealth in ways not open to poorer citizens (Parvin 2017; Piketty 2014; Winters 2011).

States in which corporations and corporate lobby organizations have disproportionate power to influence policy decisions have in general proven themselves to be less hospitable to reforms grounded in liberal egalitarian claims about redistribution, economic intervention, and the alleviation of inequality through reforms in, for instance, labor laws, tax laws, minimum wage legislation, and the provision of welfare than states in which the ability of corporations to influence political decision-making is weakened (Gilens and Page 2014; Solt 2008). The fact that business taxes are so low in the United States, workplace democracy, labor unions, and workers' rights are weak, and large corporations benefit from so many opportunities to insulate their wealth through complex legal and economic mechanisms cannot be disaggregated from the fact that business corporations in the United States are allowed relatively easy access to elected politicians, and thus are able to influence policy makers through direct lobbying and the financing of election campaigns. Similarly, the fact that the

United Kingdom and European Union more generally have stronger labor unions and workers' rights is at least partly due to the fact that lobbying and campaign finance are governed by stricter rules than in the United States.

Nevertheless, the rich in the United States, United Kingdom, and Europe have been able to secure advantageous laws that serve to protect their wealth, and increase economic and financial burdens on those further down the wealth and income distribution (Thomas 2017). As a result of their ability to leverage the power of lobbyists and special interest groups, economic elites have been able to shift the tax burden onto the less wealthy, complicate the tax code in such a way as to make its navigation dependent on expensive expert advice not available to poorer citizens, stifle initiatives designed to alleviate social and economic inequality, and establish a complex web of shell corporations and offshore tax havens that allow them to keep their wealth a secret from states and avoid paying tax (Parvin 2017; Shaxson 2011; Zucman 2015).

The failure of liberal democratic states to manage the growth of lobbying in line with democratic principles is demonstrable. Evaluated against Madison's necessary measures, we can see that, first, representative institutions as currently configured are estranged from citizens in general and poorer citizens in particular, and are not impartial but rather embody mechanisms of decision-making that give disproportionate voice to corporations and organizations that speak for the wealthy. Inequalities in voice and access are *built into* the structure of contemporary democratic governance. Second, states have failed to attend to inequalities in wealth and property ownership, resulting in the co-optation of the democratic process by the wealthy and a lack of democratic responsiveness by elected representatives to the concerns of the poor (Achen and Bartels 2016; Bartels 2016; Gilens 2014; Gilens and Page 2014; Solt 2008). Third, states have not encouraged the proliferation of interest groups necessary to guard against the emergence of dominant groups. Instead, they have presided over a decline in the number and influence of civil associations capable of representing the interests of the poor, and a reconfiguration of the public sphere that has left poorer citizens without the associational and other resources they need to participate reflectively in democratic life, gain political knowledge, and communicate their concerns effectively either individually or through representative organizations (Knight and Johnson 1998; Putnam 2001, 2015; Whiteley 2012). Furthermore, insofar as contemporary democrats are right that democracy should be understood as comprising a collection of "multiple publics," it is clear that these publics, too, have become dominated by lobby organizations representing the interests of the wealthy. Through the provision of hospitality, wealthy organizations are more able to engineer opportunities to communicate informally with decision makers, journalists, and other groups of people than ones with access to fewer resources and fewer networks.

Earlier I outlined the first aspect of the problem that lobbying poses for democracy: it is a central component of democratic governance in the contemporary era, practiced by a vast number of organizations and individuals at the domestic and international levels. Here I have outlined the second and third aspects of the problem (and indeed, the issues that make the first aspect a genuine problem): the form of elitism that has emerged in democratic states is disproportionately weighted toward the interests of the rich. The changes to the civic, economic, social, and political infrastructure of liberal democratic states outlined above have thus undermined the vision of democracy shared by the majority of democrats inside and outside the academy, including pluralists like Robert Dahl. The idea of a polyarchy in which power is distributed across a range of interest groups and organizations that represent diverse constituencies and hold one another in check has been superseded by a system in which power is distributed across a large number of organizations that represent a narrow range of interests, and in which vast swathes of the citizenry are left underrepresented and unable to form the kind of grassroots organizations on which they have traditionally relied, and that are recognized as central by the majority of democratic theorists.

Lobbying as a First- and Second-Order Problem

So what should be done to resolve this problem? And what *can* be done? Numerous academics and politicians have proposed legislative reforms aimed at introducing greater transparency as well as rectifying inequalities in access and power. While such measures are necessary, they are insufficient. The changes to the deep structure of liberal states that I have thus far described have resulted in a concentration of power in the hands of the wealthy in ways that violate democratic principles of political equality and liberty, and have served to not only exclude citizens from the democratic process but also eviscerate the democratic system of the social, civic, and associational infrastructure that citizens (and poorer ones in particular) need to participate in the democratic system, understand themselves as able to participate, or encourage them to believe that their participation is worthwhile (Parvin 2015, 2016, 2017). The fact that lobbying is now built into the core business of democratic governance means that tackling the problem requires nothing less than a fundamental reform of the core activities of the democratic state. It requires root-and-branch change, involving radical institutional reform as well as a reconfiguration of the civic support mechanisms that democracy needs to operate and flourish.

There are therefore two significant obstacles to reform: the scale of the changes that would be needed in order to wind back three-quarters of a century of democratic decline, and the fact that states are now structurally incapable of agreeing on or implementing such changes. The first is a first-order problem that concerns the concrete challenges posed to the conduct of politics and governance in liberal democratic states. The second is a second-order problem that concerns the ability of these states to resolve these problems. The first-order problem posed by lobbying is complex and wide-ranging. The second-order problem is perhaps intractable. Necessary change has not been achieved, and will not be achieved, through limited institutional reforms or new laws governing lobbying transparency, although it would also need these things. It would *in addition* require the structural reform of the democratic state, alleviation of social and economic inequalities, and rebuilding of civil society from the ground up. In Dennis Thompson's (2010) words, it would need both "constructive" and "reconstructive" change. The deep structure of the polity would need to be altered, entrenched inequalities would need to be ameliorated, and trajectories of citizen disengagement and elitism that have taken place over the past three-quarters of a century would need to be reversed. And all of this would need to be initiated and managed by states that are dominated by vested interests that would be resistant to these changes. The private interest groups that currently dominate the democratic system would need to decide collectively to engage in a process of long-term, expensive, and complex reform aimed at reducing their own power.

Powerful lobbies have repeatedly proven their reluctance to relinquish power or permit reform, however. For example, proposals to regulate the impact of private money on campaign and party activities in the United States have been consistently defeated. And statutory laws governing the activities of lobbyists are rare. Only ten "political systems throughout the democratic world" have lobbying rules in place: Australia, Canada, the European Union, Germany, Hungary, Lithuania, Poland, Taiwan, the United States, and the United Kingdom (Chari et al. 2019). Of the twenty-seven member states of the European Union, only five have national laws governing the activities of lobbyists.

Furthermore, the laws in these countries are often, at best, unfit for their purpose, or at worst, counterproductive (Parvin 2016). Governments in the United Kingdom, for instance, have over the past eighty years periodically revisited the issue of lobbying reform, usually in the wake of some new scandal (Cave and Rowell 2014). Each time, lobbyists successfully fought attempts to introduce statutory regulation, preferring instead a model of self-regulation. The UK coalition's attempt to introduce statutory regulation—via the 2014 Transparency of Lobbying, Non-Party Campaigning, and Trade Union Administration Act—is illustrative. That law, introduced in a speech at the University of East London by David Cameron in 2010 was supposed to shine "the light of transparency" on lobbying, which Cameron famously described as "the next big scandal waiting to happen" to British politics (Cave 2013). He claimed that if elected as prime minister, his government would impose tough new regulations on lobbying, including the introduction of a statutory register for anyone seeking to influence government. In its final form, the 2014 Lobbying Act not only failed to tackle the problem but it actually made it much worse by *increasing* the power of large corporations and wealthy interest groups relative to smaller campaign organizations, charities, and pressure groups (Parvin 2016). The reason for this is twofold.

First, the statutory register only requires lobbyists working for private sector consultancy firms to sign up—a group that comprises roughly 1 percent of practicing UK lobbyists. Lobbyists working in-house for large corporations were and are exempt. So while consultants working for corporate and noncorporate clients are covered, in-house lobbyists working for Google, Starbucks, law firms, tobacco and alcohol companies, pharmaceutical companies, investment banks, and trade associations like the CBI are not. Ironically, it was this fact that enabled David Cameron himself to avoid breaking lobbying laws in 2021 when he lobbied the British government on behalf of the company Greensill.

Moreover, the act only requires a minute fraction of lobbying activity to be reported. Only face-to-face meetings need to be reported, with no consideration given to any of the myriad ways in which public affairs professionals and campaigners seek to influence policy decisions (such as through media campaigns, coalition-building initiatives, and so on), and only meetings between consultants and ministers or permanent secretaries are deemed important enough. Meetings between lobbyists and other government officials, including special advisers and civil servants more junior than permanent secretaries, are excluded. To be clear, there are currently over four hundred thousand full-time civil servants working across all government departments, forty-four of whom have the title of permanent secretary or second permanent secretary. The Lobbying Act therefore succeeds only in shining the light of transparency on the activities of ninety-seven ministers, 1 percent of lobbyists, and 0.01 percent of civil servants.

Second, in addition to introducing transparency rules that do not cover the overwhelming majority of corporate lobbyists, the act imposed strict limits on the activities of smaller organizations like charities, and on the ways trade unions could campaign and raise funds. This is why the act has been dubbed the "gagging law" by critics; it forbids small organizations from political campaigning at the time that governments and members of Parliament are most receptive—the run-up to a general election—as such campaigning is deemed by the act as interfering in the electoral process. It also forbids trade unions from engaging in specific forms of political campaigning (inevitably on behalf of the Labour Party).

Recently the government has introduced new rules in addition to the Lobbying Act that forbid charities, academics, and other organizations in receipt of public funding from seeking to influence government policy (Parvin 2016). These rules in addition to those introduced in the Lobbying Act combine to silence small organizations, many of which rely on public funding, while enabling large corporations to go about their business with impunity. On the one hand, Cameron's proposal to bring lobbying under statutory regulation was radical. On the other, it was highly conservative; it misdiagnosed the problem, sought the wrong solution, and introduced even greater inequality into an already unequal system. Similar measures introduced by the European Commission and US federal government have proven just as ineffective, largely due to proposals being watered down by lobby organizations on their passage through the legislative process.

The wide and deep changes experienced by liberal democratic states that I have outlined thus far have served not only to marginalize citizens, reduce trust in democratic politics, increase political disengagement, entrench social and political inequality, and fuel the drive toward political elitism. They have also rendered it virtually impossible to implement the deep structural reforms that are necessary to resolve the problem. The elitism that characterizes liberal democratic states is now so weighted toward the interests of the wealthy that it is all but impossible for even moderate reforms to make it through the democratic process, let alone the vast and fundamental ones needed to resolve the problem. Liberal democratic institutions do not operate in accordance with democratic principles, and they are structurally incapable of reforming themselves in the ways necessary to make them do so. Cameron's coalition government was not genuinely committed to tackling lobbying (Parvin 2016). But even if it had been, its plan would have failed. The democratic system has been reconfigured in ways that make the passing of strong, effective legislation aimed at increasing transparency and accountability difficult. And even if Cameron *had* been able to pass such legislation, it would only have scratched the surface of a problem that affects all levels of democratic governance in multiple complex ways. Transparency legislation is aimed at cleaning up lobbying at the microlevel. Yet the problem, as we have seen, is at the macrolevel. We therefore arrive at an impasse.

On the one hand, it is possible and necessary to identify urgent first-order measures that would improve the situation and help to realize Madison's three-point plan. First, as well as introducing genuinely effective statutory regulation of lobbying that covers all lobbyists, we could make representative institutions more impartial by formally introducing citizens' voices at different points in the democratic system through, for example, the use of minipublics. Conclusions emanating from focus groups, deliberative assemblies and polls, and other innovations might be formally woven into the activities of select committees, for instance, or they could be introduced at a newly created stage in the legislative process (Dryzek 2012; Fishkin 2009; Goodin 2012; Parvin 2018b). Doing so would give representative organizations the space to provide representation and expertise, while creating new space for the voices of citizens whose views are not represented by these organizations. Furthermore, the decision-making process would need to be reformed to make it more hospitable to differently organized groups. Institutions would need to be capable of incorporating the concerns of different groups that may not be easily expressed through currently privileged forms of communication or within current formal rules.

Second, we would need to tackle economic inequality in order to encourage marginalized citizens back into the democratic system as well as the growth of organizations better able to represent them. Entrenched intergenerational concentrations of wealth and property ownership would need to be dismantled through higher taxes on income, wealth, and inheritance; market forces, which drive the growth of economic inequality along with the concentration of wealth and property among the richest citizens, would need to be subject to regulation and constraint; and the private financing of election campaigns and making of political donations to political parties would need to be severely curtailed, or perhaps even banned altogether and replaced with the public funding of political parties and campaigns (Rawls 1971; Thomas 2017). And politicians would need to be forbidden from accepting any hospitality from lobby groups in order to ameliorate the de facto advantages that this gives to wealthy organizations.

Third, the state would need to invest heavily in the long-term process of rebuilding civil society, particularly to support the regrowth of representative organizations capable of representing poorer citizens (Putnam 2015). That is, in Madisonian terms, it would need to encourage the growth of factional interest groups in order to diminish the structural dominance currently enjoyed by corporations and interest groups representing the wealthy. This would be a complicated and wide-ranging process, and there are feasibility concerns associated with them that I have outlined elsewhere (Parvin 2015, 2018a). Nevertheless, options might include the investment of public money into community projects and other initiatives aimed at building social capital at the local level (Whiteley 2012), public subsidy of groups that would seek to organize themselves into grassroots movements (Cohen and Rogers 1995), and creation of spaces in which citizens might meet to discuss political issues and communicate shared concerns (Gutmann and Thompson 2004).

Such measures would together go some way in aligning democratic practice and principle, and recalibrating the public sphere in a way that is in line with a Madisonian vision for the fair and just management of factional interests. Impartial institutions, supported by a more equal citizenry, would work with a diverse community of interest groups and associations capable of representing the interests of their members at the elite level while holding one another in check. Lines of communication between the citizenry and state institutions would exist, meaning that states could more effectively track the will of the people. Democracies would thus better fulfill their dual need to discover, exercise, and constrain the popular will through appropriate legislative and constitutional measures, and hence secure the liberty of citizens through self-government, and also ensure the political equality of all citizens by better including the voices of all citizens in the democratic process, and protecting against the emergence and entrenchment of dominant factions.

On the other hand, we need to recognize that it will be all but impossible to implement these reforms in the current political context. The second-order problem posed by lobbying constrains and stifles the implementation of first-order solutions. The institutions charged with the responsibility of agreeing to and implementing reform are the very same ones that are now dominated by corporations and organizations that lobby for the wealthy. States have allowed economic inequalities to translate into political inequalities, wealthy organizations to eclipse poorer ones, and a narrow range of interest groups to replace the broad citizenry in the democratic process. Citizens could in theory seek change from below, but citizens are now peripheral to the democratic process, marginalized, disengaged, and lacking the civic infrastructure to mobilize or challenge from the grass roots. States might be theoretically able to foster social capital and the emergence of grassroots movements capable of applying pressure to the established order by implementing the kind of reforms outlined above, but only once this established order has acquiesced to such measures, and only once the dominant actors have accepted that they should be subject to greater pressure. Structural reform can only begin once those who currently comprise the structure allow it to. And even if such agreement *were* possible, the kind of radical action needed to wind back three-quarters of a century of democratic decline would be far-reaching and take generations (Parvin 2015, 2020).

We can now grasp more clearly the problem posed to democracy by lobbying, and also what I meant in the beginning of the chapter when I described it as a macrolevel, three-part problem of a first and second order. Changes in the deep structure of liberal democratic states have marginalized citizens, fueled political disengagement, and afforded significant power to unelected lobby organizations. Lobby groups have eclipsed citizens in the democratic process, concentrated political power in the hands of the wealthy, and captured the political system in such a way as to make reform difficult, if not structurally impossible. Liberal democratic states have failed to manage the rise of lobbying in line with democratic principles. States have protected groups' formal rights to assemble and push for change, as is their duty. But they have failed to ensure that these rights can be meaningfully exercised by all citizens. In presiding over a decline in civil society and the social bases of grassroots politics, liberal states have failed to ensure the conditions necessary for poorer citizens to assemble or communicate their concerns to decision makers. The practice of lobbying in liberal democratic states renders these states unable to make good on their commitments to political equality and freedom as self-government.

The fact that contemporary democratic states are characterized by deep and far-reaching political inequalities associated with even deeper and more far-reaching social and economic inequalities, that these inequalities have led to a concentration of political power among those at the top end of the wealth and income distribution, that it is possible to identify possible solutions to these problems, but that these solutions face complex and perhaps even insurmountable political obstacles to their implementation, all combine to reveal the scale of the problem and our helplessness before it. I said at the start of the chapter that lobbying is arguably the most urgent of all political problems currently faced by liberal democratic states. It is hopefully now clear why I believe this is the case, and why political philosophers who are otherwise divided by deep normative disagreements can and should unite in recognizing it as a priority, and work with political activists, politicians, and the wider policy-making community to seek opportunities for real and profound long-term change. For lobbying is the problem that lies behind and exacerbates all others—the problem that needs to be resolved before any of the other problems that concern political philosophers can be addressed. Libertarians will not get the free markets they want while corporations can leverage their economic advantage to stifle competition (Munger and Villareal-Diaz 2019). Democrats will not get the politics they want while democratic regimes are hampered by distrust, citizen disengagement, and forms of governance dominated by socioeconomic elites (Parvin 2017; Thomas 2017). Epistocrats will not get the informed governance that they seek while political power is distributed according to how much money and structural influence a group or individual has rather than how much they know (Brennan 2016; Somin 2016). And egalitarians have little hope of reducing economic inequalities, increasing workplace democracy, or ensuring the fair value of basic liberties while the wealthy groups that would bear the costs of these proposals are the ones driving, or stifling, economic policy change (Anderson 2017; Baramendi and Anderson 2011; Piketty 2014; Rawls 1971; Rich 2017). The practice of lobbying imposes strict feasibility constraints on any normative prescriptions that challenge current democratic practice. Until those constraints are lifted, political philosophers should work together to seek new strategies for dismantling the unequal distribution of power that is characteristic of liberal democratic politics. At this stage, however, it is not clear how this might be done, what this solution might be, where it may come from, or even if such a bipartisan spirit might be realistically built.

Acknowledgments

I have had the pleasure of presenting these ideas at numerous workshops and conferences, including at the MANCEPT workshops in political theory, 2017; Political Philosophy Workshop, University of Cambridge, 2017; Centre for the Study of Social Justice, University of Oxford, 2018; and the Centre for the Study of Law and Society, University of California at Berkeley, 2018. I offer my thanks to Simon Kaye, John Filling, Daniel Butt, Sarah Song, and Rosann Greenspan for organizing these sessions, and everyone who participated in them.

References

Achen, Christopher H., and Larry M. Bartels. 2016. *Democracy for Realists: Why Elections Do Not Produce Responsive Government*. Princeton, NJ: Princeton University Press.

Aidt, Toke S. 2016. "Rent Seeking and the Economics of Corruption." *Constitutional Political Economy* 27 (2): 142–57.

Anderson, Elizabeth. 2017. *Private Government: How Employers Rule Our Lives (and Why We Don't Talk about It*. Princeton, NJ: Princeton University Press.

Andrews, Emily. 2015. "Civil Service Staff Numbers under the Coalition Government, from 2010 to 2015." Institute for Government, June 17. https://www.instituteforgovernment.org.uk/blog/civil-service-staff-numbers-under-coalition-government-2010-2015.

Apostolova, Vyara, Elise Uberoi, and Neil Johnston. 2017. "Political Disengagement in the UK: Who Is Disengaged?" Briefing Paper CBP7501, August. London: House of Commons.

Aristotle. 2015. *The Politics*. London: Penguin Books.

Audickus, Lukas, Noel Dempsey, and Philip Loft. 2019. "Membership of UK Political Parties." Research briefing, August 9. London: House of Commons.

Baramendi, Pablo, and Christopher J. Anderson, eds. 2011. *Democracy, Inequality, and Representation: A Comparative Perspective*. London: Russell Sage Foundation.

Bartels, Larry M. 2016. *Unequal Democracy: The Political Economy of the New Gilded Age*. 2nd ed. Princeton, NJ: Princeton University Press.

Baumgartner, Frank R., Jeffrey M. Berry, Marie Hojnacki, David C. Kimball, and Beth L. Leech. 2009. *Lobbying and Policy Change: Who Wins, Who Loses, and Why*. Chicago: University of Chicago Press.

Benhabib, Seyla, ed. 1996. *Democracy and Difference: Contesting the Boundaries of the Political*. Princeton, NJ: Princeton University Press.

Berry, Jeffrey M. 1997. *The Interest Group Society*. 3rd ed. New York: Longman.

Bevir, Mark. 2010. *Democratic Governance*. Princeton, NJ: Princeton University Press.

Birch, Sarah, Glenn Gottfried, and Guy Lodge. 2013. *Divided Democracy: Political Inequality in the UK and Why It Matters*. London: IPPR.

Boyd, Richard. 2004. *Uncivil Society: The Perils of Pluralism and the Making of Modern Liberalism*. Lanham, MD: Lexington.

Brennan, Jason. 2016. *Against Democracy*. Princeton, NJ: Princeton University Press.

Cave, Tamasin. 2013. "The Next Big Scandal: Cameron's 'Lobbying' Speech." Spinwatch, November 13. https://spinwatch.org/index.php/issues/lobbying/item/5579-the-next-big-scandal-cameron-s-lobbying-speech.

Cave, Tamasin, and Andy Rowell. 2014. *A Quiet Word: Lobbying, Crony Capitlaism, and Broken Politics in Britain*. London: Bodley Head.

Chambers, Simone. 2009. "Rhetoric and the Public Sphere: Has Deliberative Democracy Abandoned Mass Democracy?" *Political Theory* 37 (3): 323–50.

Chari, Raj, John Hogan, Gary Murphy, and Michele Crepaz. 2012. *Regulating Lobbying: A Global Comparison*. Manchester: Manchester University Press.

Cigler, Allan J., and Burkett A. Loomis. 1986. "Introduction: The Changing Nature of Interest Group Politics." In *Interest Group Politics* , edited by Allan J. Cigler and Burdett A. Loomis, 1–29. Washington, DC: Congressional Quarterly Press.

Cohen, Joshua, and Joel Rogers. 1995. *Associations and Democracy: the Real Utopias Project, Volume I*. London: Verso.

Cohen, Joshua, and Charles Sabel. 1997. "Directly-Deliberative Polyarchy." *European Law Journal* 3 (4): 313–42.

Dahl, Robert A. 1989. *Democracy and Its Critics*. New Haven, CT: Yale University Press.

Dinan, William, and David Miller. 2007. *Thinker, Faker, Spinner, Spy: Corporate PR and the Assault on Democracy*. London: Pluto Press.

Drutman, Lee. 2015. "How Corporate Lobbyists Conquered American Democracy." *Atlantic*, April 20.

Dryzek, John S. 2001. *Deliberative Democracy and Beyond: Liberals, Critics, Contestations*. Oxford: Oxford University Press.

———. 2012. *Foundations and Frontiers of Deliberative Government*. Oxford: Oxford University Press.

European Commission. 2012. *Annual Report on the Operations of the Transparency Register 2012*. Brussels: European Commission.

Fischer, Frank. 2009. *Democracy and Expertise: Re-Orienting Policy Inquiry*. Oxford: Oxford University Press.

Fishkin, James. 2009. *When the People Speak: Deliberative Democracy and Public Consultation*. Oxford: Oxford University Press.

Fraser, Nancy. 2004. *Redistribution or Recognition? A Political-Philosophical Exchange*. London: Verso.Fung, Archon. 2015. "Putting the Public Back into Governance: The Challenges of Citizen Participation and Its Future." *Public Administration Review* 25:1–10.

Gilens, Martin. 2014. *Affluence and Influence: Economic Inequality and Political Power in America*. Princeton, NJ: Princeton University Press.

Gilens, Martin, and Benjamin I. Page. 2014. "Testing Theories of American Politics: Elites, Interest Groups, and Average Citizens." *Perspectives on Politics* 12 (3): 564–81.

Goodin, Robert E. 2012. *Innovating Democracy: Democratic Theory and Practice after the Deliberative Turn*. Oxford: Oxford University Press.

Global Justice Now. 2017. *Annual Review*. https://www.globaljustice.org.uk/resource/annual-review-2016/

Gutmann, Amy, and Dennis Thompson. 2004. *Why Deliberative Democracy?* Princeton, NJ: Princeton University Press.

Habermas, Jürgen. 1996. *Between Facts and Norms: Contributions to a Discourse Theory of Law and Democracy*. Cambridge, MA: MIT Press.

Hansard Society and Electoral Commission. 2017. *Audit of Political Engagement 14*. London: Electoral Commission.

Hamilton, Alexander, John Jay, and James Madison. (1787–88) 2009. *The Federalist Papers*. https://www.gutenberg.org/files/1404/1404-h/1404-h.htm.

Hay, Colin. 2007. *Why We Hate Politics*. Cambridge, UK: Polity Press.

Hayek, F. A. 1978. *New Studies in Philosophy, Politics, Economics, and the History of Ideas*. Chicago: University of Chicago Press.

Hirst, Paul. 1994. *Associative Democracy: New Forms of Economic and Social Governance*. Cambridge, UK: Polity Press.

Hobbes, Thomas. 2008. *Leviathan*. Edited by J. C. A. Gaskin Oxford: Oxford University Press.

Holyoke, Thomas T. 2014. *Interest Groups and Lobbying: Pursuing Political Interests in America*. Boulder, CO: Westview Press.

Jacobs, Lawrence R., and Theda Skocpol, eds. 2005. *Inequality and American Democracy: What We Know and What We Need to Learn*. New York: Russell Sage Foundation.

Jordan, Grant, and William A. Maloney. 2007. *Democracy and Interest Groups: Enhancing Participation?* Basingstoke, UK: Palgrave-Macmillan.

Knight, Jack, and James Johnson. 1998. "What Kind of Political Equality Does Deliberative Democracy Require?" In *What Kind of Political Equality Does Deliberative Democracy Require?*, edited by James Bohman and William Rehg, 280–319. Cambridge, MA: MIT Press.

Knoke, David. 1986. "Associations and Interest Group." *Annual Review of Sociology* 12:1–12.

Landemore, Hélène. 2017. *Democratic Reason: Politics, Collective Intelligence, and the Rule of the Many*. Princeton, NJ: Princeton University Press.

Lessig, Lawrence. 2011. *Republic, Lost: How Money Corrupts Congress—and a Plan to Stop It*. New York: Twelve.

Levy, Jacob T. 2014. *Rationalism, Pluralism, and Freedom*. Oxford: Oxford University Press.

Lindblom, Charles E. 1977. *Politics and Markets: The World's Political-Economic Systems*. New York: Basic.

Lowy, Theodore J. 1979. *The End of Liberalism: The Second Republic of the United States*. New York: W. W. Norton.

Macedo, Stephen, Yvette Alex-Assensoh, Jeffrey M. Berry, Michael Brintnall, David E. Campbell, Luis Ricardo Fraga, Archon Fung, et al. 2005. *Democracy at Risk: How Political Choices Undermine Citizen Participation, and What We Can Do about It*. Washington, DC: Brookings Institution Press.

Madison, James. 1792. "For the *National Gazette*, 1972." Circa January 23. https://founders.archives.gov/documents/Madison/01-14-02-0176.

Mair, Peter. 2013. *Ruling the Void: The Hollowing of Western Democracy*. London: Verso.

Mansbridge, Jane, James Bohman, Simone Chambers, Thomas Christiano, Archon Fung, John Parkinson, Dennis F. Thomason, and Mark E. Warren. 2012. "A Systemic Approach to Deliberative Democracy." In *Deliberative Systems*, edited by John Parkinson and Jane Mansbridge, 1–26. Cambridge: Cambridge University Press.

Miliband, Ralph. 1969. *The State in Capitalist Society*. London: Weidenfield and Nicholson. National Audit Office. 2013. *The Role of Major Contractors in the Delivery of Public Services*. London: House of Commons.

Munger, Michael C., and Mario Villarreal-Diaz. 2019. "The Road to Crony Capitalism." *Independent Review* 23 (4): 331–44.

Parvin, Phil. 2007. "Friend or Foe? Lobbying in British Democracy." London: Hansard Society.

———. 2009. "Against Localism: Does De-Centralising Power to Communities Fail Minorities?," *Political Quarterly* 80 (3): 351–60.

———. 2011. "Localism and the Left: The Need for Strong Central Government." *Renewal* 19 (2): 37–49.

———. 2015. "Is Deliberative Democracy Feasible? Political Disengagement and Trust in Liberal Democratic States." *Monist* 98 (4): 407–23.

———. 2016. "Silencing the Critics: Charities, Lobbyists, and the Government's Quiet War on Dissent." *Renewal* 24 (3): 62–75.

———. 2017. "Democracy, Capital, and the Rise of the New Inequality." *Political Theory* 45 (6): 863–76.

———. 2018a. "Democracy without Participation: A New Politics for a Disengaged Era." *Res Publica* 23:31–52.

———. 2018b. "Representing the People: British Democracy in an Age of Political Ignorance." *Political Studies Review* 16 (4): 265–78.

________. 2020. "The Participatory Paradox: An Egalitarian Critique of Participatory Democracy." *Representation* 57 (2): 263–85.

Piketty, Thomas. 2014. *Capital in the Twenty-First Century*. Cambridge, MA: Harvard University Press.

Plato. 2007. *The Republic*. London: Penguin Books.

Putnam, Robert D. 2001. *Bowling Alone: The Collapse and Revival of American Community*. New York: Simon and Schuster.

———. 2015. *Our Kids: The American Dream in Crisis*. New York: Simon and Schuster.

Putnam, Robert D., with Robert Leonardi and Rafaella Y. Nanetti. 2005. *Making Democracy Work: Civic Traditions in Modern Italy*. Princeton, NJ: Princeton University Press.

Rauch, Jonathan. 1994. *Demosclerosis: The Silent Killer of American Government*. London: Times Books.

Rawls, John. 1971. *A Theory of Justice*. New York: Oxford University Press.

Rhodes, R. A. W. 2017. *Network Governance and the Differentiated Polity: Selected Essays, Volume 1*. Oxford: Oxford University Press.

Rich, Roland. 2017. *Democracy in Crisis: Why, Where, and How to Respond*. Boulder, CO: Lynne Rienner Publishers.

Roberts, Carys, and Mathew Lawrence. 2017. *Wealth in the Twenty-First Century: Inequalities and Drivers*. London: Institute of Public Policy Research.

Rousseau, Jean-Jacques. 2012. *Of the Social Contract and Other Political Writings*. London: Penguin Books.

Sabl, Andrew. 2015. "The Two Cultures of Democratic Theory: Responsiveness, Democratic Quality, and the Empirical-Normative Divide." *Perspectives on Politics* 13 (2): 345–65.

Schlozman, Kay Lehman, Sidney Verba, and Henry E. Brady. 2012. *The Unheavenly Chorus: Unequal Political Voice and the Broken Promise of American Democracy*. Princeton, NJ: Princeton University Press.

Schumpeter, Joseph A. 1950. *Capitalism, Socialism and Democracy*. 3rd ed. New York: Harper Colophon Books.Shaxson, Nicholas. 2011. *Treasure Islands: Tax Havens and the Men Who Stole the World* .London: Bodley Head.

Skocpol, Theda. 2003. *Diminished Democracy: From Membership to Management in American Civic Life*. Norman: University of Oklahoma Press.[not cited yet]

———. 2004. "Voice and Equality: The Transformation of American Civic Democracy." *Perspectives on Politics* 2 (4): 3–20.

Solt, Frederick. 2008. "Economic Inequality and Democratic Political Engagement." *American Journal of Political Science* 52 (1): 48–60.

Somin, Ilya. 2016. *Democracy and Political Ignorance: Why Smaller Government Is Smarter*. Stanford, CA: Stanford University Press.

Stoker, Gerry. 2006. *Why Politics Matters: Making Democracy Work*. Basingstoke, UK: Palgrave Macmillan.

Thomas, Alan. 2017. *Republic of Equals*. Oxford: Oxford University Press.

Thompson, Dennis. 2010. *The Democratic Citizen: Social Science and Democratic Theory in the 20th Century*. Cambridge: Cambridge University Press.

Tocqueville, Alexis de. (1835–40) 2003. *Democracy in America*. London: Penguin Books.

Tomasi, John. 2012. *Free Market Fairness*. Princeton, NJ: Princeton University Press.

Whiteley, Paul. 2012. *Political Participation in Britain: The Decline and Revival of Civic Culture*. Basingstoke, UK: Palgrave.

Winters, Jeffrey A. 2011. *Oligarchy*. Cambridge: Cambridge University Press.

Young, Iris Marion. 2000. *Inclusion and Democracy*. Oxford: Oxford University Press.

Zetter, Lionel. 2014. *Lobbying: The Art of Political Persuasion*. 3rd ed. London: Harriman.

Zucman, Gabriel. 2015. *The Hidden Wealth of Nations: The Scourge of Tax Havens*. Chicago: University of Chicago Press.

Afterword

POLITICAL ETHICS AND INSTITUTIONAL RENOVATION

Andrew Sabl

THIS BOOK CAME TOGETHER during unhappy years for political ethics. In Turkey and Hungary, Brazil and the Philippines, India and the United States, those years saw a resurgence of authoritarian politics, openly hostile to social pluralism and political disagreement, in democratic guise. That particular combination, which we have come to call populism, all but guarantees a massive attack on political ethics. In a grimly familiar pattern, populists in office use executive power as a political cudgel, pardoning friends while prosecuting enemies. They turn leading newspapers and the state broadcasting network (where there is one) into propaganda outlets while doing their best to threaten, weaken through regulation, co-opt, or force the sale of the opposition press. Indeed, they attack the whole idea of a loyal opposition. They use government contracts and administrative harassment to reward or obtain the loyalty of business. They label court decisions that strike down their measures as illegitimate and partisan, and eventually pack the courts with enemies of the rule of law and democratic procedure.

In the United States, Donald Trump tried to do all of these things while president. He was prevented from succeeding in most of them by durable and determined institutions: a proudly independent judiciary; an executive branch with strong institutional and professional norms; a robust, diverse, and independent (nonstate) press; two independently elected houses of Congress that served as a crucial check when—alas only when—controlled by the opposition party; and vigorous and independent state governments. The main executive agencies that welcomed authoritarianism rather than pushing back (and this is not intended as reassurance) were those that had, and had fostered, authoritarian tendencies at their very origins—chiefly Homeland Security, especially the parts tasked with policing immigration, along with the Federal Bureau of Prisons and large portions of local law enforcement. On the other hand, and (so far) unlike in the other countries named above, a president who clearly lost an election tried to keep power by inciting an armed mob to insurrection, and one of the two national political parties has become durably committed to the lie that the election was stolen as well as the belief that the insurrection was either trivial or patriotic. Not good.

This volume, however, lacks an air of crisis or doom. While we invited the authors to revise their contributions to reflect the lessons of what many of its British, Western European, and North American authors are understandably (though parochially) prone to call "the Trump era," none made radical changes. This handbook's pages, as a result, rarely convey the sense that the ground of political ethics is shifting, much less dissolving. This partly reflects the authors' academic fields: "normative" political theory and moral philosophy are primarily devoted to setting forth what ought to happen, or how things ought to go, rather than following the twists, however harrowing, of what is happening.[1] And it partly reflects temporal and political luck: shortly after our authors' contributions were finalized, Trump lost an election and gave up power (though one wishes these had not been independent events). The United States is only one country, but it is my own country, and for better or worse, something of a world bellwether. It was natural to feel guarded relief.

To my mind, though, there is a deeper reason: constitutionalism is the sea in which political ethics swims. It is not that everyone shares my position that the proper standards of political ethics are *directly* constitutional: that is, that what political figures ought to do involves understanding, and protecting, the institutions of constitutional democracy along with the less formal ethical norms and purposes that animate them (including norms and constitutional principles that uphold free speech, dissent, opposition, and peaceful agitation [Sabl 2002]). There is a looser yet deeper connection between ethics and constitutionalism as such: both are checks on political whim, the politics of immediate passions and peremptory demands, whether from above or below. Both constitutionalism and political ethics frustrate, for the sake of deeper

1. This is true even when the theorists involved are of the "realist" school—both coeditors' tendency. Realism, the kind we favor at any rate, is less about recommending what is "practical" or "feasible" than about drawing from the study of politics permanent (or at least durable) *normative insights* of a different kind than one would get from abstract philosophizing (Hall and Sleat 2017).

human commitments, the simple, in some sense *natural* politics of "I want this, now" and "we demand that, now." Even accounts of political ethics that stress the legitimate role of advocacy and partiality, as I think we should, seek to tame such partiality, and the politics of mere demand, in their rawest, most elemental form. My gut demands that politicians listen to and act on my passionate opinions while disregarding the opinions of those who oppose me. (I, after all, am passionate for justice and truth, whereas *they* are simply wrong, not to say evil.) The central tenet of political ethics, in contrast, is that my adversaries and their advocates may do what I and mine may do.

The success of politicians who practice and encourage precisely the raw, anticonstitutional and antiethical form of politics, and the approval of mass electorates that welcome that, have been bracing and even vertiginous. They brought home psychically what I and many others always acknowledged abstractly: that constitutional democracy and political ethics were never fully a matter of consensus. Because both political ethics and constitutional politics interfere with some of the most basic drives and tendencies of human nature, they require continual work and reinforcement to remind people of why they can be at once deeply frustrating and constantly necessary. I see the resilience of this book's chapters as reflecting not complacency but instead the conviction that there is no alternative to this work—to the continual task of pointing out that, and how, we can do better overall and in the long run when we say no to our raw passions and gut instincts than when we slake them.

What follows is a personal essay, not a systematic treatment. I have neither the expertise nor the space to synthesize the vast, impressive theoretical scholarship on populism; the empirical history and political science of democratic backsliding, resilience, or resurgence; or specialized work on Trump and other populist leaders. Finally, I will neither describe or prescribe the views of this volume's other contributors or its readers. My goal is to share some lessons personally learned that I hope illustrate this collection's larger purposes and themes.

Reverse Evolution

Describing contemporary societies' widespread assault on reliable knowledge, Tom Nichols (2019, 217) stresses the deliberate perversity of that assault:

> Ordinary Americans might never have liked the educated or professional classes very much, but until recently they did not widely disdain their actual learning as a bad thing in itself. It might even be too kind to call this merely

> "anti-rational"; it is almost reverse evolution, away from tested knowledge and backward toward folk wisdom and myths passed by word of mouth—except with all of it now sent along at the speed of electrons.

Though depressing enough as a summary of how we are choosing to acquire false beliefs, the diagnosis of "reverse evolution" applies more generally. For Nichols's insight—that the sifting of evidence through professional procedures (whether in law, science, or journalism) *deliberately frustrates what is natural,* namely our love of folk wisdom and knowledge transmitted via peers—is true of human institutions more broadly.

Previous work of mine portrays all of modern liberal democracy's familiar institutions—the rule of law, but also the market, the welfare state, representative democracy, political parties, and practices of toleration and free speech—as *counterintuitive*. Because they serve unknown actors' long-term ends rather than predictably furthering my desires and my group's interests right now, all of these institutions seem frustrating, even irrational. They win support only over time as and to the extent that they are seen to further a diverse set of human purposes better than their absence would. We learn, slowly and the hard way, that we do better under impartial laws than under clan warfare; better with the market than when we can trade only with people whom we know personally, or who share with us a religious, moral, or ethnic community; better under the welfare state than when relying on voluntary charity (and the moral strings, giving great personal power to the donor, that come with it); and better under representative democracy than when rival political claims are settled through violence or repeated secession (Sabl 2017).[2]

It is tempting to tell this story in the past or perfect tense: these are the institutions that we have learned to appreciate. Populism forces us to recast it in the present and future. Because our central institutions are counterintuitive and require long learning, there will always be, as we have been reminded, a constituency for attacking them: for ignoring or dismantling institutions and norms in favor of structures—or the absence of structures—that give me and people I identify with what we want, right now. The rejection of impartial institutions and the ethics they embody carries a strong, visceral appeal: the law should punish threatening outsiders while giving people like me a break. A distorted market and slanted welfare state should guarantee work and opportunity to "good people" (this means my people) while letting "those other people" face the market discipline without

2. This work draws inspiration from, without claiming to track literally, that of David Hume.

which they would choose not to work at all. And democracy should mean that the real people, people like me, win elections; when the other side "wins," the proper response is not to concede but rather to expose how it must have cheated.

These sentiments are natural. Populists merely advocate a return to the politics of indulging such sentiments by demolishing the civilized practices that sideline them. These sentiments thrive, to be sure, when liberal institutions are themselves biased, benefiting all to some extent, but some durably more than others, in ways normal politics seems unwilling to address. Yet the solution that populists offer is not to reform institutions so that they work more equitably and inclusively but instead to cynically embrace institutional unfairness—in fact intensifying and cementing it while (rhetorically at least) reversing its direction.

Polemarchan Justice and Tribal Politics

In their book tracing Trump's demolition of the presidential office, Susan Hennessey and Benjamin Wittes (2020, 176–77; cf. chap. 7) attribute to Trump the position of Polemarchus in Plato's *Republic*: justice consists of helping friends and harming enemies.[3] In an echo, probably unwitting, of what Thomas Hobbes says about the state of nature—where force and fraud are the cardinal virtues—those authors predict that a continuing "atmosphere of intense polarization" may lead future presidents to seek political gain by acting as if "hating and defeating the other side is the only virtue" (Hennessey and Wittes 2020, 290).[4]

Plato's account of Socrates's response to Polemarchus quickly (too quickly) refutes Polemarchus's definition of justice as contrary to reason. David Hume, who agreed that it was contrary to reason in some sense (the sense in which

3. "Trump evidently believes that law enforcement is personal and that the real crime is being unpopular with the predominant or governing group, being attached to the wrong political views, or being personally obnoxious to or in the way of the president himself" (Hennessey and Wittes 2020, 119). To identify Trump with Polemarchus seems more apt than identifying him with Carl Schmitt's idea that the sovereign has the power to distinguish friends (of the state) from (public) enemies, since Trump's division between friends and enemies is portrayed less as a matter of sovereignty than as one of *justice*. Those who have been prosecuted for their crimes in spite of being supporters of Trump have not just been under the would-be sovereign's protection or on the right side of his will. They have been treated, according to Trump, "unfairly," and Trump's supporters perceive *injustice*.

4. This, in turn, is an unwitting echo of Hume (1987, 33), who thought partisan passions could suspend the usual operation of ethical and political conventions; in party politics, every partisan is praised by copartisans for doing whatever harms the other side.

"reason" was shorthand for calm sentiments backed by calculation, as opposed to immediate passion), stressed that something like the Polemarchus's view was nevertheless *natural.* Human nature is "partial"; it impels us to think that we need only care, or at least care very much, about those close to us (with the corollary that the most natural political unit is something like the clan). Only long experience and painstaking socialization yield the artificial belief that my kin and my enemy should enjoy the same public treatment, which we come to call "justice" (Hume [1739–40] 2000, 3.2.1–2).

On the one hand, this process of experience and socialization, drawn across generations, is tenacious. It is so obviously useful once discovered and promulgated that citizens of all regimes, and politicians of all stripes, have an interest in cultivating this sense of justice in themselves and others, and in restoring it whenever that cultivation decays. This is why Hume (1987, 124) called the rule of law a "hardy plant." This metaphor works better, however, when the plant is merely neglected, not deliberately rooted out as endangering a tribalist monoculture. To switch metaphors, institutions that are counterintuitive are like structures that shelter us for generations, but whose demolition would—once we start considering it more seriously than we normally do or should—palpably feed immediate desires. The characters in Akira Kurosawa's film *Rashomon,* which considers the meaning of truth and justice, huddle in a cold rain, badly sheltered by a temple half of whose timbers have been dismantled. Their response, "natural" in the moment, is to remove more timbers, one by one, for firewood.

To this extent, the claim that the pro-Trump Right is politically "sterile" or thin in programmatic content (Muirhead and Rosenblum 2019, 8, 28, 31 and passim) is true, but less consequential it seems. The "program" is privative: to revert to a tribalism that is natural once the social support for impartial justice has been deliberately sapped. Populists expect that there will be more political friends on their side than on the other because the populists constitute the larger ethnoreligious tribe (for the moment anyway—and shortsightedness, along with partiality, was something that Hume rightly thought natural, with its contrary a matter of social learning). Given that, they do not *need* a "positive," "constructive" proposal. They only need a reversion to Polemarchan partiality—that is, a reversion to freedom from disinterested laws and institutions that benefit one's enemies as well as oneself.[5]

5. Compare Anne Applebaum's (2020, 33) argument that authoritarian rightists don't particularly need a new "theory" or ideology—just a desire for power along with resentment that the system does not grant them power unless they earn it through impartial rules.

Foundation and Renovation

Put differently, and inspired by (but departing from) Hume's own framework: in earlier writing I portrayed US constitutionalism as the object of universal attachment. Not only did the US Constitution provide people with common parameters for discussing political ethics—a good political role or function being one that furthered constitutional purposes (Sabl 2002)—but together with the Declaration of Independence, it also provided a common political identity. These fundamental conventions constituted a people, such that to abandon them would be to rip the country's identity up by the roots (Sabl 2012).

These two claims are, I must now admit, in tension. Combining them creates a story of constitutional allegiance that is not contradictory but rather radically unstable. On this account, the US people and its first principles of political ethics will exist if, and only if, institutions remain in force—and remain more or less compelling in daily practice, if not in conscious theory—that are counterintuitive, valued mostly in inchoate and implicit ways, and prone to lurch toward inequality unless constantly reformed. (This is a story that applies not just to the United States but also to any country that hopes for a "constitutional" or "institutional" patriotism not based solely on blood or language.) Institutions like this are prone to decay. Their survival involves not the usual metaphors of foundation ("bedrock" or "deeply rooted") but instead those of constant, necessary renovation. They resemble the Golden Gate Bridge, universally admired as a beautiful human achievement, but free from rust only if constantly repainted by crews that must start back at one end as soon as their work has reached the other. Such institutions thrive under constant reminders of their necessity (and necessary imperfection), yet are constantly subject to the impatience of intuition: "yes, but we really want this, now, and the institution stands in the way."

Nadia Urbinati's (2019, 78) masterful recent book on populism essentially portrays the relationship between the populist leader and the "people" (a "true' people" extracted from "the empirical people") as an exercise in stoking this impatience. Populism denounces and seeks to undermine all the institutions of liberal democracy on the grounds that they are frustrating, both temporally (they take too long) and normatively (they may give more rewards to people who aren't a proper part of our community than to those, like us of course, who are). Constitutional checks, on a populist view, only interfere with public opinion; populist parties see themselves as the only legitimate party rather than as part of a permanently competitive system; and populist appeals make no pretense of universality (Urbinati 2019, 61, 42, 48). Whereas constitutional political ethics thrives on a division of political labor and ethical responsibility, whereby different civic leaders articulate citizens' interests and opinions in different ways and serve as checks one another's claims (Sabl 2002), populism heaps contempt on the political vocation as such, upholding a flattened logic of "political morality" whereby "the people are considered moral because they do not hold power" (Urbinati 2019, 57; cf. 64). Whereas the logic of representative democracy is alternation in power, populists do not respect majorities, only their own majority (Urbinati 2109, 92). Against the ideal of legal impartiality, populists vindicate the old authoritarian slogan (attributed to Brazilian dictator Getúlio Vargas, reinventing Polemarchan justice), "Everything for my friends; for my enemies, the law" (quoted in Urbinati 2019, 112; cf. O'Donnell 1999).

My work on liberal institutions has portrayed them as technologies that, like our electronic and mechanical gadgets, are used by everyone, though understood by few. This benign indifference, however, is one thing. Deliberate and gleeful *attacks* on the relevant technologies are another. Nor do I draw as much solace as I once did from the irony that those who decry contemporary institutions also make pervasive use of them. While this irony enables us to mock idiosyncratic conservative romantics and to put their efforts in perspective, it does not protect us against attacks on institutions that are, despite their intellectual perversity, real, coordinated, and effective. A reactionary who uses Amazon to sell half a million copies of a book decrying technology and commerce is amusing but harmless (and will never learn their error for the reason, unhappy to them yet happy for the rest of us, that they will never get what they think they want). A band of intelligent Luddites who use their smartphones to plot the destruction of the internet is just as inconsistent but less amusing. Liberal democracy winks at the former case. Populism is the political equivalent of the latter.

Political Professionalism and Its Discontents

My first book (Sabl 2002) compared politicians to professionals (though without specialized educational credentials or licenses) who serve both clients and ethical codes; different kinds of politicians are different kinds of political professionals. It took for granted that people value professional expertise in general, and that few people wanted a world without doctors or engineers. To be sure, many denied, and still do, that politicians should be thought of as professionals. But the weaker, hypothetical claim seemed easy: *if* it made sense to see politicians as professionals, it would also make sense to value their special kind of work on our behalf, and their special expertise and skill at doing that work.

We see in our time, however, a pervasive attack on professionals of all types, whether on doctors who claim to know what does and does not cure COVID-19, lawyers who insist that claims made in court be backed by some evidence, or teachers who assign history books that flout partisan myths (as all good history books do; no myth simple and comforting enough to please a faction adequately tracks the facts). Some of the resentment is long-standing and class based; for instance, working people resent the professionals who "order them around every day" (Pitney 2018, 104) (and for once, we might note, the "working class" here imagined is not limited to white people). But as mentioned above, there are deeper causes—again grounded in "natural," folk intuitions that are flouted when the meticulously constructed alternative, namely professional expertise, is respected.

As many have noted, people enjoy the feeling of certainty that comes from repeated falsehoods (Muirhead and Rosenblum 2019, 25f.; for a depressing review of the "illusory truth effect" literature in psychology, see Brashier and Marsh 2020, 503f.).[6] Professions can be seen as organized attempts, each in its own realm, to deploy empirical verification against confirmation bias (Nichols 2019, 53–54). "Confirmation bias," though, is an anodyne term for a strong sentiment. It *feels much better* to have our immediate beliefs confirmed by those around us than to have them refuted by people who annoyingly persist in knowing more about the matters they are expert in than we do. The faith in professional expertise that combats that gut feeling requires constant reinforcement and may be hard to reinstill when lost.

To replace verification by repetition spreads conspiracies and worsens political animosity. One understressed effect, however, is to weaken *accountability* by allowing people to avoid news that would once have been of general concern. When one's news feed is curated by like-minded peers rather than professional editors, one will believe falsehoods, but also miss what would otherwise have been undisputed truths, obtruded on us *as* the news by those who in the distant past had the authority to define such. Populist rulers' opponents who ask how those rulers' supporters can possibly excuse some corruption scandal, abuse of power, or verbal expression of hatred are often asking the wrong question: to be among the ruler's core supporters is to trust only news sources that would never mention those outrages to begin with (or at the very least would mention them only glancingly, downplaying their

6. It turns out that perceived truth tracks not just how often something is repeated but also such things as whether it is presented in bold type and whether the person reading it speaks "without an accent."

importance). The result, to adapt an old bromide, is that those who know, don't care, whereas those who might care, don't know.

What is true of professional news reporting is also true of medical professionals, professional climate scientists, and so on; we can easily insulate ourselves not only from unwelcome opinions but also from unwelcome facts. Partisan polarization makes this worse. Being enthusiastic about one's own preferred candidates motivates people to act politically and seek political information. Yet being angry at the other side appears to motivate only the former (Mason 2018, 86, 125). Rage tweeting, it seems, does not require fact checking.

Partisan Spoils and Partial Access Societies

One final source of antiprofessionalism is the ambition of the unqualified. Anne Applebaum (2020, 26f.) has noted that states where one party monopolizes power allow loyalists to succeed and advance regardless of performance. Civil service laws are hollowed out or evaded; agencies and state companies are handed over to political hacks. To be "the better sort of Pole" under Poland's Law and Justice party, one need not be intelligent, skilled, qualified, or experienced; one need only believe in the same outlandish conspiracy that the ruling party believes in.

Applebaum's story might be described as the minting of a new kind of title to acquire things: *desert without merit.* To use terms familiar to students of US history, though not the history of Britain, France, or other countries that began as narrow aristocracies of birth, Poland has reinvented the nineteenth-century spoils system. Under populism now, as in the United States then, the allocation of government jobs by partisan allegiance and ethnic membership provides ordinary voters with government job opportunities at the cost of poor administration (a cost most would-be jobholders, which is to say most party activists, were and are willing to pay). Civil service reform ended the US spoils system, to such good effect that a merit civil service may be taken for granted as a political technology—again counterintuitive—that undergirds all good government. Populism, as usual, marches fearlessly forward to the past.[7]

7. Speaking of marching, one pre-Trump erosion of the merit civil service in the United States has received too little attention by political ethics scholars: the extra points given to veterans in the granting of jobs are so great that many branches of the federal government resemble the world of Robert Heinlein's *Starship Troopers*, where only veterans have civic rights. We could stand to further study the long-term effects of diffusing throughout the administrative

Describing "natural states"—those in which political status and economic incorporation are restricted to an elite—Douglass North, John Joseph Wallis, and Barry Weingast (2009, 37) summarized the opportunity structure of such a state: "Whom an individual knows and who they are matter more than what they do." (As Applebaum might dryly respond, this may sound quite appealing to those unable or unwilling to do much, yet quite happy to take on whatever affections and identities are needed to climb.) On these matters populism represents a real innovation, a sort of mass elitism that makes available to many, though far from all, a system of privilege that in aristocratic society was quite narrow. What North and his coauthors call—tellingly—a "natural" society, in which access to political and economic rights is restricted by birth and social connections, has a mass version that its original theorists did not anticipate. Precisely by creating an elite that is open to all of those, but only those, with a certain (majority) ethnic status and ideological commitment, a ruling class can cement its power by broadening its base. An open-access order is, it turns out, too meritocratic to appeal consistently to those below the median in ability. Though it certainly benefits them greatly over time, it benefits them far *less* greatly than it does the talented. A *partial*-access order, open to a large but particular subset of the population, is another matter.

Mass Despotism

Trump, again per Hennessey and Wittes (2020, 52), sought a presidency of "whim and will." This tracks, probably unwittingly, with Montesquieu's ([1748] 1989, I.1.10, 29) definition of a despotism unfettered by law, where "the prince's will," restrained by neither reasons nor institutions, effects results "as infallibly as one ball thrown against another." Fortunately, neither Trump nor other authoritarian populists who resemble him have achieved pure despotism; in the United States, outside a few areas (such as pardons), constitutional and administrative barriers prevented that. The question is why so many of these politicians' supporters seemed, and still seem, unbothered by their *attempted* despotism as well as their continued indifference to the laws and institutional checks that shield ordinary citizens from arbitrary power. Montesquieu, on the same page cited above, wrote that the subjects of a despot are reduced, like animals, to "instinct, obedience, and chastisement":

apparatus the military virtues (and civic vices) of discipline and obedience, not to mention that veteran preferences systematically advantage men over women.

each is "a creature that obeys a creature that wants." What makes people aspire to be the former?

The typical answer involves an instinct to submit to authority. Beyond this, I have suggested above that many who would have objected to attempted despotism have not properly heard about it. Two other answers, however, seem at least as plausible. As with the new spoils system, they involve the massification of what seems an inherently narrow enterprise, on the one hand, and the deliberate deconstruction of norms, on the other.

Vicarious Despotism

First, the repeated observation that Trump's most fervent supporters regard attacks on him as attacks on themselves suggests that many may come to identify with the despot so fully that his whims thrill them as if they were their own. Despotism might seem an inherently individual phenomenon, the antonym of political participation; in every polity, analytically, at most one person's arbitrary will can be unfettered (the principle that animates the rest, as Montesquieu argued, being "fear"). If the despot's will yields vicarious pleasure, though, despotism can indeed become a mass phenomenon—in citizens' heads, if not in reality.

Reverse Prefiguration

The other way that despotism can gain mass appeal is through what might be called reverse prefiguration. When a despot ignores long-standing social norms, such as against racism or misogyny, or at least rages against their constraints, this may not officially or formally change social norms, but it provides a signal that the constituted authority will not mind if the norm is flouted by others. Scholars who have called for "norm management" by government have ignored the constitutionalist's first principle: "enlightened statesmen will not always be at the helm" (Hamilton, Madison, and Jay [1788] 2001, no. 10, 45).

Unnatural Reminders

Polemarchan justice does not come unalloyed. Many populist governments also propose policies—in Trump's case, for example, a notional revival (never properly followed up on) of vocational education; in the case of Poland's Law and Justice party, generous child allowances—that would happen to benefit their partisans, but do no special harm to laws or institutions. To the extent that keeping these policies may win key constituencies back to liberal democracy, there is no reason from the standpoint of political ethics to reverse them. (In fact, there may be a strong ethical imperative to keep them.) Nor does every instance of advocacy or partiality represent a betrayal of impartial laws or principles. Weber was right that people expect a real politician to *fight*, to be an advocate, to argue not on behalf of objectively grounded normative ideals but rather on behalf of their supporters or constituents.

On the fundamental questions, however, no compromise is possible. If an institution becomes a tool for helping partisans and persecuting outsiders, it is no longer a bad institution but no institution at all. Polemarchus notwithstanding, succoring friends and harming enemies is perhaps a wry definition of justice—victor's justice—but it is no account of justice as decent societies apply it, and no principle of ethics. And reveling in the whims of the despot that oppresses you along with everyone else (yet more closely reminds you of yourself than of those whom you like less) is not a perversion of civic virtue but instead the death of civic virtue.

We could respond by giving up. Abandoning our former wisdom, we could turn to work (suitably careful and coded) on ethics under authoritarianism, and on how to avoid suffering or the worst evils when there is little opportunity to do good. From their own perspectives, in their own voices and styles, the contributors to this volume have in effect rejected that proposition. They have written under the assumption that decency and constitutional democracy are still possible and that we should chart our ethical courses accordingly.

"What is to be done?" is always a pretentious question, but never more so than when asked by academics (whose belief that we strongly influence politics is just as silly as it is durable). The question for us, as scholars and teachers, is what lessons we should publish and teach. The answer is, as with the bridge painters, that we must continue to refurbish, with a new coat of words, the constitutional structures and norms that have been corroded—all the more so if others have encouraged the corrosion on purpose. Populism does not prove that old theories about how institutions benefit everyone were wrong, merely that they were not appreciated (or that the benefits were distributed, as they typically are, unequally—which, as I noted above, should motivate reform, not demolition). Populism does not prove that the joys of domination must permanently win out over those of common and universal advantage. It does not prove that identification with a populist leader's whims must erode the calm passions that lead us to consider ethical and legal constraints on what leaders may do.

What the experience of populism does do is remind us that we are, all of us, prone to partiality and a lack of foresight. The laws, norms, practices, and principles that enable us to pursue our projects in spite of our instincts are neither written on our souls nor derived from a cosmic order; they are fostered by education and mental habit. Recognizing this may impair celestial comfort, but it fortunately enables the kind of action that academics, though not only academics, can usefully do. When we have come up with the best accounts we can of institutions and practices, we should write them down, recommend them, and teach them. If too many people are, for a time, not listening, we should write, recommend, and teach them again. That's where ethics came from to begin with.

The only ground in which political ethics in its fullest sense can flourish remains that of constitutional democracy. And the only viable response to frontal attacks on the bulwarks of constitutional democracy is to renew our efforts to shore them up, with jury-rigged and controversial measures during crises and more solid ones during breathing spells. At some times more than others, the work may be harder, but the task persists.

References

Applebaum, Anne. 2020. *Twilight of Democracy: The Seductive Lure of Authoritarianism.* New York: Doubleday.

Brashier, Nadia M., and Elizabeth J. Marsh. 2020. "Judging Truth." *Annual Review of Psychology* 71:499–515.

Hall, Edward, and Matt Sleat. 2017. "Ethics, Morality, and the Case for Realist Political Theory." *Critical Review of International Social and Political Philosophy* 20 (3): 276–90.

Hamilton, Alexander, James Madison, and John Jay. (1788) 2001. *The Federalist.* Edited by George W. Cary and James McClellan. Gideon ed. Indianapolis: Liberty Fund.

Hennessey, Susan, and Benjamin Wittes. 2020. *Unmaking the Presidency.* New York: Farrar, Straus and Giroux.

Hume, David. 1987. *Essays Moral, Political, and Literary.* Edited by Eugene F. Miller. Rev. ed. Indianapolis: Liberty Fund.

Hume, David, (1739–40) 2000. *A Treatise of Human Nature.* Ed. David Fate Norton and Mary J. Norton. Oxford: Oxford University Press.

Mason, Lilliana. 2018. *Uncivil Agreement: How Politics Became Our Identity.* Chicago: University of Chicago Press.

Montesquieu, Charles-Louis de Secondat, Baron de. (1748) 1989. *The Spirit of the Laws.* Translated by Anne M. Cohler, Basia Carolyn Miller, and Harold Samuel Stone. Cambridge: Cambridge University Press.

Muirhead, Russell, and Nancy L. Rosenblum. 2019. *A Lot of People Are Saying: The New Conspiracism and the Assault on Democracy.* Princeton, NJ: Princeton University Press.

Nichols, Tom. 2019. *The Death of Expertise: The Campaign against Established Knowledge and Why It Matters.* Oxford: Oxford University Press.

North, Douglass C., John Joseph Wallis, and Barry R. Weingast. 2009. *Violence and Social Orders: A Conceptual Framework for Interpreting Recorded Human History.* New York: Cambridge University Press.

O'Donnell, Guillermo. 1999. "Polyarchies and the (Un)Rule of Law in Latin America: A Partial Conclusion." In *The (Un)Rule of Law and the Underprivileged in Latin America,* edited by Juan E. Méndez, Guillermo O'Donnell, and Paulo Sérgio Pinheiro, 303–37. Notre Dame, IN: University of Notre Dame Press.

Pitney, John J. 2018. "Trump, Trouble, and Teaching." In *Trumping Ethical Norms,* edited by L. Sandy Maisel and Hannah E. Dineen, 99–108. New York: Routledge.

Sabl, Andrew. 2002. *Ruling Passions: Political Offices and Democratic Ethics.* Princeton, NJ: Princeton University Press.

———. 2012. *Hume's Politics: Coordination and Crisis in the* History of England. Princeton, NJ: Princeton University Press.

———. 2017. "Realist Liberalism: An Agenda." *Critical Review of International Social and Political Philosophy* 20 (3): 349–64.

Urbinati, Nadia. 2019. *Me the People: How Populism Transforms Democracy.* Cambridge, MA: Harvard University Press.

INDEX

abortion issue, 58, 95
accountability: corruption and, 175–78, 182; hierarchical model of, 153–56, 165; mutual, 207; popular model of, 153, 156–62; of representatives, 90–91, 94, 97; vocational model of, 153, 162–66; whistleblowing and, 205–10
advocacy, 28, 134. *See also* interest groups
Affordable Care and Patient Protection Act, 164n14
Afghanistan War, 193, 197–98
Agamben, Giorgio, 17, 220–21
agency, 69; corruption and, 174–75; legitimacy and, 127–28; whistleblowing and, 194–95, 198–200, 202, 210. *See also* autonomy
agent-centric leadership model, 105, 108–13
Alexander, Larry, 224, 225
Algerian independence, 6–7
Alien and Sedition Acts (1798), 142
Allen, Jonathan, 15, 93
Americans with Disabilities Act (1990), 164n14
Amnesty International, 245–46
Anders, Gerhard, 183
animal rights, 134
Ankersmit, Frank R., 56, 57
anti-intellectualism, 267–68
Applbaum, Arthur, 153, 162–63
Applebaum, Anne, 270n5, 274, 275
Appleby, Paul, 154
approval ratings, 69, 82, 87, 111, 267
arbitration, 48–51, 55–59
Archard, David, 7–8
Arendt, Hannah, 21; on factual truth, 36; on leadership, 111–12; on rational truth, 36, 41
Aristotle, 55–56, 238
Armstrong, Robert, 22n1, 154
Arusha Declaration (1967), 180–81
Assange, Julian, 193, 199
authoritarianism, 30, 142, 218–20; antiauthoritarianism and, 150–51; clientelism and, 183; demagogues and, 113, 122; despotism and, 275–76; ideology of, 270n5; Milgram experiments on, 155; populist, 18–19, 184, 265–78; Roman dictatorship and, 219
autonomy, 15, 84, 89, 100; democratic norm of, 94–95; Kant on, 26. *See also* agency
Axelrod, Robert, 109n3

Barber, Benjamin, 118
Bauman, Zygmunt, 97–99
Beerbohm, Eric, 15–16, 104–23
Bell, Derrick, 87
Bellamy, Richard, 14, 21–42, 54–57, 60–61
Benjamin, Martin, 59, 69–70
Benjamin, Walter, 220
Bentham, Jeremy, 42
Berlin, Isaiah, 5n3
Bermeo, Nancy, 90–91
Biden, Joe, 132, 142
Blair, Tony, 30n2, 32n3, 36n4
Bocchiola, Michele, 17, 193–210
Boehner, John, 140
Brazil, 265, 272
Brexit, 76, 83, 130
bribery, 21–22, 148, 170, 174. *See also* corruption

"bully pulpit," 120
bureaucracy. *See* civil servants
Burke, Edmund, 52, 61, 107
Burnet, Gilbert, 51
Burns, James MacGregor, 110n5
Bush, George W., 132

Calhoun, Cheshire, 70n2
Calvert, Randall, 112–13
Cameron, David, 254–56
campaigning, 45, 87; financing of, 132, 143–44, 171, 183–84, 186–87; lobbying and, 241, 245–47, 250–57; on party platform, 79, 128, 139–40
Canada, 230, 253; civil service code of, 148n2; Emergencies Act of, 228; SARS crisis in, 232n10
Ceva, Emanuela, 17, 193–210
Chamberlain, Neville, 53–54, 57–58
Chari, Raj, 240
charisma, 35, 108, 117–18
charities, 215–16, 241, 255
Charkaoui v. Canada (2007), 230
Charron, Pierre, 50
Cheney, Dick, 132n4
Chesterton, G. K., 55
Chilcot, John, 32n3
China, 232n10
Chomsky, Noam, 83
Christian Democratic parties, 129–30
Churchill, Winston, 58
Civil Rights Act (1964), 106, 130–31
civil rights movement, 115–17, 121, 245
civil servants, 16–17, 147–67, 274; allegiances of, 149; Armstrong on, 154–55; conflicts of interest among, 172, 178–84; corruption by, 148, 166–67; government codes for, 147–48, 179, 195–96; lobbying of, 254–55; performance measures of, 158–59. *See also* public administration ethics
Civil War (US), 114
Clean Air Act (1967), 164n14
Clemenceau, Georges, 41
clientelism, 138–39, 183, 202–3
climate change, 37, 38, 229
Clinton, Bill, 131, 156n8
Clinton, Hillary, 98, 142
Coady, C. A. J., 12–13
coalitions, 133, 143
coauthority, 120–22
Cold War, 24, 52, 173
collective action, 109, 123, 238; problems of, 160–61, 165–66, 186–87
Committee on Standards in Public Life (UK), 72–74, 185
common good, 134, 149, 154; cooperation for, 133, 143; self-interest versus, 22
compatibility testing, 118–22
compliance, 148, 174, 178; integrity and, 151n4, 186–89; with public reason, 137; with quarantines, 232n10
compromise, 14–15, 45–62; arbitration and, 48–51, 55–59; Bellamy on, 54–57, 60–61; as contract, 50; "creative," 56; democracy and, 53, 55–57; etymology of, 47–49; "fair," 55; Morley on, 52–53; partisanship and, 138–42; "principled," 59–62, 77; as process, 57; T. V. Smith on, 53–54
Condorcet, Marquis de, 40
confirmation bias, 273
conflicts of interest, 100, 172, 178–84
Constant, Benjamin, 25–27
Constitution (US), 133, 163, 266, 271; Bill of Rights to, 22, 131, 268; Fourteenth Amendment to, 86–87
Converse, Philip, 130–31
Cooper, Terry, 152–53
cooperation, 109–13; for common good, 133, 143; coordination and, 112–13
corporations: ethics of, 16–17, 147–67; lobbying by, 249–50, 254, 259; personhood of, 87; "scientific" management of, 162n11
corruption, 17, 170–89; bribery and, 21–22, 148, 170, 174; by civil servants, 148, 166–67; economic approaches to, 173–75, 184; lobbying and, 236, 248; principal-agent model of, 174–75, 184; World Bank on, 173. *See also* whistleblowing

Cottingham, John, 68
coup d'état, 148
COVID-19 pandemic, 141, 217, 229, 273
Cruz, Ted, 98
Cubbon, Brian, 155

Dahl, Robert, 252
dark matter, 37
Darwall, Stephen, 207n6
David-Barrett, Elizabeth, 17, 170–89
Davis, Michael, 204
deception. *See* lying
Declaration of Independence (US), 271
De George, Richard, 202, 204
demagogues, 113, 122. *See also* authoritarianism
democracy, 35, 90–91, 126–44; Athenian, 1–2, 56; Barber on, 118; Bentham on, 42; bureaucratic values versus, 152; compromise and, 53, 55–57; definitions of, 240, 242; direct, 82, 118, 127n2; equality and, 240, 251–52, 258–59; liberalism and, 123; lobbying as threat to, 18, 236–59; "noble lie" of, 22–24; "paradox" of, 142; representative, 56, 82–100, 268
"democratic constancy," 108
Democratic Party (US), 130–33
Denhardt, Kathryn, 164
deontology, 10–12, 17, 61, 214, 224–27
despotism, 18, 275–76. *See also* authoritarianism
dictatorship, 218–20. *See also* authoritarianism
dirty hands dilemma, 4–14; Archard on, 7–8; "democratic," 8n5; Thompson on, 88; Walzer on, 5–7, 11, 65, 88, 105–6, 225; Williams on, 68–69, 106
disaster management, 217. *See also* emergency situations
discretionary power, 87, 107, 206–7, 221; of civil servants, 158, 166; corruption of, 175; of leaders, 114, 122, 148, 214
disdainful distraction tactic, 84, 98–100
Dodd-Frank Wall Street Reform and Consumer Protection Act (2010), 197n3
Dovi, Suzanne, 15, 82–100
Downs, Anthony, 130, 132
Dresden firebombing, 226
Du Bois, W. E. B., 121n11
Dyzenhaus, David, 215, 228–30, 232

Ebola virus, 218, 222n3
Egypt, 222n2
Eichmann, Adolf, 154n7
Eigen, Peter, 173
Eisenhower, Dwight, 115–16
Ekeh, Peter, 183
Ellis, Anthony, 224
emergency situations, 17–18, 213–32; definition of, 213; legitimacy in, 230–32; rule of law and, 18, 214, 215, 221, 227–30, 232; Schmitt on, 219
e pluribus unum, 133
equality, 48, 119–20; Arendt on, 111–12; democracy and, 240, 251–52, 258–59; freedom and, 138; racial, 120
Erdoğan, Recep Tayyip, 140, 176, 265
Essex Centre for the Study of Integrity, 67
ethical obliviousness, 84, 93–100
Eyre, Edward John, 140

fake news, 21, 35, 42, 273–74
Farm Bill (US), 139
Fatovic, Clement, 231–32
Fidesz party (Hungary), 130
Fight for $15 movement, 122
Finland, 130
Five Star Movement (Italy), 83
"flex organizations," 183
Fourteenth Amendment (US), 86–87
France, 130, 229
Frankfurt, Harry, 38, 96
Friedrich, Carl, 154, 162n11
Friends of the Earth, 245–46
Frohlich, Norman, 112
Fuller, Lon, 230
Fumurescu, Alin, 14–15, 45–62

Galston, William, 65, 78
Gandhi, Indira, 222n2
Gauthier, David, 54, 55

German political parties, 130. *See also* Nazi Germany
gerrymandering, 87, 141, 143–44
Geuss, Raymond, 182
Ghana, 183
global warming, 37, 38, 229
Goldwater, Barry, 138
Goodin, Robert, 30
Google, lobbying by, 249–50, 254
Grant, Ruth, 165n16
Great Recession (2008), 132
Greenpeace, 245–46
Gross, Oren, 215, 227–29
Guantánamo Bay, Cuba, 198
Guizot, François, 57
Gutmann, Amy, 45

Habermas, Jürgen, 134
Hall, Edward, 1–19, 65–80
Hallowell, John H., 54
Hamas, 58
Hamilton, Alexander, 105, 117, 276
Hampton, Jean, 117–18
Harris, Arthur, 226
Hayek, F. A., 55, 241n1
Heath, Joseph, 16–17, 147–67
Hegel, G. W. F., 51
Heinlein, Robert, 274n7
Hennessey, Susan, 269, 275
Hesiod, 24
Hickox, Kaci, 222n3
Himmler, Heinrich, 79
Hitler, Adolf, 53–54, 57–58
Hobbes, Thomas, 50–53, 107, 238, 269; Gauthier and, 54; Hampton and, 117–18; on selection of leaders, 117–18
Homeland Security Department, 266
Hume, David, 111n7, 116n10, 269–71
Hungary, 130, 176, 265
hurricanes, 213, 217, 218, 229

identity politics, 46, 58–60, 62
Illing, Sean, 90–91
inclusivity, 128–33, 141
Independents, 127–28, 131
India, 140, 222n2, 265
individualism, 49–50
integrity, 15, 65–80; Martin Benjamin on, 69–70; compliance and, 151n4, 186–89; etymology of, 68; Carol Lewis on, 150n4; messiness of, 80; as positive ideal, 74–79; public, 72–74, 147, 184–88; questionnaire on, 67; Bernard Williams on, 68–69
interest groups, 28, 134, 238–39, 247–48
International Covenant on Civil and Political Rights, 223
intersectionality, 86
Iraq War, 6–7, 132, 193, 197–98; Blair on, 32n3, 36n4
Irish Republican Army, 31
Isaacson, Walter, 114
Israel, 58
Italy, Five Star Movement of, 83

Jacobs, Leslie, 232n10
Jamaica, 140
Jefferson, Thomas, 229
Jeffords, Jim, 132n4
Johnson, Boris, 76
Johnson, Lyndon, 41n5, 130–31
just war, 26

Kant, Immanuel, 10, 25–27, 151, 225
Kennedy, John F., 104, 115–16, 119–20
Kenyan Constitution, 185–86
Keohane, Robert, 165n16
Key, V. O., Jr., 127
Khan, Sadiq, 229n8
King, Martin Luther, Jr., 115–17, 121
Korean War, 228n6
Kurosawa, Akira, 270

labor unions, 133–34, 241, 250–51
L'Aquila earthquake (2009), 218
Larmore, Charles, 55
lawyers, 82, 119, 201; lying by, 27–29, 39; morality of, 12–13
Lazar, Nomi Claire, 17–18, 213–32

leadership, 15–16, 104–23; action-centric model of, 109; agent-centric model of, 105, 108–13; Arendt on, 111–12; Barber on, 118; charismatic, 108, 118; coauthority of, 120–21; Du Bois on, 121n11; follower-centric model of, 105, 110–13; Hobbesian, 117–18; independence of, 104; Philp on, 112, 114; Pitkin on, 118–19; problem-solving and, 105–6, 116; risks of, 109–10; sacrificial role of, 106–7; Schumpeter on, 110–11; selection of, 111, 117–19; shared agency model of, 113–18; virtue-theoretic model of, 108–9; Walzer on, 106, 120; Weber on, 108
Leftwich, Adrian, 183
legitimacy, 165–66, 176; agency and, 127–28; in emergency situations, 230–32; of partisanship, 133
Le Pen, Marine, 130
Lessig, Lawrence, 248
Lewis, Carol, 150n4
LGBTQ+ community, 58, 60n9
liberalism, 271–72; compromise and, 55; democracy and, 123; lobbying and, 238, 246, 248; New Deal, 131
libertarianism, 83, 171, 238, 259
Lincoln, Abraham, 61n10, 114, 120
living wage movement, 122
lobbying, 18, 134, 236–59; definition of, 240; Madison and, 238–39, 248, 251, 256, 257; money spent on, 247; reform of, 252–59; rise of, 241–46; scope of, 246–47
Loevy, Karin, 231
Louisiana Purchase, 229
lying, 7, 14, 21–42, 65, 215; Constant versus Kant on, 25–27; definitions of, 27–29; "economical with the truth" and, 22; by lawyers, 12–13, 27–29, 39; Machiavelli on, 24–25, 88; Mearsheimer on, 42; "noble," 22–24; "strategic," 31–32

Machiavelli, Niccolò, 59–60; on ends/means, 4–5; on lying, 24–26, 32, 88
Mackie, Gerry, 111
Madison, James, 238–39, 248, 251, 256–57, 276
Maduro, Nicolás, 100
Mafia code of silence (*omertà*), 12, 13
Mainwaring, Scott, 91
Mair, Peter, 129
Major, John, 31
Malawi, 183
malpractice, medical, 162, 201
Mandela, Nelson, 121
Manning, Chelsea, 193, 194, 197–200, 205, 209–10
Margalit, Avishai, 57–59
marriage, same-sex, 58
Martin, Oliver, 53
Marx, Karl, 176
Mass Observation Archive (UK), 82–83
May, Simon Căbulea, 60, 61
Mayer, Jane, 6n4
McCain, Jesse, 15, 82–100
Mearsheimer, John, 31, 33, 41
Mendus, Susan, 77, 79
Mexican border wall, 46
Milgram, Stanley, 155
Mill, John Stuart, 52
millennials, 47
minimum wage, 122
Montaigne, Michel de, 50
Montesquieu, Charles de, 275–76
moon shot, 115–16, 119–20
Moore, Michael, 224
"moral blindness," 97–98
Morant Bay rebellion (1865), 140
Morley, John, 52–53, 61
Muirhead, Russell, 16, 126–44
Mulvaney, Mike, 46
Munich Agreement (1938), 53–54, 57–58

NASA, 119–20
Nash equilibria, 187
National Emergencies Act (US), 228n6
National Front party (France), 130
nationalist parties, 130
Nazi Germany, 53–54, 57–58, 79, 154–55
"negative morality," 15
Netherlands, 134, 209n7

Neustadt, Richard, 109n2
New Deal liberalism, 131
Newey, Glen, 29, 33
new public management movement (UK), 157–59, 181
Nichols, Tom, 267–68
Nielsen, Kai, 10, 11
Nietzsche, Friedrich, 78
"noble lie," 22–24
nonderogable rights, 223–24
normative ethics, 151
North, Douglass, 275
Nyerere, Julius, 180–81

Obama, Barack, 132, 164n14
Orbán, Viktor, 130, 176, 253, 265
Organization for Economic Cooperation and Development (OECD), 173, 181, 243
orphanages, 216
"output legitimacy," 16–17
Overeem, Patrick, 61
Oxfam (organization), 247

Pareto efficiency, 166
Parrish, John, 8–9
partisanship, 2, 126–44, 277–78; common good and, 133–34; comprehensiveness of, 133–38, 141; compromise and, 138–42; Hume on, 269–70; inclusivity of, 128–33, 141; interest groups and, 238; justification of, 136–37; legitimacy of, 133; Madison on, 238–39, 248, 251, 256, 257; moral distinctiveness of, 143–44; populism and, 270; Rawls on, 164n13; Trump and, 140–42
Parvin, Phil, 18, 236–59
patronage jobs, 138–39, 183, 202–3
Pelosi, Nancy, 46
Pentagon Papers, 41
performance measures, 158–59
Philippines, 265
"philosophy of nudge," 187
Philp, Mark, 17, 72–73, 112, 114, 170–89
phronesis (practical wisdom), 61
Pitkin, Hanna, 89, 106–7, 118–19
Plato, 54, 238, 269–70; on demagogues, 122; on noble lie, 24; on Sophists, 24, 35–36
Plotke, David, 83
Poland, 253, 274, 276–77
police brutality, 175
political parties, 140–42, 268. *See also* partisanship
populism, 82–83, 122, 130; authoritarian, 18–19, 184, 265–78; public administrators and, 156, 161; Thatcher and, 157–58; Trump and, 140, 142, 176
Postman, Neil, 91–92, 97
principal-agent theory of corruption, 174–75, 184
prisons, 134, 198, 266
professional ethics, 149–55, 157, 162–66
public administration ethics, 16–17, 72–74, 147–67; best practices for, 162, 166–67; conflicts of interest and, 172, 178–84; hierarchical model of, 153–56, 165; incentives for, 158–59, 167, 174, 187, 197n3; popular model of, 153, 156–62; vocational model of, 153, 162–66. *See also* civil servants
public reason politics, 134–38

Rawls, John, 37, 57, 134–35, 137, 164
Read, James H., 109
Reagan, Ronald, 131
refugee status, 221
reinventing government movement (US), 157
renaissance of twelfth century, 47
representatives, 15, 85–100; accountability of, 90–91, 94, 97; Barber on, 118; disdainful distraction tactics of, 15, 84, 98–100; ethical qualities of, 85–91; independence of, 104; leadership and, 15–16, 104–23; Machiavellian ethics of, 88; Schumpeter on, 111; self-contradiction by, 15, 84, 95–98; unethical qualities of, 91–100
Republican Party (US), 130–33, 140
reverse evolution, 267–69
reverse prefiguration, 276
Richelieu, Cardinal, 50
right to know, 150

Rittel, Horst, 216
Roach, Kent, 230
Rockefeller, Nelson, 138
Rohr, John, 149, 152
Romanticism, 56
Roosevelt, Theodore, 120
Rosenblum, Nancy L., 16, 126–44
Rothstein, Bo, 172
Rousseau, Jean-Jacques, 238
Rove, Karl, 132
rule of law, 88, 165, 170–71, 214, 265, 268; civil servants and, 148; emergencies and, 18, 215, 221, 227–30, 232; Hume on, 270; Trump and, 99–100; Vargas on, 272
rules of war, 26, 225
Russell, Bertrand, 5n3

Sabl, Andrew, 1–19, 265–78; on "democratic constancy," 108; on governing office ethics, 61; on "middle virtues," 108; on political integrity, 77; on populism, 18–19; on "principled compromise," 59; on representatives' duties, 91
Saint-Simon, Henri de, 176
Sanders, Bernie, 76
Sanson, Charles-Henri, 154n7
SARS (severe acute respiratory syndrome) pandemic, 217, 218, 232n10
Sartre, Jean-Paul, 5, 105
Saward, Michael, 89–90, 95
Scharpf, Fritz, 165–66
Schattschneider, E. E., 126, 141, 144
Scherkoske, Greg, 69
Schmitt, Carl, 215, 218–21, 225–26, 231, 269n3
Schumpeter, Joseph, 110–11
sedition, 142
self-contradiction, 84, 95–99
Shalit, Gilad, 58
Shapiro, Ian, 165
Shklar, Judith, 123
Singapore, 217
Skocpol, Theda, 249
Smith, Thomas Verner, 53
Snowden, Edward, 193
social contract, 33, 51, 53n4
Social Democratic parties, 129–30
Sophists, 24, 35–36
Southern Christian Leadership Conference (SCLC), 121
Stalin, Joseph, 58
standards of care, 162
Stanley, Jason, 83
Stark, Andrew, 180
Stowe, Harriet Beecher, 60n9
Strauss, Leo, 24
Straw, Jack, 73–74
Sweden's New Democrats, 130

Tanzania, 180–81
Tea Party (US), 139
Thatcher, Margaret, 157–59
Thieme, Marianne, 134
Thompson, Dennis, 90, 109n3, 253; on administrative responsibility, 152–53; on dirty hands dilemma, 88; on participatory government, 157, 160
Thuderoz, Christian, 58
Tocqueville, Alexis de, 129
toleration, 108, 268
Tomasi, John, 241n1
torture, 6–10, 88, 224
transnational institutions, 165n16
transparency, 22, 33, 88; corruption and, 172, 173; lobbyists and, 246, 254–56; political autonomy and, 89; Trump and, 94
Transparency International, 173, 174
Truex, Rory, 182
Trump, Donald, 3, 76, 132, 265–66, 269, 275–76; on abortion, 95; approval ratings of, 82; Clinton and, 98; conflicts of interest of, 100; COVID-19 pandemic and, 141; ethical obliviousness of, 94–100, 269n3; populism of, 140–42, 176, 269–70; transparency and, 94; US-Mexican border wall of, 46; working-class supporters of, 87
trust, 42, 87, 175
trustee/delegate paradigm, 85, 90
Turkey, 140, 176, 265

Union of Soviet Socialist Republics (USSR), 24, 52, 58, 173
unions. *See* labor unions
United Kingdom, 82–83, 154, 230, 242–43; Brexit and, 76, 83, 130; Committee on Standards in Public Life of, 72–74, 185; lobbyists in, 246–47, 254–55; new public management movement in, 157–59, 181
University of Essex, 67
Urbinati, Nadia, 83
utilitarianism, 10–12, 68–69, 151; of emergencies, 214, 224, 226–27; of torture, 9–10, 224

Vargas, Getúlio, 272
Venezuela, 100
vicarious despotism, 18, 276
Vietnam War, 41
virtue theory, 151
Voting Rights Act (1965), 130

Waldron, Jeremy, 127
Walmart, 249
Walzer, Michael, 13, 55, 215; on dirty hands dilemma, 5–7, 11, 65, 88, 105–6, 225; Gross and, 229; on just wars, 225; Kant and, 225; on leaders, 106, 120; Schmitt and, 225–26
war: crimes of, 154–55; rules of, 26, 225
Washington, Booker T., 120
Washington, George, 117
Weber, Max, 60, 277; on bureaucracy, 154; on charisma, 108; on political integrity, 75, 77, 78; on "spiritual proletarianization," 2; on state violence, 7
Weinstock, Daniel, 60, 61
Wellstone, Paul, 132n4
whistleblowing, 17, 193–210; definition of, 194; duty of, 17, 199–201, 209–10; elements of, 194–97; evidence of, 202; journalists and, 199; justifications of, 200–209; motives for, 197; rewards for, 197n3. *See also* corruption
WikiLeaks, 193, 199, 209–10
Wildavsky, Aaron, 138
Wilde, Oscar, 55
Williams, Bernard, 7, 13–14, 39; on dirty hands dilemma, 68–69, 106; on "ground projects," 69; on lying, 65
Williamson, Oliver, 155–56
Wilson, Woodrow, 154
"wisdom of the crowds," 40
Wittes, Benjamin, 269, 275
Wittgenstein, Ludwig, 118
Wolff, Robert Paul, 45–46
World Bank, 173

Xenophon, 24

Ypi, Lea, 75–76
Yugoslavia, 52

Zacka, Bernardo, 148
Zika virus, 217
Žižek, Slavoj, 83

A NOTE ON THE TYPE

This book has been composed in Arno, an Old-style serif typeface in the classic Venetian tradition, designed by Robert Slimbach at Adobe.

CPSIA information can be obtained
at www.ICGtesting.com
Printed in the USA
JSHW042223140722
28096JS00004B/4

9 780691 241135